A Reading/Language Arts Program

Macmillan/McGraw-Hill

Contributors

Time Magazine

RFB&D 
learning through listening

Students with print disabilities may be eligible to obtain an accessible, audio version of the pupil edition of this textbook. Please call Recording for the Blind & Dyslexic at 1-800-221-4792 for complete information.

A

The McGraw·Hill Companies

Macmillan/McGraw-Hill

Published by Macmillan/McGraw-Hill, of McGraw-Hill Education, a division of The McGraw-Hill Companies, Inc., Two Penn Plaza, New York, New York 10121.

Printed in the United States of America

1 2 3 4 5 6 7 8 9 006/055 13 12 11 10 09

A Reading/Language Arts Program

Program Authors

Dr. Diane August
Senior Research Scientist, Center for Applied Linguistics
Washington, D.C.

Dr. Donald R. Bear
University of Nevada, Reno
Reno, Nevada

Dr. Janice A. Dole
University of Utah
Salt Lake City, Utah

Dr. Jana Echevarria
California State University, Long Beach
Long Beach, California

Dr. Douglas Fisher
San Diego State University
San Diego, California

Dr. David J. Francis
University of Houston
Houston, Texas

Dr. Vicki L. Gibson
Educational Consultant, Gibson Hasbrouck and Associates, Massachusetts

Dr. Jan E. Hasbrouck
Educational Consultant – J.H. Consulting
Los Angeles, California

Dr. Scott G. Paris
Center for Research and Practice, National Institute of Education
Singapore

Dr. Timothy Shanahan
University of Illinois at Chicago
Chicago, Illinois

Dr. Josefina V. Tinajero
University of Texas at El Paso
El Paso, Texas

Mc Graw Hill Macmillan/McGraw-Hill

Program Authors

Dr. Diane August

Center for Applied Linguistics, Washington, D.C.

- Principal Investigator, Developing Literacy in Second-Language Learners: Report of the National Literacy Panel on Language-Minority Children and Youth
- Member of the New Standards Literacy Project, Grades 4–5

Dr. Donald R. Bear

University of Nevada, Reno

- Author of *Words Their Way* and *Words Their Way with English Learners*
- Director, E.L. Cord Foundation Center for Learning and Literacy

Dr. Janice A. Dole

University of Utah

- Investigator, IES Study on Reading Interventions
- National Academy of Sciences, Committee Member: Teacher Preparation Programs, 2005–2007

Dr. Jana Echevarria

California State University, Long Beach

- Author of *Making Content Comprehensible for English Learners: The SIOP Model*
- Principal Researcher, Center for Research on the Educational Achievement and Teaching of English Language Learners

Dr. Douglas Fisher

San Diego State University

- Co-Director, Center for the Advancement of Reading, California State University
- Author of *Language Arts Workshop: Purposeful Reading and Writing Instruction* and *Reading for Information in Elementary School*

Dr. David J. Francis

University of Houston

- Director of the Center for Research on Educational Achievement and Teaching of English Language Learners (CREATE)
- Director, Texas Institute for Measurement, Evaluation, and Statistics

Dr. Vicki Gibson

Educational Consultant Gibson Hasbrouck and Associates, Massachusetts

- Author of *Differentiated Instruction: Grouping for Success*

Dr. Jan E. Hasbrouck

Educational Consultant JH Consulting, Los Angeles

- Developed Oral Reading Fluency Norms for Grades 1–8
- Author of *The Reading Coach: A How-to Manual for Success*

Dr. Scott G. Paris

Center for Research and Practice, National Institute of Education, Singapore

- Principal Investigator, CIERA, 1997–2004

Dr. Timothy Shanahan

University of Illinois at Chicago

- Member, National Reading Panel
- President, International Reading Association, 2006
- Chair, National Literacy Panel and National Early Literacy Panel

Dr. Josefina V. Tinajero

University of Texas at El Paso

- Past President, NABE and TABE
- Co-Editor of *Teaching All the Children: Strategies for Developing Literacy in an Urban Setting* and *Literacy Assessment of Second Language Learners*

Consulting and Contributing Authors

Dr. Adria F. Klein
Professor Emeritus,
California State University,
San Bernardino

- President, California Reading Association, 1995
- Co-Author of *Interactive Writing* and *Interactive Editing*

Dolores B. Malcolm
St. Louis Public Schools
St. Louis, MO

- Past President, International Reading Association
- Member, IRA Urban Diversity Initiatives Commission
- Member, RIF Advisory Board

Dr. Doris Walker-Dalhouse
Minnesota State University,
Moorhead

- Author of articles on multicultural literature and reading instruction in urban schools
- Co-Chair of the Ethnicity, Race, and Multilingualism Committee, NRC

Dinah Zike
Educational Consultant

- Dinah-Might Activities, Inc. San Antonio, TX

Program Consultants

Kathy R. Bumgardner
Language Arts Instructional Specialist
Gaston County Schools, NC

Elizabeth Jimenez
CEO, GEMAS Consulting
Pomona, CA

Dr. Sharon F. O'Neal
Associate Professor
College of Education
Texas State University
San Marcos, TX

Program Reviewers

Mable Alfred
Reading/Language Arts Administrator
Chicago Public Schools, IL

Suzie Bean
Teacher, Kindergarten
Mary W. French Academy
Decatur, IL

Linda Burch
Teacher, Kindergarten
Public School 184
Brooklyn, NY

Robert J. Dandorph
Principal
John F. Kennedy Elementary School
North Bergen, NJ

Suzanne Delacruz
Principal, Washington Elementary
Evanston, IL

Carol Dockery
Teacher, Grade 3
Mulberry Elementary
Milford, OH

Karryl Ellis
Teacher, Grade 1
Durfee School, Decatur, IL

Christina Fong
Teacher, Grade 3
William Moore Elementary School
Las Vegas, NV

Lenore Furman
Teacher, Kindergarten
Abington Avenue School
Newark, NJ

Sister Miriam Kaeser
Assistant Superintendent
Archdiocese of Cincinnati
Cincinnati, OH

LaVonne Lee
Principal, Rozet Elementary School
Gillette, WY

SuEllen Mackey
Teacher, Grade 5
Washington Elementary School
Decatur, IL

Jan Mayes
Curriculum Coordinator
Kent School District
Kent, WA

Bonnie Nelson
Teacher, Grade 1
Solano School, Phoenix, AZ

Cyndi Nichols
Teacher, Grade K/1
North Ridge Elementary School
Commack, NY

Sharron Norman
Curriculum Director
Lansing School District
Lansing, MI

Renee Ottinger
Literacy Leader, Grades K–5
Coronado Hills Elementary School
Denver, CO

Michael Pragman
Principal, Woodland Elementary School
Lee's Summit, MO

Carol Rose
Teacher, Grade 2
Churchill Elementary School
Muskegon, MI

Laura R. Schmidt-Watson
Director of Academic Services
Parma City School District, OH

Dianne L. Skoy
Literacy Coordinator, Grades K–5
Minneapolis Public Schools
Minneapolis, MN

Charles Staszewski
ESL Teacher, Grades 3–5
John H. William School, No. 5
Rochester, NY

Patricia Synan
New York City Department of Education

Stephanie Yearian
Teacher, Grade 2
W. J. Zahnow Elementary
Waterloo, IL

Unit 3 The Big Question

How did you travel to school today?

Enduring Understanding and Essential Questions

In this unit, children will read and write about how they travel. As they progress through the unit, they will also develop and apply key comprehension skills that good readers use as they read.

Big Idea	Enduring Understanding	Essential Questions
Theme: Transportation	There are many ways to travel from one place to another.	How did you travel to school today?

Comprehension	Enduring Understanding	Essential Questions
Make and Confirm Predictions Week 1	Good readers use different parts of a story to predict what might happen.	What can you predict about the story using the title and illustrations?
Classify and Categorize Week 2	Good readers understand the different ways information is organized in a story.	How can the way the author organized the information help you understand the story?
Identify Character and Plot Week 3	Good readers understand the important parts of a story.	Who are the characters in the story? What events happened in the story?

Theme: Transportation

Planning the Unit

Teaching the Unit

Wrapping Up the Unit

Additional Resources

Unit Theme Opener

Literature Selections

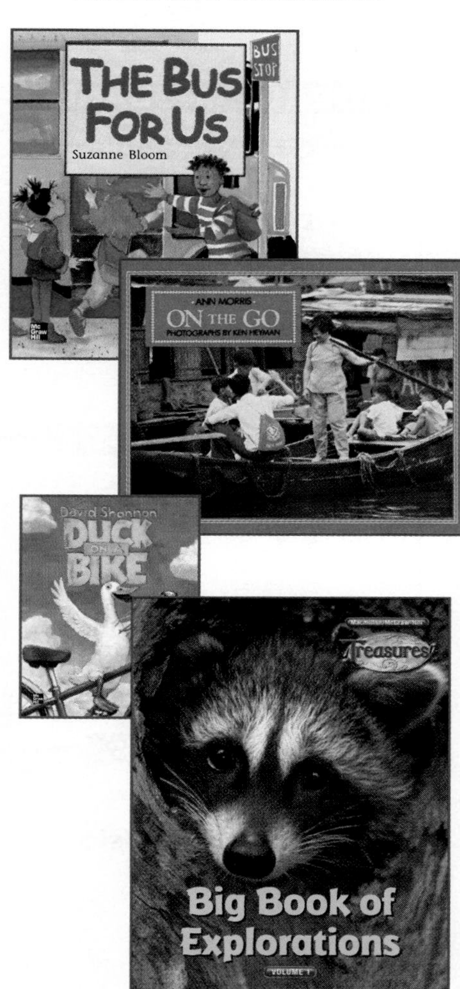

Unit Assessment

Unit 3 Contents

Unit 3 Planner

Theme: Transportation

Unit Theme Opener, page xvi

Big Book

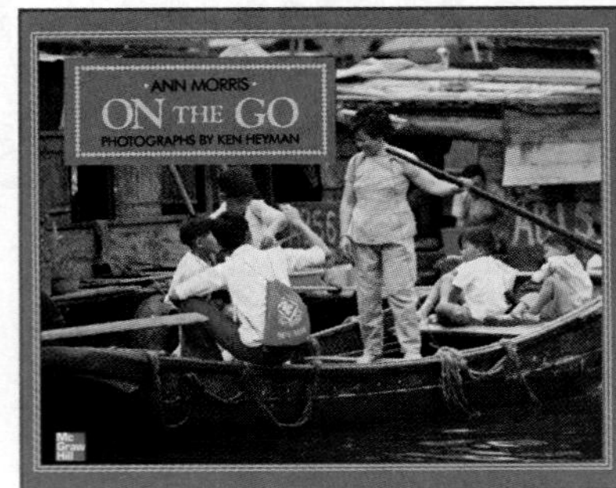

Big Book

	WEEK 1	WEEK 2
ORAL LANGUAGE • Oral Vocabulary • Phonemic Awareness	**Theme** Getting Around Town **Phonemic Awareness** Phoneme Isolation (/t/) Phoneme Categorization (/t/) Phoneme Blending	**Theme** Traveling Far and Near **Phonemic Awareness** Phoneme Isolation Phoneme Blending Phoneme Categorization
WORD STUDY • Phonics	**Phonics** Introduce /t/*t*	**Phonics** Introduce /i/*i*
• High-Frequency Words	**High-Frequency Word** *see*	**High-Frequency Word** *go*
READING • Listening Comprehension	**Comprehension** **Strategy:** Recognize Story Structure **Skill:** Make and Confirm Predictions	**Comprehension** **Strategy:** Recognize Text Structure **Skill:** Classify and Categorize
• Fluency	**Fluency** Build Fluency: Word Automaticity Echo-Read, Read for Fluency	**Fluency** Build Fluency: Word Automaticity Echo-Read, Choral-Read, Read for Fluency
• Leveled Readers	Approaching *Bear Goes to Town* On Level *Tig Can See* Beyond *How They Go* ELL *Tiger Can See*	Approaching *Pig's Trip* On Level *Pig On Wheels* Beyond *Chip Likes Nuts* ELL *Go Pig!*
LANGUAGE ARTS • Grammar • Writing	**Grammar** Action Words **Writing** Sentence Frame	**Grammar** Action Words **Writing** Poster

Read-Aloud Trade Book

WEEK 3

Theme
Wheels All Around

Phonemic Awareness
Phoneme Identity
Phoneme Categorization
Phoneme Blending

Phonics
Review /t/*t*

High-Frequency Words
see, *go*

Comprehension
Strategy: Recognize Story Structure
Skill: Identify Character, Plot

Fluency
Build Fluency: Word Automaticity
Echo-Read, Choral-Read, Read for Fluency

Approaching *See It Go Up*

On Level *Fast or Slow?*

Beyond *The Train Trip*

ELL *See It Go*

Grammar and Writing
Action Words, Book Title

Half-Day Kindergarten

Use the chart below to help plan your half-day kindergarten schedule. Choose Small Group and Workstation Activities as your time allows during the day.

ORAL LANGUAGE

- **Phonemic Awareness**
- **Build Background**
- **Oral Vocabulary**

WORD STUDY

- **Phonics:** /t/*t*, /i/*i*
- **High-Frequency Words:** *see, go*

READING

- **Share the Big Books:** *The Bus for Us; On the Go*
- **Read-Aloud Trade Book:** *Duck on a Bike*
- **Read-Aloud Anthology**
- **Big Book of Explorations**
- **Fluency Practice**

LANGUAGE ARTS

- **Shared Writing**
- **Interactive Writing**
- **Independent Writing**

INDEPENDENT PRACTICE

- **Activity Book Pages**
- **Practice Book Pages**
- **Handwriting Practice**

Theme: Transportation

Unit 3 Resources

Literature

Big Book

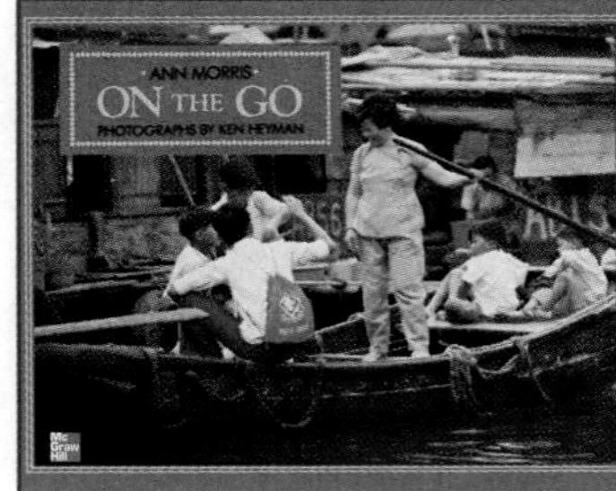

Big Book

Read-Aloud Trade Book

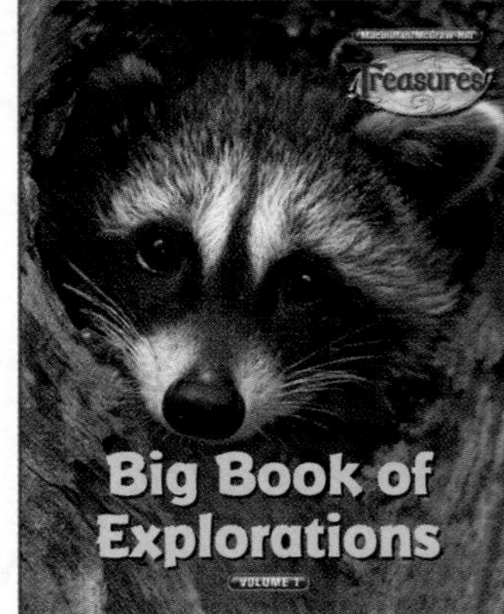

Big Book of Explorations (2)

Pre-decodable Readers

Approaching Level

On Level

Beyond Level

ELL

Leveled Readers

Read-Aloud Anthology
Includes Plays for Readers Theater

Oral Vocabulary Cards
(30 sets)

Retelling Cards

Teaching Support

Teacher's Edition

Teacher's Resource Book

Home-School Connection

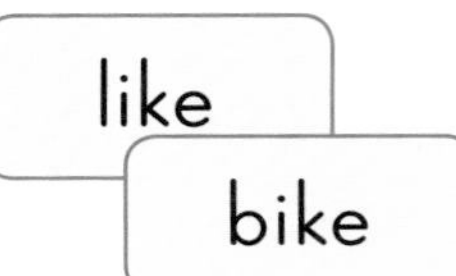

High-Frequency Word Cards

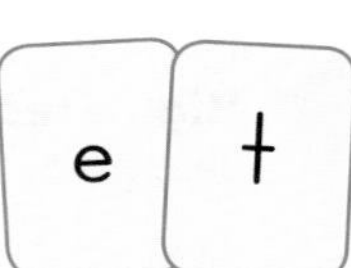

Word-Building Cards

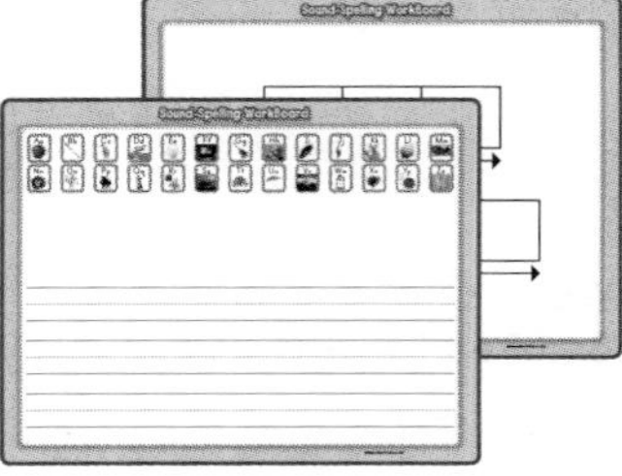
Sound-Spelling WorkBoards

Puppet

Sound-Spelling Cards

Photo Cards

Unit 3 Resources

Teaching Chart

Student Practice

Activity Book

Practice Book

Handwriting
- Ball and Stick
- Slant

Literacy Workstation Flip Charts

Differentiated Resources

English Language Learners

ELL Resource and Practice Books

Visual Vocabulary Resources

Response to Intervention

- Phonemic Awareness
- Phonics
- Vocabulary
- Comprehension
- Fluency

Tier 3

Assessment

Unit Assessment

Assess Unit Skills
- Phonemic Awareness
- Phonics
- High-Frequency Words
- Listening Comprehension

Class Management Tools

How-to Guide

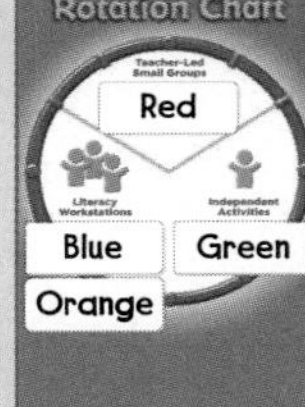

Rotation Chart

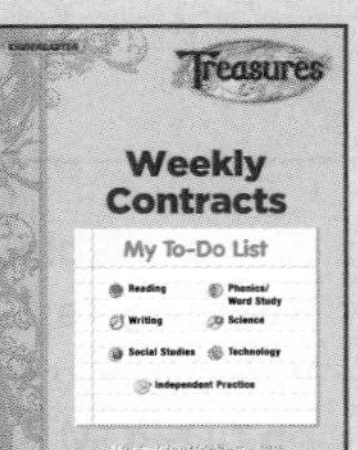

Weekly Contracts

Digital Solutions

Go to  http://connected.mcgraw-hill.com Online Center

☑ Prepare/Plan

ONLINE www.macmillanmh.com

Teacher's Edition Online

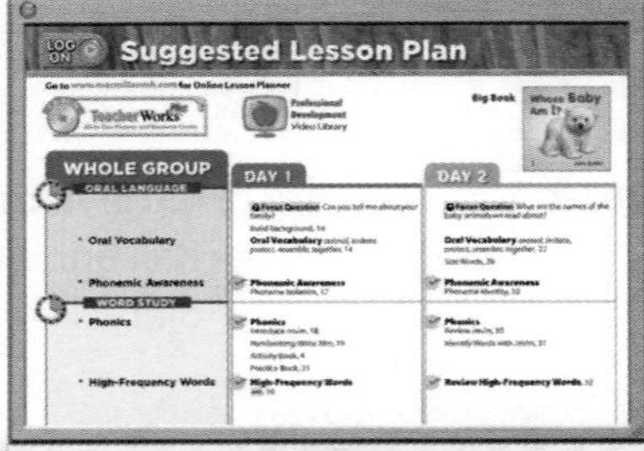

TeacherWorks Plus
All-In-One Planner and Resource Center

Available on CD-ROM
- Interactive Teacher's Edition
- Printable Weekly Resources

Implementation Modules

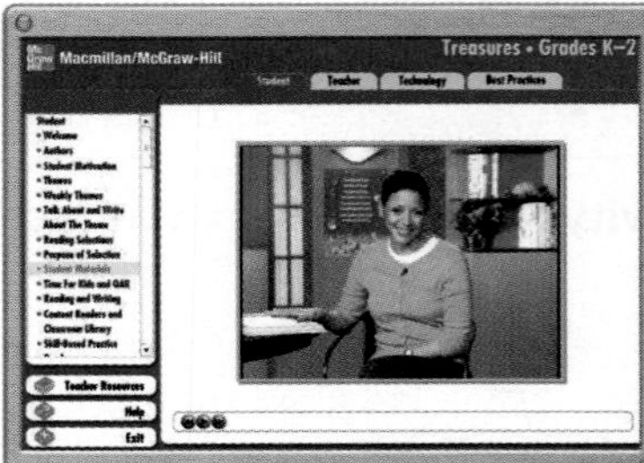

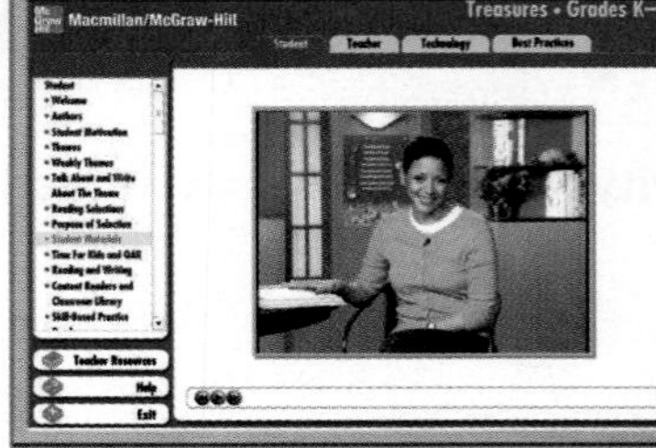

- Support on how to implement the reading program

Balanced Literacy Planner

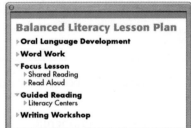

- Create customized weekly balanced literacy planners

ELL Strategies

- Teaching strategies for English Language Learners

Reading Video Library

- Video clips of instructional routines

Leadership Handbook

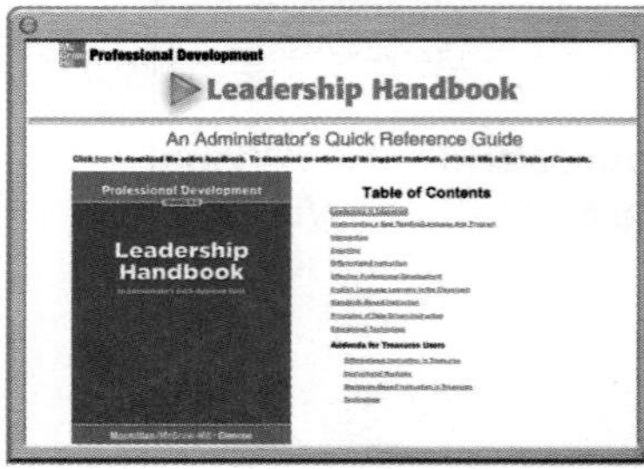

- Professional development for school principals

☑ Teach/Learn

ONLINE www.macmillanmh.com

Animated Activities

- Animated comprehension activities

Classroom Presentation Toolkit

- Weekly transparencies, graphic organizers, and guided instruction and practice

Additional Professional Development

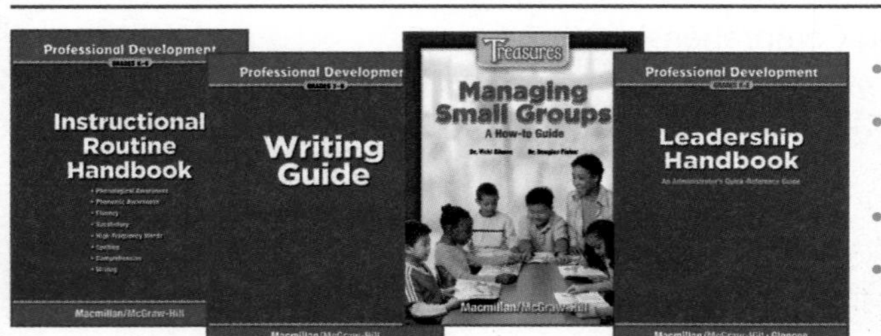

- **Instructional Routine Handbook**
- **Writing Professional Development Guide**
- **Managing Small Groups**
- **Leadership Handbook:** *An Administrator's Quick Reference Guide*

Also available **Reading Yes!** Video Workshops on CD-ROM

Leveled Reader Database

- Search and print Leveled Reader titles

Weekly Activities

- Oral Language
- Research Roadmap
- Research and Inquiry
- Vocabulary and Spelling
- Author and Illustrator

Assess

ONLINE www.macmillanmh.com

Progress Monitoring

Unit 1 Reteaching and Intervention Opportunities

- Prescriptions for Reteaching
- Student Profile System

Online and CD-ROM materials are **Interactive White Board Ready!**

IWB

Available on CD

- **Listening Library**
- **Sound Pronunciation**

- **New Adventures with Buggles and Beezy**

Diagnostic Assessment

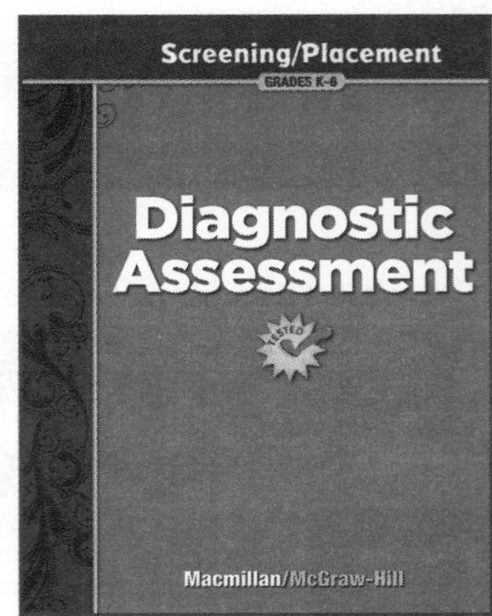

Screening, Diagnosis, and Placement

Use your state or district screener to identify children at risk. In addition, see tests in the **Diagnostic Assessment** book for information on determining the proficiency of children according to specific skills. Use the results to place children in the program.

- Diagnostics should be given at the beginning of the school year after you have had time to observe children and they become familiar with classroom routines. Use the diagnostics to determine children in need of intervention or to identify specific prerequisite skill deficiencies that you need to teach during Small Group differentiated instruction time.

Progress Monitoring Assessment

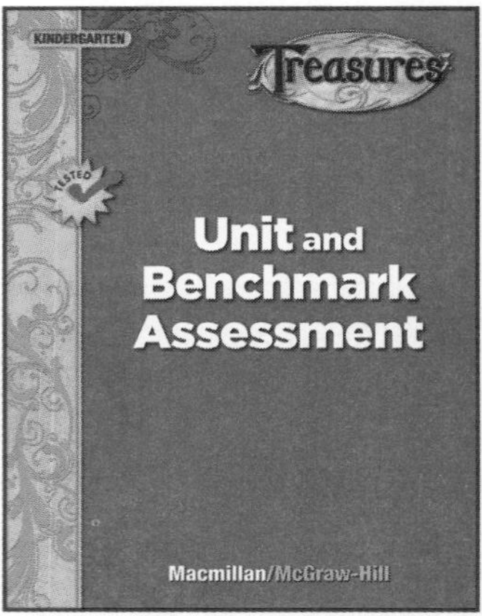

Meeting Grade-Level Expectations

Use these tests at the end of each unit (every 3 weeks). Multiple questions and next-steps information are provided.

Ongoing Informal Assessments

- Daily Quick Check Observations

Formal Assessments

- **Unit Assessment**

Benchmark Assessment

Give once a year to determine whether children have mastered the grade-level content standards and to document long-term academic growth.

Test Alignment

GRADE K UNIT 3 ASSESSED SKILLS	TerraNova/ CAT 6	SESAT	TPRI	DIBELS*
COMPREHENSION STRATEGIES AND SKILLS				
• Strategies: Recognize text/story structure	◆	◆	◆	◆
• Skills: Make and confirm predictions, Classify and categorize, Identify character and plot	◆	◆	◆	◆
VOCABULARY/HIGH-FREQUENCY WORDS				
• Shape and sound words				
• *see, go*	◆	◆	◆	◆
PHONEMIC AWARENESS				
• Phoneme isolation (initial and final /t/, initial and medial /i/)	◆	◆	◆	◆
• Phoneme blending (/t/, short /i/)	◆	◆	◆	◆
PHONICS				
• *t, i*	◆	◆	◆	◆
TEXT FEATURES				
• Photographs, Labels, Maps				
GRAMMAR				
• Verbs				

*Data from DIBELS serve as indicators of overall reading comprehension performance, not specific skills.

KEY

TerraNova/CAT 6	TerraNova, The Second Edition
SESAT	Stanford Early School Achievement Test
TPRI	Texas Primary Reading Inventory
DIBELS*	Dynamics Indicators of Basic Early Literacy Skills

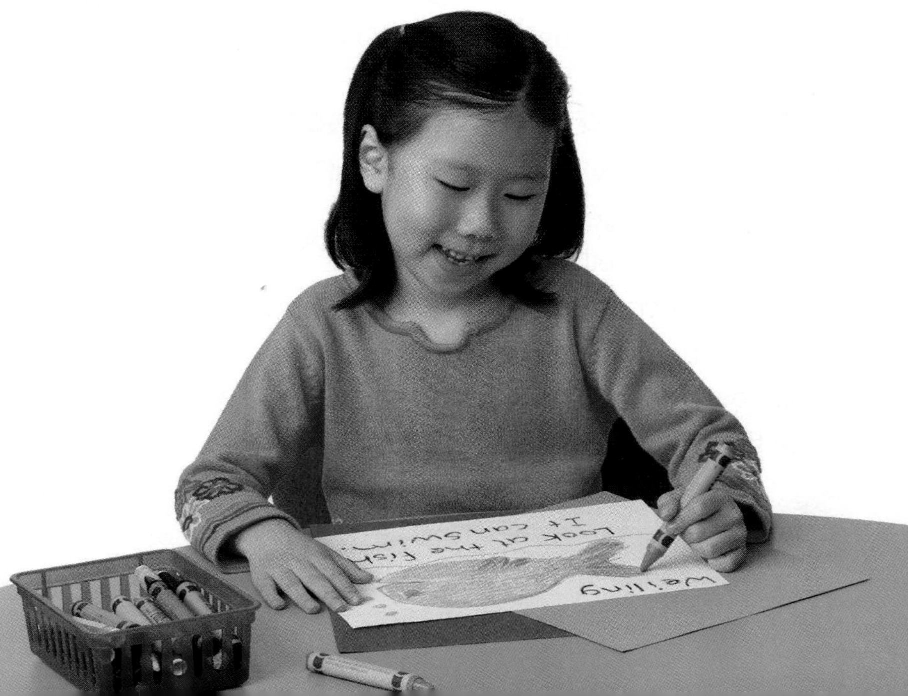

Theme Project: On the Move

Build Background

Sing the theme song. Then guide children to generate questions related to the theme and topic of class-wide interest. For example: *What is your favorite way to travel? How did you travel to school today?*

AUDIO CD
The Little
Red Caboose
Oh, the little red caboose,
little red caboose,
Riding behind the train!
Little red caboose,
little red caboose,
Riding behind the train!

Song on Listening Library Audio CD

Research and Inquiry

Self-Selected Theme Project

Planning a Project

What do I want to learn about transportation?

- Use the **Photo Cards** to show modes of transportation.
- Ask children to choose an unusual way they might want to travel to school and discuss what sources in the classroom they can use to find out about transportation.
- Refer to the **Big Book** *On the Go* and a picture dictionary.

Doing the Project

- Guide children to use the picture dictionary and Big Book to gather evidence.

Document and Evaluate Research

How can I share what I have learned?

You might suggest:

- a show-and-tell presentation
- an arts or craft project using pictures and writing

Help children decide what materials they will need for their presentation.

See the Unit Closer on pages 770–771.

Research Strategy

A **Picture Dictionary** shows many different places, people, and things.

Use the picture dictionary to gather ideas for a project.

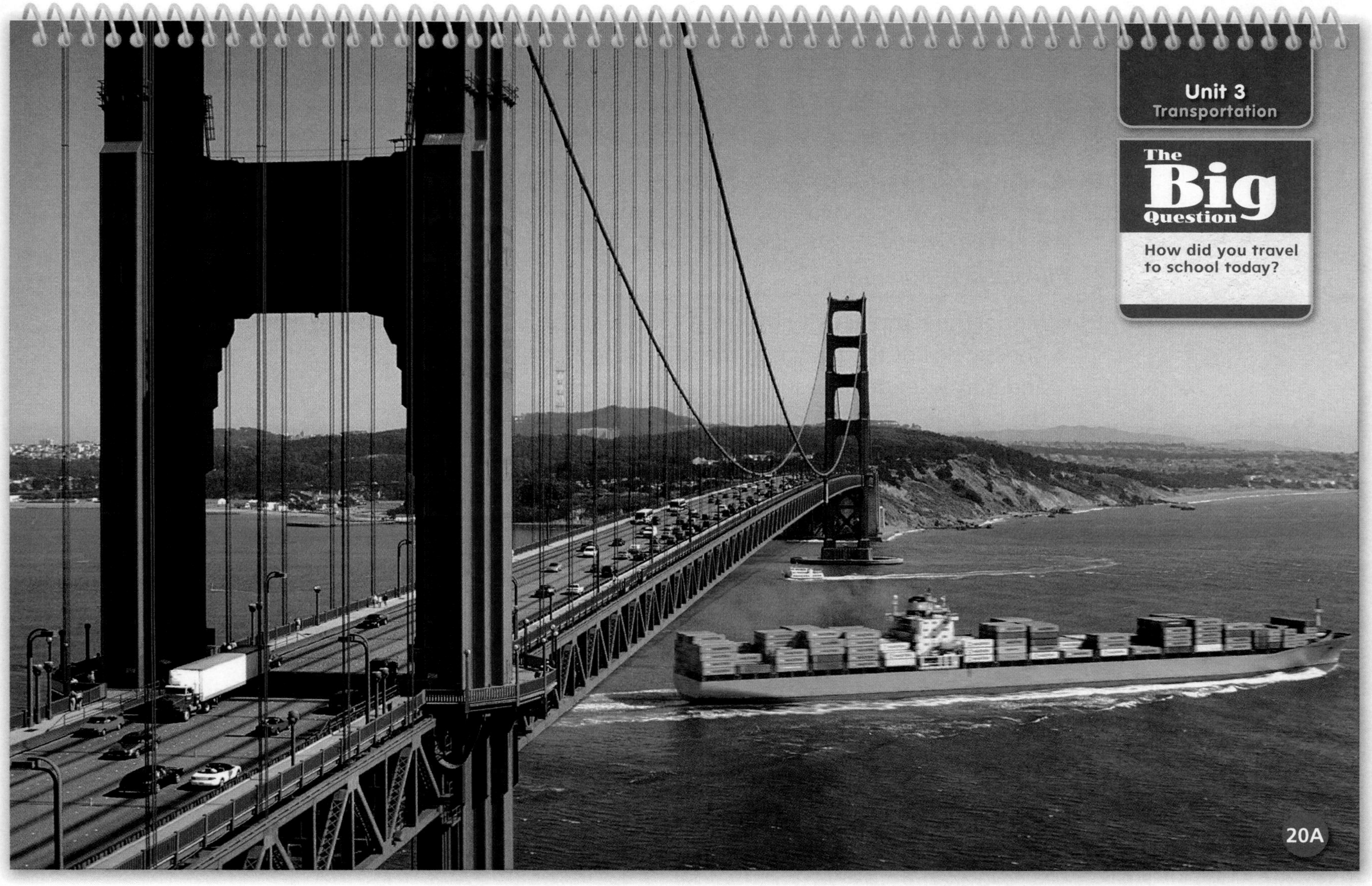

Unit 3
Transportation
The Big Question
How did you travel to school today?
20A

Teaching Chart 20A

Introduce Theme Project

TRANSPORTATION

Let's look at this photo. It is a bridge with different kinds of vehicles traveling on it. I see trucks and cars. I also see a ship traveling on the water. Point to the bridge, the cars, the trucks, and the ship. *How many ways can people travel?*

Look at the photograph together as you discuss the following:

- Ask: *What is your favorite way to travel?*
- Ask: *How do you get to school every day?*
- *Throughout this unit, we will be learning about transportation, getting around town, traveling near and far, and wheels that go round and round.*

Connect to Content

Gifted Talented

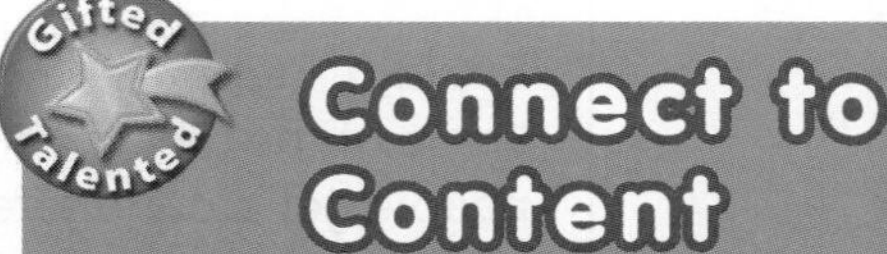

Social Studies

Share with children that people use different forms of transportation to get to their jobs. Some people can walk, while others need to use a car or a train. Tell children that throughout the unit, they can create a model of their neighborhood showing different kinds of transportation as well as a bridge that connects one neighborhood to another.

Connect to Content

Activity: How Far?

Ask: *What would happen if we put a toy car at the top of a playground slide?*

- Model the ramp activity by using a book and one block. Put the toy car at the top of the ramp and gently let go. Measure the distance from the bottom of the ramp to the back of the car with blocks.
- Have children use a one-block and a two-block ramp in the experiment and record their findings.
- Repeat the experiment using different toy cars.

Use Media

Help children

- understand the main idea or message in visual media;
- respond to visual messages by distinguishing between fantasy and reality in stories, videos, and television programs.

Minilesson

Identifying Traffic Signs

Explain Signs are all around us. They alert us to where we are. Some of the most common signs are **traffic signs**. These signs help people get around safely. They tell us when to stop, when to slow down, when to watch for children, when we are near a school, and how fast to travel.

Discuss Ask: *What traffic signs have you seen around town?* (stop, railroad crossing, speed limit, do not enter, school zone, etc.)

Apply Provide children with shape patterns for several different traffic signs. Have children trace, color, cut out and label their signs to match an actual traffic sign. Hang the signs around the classroom.

Connect to Content

Activity: Then and Now

Ask: *How did people travel in the past?*

- Have children cut out pictures or create drawings of transportation then and now.
- Ask them to sort their pictures into travel then/ travel now using a two-column chart.
- Create a class mural that shows different modes of transportation from the past and from today.

Character Building: Caring

Use the class mural to discuss easier ways for a physically challenged person to travel.

Minilesson

Writing Captions

Explain Pictures in books often have sentences underneath them that describe the pictures. They also give us more information about what the pictures are about. These sentences are called **captions**.

Discuss Ask: *What kind of information might be helpful to have in a caption?* (Who is in the picture? What does the picture show? Where was the picture taken?)

Apply Have children choose one of the pictures or drawings from the Travel Then/Travel Now project. Then guide children to write a caption that describes the picture. Display the captions with the class mural.

LOG ON FIND OUT

Research For technology research and presentation strategies, see the Computer Literacy lesson on pages 768–769. For additional research and inquiry, go to **www.macmillanmh.com**.

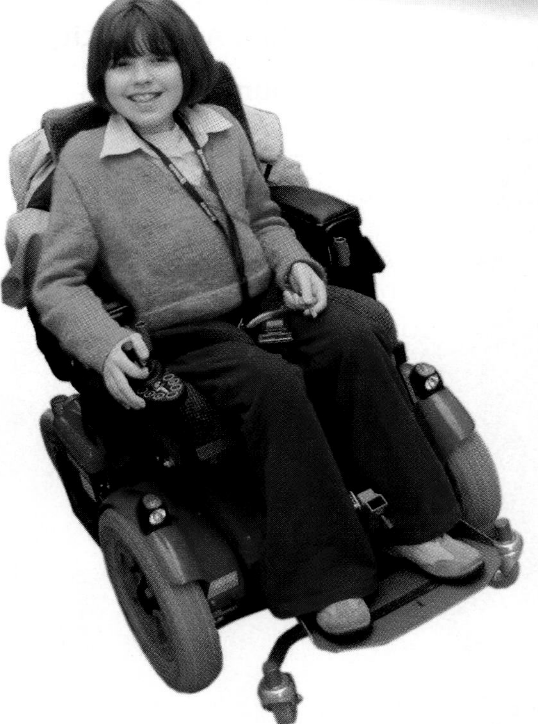

Week 1 ★ At a Glance

Priority Skills and Concepts

Comprehension

- **Genre:** Fiction, Nonfiction, Fable
- **Strategy:** Recognize Story Structure
- **Skill:** Make and Confirm Predictions
-  **Skill:** Identify Characters

High-Frequency Word

- ***see***

Oral Vocabulary

- **Build Robust Vocabulary:** ***continue***, ***glide***, ***rapidly***, ***transportation***, ***vehicles***

Fluency

- **Word Automaticity**
- **Sound-Spellings**

Phonemic Awareness

- **Phoneme Isolation**
- **Phoneme Blending**
- **Phoneme Categorization**

Phonics

- ***Tt***

Grammar

- **Action Words (Verbs)**

Writing

- **Sentences**

Key

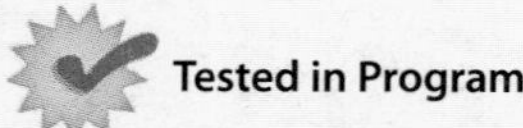 **Tested in Program**

 **Review Skill**

Digital Learning

Digital solutions to help plan and implement instruction

Teacher Resources

ONLINE www.macmillanmh.com

- **Teacher's Edition**
  - Lesson Planner and Resources also on CD-ROM
- **Professional Development**
  - Video Library

TeacherWorks Plus

Student Resources

ONLINE www.macmillanmh.com

- **Leveled Reader Database**
- **Activities**
  - Oral Language Activities
  - Phonics Activities
  - Vocabulary/Spelling Activities

Listening Library

- Recordings of Literature Big Books, Read-Aloud Trade Books, and Leveled Readers

Weekly Literature

Theme: Getting Around Town

Student Literature

A mix of fiction and nonfiction

Big Book

Genre Fiction

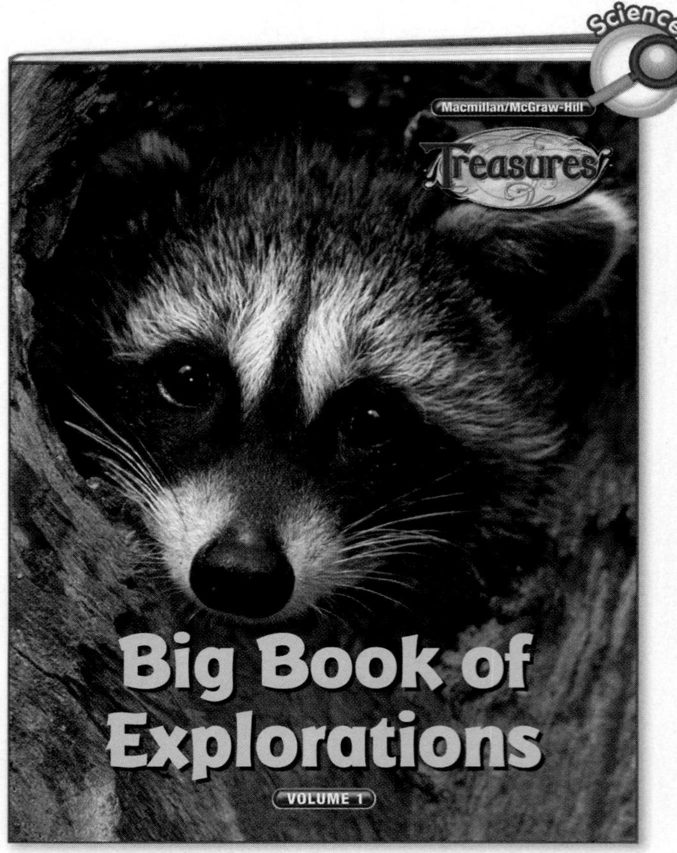

Big Book of Explorations

Genre Expository

Support Literature

Interactive Read-Aloud Anthology

Genre Fable

Oral Vocabulary Cards

- Listening Comprehension
- Build Robust Vocabulary

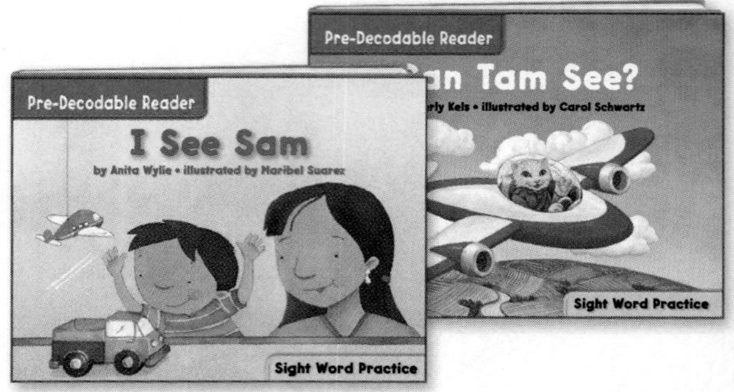

Pre-decodable Readers

Resources for Differentiated Instruction

Leveled Readers

GR Levels Rebus-D

Genre	Fiction

- Same Theme
- Same Vocabulary/Phonics
- Same Comprehension Skills

Approaching Level

On Level

Beyond Level

ELL

Leveled Reader Database
Go to www.macmillanmh.com.

Practice

Activity Book

Practice Book

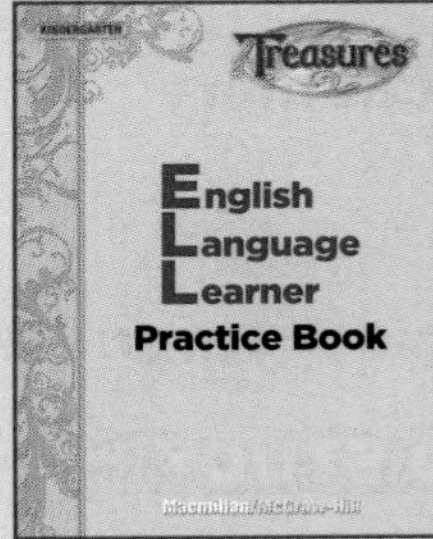
ELL Practice Book

Response to Intervention

- Phonemic Awareness
- Phonics
- Vocabulary
- Comprehension
- Fluency

Unit Assessment

Assess Unit Skills

- Phonemic Awareness
- Phonics
- High-Frequency Words
- Listening Comprehension

HOME-SCHOOL CONNECTION

- Family letters in English and Spanish
- Take-home stories and activities

LOG ON Suggested Lesson Plan

Go to www.macmillanmh.com for Online Lesson Planner

Professional Development Video Library

Big Book

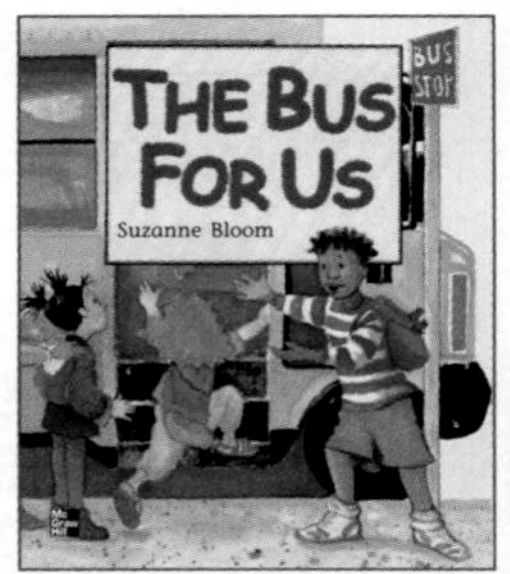

WHOLE GROUP	DAY 1	DAY 2
ORAL LANGUAGE • Oral Vocabulary • Phonemic Awareness	**Focus Question** What things do you see that move around town? Build Background, 526 **Oral Vocabulary** *continue, glide, rapidly, transportation, vehicle,* 526 **Phonemic Awareness** Phoneme Isolation, 529	**Focus Question** What did you see when we read *The Bus for Us*? **Oral Vocabulary** *continue, glide, rapidly, transportation, vehicle,* 534 Shape Words, 541 **Phonemic Awareness** Phoneme Blending, 542
WORD STUDY • Phonics • High-Frequency Words	**Phonics** Introduce /t/*t*, 530 Handwriting: Write *Tt*, 531 Activity Book, 4 Practice Book, 61 **High-Frequency Words** *see*, 528 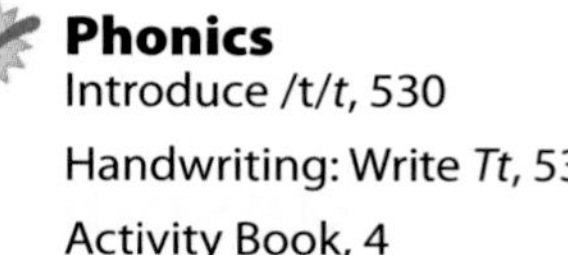	**Phonics** Review /t/*t*, 542 Blend with /t/*t*, 543 **Review High-Frequency Words**, 544
READING • Listening Comprehension • Apply Phonics and High-Frequency Words • Fluency	**Share the Big Book** *The Bus for Us* **Strategy:** Recognize Story Structure, 527 **Skill:** Make and Confirm Predictions, 527  Big Book	**Reread the Big Book** *The Bus for Us* **Strategy:** Recognize Story Structure, 536 **Skill:** Make and Confirm Predictions, 536 Big Book Retell, 540 **Pre-decodable Reader:** *I See Sam*, 544 Activity Book, 5 Practice Book, 62 **Fluency** Echo-Read, 541
LANGUAGE ARTS • Writing • Grammar	**Shared Writing** A List, 533 **Grammar** Action Words (Verbs), 532	**Interactive Writing** Sentences, 545
ASSESSMENT • Informal/Formal	Quick Check Phonemic Awareness, 529	Quick Check Comprehension, 540

SMALL GROUP Lesson Plan — Differentiated Instruction 520–521

Priority Skills

Phonemic Awareness/Phonics	High-Frequency Words	Oral Vocabulary	Comprehension
/t/t	*see*	Shape Words	**Strategy:** Recognize Story Structure **Skill:** Make and Confirm Predictions

Half-Day Kindergarten

Teach Core Skills
Focus on tested skill lessons, other lessons, and small group options as your time allows.

DAY 3

Focus Question What can you see from a car?

Oral Vocabulary *continue, glide, rapidly, transportation, vehicle*, 546

Oral Vocabulary Cards: "How Partridge Built Canoes"

Phonemic Awareness
Phoneme Isolation, 551

Phonics
Review, 552
Blend with /t/*t*, 553
Read Words, 553

High-Frequency Words
see, 550
Activity Book: "I See Sam," 7–8
Practice Book, 63–64
Read for Fluency, 550

Read the Big Book of Explorations
"Signs in the Park," 33–36

Text Feature:
Use Photographs, 548

Big Book of Explorations

Independent Writing
Prewrite and Draft Sentences, 555

Grammar
Action Words (Verbs), 554

Quick Check High-Frequency Words, 550

DAY 4

Focus Question What are some of the fastest things you see around town?

Oral Vocabulary *continue, glide, rapidly, transportation, vehicle*, 556

Shape Words, 559

Phonemic Awareness
Phoneme Blending, 560

Phonics
Picture Sort, 560
Blend with /t/*t*, 561
Activity Book, 9
Practice Book, 65

Review High-Frequency Words, 562

Interactive Read Aloud
Listening Comprehension, 558

Read Aloud: "The Turtle and the Rabbit"

Pre-decodable Reader:
Can Tam See?, 568

Read Aloud

Independent Writing
Revise and Edit Sentences, 563

Quick Check Phonics, 561

DAY 5
Review and Assess

Focus Question What did you see in our books this week?

Oral Vocabulary *continue, glide, rapidly, transportation, vehicle*, 564

Shape Words, 566

Phonemic Awareness
Phoneme Categorization, 567

Phonics
Read Words, 568
Dictation, 568
Activity Book, 12

High-Frequency Words
see, *a*, *like*, *we*, *the*, 566

Read Across Texts
Strategy: Recognize Story Structure, 565
Skill: Make and Confirm Predictions, 565
Activity Book, 11

Fluency Word Automaticity, 566

Independent Writing
Publish and Present Sentences, 569

Weekly Assessment, 596–597

Differentiated Instruction

What do I do in small groups?

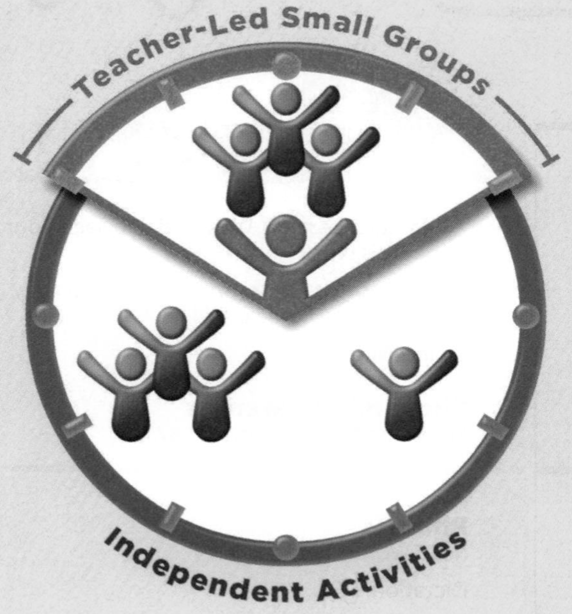

Focus on Skills

IF... **children need additional instruction, practice, or extension based on your Quick Check observations for the following priority skills**

 **Phonemic Awareness**
Phoneme Isolation, Blending, Categorization

 **Phonics**
Tt

 **High-Frequency Words**
see

Comprehension
Strategy: Recognize Story Structure
Skill: Make and Confirm Predictions

THEN...

Approaching	Preteach and
ELL	Reteach Skills
On Level	Practice
Beyond	Enrich and Accelerate Learning

Suggested Small Group Lesson Plan

	DAY 1	DAY 2
Approaching Level • **Preteach/Reteach** Tier 2 **Tier 2 Instruction**	• Oral Language, 570 • High-Frequency Words, 570 ELL High-Frequency Words Review, 570 • Phonemic Awareness, 571 • Phonics, 571 ELL Sound-Spellings Review, 571	• High-Frequency Words, 576 ELL • Pre-decodable Reader, 576 • Phonemic Awareness, 577 • Phonics, 577
On Level • **Practice**	• High-Frequency Words, 572 • Phonemic Awareness/Phonics, 572 ELL	• Pre-decodable Reader, 578
Beyond Level • **Extend/Accelerate** Gifted and Talented **Gifted and Talented**	• High-Frequency Words/Vocabulary, 573 ELL Expand Oral Vocabulary, 573 • Phonics, 573	• Pre-decodable Reader, 578
ELL • **Build English Language Proficiency** • **See ELL in other levels.**	• Oral Language Warm-Up, 574 • Academic Language, 574 • Vocabulary, 575	• Access to Core Content, 579

Focus on Leveled Readers

Levels Rebus–D

Approaching

On Level

Beyond

ELL

Manipulatives

Sound-Spelling WorkBoards

Sound-Spelling Cards

Photo Cards

High-Frequency Word Cards

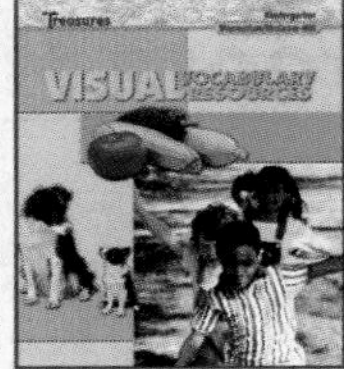

Visual Vocabulary Resources

Additional Leveled Readers

Leveled Reader Database

www.macmillanmh.com

Search by

- Comprehension Skill
- Content Area
- Genre
- Text Feature
- Guided Reading Level
- Reading Recovery Level
- Lexile Score
- Benchmark Level

Subscription also available

DAY 3	DAY 4	DAY 5
• High-Frequency Words, 580 ELL • Phonemic Awareness, 580 • Phonics, 581 • Pre-decodable Reader, 581	• Phonemic Awareness, 584 • Phonics, 584 ELL • Leveled Reader Lesson 1, 585	• Phonemic Awareness, 590 • Phonics, 590 ELL • Leveled Reader Lesson 2, 591 • High-Frequency Words, 591
• Phonics, 582	• Leveled Reader Lesson 1, 586 ELL	• Leveled Reader Lesson 2, 592
• Phonics, 582	• Leveled Reader Lesson 1, 587 Analyze, 587	• Leveled Reader Lesson 2, 593 ELL • Expand Vocabulary, 593
• Access to Core Content, 583 • Grammar, 583	• Leveled Reader, 588–589	• Fluency, 594 • High-Frequency Words, 595 • Writing, 595

What do I do with the rest of my class?

- Activity Book
- Practice Book
- ELL Practice Book
- Leveled Reader Activities
- Literacy Workstations
- Online Activities
- Buggles and Beezy

Classroom Management Tools

Weekly Contract

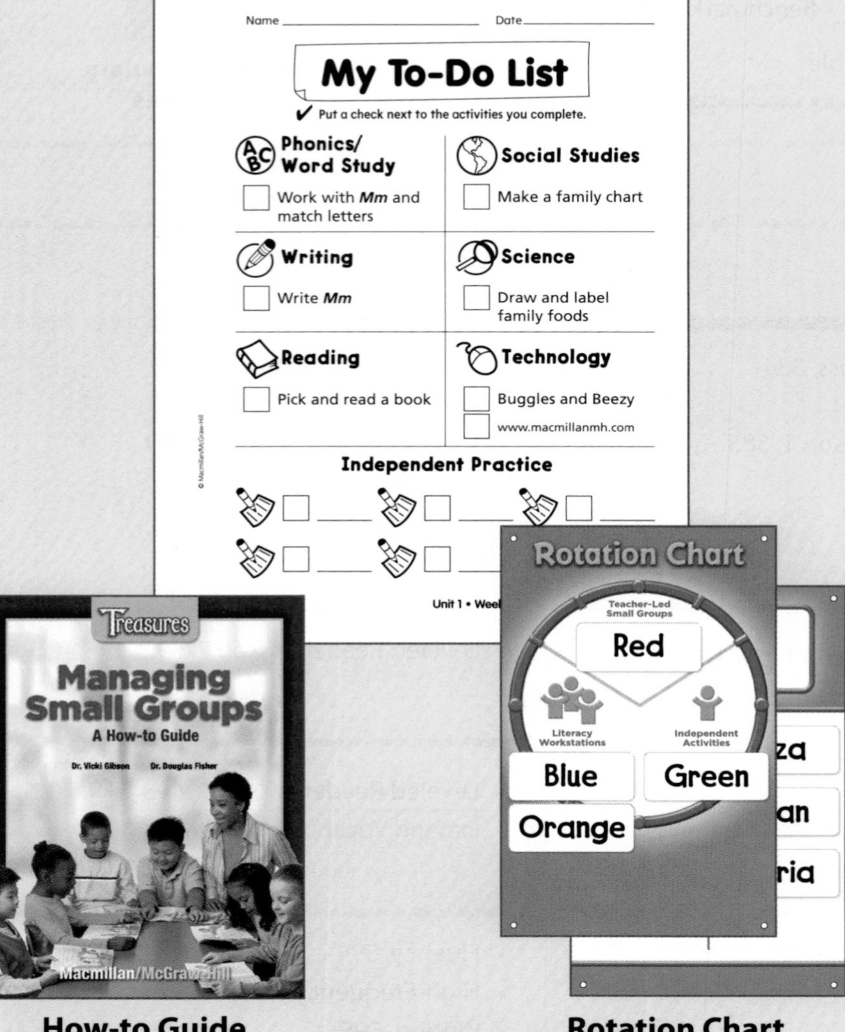
Name ______ Date ______

My To-Do List

✔ Put a check next to the activities you complete.

Phonics/ Word Study	Social Studies
☐ Work with *Mm* and match letters	☐ Make a family chart
Writing	**Science**
☐ Write *Mm*	☐ Draw and label family foods
Reading	**Technology**
☐ Pick and read a book	☐ Buggles and Beezy ☐ www.macmillanmh.com

Independent Practice

☐ ____ ☐ ____ ☐ ____

☐ ____ ☐ ____

Unit 1 • Week

How-to Guide

Rotation Chart

Digital Learning

- Match Letters
- Match Letters to Sounds
- Blend Words

- Read Other Books by the Author or Illustrator

Practice

Activity Book

Practice Book

ELL Practice Book

ONLINE INSTRUCTION www.macmillanmh.com

Oral Language Activities

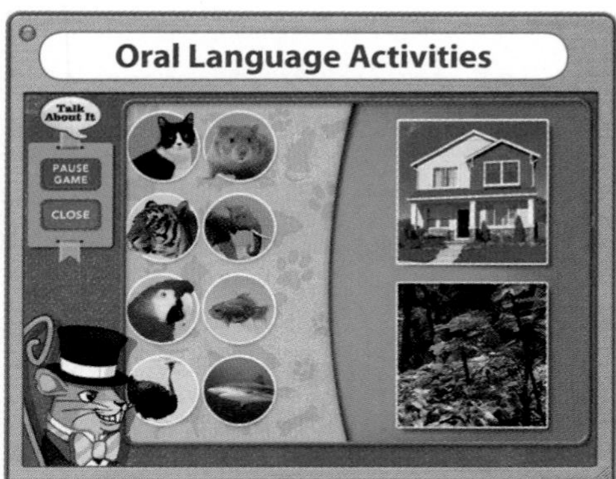

- Focus on Unit Vocabulary and Concepts
- English Language Learner Support

Vocabulary/Spelling Activities

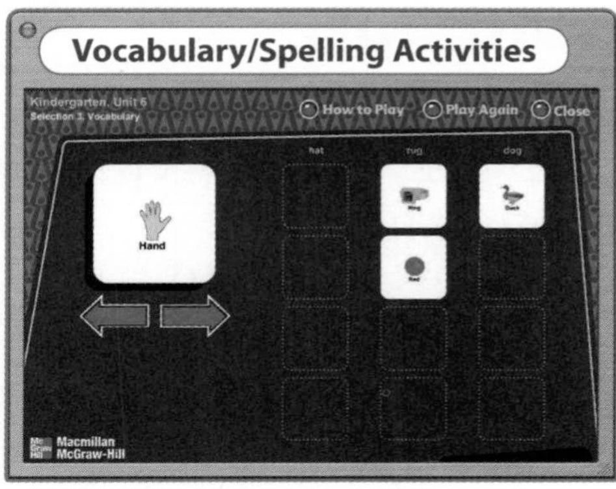

- Differentiated Lists and Activities

Leveled Reader Database

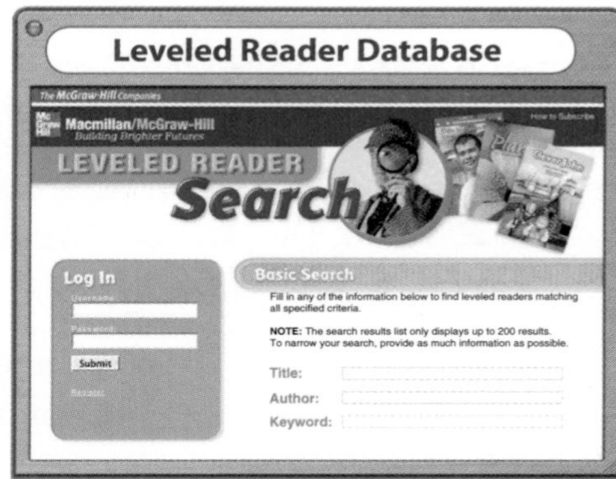

- Leveled Reader Database
- Search titles by level, skill, content area, and more

Available on CD

LISTENING LIBRARY
Recordings of selections
- Literature Big Books
- Read-Aloud Trade Books
- Leveled Readers
- ELL Readers

NEW ADVENTURES WITH BUGGLES AND BEEZY
Phonemic awareness and phonics activities

Leveled Reader Activities

Approaching

On Level

Beyond

Tiger Can See

ELL

See inside cover of all Leveled Readers.

Literacy Workstations

See lessons on pages 524–525.

Teacher-Led Small Groups
Independent Activities

What do I do with the rest of my class?

Reading

Objectives

- Compare books by the same author
- Read and respond to a book

Phonics/Word Study

Objectives

- Sort pictures by initial sounds and letters /m/*m*, /p/*p*, /t/*t*
- Form words that begin with the letters *m*, *p*, *s*, *t*

Reading
Read an Author
20 Minutes
Read books by the same author.
Raffi
Donald Crews
Suzanne Bloom
❶ Pick an author.
❷ Read the books.
❸ Talk about them.
Do More
• How were the characters in each book like each other?
• What else might the author write about?
Raffi
For more book titles, go to the Meet the Author/ Illustrator page on www.macmillanmh.com
13
© Macmillan/McGraw-Hill

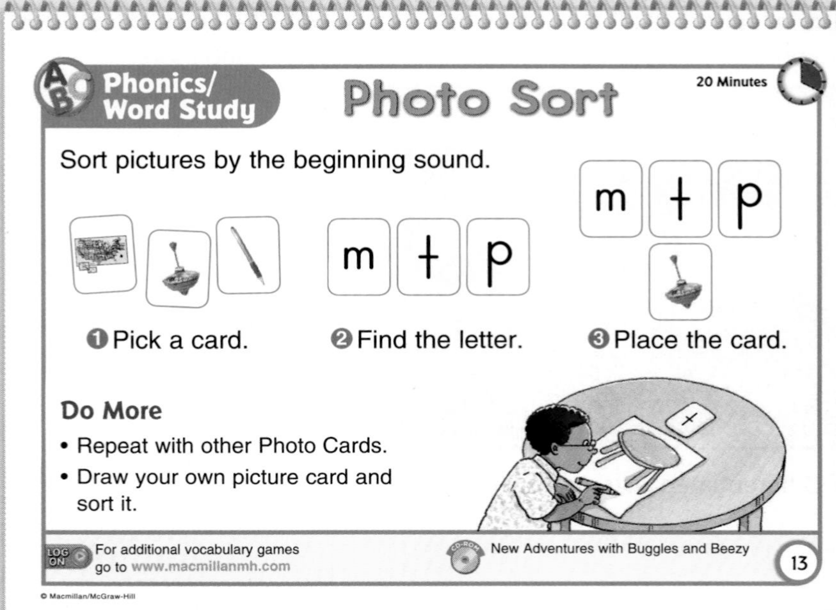
Phonics/ Word Study
Photo Sort
20 Minutes
Sort pictures by the beginning sound.
m t p
m t p
❶ Pick a card.
❷ Find the letter.
❸ Place the card.
Do More
• Repeat with other Photo Cards.
• Draw your own picture card and sort it.
For additional vocabulary games go to www.macmillanmh.com
New Adventures with Buggles and Beezy
13
© Macmillan/McGraw-Hill

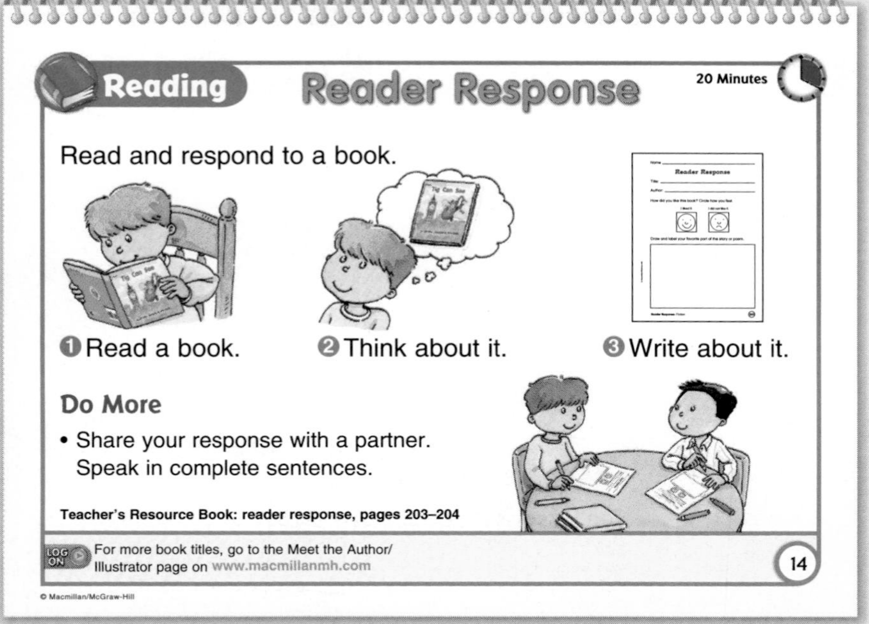
Reading
Reader Response
20 Minutes
Read and respond to a book.
❶ Read a book.
❷ Think about it.
❸ Write about it.
Do More
• Share your response with a partner. Speak in complete sentences.
Teacher's Resource Book: reader response, pages 203–204
For more book titles, go to the Meet the Author/ Illustrator page on www.macmillanmh.com
14
© Macmillan/McGraw-Hill

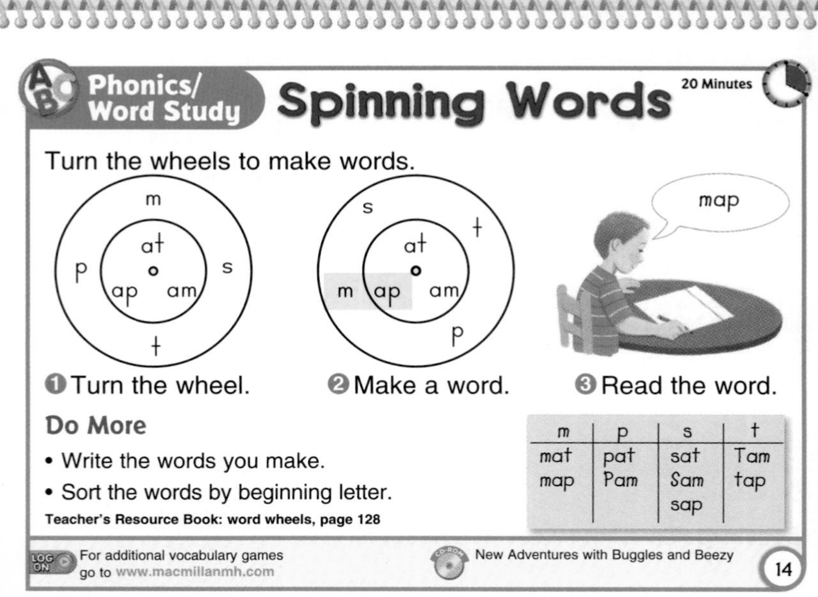
Phonics/ Word Study
Spinning Words
20 Minutes
Turn the wheels to make words.
map
❶ Turn the wheel.
❷ Make a word.
❸ Read the word.
Do More
• Write the words you make.
• Sort the words by beginning letter.
m | p | s | t
mat map | pat Pam | sat Sam sap | Tam tap
Teacher's Resource Book: word wheels, page 128
For additional vocabulary games go to www.macmillanmh.com
New Adventures with Buggles and Beezy
14
© Macmillan/McGraw-Hill

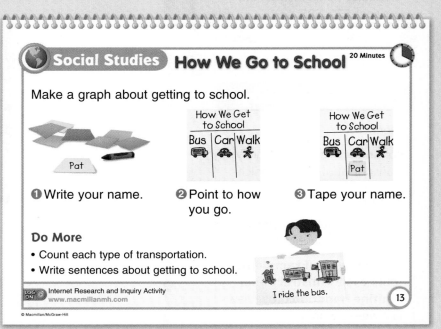

Literacy Workstation Flip Charts

Writing

Objectives

- Write sentences about a vehicle
- Identify and label pictures that begin with the letter *Tt*

Content Literacy

Objectives

- Use magnets to move around a map
- Make a graph about getting to school

Writing — **Write Sentences** — 20 Minutes

Write about a vehicle.

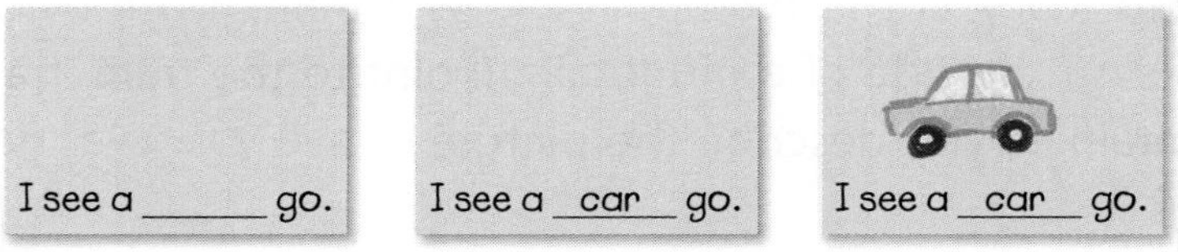

❶ Write the sentence. ❷ Finish the sentence. ❸ Draw a picture.

Do More

- Write another sentence about your vehicle. Begin your sentence with a capital letter.

13

Science — **Magnets on the Move** — 20 Minutes

Use magnets to move around a map.

❶ Make a map. ❷ Place the map. ❸ Move a magnet.

Do More

- Find out what else magnets can move.

Internet Research and Inquiry Activity
www.macmillanmh.com

14

Writing — **Label with Tt** — 20 Minutes

Make a T. Label Tt items from magazines.

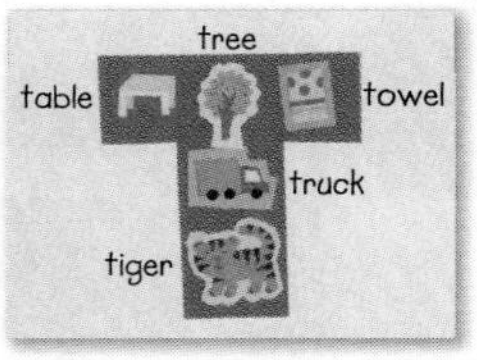

❶ Find Tt items. ❷ Cut out the Tt items. ❸ Glue and label them.

Do More

- Find and label more Tt items.
- Hunt for T and t in books.

14

Social Studies — **How We Go to School** — 20 Minutes

Make a graph about getting to school.

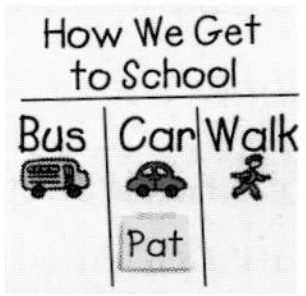

❶ Write your name. ❷ Point to how you go. ❸ Tape your name.

Do More

- Count each type of transportation.
- Write sentences about getting to school.

Internet Research and Inquiry Activity
www.macmillanmh.com

13

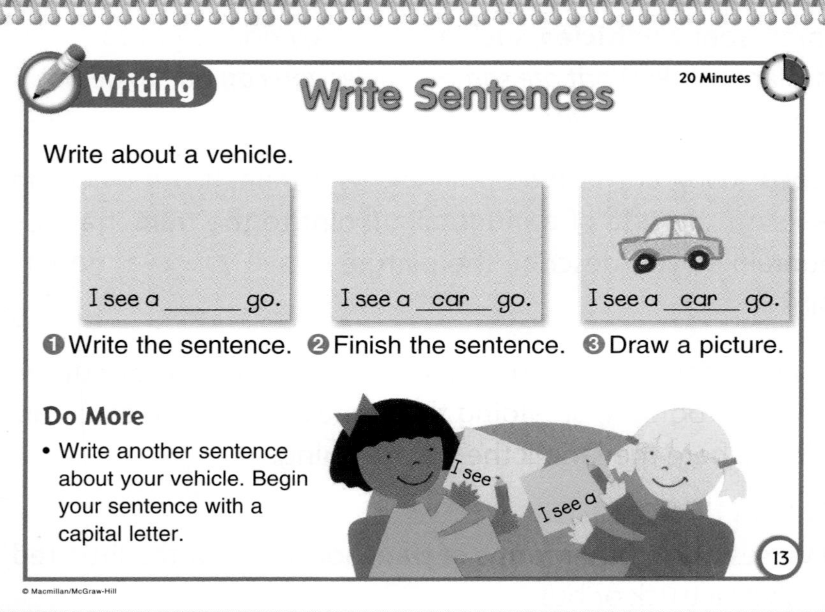

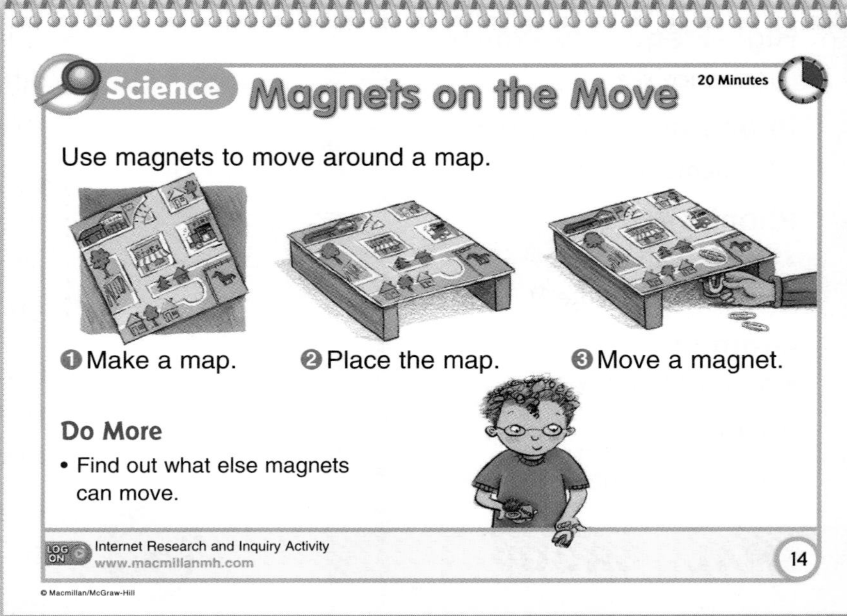

Day 1 At a Glance

WHOLE GROUP

Oral Language
- Build Background

Comprehension
- Read *The Bus for Us*
- Strategy: Recognize Story Structure
- Skill: Make and Confirm Predictions

High-Frequency Words
- Introduce *see*

Phonemic Awareness
- Phoneme Isolation

Phonics
- Introduce /t/*t*
- Handwriting: Write *Tt*

Grammar
- Action Words (Verbs)

Writing
- Shared Writing: A List

SMALL GROUP

- Differentiated Instruction, pages 570–595

Oral Vocabulary

Week 1

continue glide rapidly transportation vehicle

Review

grateful include problem solve thoughtful

Use the **Define/Example/Ask** routine in the **Instructional Routine Handbook** to review last week's words.

Oral Language

Build Background: *Getting Around*

INTRODUCE THE THEME

Tell children that this week they will be talking and reading about the forms of **transportation**—such as buses, trains, or cars—that people use to get to places.

Write the following question on the board: *What things do you see that move around town?* Track the print as you read aloud the question. Help children recognize that spoken words can be represented by print. Then prompt children to answer the question.

ACCESS PRIOR KNOWLEDGE

- Ask children about **vehicles**, such as cars, they ride to get to different places. Ask: *What are some vehicles you can ride to get to school? To friends? To family?*

Think Aloud Look at this picture. It shows a train. It is moving on train tracks on the side of a mountain. (Point to the train, tracks, and mountain as you describe the picture.) Have you ever ridden on a train?

- Look at the photograph together and sing the song. Talk about the train in the photograph, providing the name and color of each car. Ask children where they think the train is going.

INNOVATE ON THE SONG

Write new verses using other forms of transportation for the little red caboose, such as a truck or bus.

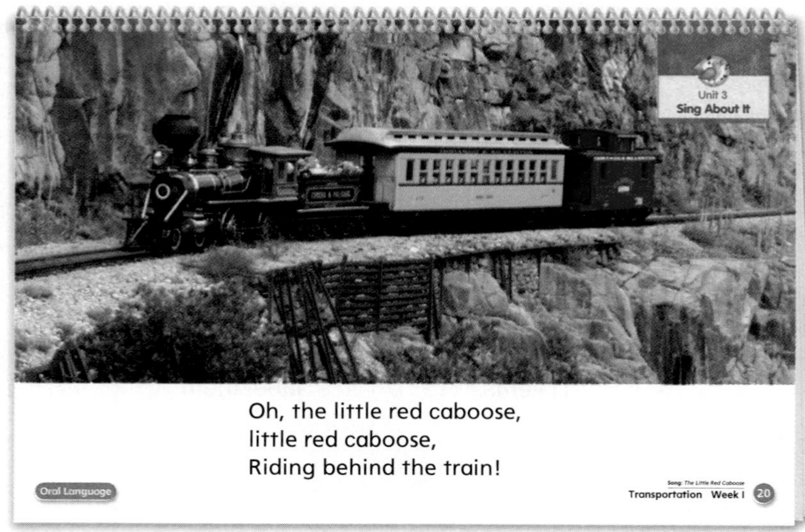

Teaching Chart 20

Share the Big Book

Listening Comprehension

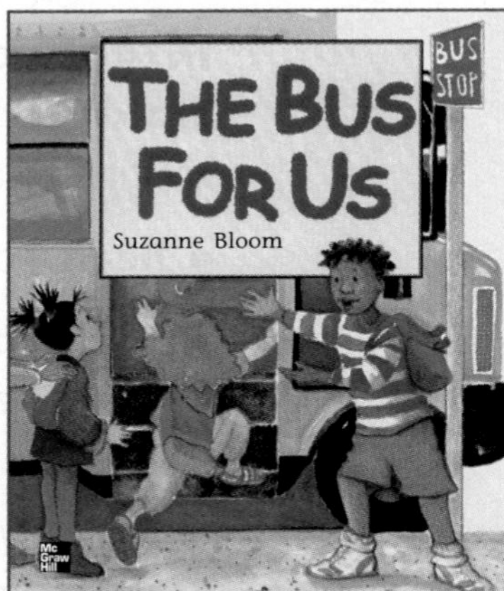

Big Book

PREVIEW Display the cover. Guide children to make an inference based upon the cover. *I see a bus with some children getting on. Where might they be going? Now let's read about the bus, a type of* ***vehicle****.*

Read the title and the name of the author/illustrator as you track the print.

GENRE: LITERARY TEXT/FICTION Tell children that this story is **fiction**, which means it did not really happen.

STRATEGY Recognize Story Structure

EXPLAIN/MODEL Remind children that they can use a book's structure to figure out what will come next as they read and listen.

Think Aloud Sometimes the structure of a book follows a pattern. Can you tell me what comes next in this pattern: *Hello, good-bye; hello, good-bye; hello* . . . ? I know that the next word is *good-bye* because I see that the pattern is *hello, good-bye*. As we read the book, we will be paying attention to its pattern.

SKILL Make and Confirm Predictions

EXPLAIN/MODEL Tell children that now they will learn how to check to see if the predictions they make are correct. Display pages 4–5.

Think Aloud I will try to figure out what vehicle is coming. I think it is a taxi because I see what looks like the front of a yellow taxi. Let's turn the page to see if I was right. Yes, it is a taxi.

Read the Big Book

SET PURPOSE Tell children to pay attention to the structure of the book to figure out what will come next. Use the **Define/Example/Ask** routine to teach the story words on the inside back cover.

Respond to Literature

MAKE CONNECTIONS Discuss the book. Have children make connections to their own experiences and to the larger community.

Objectives

- Discuss the theme
- Understand that spoken words can be represented in print for communication
- Use oral vocabulary words *vehicle* and *transportation*
- Listen and respond to a story
- Recognize story structure/ make and confirm predictions

Materials

- Teaching Chart 20
- Big Book: *The Bus for Us*

ELL

Use the **Interactive Question-Response Guide** for *The Bus for Us,* **ELL Resource Book** pages 62–69, to guide children through a reading of the book. As you read *The Bus for Us,* make meaning clear by pointing to the pictures, demonstrating word meanings, paraphrasing text, and asking children questions.

Digital Learning

Story on **Listening Library Audio CD**

Objectives

- Read the high-frequency word *see*
- Review the high-frequency words *a, like, the, we*
- Identify the word *see* in the text and speech
- Follow oral directions in sequence

Materials

- High-Frequency Word Cards: *a, like, see, the, we*
- Teaching Chart 21

ELL

Reinforce Vocabulary Display the **High-Frequency Word Cards** *a, like, see, the, we.* Point to classroom objects and groups of children as you use the high-frequency words in sentences such as the following: *I see a big book. Do you see a big book?* (Yes, we see a big book.) *I like the big book. Do you like the big book?* (Yes, we like the big book.) Repeat with other objects.

High-Frequency Words

see

see

INTRODUCE Display the **High-Frequency Word Card** for **see**. Use the **Read/Spell/Write** routine to teach the word.

- **Read** Point to and say the word *see. This is the word* see. *I* see *a book.*
- **Spell** *The word* see *is spelled* s-e-e. *What's the first sound in* see? *That's right. The first sound in* see *is /s/. That's why the first letter is* s. *After the* s, *I see two* e*'s. Let's read and spell* see *together.*
- **Write** *Now let's write the word* see *on our papers. Let's spell aloud the word as we write it:* see, s-e-e.

REVIEW *a, like, the, we* Display each card and have children read the word. Repeat several times.

a | like | we | the

READ THE RHYME AND CHIME Tell children to point to *see* each time they see it. Repeat the rhyme together for fluency. Add *see* to the class Word Wall.

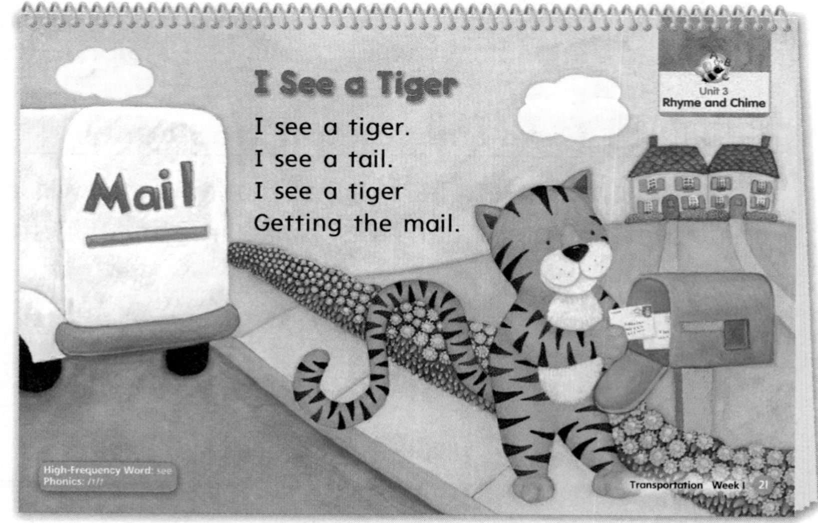

I See a Tiger
I see a tiger.
I see a tail.
I see a tiger
Getting the mail.
Mail
Unit 3
Rhyme and Chime
Transportation Week 1 21

Teaching Chart 21

For Tier 2 instruction, see page 570.

TIME TO MOVE!

Have children act out "See me" sentences by following simple 1- and 2-step oral directions in sequence. "See me jump." "See me hop." "See me touch my toes."

Phonemic Awareness

Phoneme Isolation

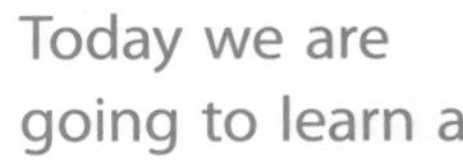

Model

Display the **Photo Card** for *turtle*.

Repeat with the Photo Card for *teeth*.

Today we are going to learn a new sound. Listen for the sound at the beginning of *turtle*: /t/. *Turtle* has /t/ at the beginning. Say the sound with me: /t/. What is the sound? We'll tap the top of our heads when we hear /t/ at the beginning of a word.

Read the "I See a Tiger" Rhyme and Chime again. Have children tap every time they hear /t/.

I see a tiger.
I see a tail.
I see a tiger
Getting the mail.

Review /s/, /p/

Display the Photo Card for *sock*.

Repeat for *pen*.

This is a *sock*. The beginning sound in *sock* is /s/. What is the sound?

Guided Practice/Practice

Display and name the Photo Cards. Children identify initial sounds. Guide practice with the first card, using the same routine. Continue orally with the words *tub*, *take*, *time*, *sad*, *sail*, *pet*, and *puppy*.

Say each picture name with me. Tell me the sound you hear at the beginning of the word.

Quick Check

Can children identify the initial /t/ sound?

During **Small Group Instruction**

If No → **Approaching Level** Provide more practice isolating beginning sounds, page 571.

If Yes → **On Level** Blend sounds to form words with /t/, page 572.

Beyond Level Blend sounds to form words with /t/, page 573.

Objectives

- Identify initial sound /t/
- Review initial /s/ and /p/

Materials

- Photo Cards: *pen, pizza, soap, sock, table, teeth, toothbrush, turtle*

ELL

Pronunciation Display and have children name Photo Cards from this and prior lessons to reinforce phonemic awareness and word meanings. Point to a card and ask: *What do you see?* (a turtle) *What is the sound at the beginning of the word* turtle? (/t/) Demonstrate the correct way to say /t/. Display articulation photos on small **Sound-Spelling Cards**. Repeat with Photo Cards with words that begin with /p/ and /s/.

Objectives

- Match the letter *t* to the /t/ sound
- Handwriting: Write *Tt*

Materials

- Sound-Spelling Card: *Turtle*
- Teaching Chart 21
- Word-Building Cards
- Handwriting
- Handwriting Teacher's Edition
- Activity Book, p. 4
- Practice Book, p. 61

ELL

Variations in Languages
Speakers of Vietnamese and Hmong may have difficulty perceiving and pronouncing /t/. Use the Approaching Level Phonics lessons for additional pronunciation and decoding practice.

Sound Pronunciation

See **Sound Pronunciation CD** for a model of the /t/ sound. Play this for children needing additional models.

Phonics

Introduce /t/*t*

Model

Display the *Turtle* **Sound-Spelling Card**.

This is the *Turtle* card. The sound is /t/. The /t/ sound is spelled with the letter *t*. Say it with me: /t/. This is the sound at the beginning of the word *turtle*. Listen: /t/, /t/, /t/ . . . *urtle*, *turtle*. What is the name of this letter? What sound does this letter stand for?

Read the "I See a Tiger" Rhyme and Chime. Point out that the word *Tiger* in the title begins with the letter *T*. Reread the title. Model placing a self-stick note below the *T* in *Tiger*.

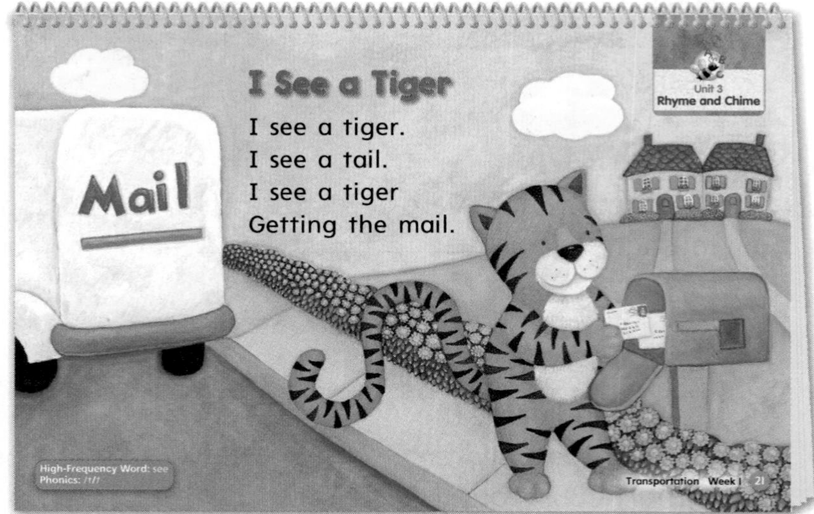

Teaching Chart 21

Guided Practice/Practice

Read the rest of the rhyme. Stop after each line. Children place self-stick notes below words that begin with *t*. Guide practice with *tiger* in line 1. Repeat with *s*.

Let's put a sticky note below the word in the line that begins with the letter *t*. The word *tiger* begins with the letter *t*.

Which word begins with the letter *s*?

Yes, the word *see* begins with the letter *s*.

For Tier 2 instruction, see page 571.

Build Fluency: Sound-Spellings

Display the following **Word-Building Cards**: *a, m, p, s, t*. Have children chorally say each sound. Repeat and vary the pace.

Handwriting: Write *Tt*

MODEL Model holding up your writing hand. Say the handwriting cues below as you write the capital and lowercase forms of *Tt* on the board. Identify the forms of the letter for children. Then trace the letters on the board and in the air as you say /t/.

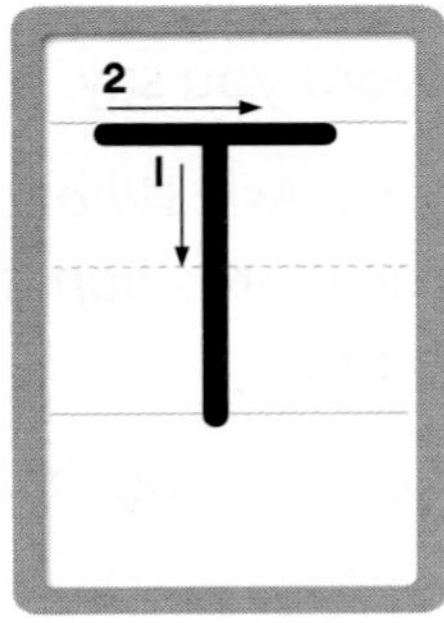

Straight down. Go back to the top. Straight across.

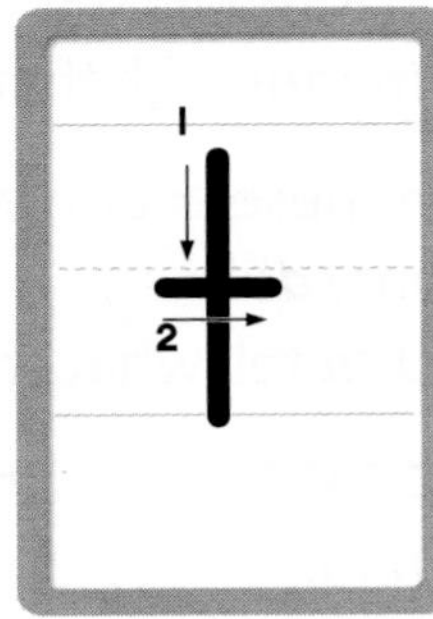

Start at the top line. Straight down. Go to the dotted line. Straight across.

PRACTICE Ask children to hold up their writing hand.

- Say the cues together as children trace with their index finger the letters you wrote on the board. Have children identify the uppercase and lowercase forms of the letter.
- Have children write *T* and *t* in the air as they say /t/ multiple times.
- Distribute handwriting practice pages. Observe children's pencil grip and paper position, and correct as necessary. Have children say /t/ every time they write the letter *t*.

Check that children form letters starting at the top and moving to the bottom. See **Handwriting Teacher's Edition** for ball-and-stick and slant models.

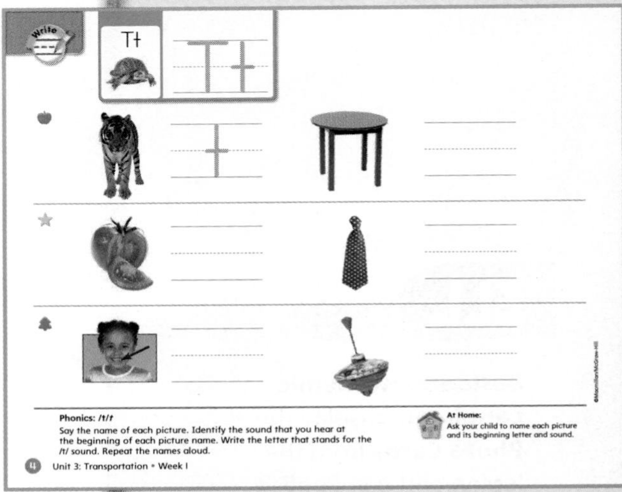

Activity Book, page 4
Practice Book, page 61

Objectives

- Recognize action words (verbs)
- Use past and future tenses when speaking

Materials

- Big Book: *The Bus for Us*
- Photo Cards: *balloon, dog, helicopter, jet, man*

Grammar

Action Words (Verbs)

MODEL Use the **Big Book** *The Bus for Us* to introduce action words. Point to illustrations as you say these sentences: *We see a taxi. We see a tow truck.* Then ask: *What are we doing?*

- Have children gesture using binoculars to see. *I see a lot.* Point to other story illustrations and have children say: *We see a* ________. Then ask: *What do we do?* (see)

Ask children to stand. Explain that you will say a word and then point to someone. Tell that child to act out the word you say.

- Use these action words: *hop, smile, clap, sit.* Ask: *What does [child's name] do?* (He/She hops.) Explain that the words *hop, smile, clap,* and *sit* tell what someone or something does.

PRACTICE Show **Photo Cards** for *jet, helicopter, dog, balloon,* and *man*.

- Have children identify each picture. Model using each picture name in a sentence that includes an action word, such as:

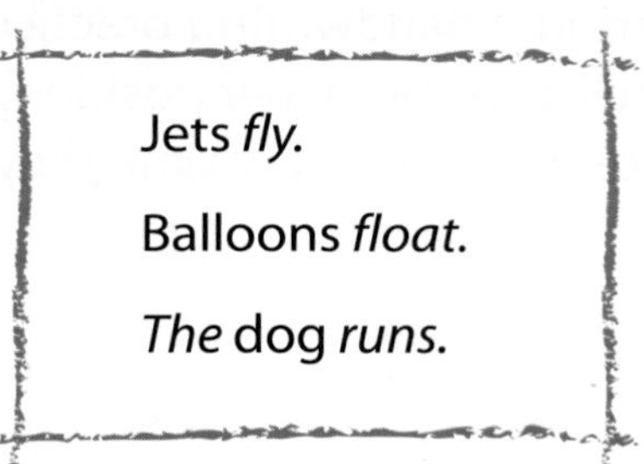

Jets *fly.*

Balloons *float.*

The dog *runs.*

- After each sentence, ask children which word tells what the person or object is doing. Then have children make up their own sentences about the people and objects in the pictures. Guide them to name the action word and to use complete sentences.

ELL

Basic and Academic Language Display the **Photo Cards** from the lesson and pair English Language Learners with fluent speakers. Have partners make up sentences with the picture names and a verb. Write their sentences, read them with children, and say: *Tell me the action word, or verb, in your sentence.*

Writing

Shared Writing: A List

BRAINSTORM

Remind children that in the **Big Book** *The Bus for Us*, they learned that there are many kinds of **vehicles** on the road. Ask children to name some of them.

WRITE

- Create a list as shown below. Read the heading aloud as you track the print. Point out the high-frequency word *see*.
- Tell children that they will make a list of the vehicles they saw in the book as well as other vehicles they have seen.
- List children's ideas. Read the completed list together.
- Point out how the words are written one under the other. Say: *A list helps us remember information and ideas.*
- Save the list to refer to in other writing activities this week.

Vehicles I See

taxi
tow truck
fire engine
ice-cream truck
garbage truck
backhoe
school bus
ambulance
bicycle
car
train
airplane

Write About It

Have children draw a picture of a bus or a truck. Tell them to include as many details as they can. Help them label their picture.

Objective

- Write a list

Materials

- Big Book: *The Bus for Us*

5-Day Writing

Sentences	
DAY 1	Shared: A List
DAY 2	Interactive: Sentences
DAY 3	Independent: Prewrite and Draft Sentences
DAY 4	Independent: Revise and Edit Sentences
DAY 5	Independent: Publish and Present

ELL

Prewriting Planning
Provide the **Big Book** for children to use. Help them point to and name vehicles, such as a bus, a truck, or another form of transportation, before they begin working on their journal entries. Help them label their drawings.

Transitions That Teach

While children wait in line, have them name types of **transportation**.

DAY 2
At a Glance

WHOLE GROUP

Oral Language
- Build Robust Vocabulary

Comprehension
- Reread *The Bus for Us*
- Strategy: Recognize Story Structure
- Skill: Make and Confirm Predictions
- Fluency: Echo-Read

Vocabulary
- Shape Words
- Story Words: *tow truck, backhoe*

Phonemic Awareness
- Phoneme Blending

Phonics
- Review /t/*t*
- Blend with /t/*t*
- Pre-decodable Reader: *I See Sam*

Writing
- Interactive Writing: Sentences

SMALL GROUP

- Differentiated Instruction, pages 570–595

Oral Vocabulary

Week 1

continue glide rapidly transportation vehicle

Review

grateful include problem solve thoughtful

Use the **Define/Example/Ask** routine in the **Instructional Routine Handbook** to review last week's words.

Oral Language

Build Robust Vocabulary

INTRODUCE WORDS

Tell children that today you are going to talk about the forms of transportation in *The Bus for Us. Transportation is the way people get from one place to another. The form of transportation that I used to get to school was my car. What transportation did you use today? Did you ride in a vehicle?* Read pages 5–9 aloud.

Vocabulary Routine

Use the routine below to discuss the meaning of each word.

Define: **Transportation** is a way to move people or things from one place to another. Say the word with me.
Example: A subway is a type of transportation for people living in cities.
Ask: What kind of transportation do you use to get to school?

Define: A **vehicle** is something used to carry people or things. Say the word with me.
Example: A canoe is a good vehicle for crossing a lake.
Ask: Can you name some vehicles that go on land?

CREATE A CHART

Create a two-column chart, or use **Teaching Chart G3**. Write the headings as shown. Read the chart together as you track the print. *First, Tess sees a taxi. I will write* taxi *on the chart. What does a taxi do?* Have children share information and ideas to help you complete the chart. Guide them to speak audibly as they use complete sentences. Recast children's responses using complete sentences as needed.

Vehicle	What It Does
taxi	takes people around town
tow truck	hauls away cars
fire engine	takes firefighters to fires
ice-cream truck	carries ice cream to sell

Listen for Rhyme

IDENTIFY RHYME

Tell children that words rhyme when they have the same ending sounds. *The word* way *rhymes with* day. Tell children *way* and *day* end with the sounds for /ay/, *ay*. Guide children to recognize the rhyming pairs in the song. Then guide them to distinguish rhyming pairs from non-rhyming pairs of words. Use the following words from the song: *plane/train* (rhyming pair), *bike/van* (non-rhyming pair), *van/sedan* (rhyming pair).

SING ABOUT TRANSPORTATION

Let's sing a fun song about transportation, or the way people move from one place to another. Play the song "Transportation Is the Way!" using the **Listening Library Audio CD**. Then teach children the words and sing the song together.

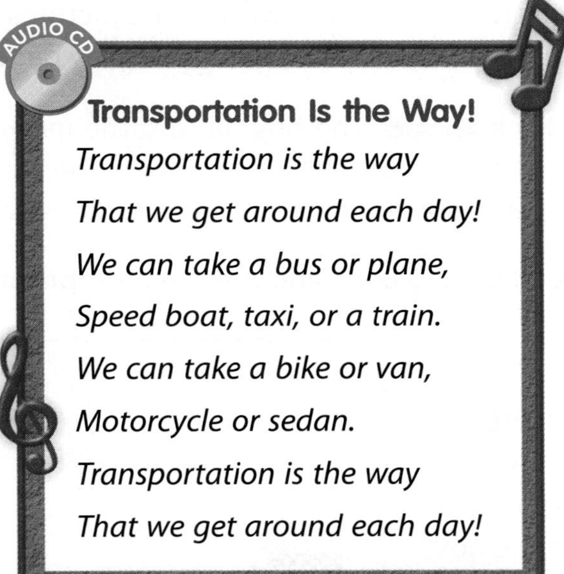

Transportation Is the Way!

Transportation is the way
That we get around each day!
We can take a bus or plane,
Speed boat, taxi, or a train.
We can take a bike or van,
Motorcycle or sedan.
Transportation is the way
That we get around each day!

ELL ENGLISH LANGUAGE LEARNERS

Beginning

Confirm Understanding Review oral vocabulary from prior lessons using the **Big Book** *The Bus for Us*. For example, display the page that shows the tow truck. Say: *This is a tow truck. What vehicle is this?* (a tow truck) Repeat with other pages.

Intermediate

Enhance Understanding Display the same page from the **Big Book** and ask: *What kind of vehicle is this?* (It's a tow truck.) *What does a tow truck do?* (A tow truck pulls cars that don't work.) Guide children to answer in complete sentences.

Advanced

Share Preferences Ask children about the vehicle they would most like to ride in or drive and tell why. Help them answer by completing the sentence frame *I would like to* ________ *a* ________ *because* ________. Write the completed sentences on the board. Read them together.

Objectives

- Discuss the theme
- Use oral vocabulary words *vehicle* and *transportation*
- Complete a chart
- Distinguish rhyming pairs from non-rhyming pairs of words

Materials

- Big Book: *The Bus for Us*
- Graphic Organizer; Teaching Chart G3
- Listening Library Audio CD

Digital Learning
AUDIO CD
Song on Listening Library Audio CD

Objectives

- Identify parts of a book
- Recognize story structure
- Make and confirm predictions
- Respond to a story
- Retell a story
- Develop fluency

Materials

- Big Book: *The Bus for Us*
- Retelling Cards
- Activity Book, p. 5
- Practice Book, p. 62

Big Book

Story on **Listening Library Audio CD**

ELL

Gesture and Talk
Use gestures and other strategies to help make the text comprehensible.

pp. 4–5
taxi: Ask children to share how to say *taxi* in their native languages.

Reread the Big Book

Listening Comprehension

CONCEPTS ABOUT PRINT Display the book. Point to the cover. *This is the cover.* Read the title aloud as you track the print. Have children tell what they remember about the story.

STRATEGY Recognize Story Structure

Explain to children that they used the structure of the **Big Book** to help them predict what would happen next. Guide them to recall how the book is organized.

SKILL Make and Confirm Predictions

Tell children that you will use the pictures and words to help you to guess what will happen next. Display pages 16–23.

Think Aloud The boy has a turtle in his box. Now the turtle is climbing out of the box. I think the turtle will try to crawl away. Let's turn the page. Yes, the turtle is crawling away.

Read the Big Book and use the prompts on the inside covers.

pages 2–3

STORY STRUCTURE
Think Aloud Tess is asking Gus a question. I think that on the next page, he will answer it. Let's see.

pages 4–5

STORY STRUCTURE
Think Aloud Yes, on this page Gus answers Tess's question. I wonder what will be on the next page.

Develop Comprehension

pages 6–7

MAKE PREDICTIONS

Think Aloud Tess asked if this is a bus. The picture does not look like a bus. It looks like the front of some kind of truck. I think Gus is going to say, "No." Let's see.

pages 8–9

MAKE PREDICTIONS

Think Aloud Gus did say, "No." It was not a bus.

PHONICS

- *What words on this page start with the /t/ sound?* (Possible answers: *Tess, tow, truck*)

pages 10–11

MAKE PREDICTIONS

- *Do you think this is a bus? What do you think it is?*

STORY STRUCTURE

- *Tess asked a question on this page. What do you think will happen on the next page?*

pages 12–13

MAKE PREDICTIONS

- *It was a fire engine. What do you think will happen next?* (Possible answer: Tess will see something else. She will ask if it is the bus.)

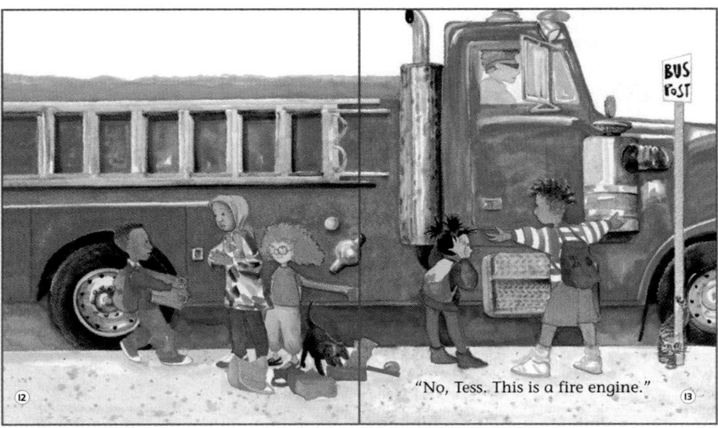

Comprehension

Recognize Story Structure

- (pages 2–5) Tess is asking Gus a question. I think that on the next page he will answer it. Let's see. Yes, on this page Gus answers Tess's question.

Make Predictions

- (pages 8–9) Tess asked if this is a bus. Do you think this is a bus? What do you think it is?

Story Words

(page 9) tow (page 25) backhoe

About the Author/Illustrator: Suzanne Bloom

When Suzanne Bloom isn't waiting for the school bus with her sons, she is illustrating people and pigs. Her illustrations appear in a number of books, including *My Special Day at Third Street School*, about an author's exciting school visit, and *No Place for a Pig*, about raising a little pig in the big city.

Big Book Inside Back Cover

ELL

pp. 8–9

tow truck: When my car is broken and I can't drive, I call a tow truck to take it away. Would I need a big tow truck or a little tow truck to take away a school bus?

pp. 12–13

fire engine: Point to the fire engine. Make an emergency vehicle siren sound and say *fire engine*. Have children repeat.

Text Evidence

Story Structure

Explain Remind children that when they answer a question they will need to find evidence in the text to support their answer.

Discuss Tell children that they can use a book's structure to figure out what will come next as they read. Have children reread pp. 14–21. Ask: *What happened on the next page after the question, "Is that the bus for us?" was asked?*

ELL

pp. 16–17
ice-cream truck: Point to the ice cream on the page. Tell children to join you in acting out eating ice cream. Say: *I eat ice cream from the ice-cream truck*. Have children repeat after you.

pp. 20–21
garbage truck: Point to the part of the illustration that shows garbage. Point to the classroom garbage can and say *garbage*.

Develop Comprehension

pages 14–15

ILLUSTRATOR'S CRAFT

- *Why do you think the illustrator shows only the front of each **vehicle**?* (Possible answer: Showing a little part makes us figure out what the vehicle is.)

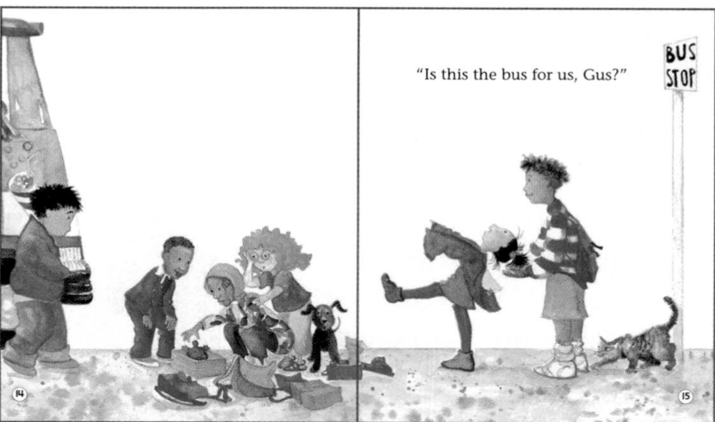

pages 16–17

MAKE PREDICTIONS

- *The dog sees the cat, and the cat looks scared. What do you think will happen next? Let's turn the page to find out.* (Possible answer: The cat will run away, and the dog will chase the cat.)

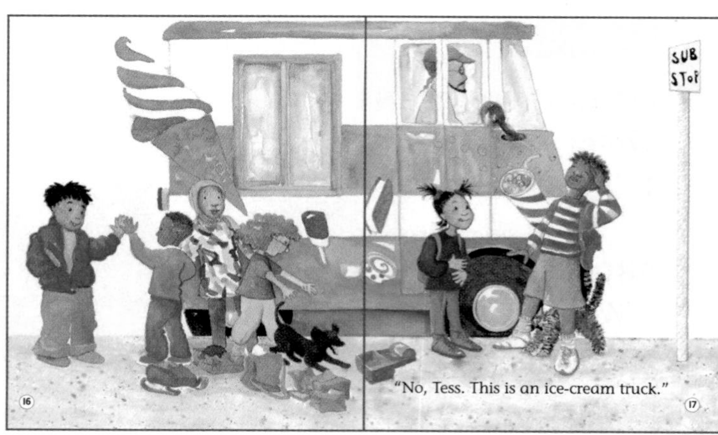

pages 18–19

CONCEPT WORDS: COLOR WORDS

- *What color words would you use to describe the children's clothing?* (Possible answers: *red, yellow, blue, pink, green, purple, white, orange*)

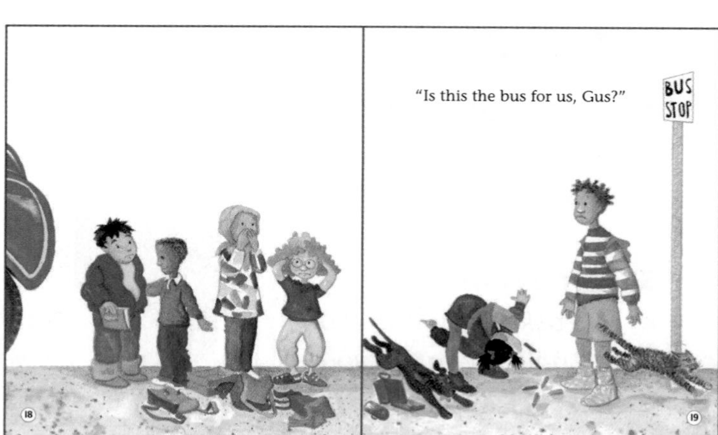

pages 20–21

CONCEPTS ABOUT PRINT

- *Can you point to the first word on this page? Can you point to the last word?*

STORY STRUCTURE

- *Gus answered a question on this page. What do you think will happen on the next page?*

pages 22–23

VISUALIZE

Think Aloud I see part of something. It looks like the bucket on the front of a machine. I think if I could see the rest, I would see a part that a person sits in.

pages 24–25

HIGH-FREQUENCY WORD

- *Can you find the word* a?

CULTURAL PERSPECTIVES

Think Aloud The boy and the girl on the far left are speaking in sign language. This shows us that many different languages are spoken at school.

ELL

pp. 24–25
backhoe: Use your arm and scooped hand to pretend you are digging in the ground. Have children repeat the action and word.

pages 26–27

MAKE PREDICTIONS

- *Where do you think children will go when the bus comes? Why?* (Possible answer: They will go to school. They are carrying things that children take to school.)

pages 28–29

IDENTIFY CHARACTER

- *How do you think Tess feels? Why?* (Possible answer: She feels happy because the bus came at last.)

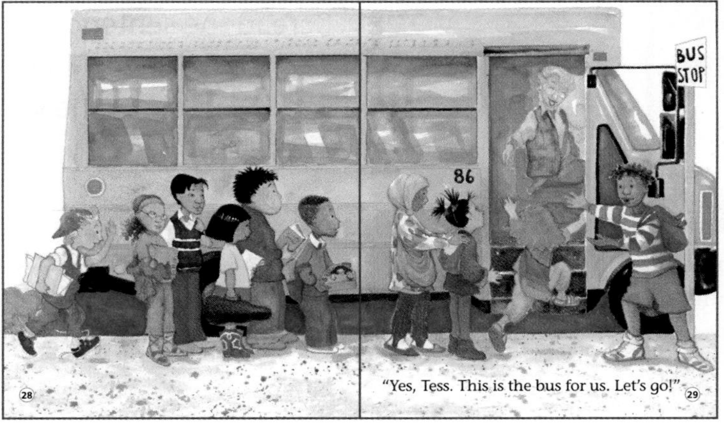

Respond to Literature

TALK ABOUT IT Have children talk about the words and illustrations that they liked and refer to the book as they answer the questions. Help them to speak audibly and in complete sentences.

- *What did you use to predict what* ***vehicle*** *Tess saw each time?* (the pictures that showed the front of each vehicle) LOCATE
- *How could you tell what Tess and Gus were going to say?* (The words followed the same pattern throughout the book.) CONNECT
- *Why might the author have chosen to write a story about vehicles? Which vehicles transport people? Which vehicles are used to do work?* COMBINE

Activity Book, page 5
Practice Book, page 62

Retell

GUIDED RETELLING

Remind children that as they listened to *The Bus for Us*, they used the words and the illustrations to understand the story. *Now you will use the pictures on these cards to retell the story.*

Retelling Cards

- Display **Retelling Card 1**. Based on children's abilities, use the Guided, Modeled, or ELL prompts.
- Repeat the procedure with the rest of the Retelling Cards, using the prompts to guide children's retelling. Then discuss the story. Ask: *What did you learn about different vehicles and different kinds of* ***transportation****? Did you like the story? Why or why not?*
- Have children dramatize their favorite part of the story. Have them describe their actions in complete sentences.

Retelling Rubric

4 Excellent

Retells the selection without prompting, in sequence, and using supporting details. Clearly describes the setting, main characters, and complete plot.

3 Good

Retells the selection with little guidance, in sequence, and using some details. Generally describes the setting, main characters, and plot.

2 Fair

Retells the selection with some guidance, mostly in sequence, and using limited details. Partially describes the setting, main characters, and plot.

1 Unsatisfactory

Retells the selection only when prompted, out of sequence, and using limited details. Does not describe the main characters or plot.

Fluency: Echo-Read

MODEL Reread the sentence on pages 2–3 of *The Bus for Us*, emphasizing the word *this*. Then reread the sentence on pages 4–5, emphasizing the name of the vehicle (*taxi*). Reread pages 6–12 and have children echo-read as you track the print.

Quick Check

Can children make and confirm predictions to help understand a story?
Can children begin to retell the main events from the story?

Vocabulary

Shape Words

Chant the following jingle:

Red is a circle.

Blue is a square.

Yellow is a triangle.

Green is a rectangle.

We see shapes everywhere!

- Repeat the first line and tell children what word names a shape. Ask children to name other things that are circles. Repeat with the remaining lines.
- Have children page through the **Big Book** *The Bus for Us*. Ask them to find circles, squares, rectangles, and triangles. Have children repeat the shape names as rapidly as they can.

NAME SHAPE WORDS Have children locate and name different shapes in the classroom.

Story Words: *tow truck*, *backhoe*

- Display pages 8–9 of *The Bus for Us* and point out the picture of the tow truck. *What does a tow truck do?* Explain that the word *tow* means "to pull." *A tow truck pulls other **vehicles**.*

COMPOUND WORDS Display pages 24–25 of *The Bus for Us* and point out the picture of the backhoe. Explain that the word *backhoe* is a compound word and has two parts, *back* and *hoe*. *A hoe is a tool for digging. A backhoe is a tractor that digs up dirt.*

TIME TO MOVE!

Children can work together to stand in the shape of a circle, a triangle, a rectangle, and a square. Challenge them to think of other ways to make those shapes with their bodies.

Objectives

- Use shape words *circle, square, rectangle, triangle*
- Learn the story words *tow truck, backhoe*
- Identify compound words

Materials

- Big Book: *The Bus for Us*
- Activity Book, p. 6

Digital Learning

LOG ON For children who need additional language support and oral vocabulary development, use the activities found at **www.macmillanmh.com**.

ELL

Reinforce Meaning Point to classroom objects that match the shapes. Say: *This clock is in the shape of a circle.* Move your finger around the edge of the clock. *What other object you know is shaped like a circle?* (a tire) Repeat with square, triangle, and rectangle.

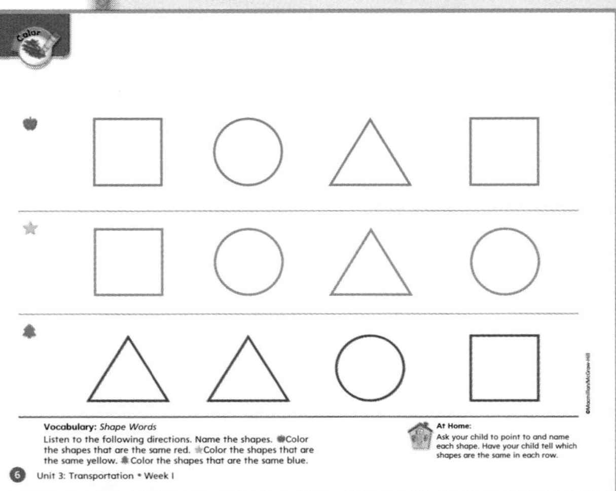

Color

Vocabulary: *Shape Words*
Listen to the following directions. Name the shapes. Color the shapes that are the same red. Color the shapes that are the same yellow. Color the shapes that are the same blue.

At Home: Ask your child to point to and name each shape. Have your child tell which shapes are the same in each row.

6 Unit 3: Transportation • Week 1

©Macmillan/McGraw-Hill

Activity Book, page 6

Objectives

- Orally blend sounds to form words
- Match letter *t* to sound /t/
- Blend sounds in words with *t*

Materials

- Puppet
- Word-Building Cards
- pocket chart

Phonemic Awareness

Phoneme Blending

Model

Use the **Puppet** to model how to blend the sounds in the word *tap*.

Repeat the routine with *tan*.

Happy is going to say the sounds in a word. Listen to Happy as he says each sound: /t/ /a/ /p/. Happy can blend these sounds together: /taaap/, *tap*. Say the sounds with Happy: /t/ /a/ /p/, /taaap/. Now say the word with Happy: *tap*.

Guided Practice/Practice

Say the sounds. Children blend the sounds to form words.

Guide practice with the first word, using the same routine.

Happy is going to say the sounds in a word. Listen to Happy as he says each sound. You will repeat the sounds, then blend them.

/t/ /a/ /g/ /p/ /a/ /n/ /t/ /a/ p/

/t/ /a/ /m/ /s/ /a/ /m/ /p/ /a/ /m/

Phonics

Review /t/*t*

Model

Hold up **Word-Building Card** *t*.

Repeat the routine for the letters *p*, *a*.

This is the letter *t*. The letter *t* stands for /t/. What is the letter? What does this letter stand for?

Say the word. Write the letter *t*.

Repeat with *pin*.

Listen as I say a word: *turtle*. *Turtle* has /t/ at the beginning.

The letter *t* stands for /t/. I'll write *t*.

Guided Practice/Practice

Children write the letter that stands for the beginning sound. Do the first word with children.

Listen as I say a word. Write the letter that stands for the beginning sound.

pack am tall tin pat

tag pail add pan take

Build Fluency: Sound-Spellings

Display the following **Word-Building Cards**: *a, m, p, s, t*. Have children chorally say each sound. Repeat and vary the pace.

Blend with /t/*t*

Model

Place **Word-Building Card** *t* in the pocket chart.

This letter is *t*. The letter *t* stands for the /t/ sound. Say /t/.

Place Word-Building Card *a* next to *t*. Move your hand from left to right.

This is the letter *a*. The letter *a* stands for the /a/ sound. Listen as I blend the two sounds together: /taaa/. Now you blend the sounds with me. (/taaa/)

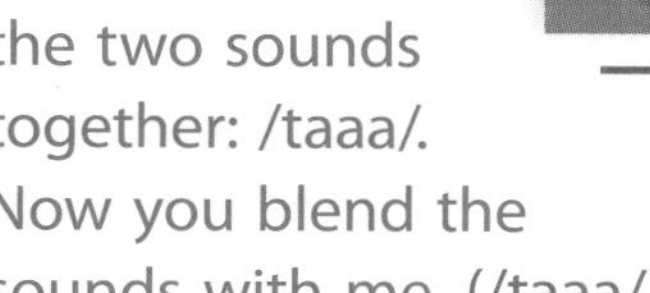

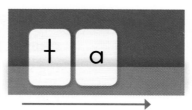

Place Word-Building Card *p* next to *ta*. Move your hand from left to right.

This is the letter *p*. The letter *p* stands for the /p/ sound. Listen as I blend the three sounds together: /taaap/. What is the word? (/taaap/)

Repeat with *Tam*.

Guided Practice/Practice

Children blend sounds to form words. Guide practice with the first word, using the routine.

Pam	Sam	am
tap	Tam	sap

For Tier 2 instruction, see page 576.

ELL

Reinforce Meaning Review the meaning of words in the Guided Practice. Model saying each word and ask children to repeat. Help them explain what each word means. For example, tap a pencil on the table as you say *tap*.

Objectives

- Read the word *see*
- Review the words *see, can, a, the*
- Reread for fluency

Materials

- Pre-decodable Reader: *I See Sam*
- High-Frequency Word Cards: *a, can, see, the*
- pocket chart

Pre-decodable Reader

Read *I See Sam*

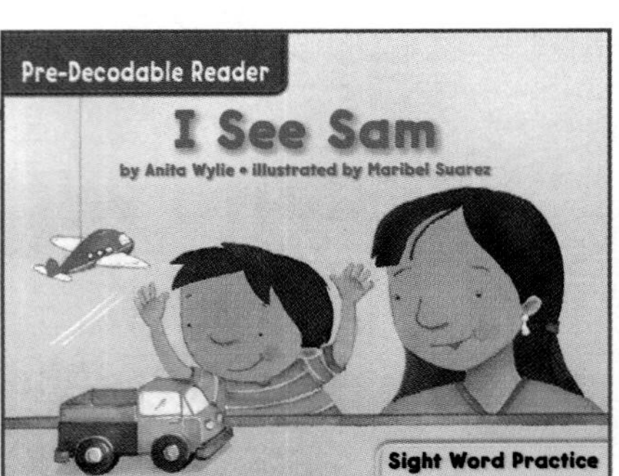

I See Sam

REVIEW HIGH-FREQUENCY WORDS Display **High-Frequency Word Cards** for **see**, **can**, **a**, and **the** in the pocket chart. Review the words using the **Read/Spell/Write** routine.

MODEL CONCEPTS ABOUT PRINT Demonstrate book handling. Guide children to follow along with their books. *I hold the book so that the cover is on the front and the words are not upside down. Then I turn each page as I read it.*

PREDICT Ask children to describe the cover illustration. *Do you think the story will be a made-up story or one that could really happen. Why?*

FIRST READ Point out the rebus and discuss what it stands for. Have children point to each word, saying the sight words quickly. Children should chorally read the story the first time through.

DEVELOP COMPREHENSION Ask the following:

- *Look at page 7. What do you like?* (the plane)
- *Look at page 8. Who do you see?* (Sam)

SECOND READ Have partners reread the book together. Circulate, listen in, and provide corrective feedback.

I see a [boat].

2

I like the [boat].

3

I see a [train].

4

I like the [train].

5

I see a [plane].

6

I like the [plane].

7

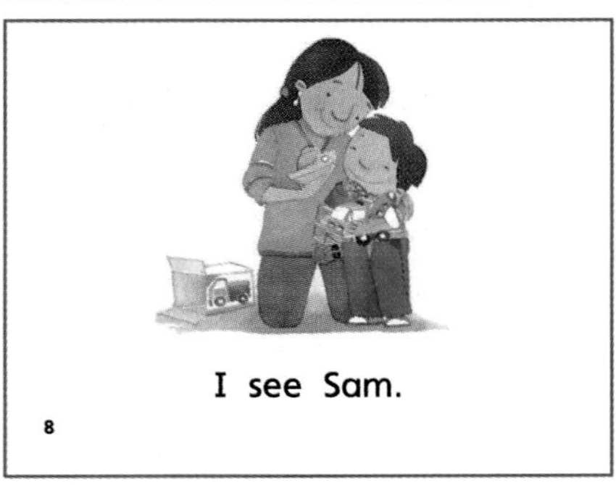

I see Sam.

8

Pre-decodable Reader

Writing

Interactive Writing: Sentences

REVIEW

- Display and read aloud the list that children created for yesterday's Shared Writing activity.

WRITE

- Tell children that today they will list some shapes they see on pages 4–5 of the **Big Book** *The Bus for Us*. *I see a square on a taxi, so I will write* square *on our list.* Generate ideas through class discussion by having children identify and discuss ideas about circles, rectangles, and triangles on other pages of the book.
- Tell children that now they are going to write a sentence about a **vehicle** and a shape. Collaborate with children to write the sentence frame. For example, have children write the word *see*.

I see a _____ on a _____.

- Read the sentence together as you track the print. Have children suggest a vehicle from the Day 1 list and a shape from today's list to complete the sentence. Write the words to complete the sentence.
- Have children help by writing all of the letters they know. Have them confirm spelling by looking at the Word Wall.
- Extend the activity by working with children to write a short rebus story about one of the vehicles. Have children check that their story makes sense and is in correct chronological order. Guide them as needed.
- Explain to children that a caption is a description written for a picture. Then have them complete the activity below.

Write About It

Have children draw in their Writer's Notebooks. Suggest that they draw a picture showing them on a vehicle they like. Guide them to write a caption for their drawings using the sentence *I like a* ____________.

Objectives

- Write sentences by generating ideas through class discussion
- Dictate sentences to tell a story
- Write captions

Materials

- Shared Writing list from Day 1
- Big Book: *The Bus for Us*

5-Day Writing

Sentences	
DAY 1	Shared: A List
DAY 2	Interactive: Sentences
DAY 3	Independent: Prewrite and Draft Sentences
DAY 4	Independent: Revise and Edit Sentences
DAY 5	Independent: Publish and Present

ELL

Reinforce Vocabulary Use illustrations in the **Big Book** to review words that name vehicles and colors. For example, display pages 12–13. Ask: *What color is the fire engine?* Display pages 10–11. Ask *What shape is the tire?* Then model completing a sentence frame.

Transitions That Teach

While packing up, have children name **vehicles** they know.

Day 3 At a Glance

WHOLE GROUP

Oral Language
- Build Robust Vocabulary
- Oral Vocabulary Cards: "How Partridge Built Canoes"

Comprehension
- Read "Signs in the Park"
- Text Features: Maps

High-Frequency Words
- Review *see*

Phonemic Awareness
- Phoneme Isolation

Phonics
- Identify /t/*t*
- Blend with /t/*t*

Grammar
- Action Words (Verbs)

Writing
- Independent Writing: Prewrite and Draft Sentences

SMALL GROUP
- Differentiated Instruction, pages 570–595

Additional Vocabulary
To provide 15–20 minutes of additional vocabulary instruction, see Oral Vocabulary Cards 5-Day Plan. The pre- and posttests for this week can be found in the **Teacher's Resource Book**, pages 218–219.

Oral Language

Build Robust Vocabulary

BUILD BACKGROUND

Introduce the story "How Partridge Built Canoes" using **Oral Vocabulary Card 1** and read the title aloud. *Have you ever traveled on water? In what type of vehicle did you travel?* Ask children to tell what they think will happen in the story.

- Read the story on the back of the cards. Pause at each oral vocabulary word and read the definition. You may wish to check children's understanding using the Activate Background Knowledge, Words with Multiple Meanings, and Compare and Contrast prompts.

Oral Vocabulary Cards

Vocabulary Routine

Use the routine below to discuss the meaning of each word.

Define: **Glide** means "to move smoothly and easily." Let's say the word.
Example: We watched an eagle glide through the air.
Ask: What are some things that glide in the sky?

Define: When you **continue** doing something, you keep on doing it. Say the word with me.
Example: The runners will continue running until they reach the finish line.
Ask: If it is bedtime, should you continue playing or stop to get ready for bed? Why?

Define: **Rapidly** means "very quickly." Say the word with me.
Example: When it started to rain, Greg walked rapidly into his house.
Ask: What might happen if someone eats rapidly?

- Use the routine on Card 1 to review the words **transportation** and **vehicle**.

- Review last week's words: *grateful*, *include*, *problems*, *solve*, and *thoughtful*.

Listen for Rhyme

IDENTIFY RHYME

Tell children that they will sing another song about transportation. Play the rhyme and ask children to join in. Explain that the word *ground* rhymes with *around* because they both end in *-ound*. Then guide children to name which of the following words rhymes with *so: go, ride,* or *hum*. (*go*)

Let's Ride

Time to take a little ride.

Open the door and get inside.

Open door and sit.

Now the engine starts to hum.

Shakes a bit, goes brr . . . brrum!

Hum, shake.

Then the tires go around.

Rolling faster on the ground.

Make circles in air with arms.

Turn the steering wheel just so.

Turn steering wheel.

To take us where we want to go.

Objectives

- Discuss the theme
- Recognize rhyme
- Use oral vocabulary words *continue, glide, rapidly, transportation*, and *vehicle*
- Listen and respond to a folktale

Materials

- Oral Vocabulary Cards: "How Partridge Built Canoes"

Song on **Listening Library Audio CD**

Objectives

- Retell and respond to expository text
- Identify places where signs and symbols are used (parks, streets, maps)
- Tell what information is presented on traffic signs and map symbols

Materials

- Big Book of Explorations, Vol. 1: "Signs in the Park"

Content Vocabulary

symbol drawings that stand for real things

map a drawing of an area that shows where different places are

key part of a map that tells you what different symbols mean

Use a Picture Dictionary Guide children to look up the content words in a picture dictionary.

Informational Text

Genre

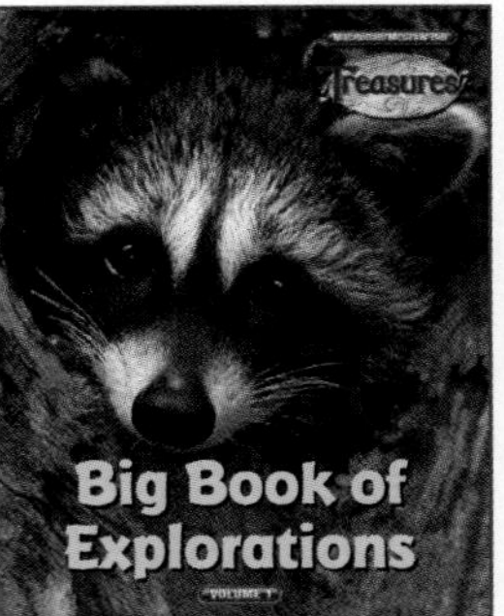

Big Book of Explorations

INFORMATIONAL TEXT: EXPOSITORY Have children point to the title and name of the author. Read them aloud while tracking print. Access children's prior knowledge about traffic signs by asking them to tell about any they have seen while riding in a car or bus. Tell children that this nonfiction photo essay is **expository text**. Tell them they will learn about signs and maps and some places where they are used.

READ "SIGNS IN THE PARK"

- **Preview and Predict** Page through the book and point out the signs and maps with children. *What do you think this will be about?*
- **Content Vocabulary** Introduce and discuss the vocabulary words.
- **Text Feature: Maps** *Maps show us where different places are in an particular area. They can also show us how to get from one place to another.*

CONTENT FOCUS

- As you read pages 33–34 aloud, pause to discuss the meanings of each sign you might see in a park. Explain that even if you could not read the words, each sign has a symbol, or drawing, that shows what the sign is about. Discuss the symbols used on the signs (wheelchair, litter basket, bicycle, and playground slide).
- As you read page 35, discuss the meanings of the various traffic signs and signals. Mention the use of shape and color to give information. For example, no matter where you go, a red octagon with the letters *S-T-O-P* always means that drivers must come to a full stop. Discuss the use and meaning of colors on street and traffic signals as well (red—stop, green—go, and yellow—caution).
- Turn to page 36. Identify the map shown as Texas. Review the symbols used on the map key. Point out the use of colored symbols to represent land and water features.
- Point to the place on the map where your school is probably located. Have children point to cities, land, or water features that are nearest to your school.

page 33

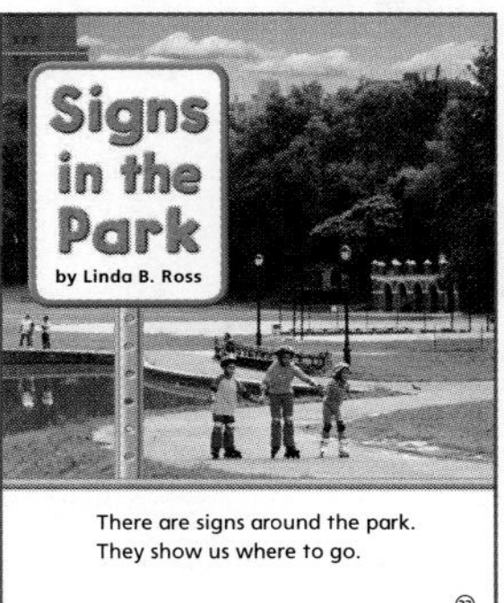

There are signs around the park.
They show us where to go.

pages 34–35

ACCESSIBLE ENTRANCE
PITCH IN
STEEP HILL
PLAYGROUND

They tell us what to do.
What do the signs say?

STOP
ONE WAY

There are signs and signals on streets.
They show us where to go.
They show us when to stop and go.

page 36

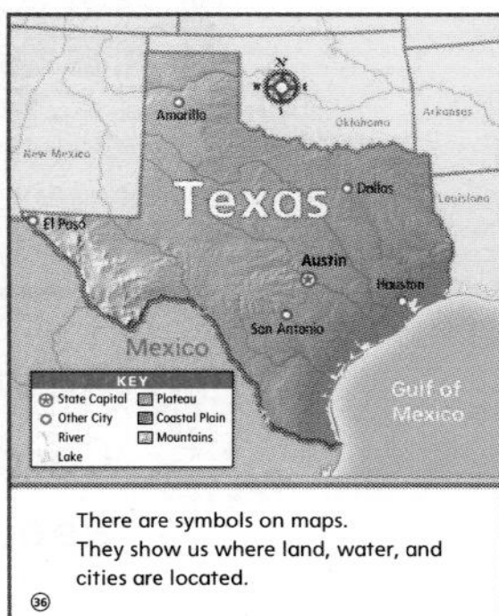

There are symbols on maps.
They show us where land, water, and cities are located.

Retell and Respond

- *What are some places where signs and symbols are used?* (in parks, on streets, on maps)
- *What are some things street signs show us?* (where to go, when to stop, when to go)
- *What are some things symbols on maps show us?* (the location of cities, rivers, lakes)

Connect to Content

Street Map

- Discuss the streets and landmarks around the school, such as trees, fire hydrants, flagpoles, or corner mailboxes.
- Have children brainstorm three symbols they can use to represent three things found on the street, such as their school, a stop sign, and a bus stop.
- Ask them to draw a map of the street. Have them use both picture symbols and words in the key to the map.

ELL

Beginning

Use Pictures Turn to page 36. Point to the symbol of the river on the key and explain that it stands for a river. Discuss what rivers look like. *Why is the symbol for rivers blue?* Locate the rivers on the map with children. Continue for other map symbols.

Intermediate

Identify Map Features After reading page 36, ask questions to reinforce vocabulary and key concepts. Have children describe the landforms, bodies of water, and other features indicated on the map. Match the descriptions with the symbols and then point to the feature on the map. For example: *Many people live here.* (city)

Advanced

Map Study Have children study the map on page 36. Ask them to look at the map and describe a trip from El Paso to the Gulf of Mexico in terms of highways, lakes, rivers, plateaus, plains, and cities that might be seen along the way.

Objective

- Read the high-frequency word *see*

Materials

- High-Frequency Word Cards: *a, can, I, see*
- Photo Cards: *bike, bus, helicopter*
- index card with period mark
- pocket chart
- Activity Book, pp. 7–8
- Practice Book, pp. 63–64

Activity Book, pages 7–8
Practice Book, pages 63–64

High-Frequency Words

see

see

REVIEW Display the **High-Frequency Word Card** for **see**. Review the word using the **Read/Spell/Write** routine.

Repeat the routine for the words **I**, **can**, and **a**.

APPLY Build sentences in the pocket chart using High-Frequency Word Cards and **Photo Cards**. Have children point to the high-frequency words. Use the sentence below and the following: *I can see a helicopter. I can see a bike.*

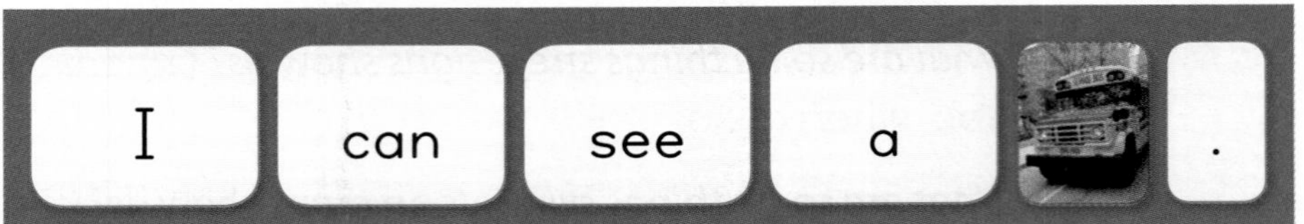

READ FOR FLUENCY Chorally read the Take-Home Book with children. Then have them reread the book to review high-frequency words and build fluency.

Quick Check

Can children read the word *see*?

During **Small Group Instruction**

If No → **Approaching Level** Provide additional practice reading the word *see*, page 580.

If Yes → **On Level** Children can read the Take-Home Book.

Beyond Level Children can read the Take-Home Book.

TIME TO MOVE!

Have children gesture holding binoculars in front of their eyes as they "focus" on where they would *see* a plane (up in the sky), a car (on a road, on a bridge), or a bicycle (on a path). Ask them to look out the window and look for and name vehicles. *I* see *a bus.*

Phonemic Awareness

Phoneme Isolation

Model

Display the **Photo Card** for *turtle*.

Listen for the beginning sound in *turtle*. Say the word with me: *turtle*. *Turtle* has /t/ at the beginning: /t/, /t/, *turtle*. Say the /t/ sound with me: /t/. What is the sound? (/t/)

Display the Photo Card for *nest*.

Now we are going to listen for the ending sound in *nest*. Say the word with me: *nest*. (Clearly enunciate and emphasize the ending sound.) *Nest* has /t/ at the end. Listen carefully: *nest*, /t/. Say the sound with me: /t/. What is the sound? (/t/)

Repeat with *tiger* and *jet*.

Guided Practice/Practice

Display the Photo Cards. Children identify initial and final /t/. Guide practice with the first card.

Say the name of the picture with me. If the picture name begins with /t/, point to the *turtle*. If the picture name ends with /t/, point to the *nest*.

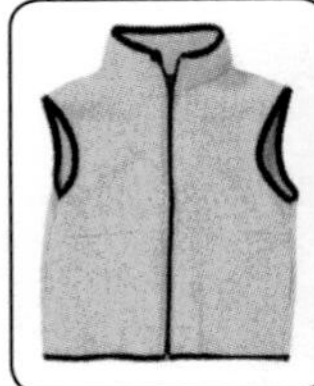

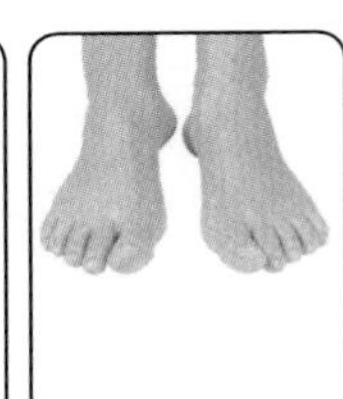

Objective

- Identify initial and final /t/

Materials

- Photo Cards: *feet, hat, jet, nest, table, teeth, tiger, top, turtle, vest*

Objectives

- Identify final /t/*t* in words
- Review final /p/*p*, /s/*s* in words
- Blend sounds in words with /t/*t*
- Read simple one-syllable words

Materials

- Word-Building Cards
- pocket chart

Phonics

Review

Model

Display **Word-Building Card** *t*. — This is the letter *t*. The letter *t* stands for the /t/ sound you hear at the end of *net*.

Repeat for *p* and *s*.

Say a word. Point to *t*. — I will say a word: *lit*. The word *lit* has /t/ at the end. I will point to the letter *t* because *lit* has the /t/ sound at the end.

Guided Practice/Practice

Children point to the letter that stands for the final sound. Guide practice with the first word. — Point to the letter that stands for the sound at the end of the word.

top	cat	bus	rip
lap	jet	yes	pot

Build Fluency: Sound-Spellings

Display the following Word-Building Cards: *a, m, p, s, t*. Have children chorally say each sound. Repeat and vary the pace.

For Tier 2 instruction, see page 581.

Blend with /t/*t*

Model

Place **Word-Building Card** *P* in the pocket chart.

This letter is capital *P*. It stands for /p/. Say /p/.

Place Word-Building Card *a* next to *P*. Move your hand from left to right.

This letter is *a*. It stands for /a/. Listen as I blend the two sounds together: /paaa/. Now you say it. (/paaa/)

Place Word-Building Card *t* next to *Pa*. Move your hand from left to right.

This is *t*. It stands for /t/. Listen as I blend the three sounds together: /paaat/, *Pat*. Now you say it. (/paaat/, *Pat*)

Repeat with *mat*.

Guided Practice/Practice

Children blend with /t/. at sat tap Tam

Read Words

Apply

Write the words and sentences. Guide practice with the first word, using the **Sound-by-Sound Blending Routine**.

Read the sentences with children.

tap
sat
Pat
Pat sat.
I see Pat tap.

Corrective Feedback

Blending: Sound Error Model the sound that children missed, then have them repeat the sound. For example, for the word *sat*, say: *My turn.* Tap under the letter *t* in the word *sat* and say: *Sound? What's the sound?* Then return to the beginning of the word. Say: *Let's start over.* Blend the word with children again.

ELL

Minimal Contrasts Spanish speakers and others may need extra practice pronouncing short vowels /a/ and /o/. Contrast words with the /a/ sound and the /o/ sound, such as *tap* and *top* and *Pat* and *pot*. Have children repeat the words after you. Note how the shape of your mouth changes when you make each sound. Reinforce the meaning of *tap* by asking children to tap their fingers. Demonstrate meaning of other one-syllable words from this lesson.

Objective

- Recognize action words (verbs)

Materials

- Big Book: *The Bus for Us*

Grammar

Action Words (Verbs)

MODEL Use the **Big Book** *The Bus for Us* to review action words. Point to illustrations as you say these sentences: *We ride in a taxi. We ride in a bus.* Then ask: *What are we doing?* Then point to other story illustrations and have children say: *We ride in a* ________. Then ask: *What do we do?* (ride)

- Ask children to stand. Explain that you will say a word and then point to someone. Tell that child to act out the word you say.
- Use these action words: *pedal, drive, bounce, fly*.

What does Pedro do? (Pedro pedals.) Explain that *pedal, drive, bounce,* and *fly* are words that tell what someone or something does.

PRACTICE Then page through the remaining pages in *The Bus for Us* Point out the action words in the text with children.

- Say sentences about the illustrations. Have children repeat the sentence. Help them identify the action word. Say these sentences and others: *The boy* talks. *The bus driver* drives.
- Then have children make up their own complete sentences about the people and objects in the pictures. Guide them to name the action word in each sentence.

ELL

Basic and Academic Language Write the verbs *ride, drive, pedal,* and *walk.* Use each in a sentence and use gestures to demonstrate their meaning. Pair English Language Learners with fluent speakers. Have partners make up sentences using the verbs listed. Write their sentences, read them chorally, and say: *Tell me what word in your sentence is the action word or verb.*

Writing

Independent Writing: Sentences

Display the lists of **vehicles** and shapes that children created in the Days 1 and 2 Writing activities.

BRAINSTORM
Have children name their favorite vehicle from the **Big Book** *The Bus for Us* and the shapes on the vehicle. Ask children to think of other vehicles they have seen and the shapes on those vehicles. Add children's ideas to the lists.

PREWRITE
Write the sentence frame. Read it aloud as you track the print.

I see a ______ on a ______.

- Draw a shape on the first blank and then write the name of a vehicle on the second one to complete the sentence. Share your sentence with children. Have children chorally repeat.
- Have children choose a vehicle and shape to write about.

DRAFT
Distribute paper, pencils, and crayons. Have children write their own name on the top of the paper.

- Guide children to write the sentence frame as shown.
- Tell children to a draw a shape on the first blank and to write the name of a vehicle on the second blank to complete the sentence.
- Collect and save children's work to use tomorrow.

Write About It

Tell children to draw in their Writer's Notebooks. Suggest that they draw a place they like to go to on the bus. Guide them to label their drawings.

Objectives

- Write a sentence
- Use letter knowledge to write letters in a word
- Draw a picture

Materials

- Interactive Writing from Day 2
- Big Book: *The Bus for Us*

5-Day Writing

Sentences	
DAY 1	Shared: A List
DAY 2	Interactive: Sentences
DAY 3	Independent: Prewrite and Draft Sentences
DAY 4	Independent: Revise and Edit Sentences
DAY 5	Independent: Publish and Present

ELL

Reinforce Meaning Use the chart from the Day 1 Writing activity. Ask children to draw a simple vehicle next to its name. Have them say each vehicle name with you. Then ask children which is their favorite vehicle and why.

Transitions That Teach

While children wait in line, have them tell about something they would like to **continue** doing tomorrow.

Day 4 At a Glance

WHOLE GROUP

Oral Language
- Build Robust Vocabulary

Comprehension
- Read-Aloud: "The Turtle and the Rabbit"

Vocabulary
- Shape Words
- Story Words: *tow truck, backhoe*

Phonemic Awareness
- Phoneme Blending

Phonics
- Picture Sort
- Blend with /t/*t*
- Pre-decodable Reader: *Can Tam See?*

Writing
- Independent Writing: Revise and Edit Sentences

SMALL GROUP

- Differentiated Instruction, pages 570–595

Oral Language

Build Robust Vocabulary

TRANSPORTATION THAT GOES FAST OR SLOW
Talk about fast ways to get around town and slower ways to get around. *What would you ride around town if you were in a hurry and needed to get somewhere* **rapidly**? *How would you get around if you wanted to take your time? Tell about different* **vehicles**.

CREATE A CHART Draw the chart as shown below, or use **Teaching Chart G3**. Discuss fast and slow forms of **transportation**. Use words and concepts that will be introduced in "The Turtle and the Rabbit."

Think Aloud You can get around town quickly, or you can travel a little more slowly. One fast way to get around town is to ride in a car, so I'll put *car* on our chart under *Fast*. Another way to get around town is to *walk*. I'll put that under *Slow*.

Have children speak audibly and clearly to name other ways to get around town fast and ways to travel a little more slowly. Add their ideas to the chart.

How to Get Around Town

Fast	Slow
car	walk
taxi	bike
bus	skates

ELL ENGLISH LANGUAGE LEARNERS

Beginning

Confirm Understanding
Tell children to walk around the room slowly saying the word *slow*. Then have them walk as fast as they can saying the word *fast*. Ask: *Are you moving slowly? Are you moving rapidly?*

Intermediate

Enhance Understanding
Use questions to help children make simple comparisons. For example: *Which is faster, to ride in a car or to walk? Which is slower, to ride around town in a bus or on a bike?*

Advanced

Share Preferences
Tell children to describe their favorite way to get around town with their family.

Listen for Rhyme

IDENTIFY RHYME

Remind children that words rhyme when they have the same ending sounds. *The word* way *rhymes with* day. Tell children *way* and *day* end with the sound: /ā/*ay*. Have children generate more words that rhyme with *way* and *day*.

TRANSPORTATION SONG

Tell children that they will sing "Transportation Is the Way!" the song they learned about transportation. Play the song and have children join in. Then ask children to name and describe all the forms of transportation they have learned.

AUDIO CD

Transportation Is the Way!

Transportation is the way
That we get around each day!
We can take a bus or plane,
Speed boat, taxi, or a train.
We can take a bike or van,
Motorcycle or sedan.
Transportation is the way
That we get around each day!

Objectives

- Generate rhyme
- Discuss fast and slow ways to travel
- Complete a chart
- Use oral vocabulary words *continue, glide, rapidly, transportation*, and *vehicle*

Materials

- Graphic Organizer; Teaching Chart G3

Oral Vocabulary

Have children use each word in a sentence about this week's stories.

continue
glide
rapidly
transportation
vehicle

Review Work with children to review last week's words. Provide a sentence starter for children to repeat and complete, such as *I am grateful that I* ______.

grateful
include
problem
solve
thoughtful

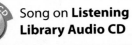

Song on **Listening Library Audio CD**

Objectives

- Listen and respond to literary text, a fable
- Recognize recurring phrases in traditional text

Materials

- Read-Aloud Anthology: "The Turtle and the Rabbit," pp. 45–48
- Story Patterns; Teacher's Resource Book, pp. 171–198

ELL

Develop Vocabulary Show the illustrations of a rabbit and a turtle in the story. Say *rabbit* quickly while running in place. Say *turtle* slowly, *tuuurtle*, while miming a turtle's slow walk. Have children join in echoing the words and imitating the actions. Show children the **Photo Cards** for *turtle* and *rabbit*. Have them repeat the picture names.

Readers Theater

BUILDING LISTENING AND SPEAKING SKILLS
Distribute copies of "Catch a Little Rhyme," Read-Aloud Anthology pages 163–164. Have children practice performing the play throughout the unit. Assign parts and have children present the play or perform it as a dramatic reading at the end of the unit.

Interactive Read Aloud

Listening Comprehension

Read Aloud

GENRE: LITERARY TEXT/FICTION
Explain that "The Turtle and the Rabbit" is a **fable**. *A fable is a very old story that teaches a lesson. What other fables have you heard?* ("The Bundle of Sticks," "The Lion and the Mouse") *What were the lessons?* Tell children that some fables begin the same way as this fable does, "Once there was…"

CULTURAL PERSPECTIVES
Tell children that "The Turtle and the Rabbit" is an Aesop's fable. Aesop was a man who lived long ago. He told many stories. In some retellings the story is called "The Tortoise and the Hare."

READ "THE TURTLE AND THE RABBIT"

- **MODEL ASKING QUESTIONS ABOUT STORY STRUCTURE** Use the Think Alouds provided at point of use in the fable.
- **MODEL FLUENT READING** Read aloud the fable with fluent expression. Point out that how you read the dialogue helps the listener understand what the characters say and how they feel.
- **EXPAND VOCABULARY** See page 45 of the **Read-Aloud Anthology** to teach new words using the **Define/Example/Ask** routine.

Respond to Literature

TALK ABOUT IT Ask children to retell a main event in the fable. Then ask: *Who could run faster: the rabbit or the turtle? Why did the rabbit lose the race? Why did the turtle win? What can you learn from this fable?*

Write About It

Have children draw their favorite part of the race between the turtle and the rabbit. Guide them to write a label or a sentence about their drawing.

Vocabulary

Shape Words

REVIEW SHAPES

Give each child an index card with the drawing of a shape. *I am going to read you a story. When you hear your shape word, hold up your card.* Read the following story:

One day Tess and her class went on a shape walk. The children had to find a circle, *a* square, *a* rectangle, *and a* triangle. *The roof on the house was a* triangle. *She saw a street sign in the shape of a* rectangle. *The sign hanging in front of a store was a* square. *Tess went in the store to find another* square *and a* circle. *A box of crackers was a* square. *But where would she find a* circle? *Tess bought a lollipop!*

Repeat the names of the shapes with children. Guide children to sort their index cards by shape. Then go on a shape walk through the classroom or school. Have children dictate their observations to help you write a class report.

Story Words: *tow truck, backhoe*

Page through *The Bus for Us* and have children point out the *tow truck* and the *backhoe*. Have children describe what each word means.

COMPOUND WORDS

Remind children that compound words are made up of shorter words. Guide children to recognize the two words *back* and *hoe* in the word *backhoe*.

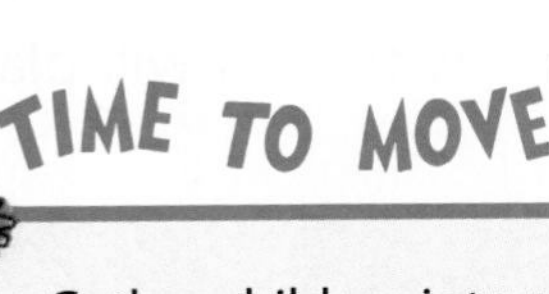

Gather children into a circle and have them hold hands. Next arrange them in the shape of a square, triangle, and rectangle.

Objectives

- Use shape words *circle, triangle, square, rectangle*
- Review story words *tow truck, backhoe*
- Recognize compound words

Materials

- shapes hand drawn on index cards (circle, square, rectangle, triangle)
- Big Book: *The Bus for Us*

ELL

Reinforce Vocabulary
Point to the illustration of the taxi on pages 4–5 of the **Big Book**. Ask children to look for as many shapes as they can in the picture of the taxi and report their findings. (Here is a circle. Here is a rectangle., etc.) Tally the results on the board. Make sure there is at least one of each shape.

Objectives

- Orally blend sounds to form words
- Sort pictures by initial sound/letter

Materials

- Puppet
- Word-Building Cards
- pocket chart
- Photo Cards: *anchor, ant, penguin, saw, soup, teeth, top*

Phonemic Awareness

Phoneme Blending

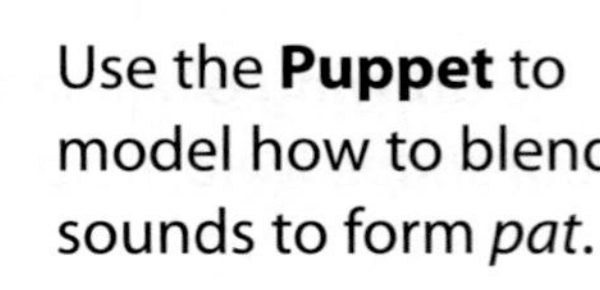

Model

Use the **Puppet** to model how to blend sounds to form *pat*.

Happy is going to say the sounds in a word. Listen to Happy: /p/ /a/ /t/. Happy can blend these sounds together: /paaat/, *pat*. Say the sounds with Happy: /p/ /a/ /t/, /paaat/, *pat*. Now say the word with Happy: *pat*.

Repeat with *sat*.

Guided Practice/Practice

Children blend sounds to form words.

Guide practice with the first word, using the same routine.

Happy is going to say the sounds in a word. Listen to Happy as he says each sound. Then blend the sounds to say the word.

/t/ /a/ /g/	/m/ /a/ /t/	/a/ /t/
/s/ /a/ /t/	/t/ /a/ /p/	/s/ /ā/ /l/

Phonics

Picture Sort

t

Model

Place **Word-Building Card** *t* in the pocket chart.

This is the letter *t*. The sound for this letter is /t/.

Follow the routine for *s*, *p*, and *a*.

This is the letter *s*. The sound for this letter is /s/.

Hold up the **Photo Card** for *top*.

Here is the picture of a *top*. *Top* begins with /t/. I will place *top* under the letter *t*.

Follow the routine for *saw*.

Guided Practice/Practice

Children sort the Photo Cards. Guide practice with the first card, using the routine.

Build Fluency: Sound-Spellings

Display the following **Word-Building Cards**: *a, m, p, s, t*. Have children chorally say each sound. Repeat and vary the pace.

Blend with /t/*t*

Model

Place **Word-Building Card** *s* in the pocket chart.

This letter is *s*. The letter *s* stands for the /s/ sound. Say /s/.

Place Word-Building Card *a* next to *s*. Move your hand from left to right.

This letter is *a*. The letter *a* stands for the /a/ sound. Listen as I blend the two sounds together: /sssaaa/. Now blend the sounds with me. (/sssaaa/)

Place Word-Building Card *t* next to *sa*. Move your hand from left to right.

Repeat the routine with *tap*.

This letter is *t*. The letter *t* stands for /t/. Listen as I blend the three sounds together: /sssaaat/, *sat*. Now you blend the sounds with me. (/sssaaat/, *sat*)

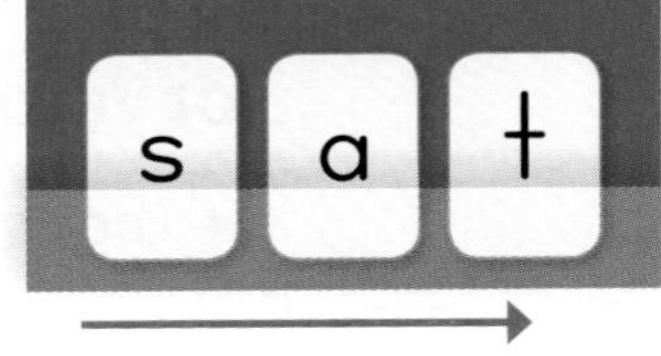

Guided Practice/Practice

Children blend sounds to form words.

at mat pat Pam

For Tier 2 instruction, see page 584.

Corrective Feedback

Blending: Sound Error Model the sound that children missed, then have them repeat the sound. For example, for the word *sat*, say: *My turn.* Tap under the letter *t* in the word *sat* and say: *Sound? What's the sound?* Then return to the beginning of the word. Say: *Let's start over.* Blend the word with children again.

Objective

- Blend sounds to form words with *s, a, t, m, p*

Materials

- Word-Building Cards
- pocket chart
- Activity Book, p. 9
- Practice Book, p. 65

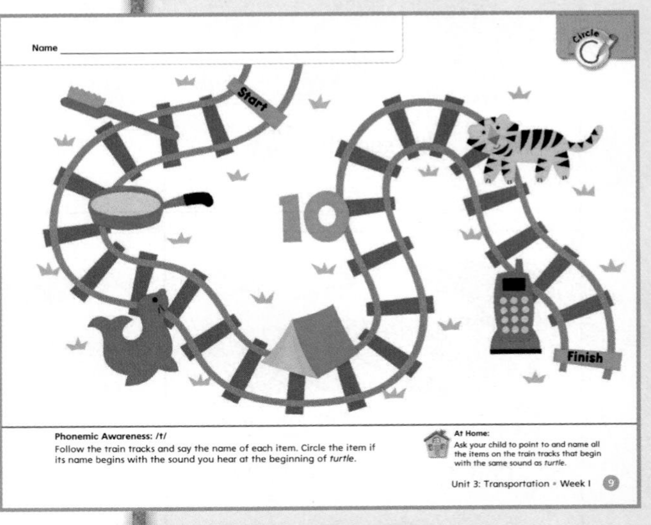

Activity Book, page 9
Practice Book, page 65

Objectives

- Read decodable words with /t/*t*
- Read the word *see*
- Review the words *see, can, the*
- Reread for fluency
- Make a prediction

Materials

- Pre-decodable Reader: *Can Tam See?*
- High-Frequency Word Cards: *can, see, the*
- pocket chart

Pre-decodable Reader

Read *Can Tam See?*

Can Tam See?

REVIEW Display **High-Frequency Word Cards** for **see**, **can**, and **the** in the pocket chart. Use the **Read/Spell/Write** routine to review each word.

MODEL CONCEPTS ABOUT PRINT Demonstrate book handling. Guide children to follow along with their books. *I hold the book so that the cover is on the front and the words are not upside down. I open the book by turning the cover. Then I turn each page as I read it.*

PREDICT Have children describe the illustration on the cover. Ask: *Do you think the story will be a real or made-up story? Why?*

FIRST READ Point out the rebus and discuss what it stands for. Have children point to each word, sounding out the decodable words and saying the sight words quickly. Children should chorally read the story the first time through.

DEVELOP COMPREHENSION Ask the following:

- *Look at page 7. What did you think would happen next?*
- *Look at page 8. What did happen next?*

SECOND READ Have partners reread the book together.

Can Tam see the ?
boat
2

Can Tam see the ?
train
4

Can Tam see the ?
jet
6

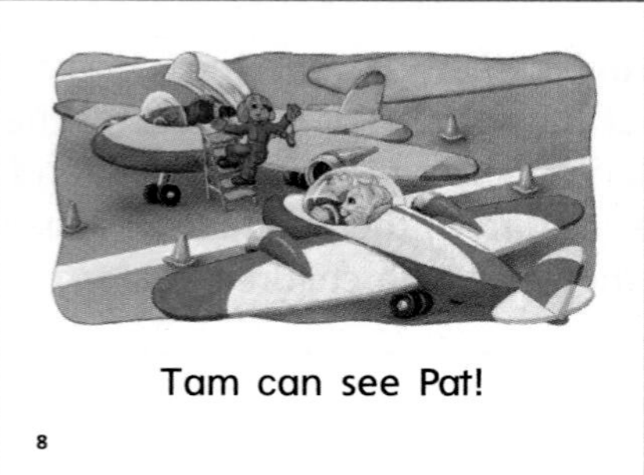

Tam can see Pat!
8

Pre-decodable Reader

Writing

Independent Writing: Sentences

REVISE AND EDIT

Distribute children's sentences from Day 3. Have them reread their sentences and check for the following:

- Does my sentence name the **vehicle**?
- Did I draw a picture of a shape in the sentence?
- Did I draw a picture of the vehicle?

PARTNERS

Circulate and help children as they review and self-correct their sentences. Have children share their sentences with a partner.

Diana
I see a
on a garbage truck.

Write About It

Have children draw anything they wish. If they have difficulty thinking of a topic, suggest they draw a picture of themselves on a school bus. Guide them to label their drawings.

Objectives

- Revise and edit sentences
- Use letter knowledge to write letters in a word

Materials

- children's writing from Day 3

5-Day Writing

Sentences	
DAY 1	Shared: A List
DAY 2	Interactive: Sentences
DAY 3	Independent: Prewrite and Draft Sentences
DAY 4	Independent: Revise and Edit Sentences
DAY 5	Independent: Publish and Present

ELL

Use New Language Use the example to model sharing a sentence with a partner about a shape you can see on a vehicle. For example, as you point, say: *This is a picture of the square I see on a garbage truck. This is a picture of the garbage truck.*

Transitions That Teach

While packing up, have children tell about ways that people, animals, or things **glide**.

Day 5 At a Glance

WHOLE GROUP

Oral Language
- Build Robust Vocabulary

Comprehension
- Strategy: Recognize Story Structure
- Skill: Make and Confirm Predictions
- Read Across Texts

Vocabulary
- High-Frequency Word *see*
- Build Fluency
- Shape Words

Phonemic Awareness
- Phoneme Categorization

Phonics
- Read Words
- Dictation

Writing
- Independent Writing: Publish and Present

SMALL GROUP

- Differentiated Instruction, pages 570–595

Review and Assess

Oral Language

Build Robust Vocabulary

REVIEW WORDS

Review this week's oral vocabulary words with children. Explain that all of the words will be used to discuss winning a race. Talk about what it means to win a race. *A race is a when two or more people compete to see who can run, move, or ride the fastest.*

Use the following questions to check children's understanding:

- What type of **transportation** could be used to win a race?
- What might a **vehicle** look like that could win a race?
- Why would someone like to drive **rapidly** in order to win a race?
- What could it look like for a vehicle that **glides** to win a race?
- Should a vehicle **continue** to drive until it reaches the finish line in order to win a race? Why?

REVIEW SONGS AND RHYMES ABOUT TRANSPORTATION

Sing the song "Transportation Is the Way!" and have children sing along. Have children name and describe each form of transportation. Then recite the rhyme "Let's Ride" with children. Have children name the words that rhyme. Then have them generate more words that rhyme with words read from the song and rhyme. For example, ask: *What rhymes with* car?

Review and Assess
Comprehension

STRATEGY Recognize Story Structure

REFLECT ON THE STRATEGY Remind children that they have learned how to use the pattern or the structure of the story to understand what happens.

Think Aloud I can think about the pattern in the story or the way the story is organized to figure out what will happen next.

SKILL Make and Confirm Predictions

Lead children in reviewing how they used the skill of making and confirming predictions as they read *The Bus for Us* and "The Turtle and the Rabbit."

- *What helped you guess what **vehicle** Tess and Gus would see next?* (the pattern of the story and the illustrations)
- *What helped you guess who would win the race, the rabbit or the turtle?* (the characters and the story events)
- *When you figured out what could happen next, were you right?*

Reading Across Texts

Create a chart like the one below to make connections between ideas in the fiction book *The Bus for Us* and the expository article "Signs in the Park." You may wish to add another column for "The Turtle and the Rabbit."

The Bus for Us	Signs in the Park
fiction	expository
illustrations	photographs
about a made-up girl and boy	about real signs seen in parks
about types of transportation used	about types of signs used

Objectives

- Review the strategy and skill
- Compare genres
- Listen and share information

Materials

- Big Book: *The Bus for Us*
- Read-Aloud Anthology: "The Turtle and the Rabbit," pp. 45–48
- Big Book of Explorations, Vol. 1: "Signs in the Park"
- Activity Book, p. 11

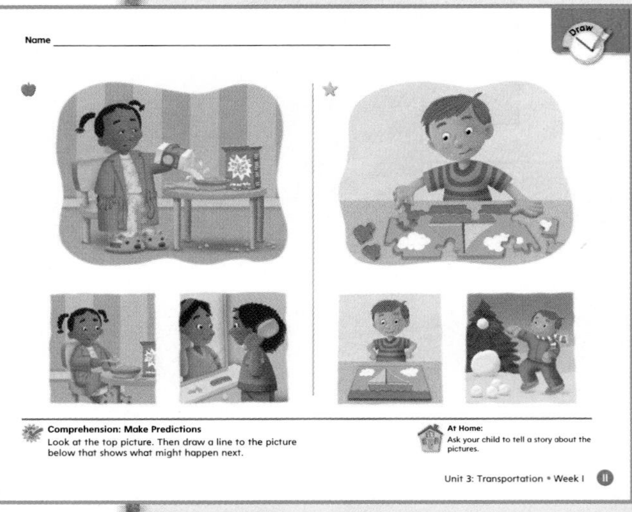

Activity Book, page 11

Objectives

- Review the high-frequency words *a, like, see, the, we*
- Review shape words *circle, triangle, square, rectangle*

Materials

- High-Frequency Word Cards: *a, like, see, the, we*
- High-Frequency Word Cards; Teacher's Resource Book
- hand drawn shapes and shape words on index cards: *circle, triangle, square, rectangle*
- Big Book: *The Bus for Us*

Fluency

Connected Text Have children reread this week's **Pre-decodable Readers** with a partner. Circulate, listen in, and note those children who need additional instruction and practice reading this week's decodable and sight words.

Pre-Decodable Reader
Can Tam See?
Pre-Decodable Reader
I See Sam
Sight Word Practice

Review and Assess

Vocabulary

High-Frequency Words

Distribute one of the following **High-Frequency Word Cards** to each child: **see**, **a**, **like**, **we**, **the**. Say: *When you hear the word that is on your card, stand and hold up your Word Card.*

- We like *to go out for recess.*
- *I can climb* the *monkey bars.*
- *From* the *top, I can* see the *playground.*
- *Is there* a *sandbox to play in?*
- *Yes,* we *can play in* the *sandbox today.*

Build Fluency: Word Automaticity

Rapid Naming Display the High-Frequency Word Cards. Point quickly to each card, at random, and have children read the word as fast as they can.

see	a	like	we	the

Shape Words

Distribute the index cards with shape words and drawings to children. Page through the **Big Book** *The Bus for Us*. Ask children to sort the shapes by placing them on the shapes on the vehicles in the book.

circle | triangle | rectangle | square

TIME TO MOVE!

Distribute the shape index cards. Then group children according to the shape they have: *Triangles, go to the window. Circles, go to the reading center.*

Review and Assess

Phonemic Awareness

Phoneme Categorization

Guided Practice

Display the **Photo Cards** for *teeth*, *sock*, and *top*.

I will say three picture names. Which picture names begin with the same sound? *Teeth*, *sock*, and *top*. *Teeth* and *top* begin with the same sound, /t/. *Sock* does not begin with the /t/ sound. It does not belong.

Practice

Children identify the picture name that does not begin with the same sound.

Use these sets of cards: *soap, penguin, seal*; *pizza, pen, table*; *saw, tiger, toothbrush*.

I will show you three cards. Tell me which picture does not belong.

Objective

- Categorize or group words with the same beginning sounds

Materials

- Photo Cards: *pen, penguin, pizza, saw, seal, soap, sock, table, teeth, tiger, toothbrush, top*

Objectives

- Review sound-spellings for /t/t, /s/s, /p/p
- Read simple one-syllable words
- Use letter-sound correspondences to spell

Materials

- Word-Building Cards
- pocket chart
- 4 index cards with: *We*, *see*, *Pat*, period mark
- 4 index cards with: *See*, *Pat*, *tap*, period mark
- WorkBoard Sound Boxes; Teacher's Resource Book, p. 136
- markers
- Activity Book, p. 12

Activity Book, page 12

Review and Assess

Phonics

Build Fluency: Sound-Spellings

Rapid Naming Display the following **Word-Building Cards**: *a, m, p, s, t*. Have children chorally say each sound. Repeat and vary the pace.

Read Words

Apply

Distribute the first set of cards. Have children stand in sequence.

Let's read the sentence together. *We see Pat.*

Repeat, using the other set of cards.

Let's read the sentence together. *See Pat tap.*

Dictation

Dictate the following sounds for children to spell.

Listen as I say a sound. Repeat the sound, then write the letter that stands for the sound.

/t/ /s/ /m/ /a/ /p/

Then dictate the words for children to spell. Model for children how to use the **Sound Boxes** to segment the word. Have them repeat.

Now let's write some words. I will say a word. I want you to repeat the word, then think about how many sounds are in the word. Use your Sound Boxes to count the sounds. Then write one letter for each sound you hear.

at sat mat pat Sam Pam

Write the letters and words on the board for children to self-correct.

Review and Assess
Writing

Independent Writing: Sentences

PUBLISH
Explain to children that you will gather their sentences about **vehicles** to make a class book.

- Brainstorm ideas for a title, such as "Vehicles We See."
- Have a few children work on a cover for the book. Write the title on the cover.
- Make holes along the edges of the cover and each page.
- Bind the pages together with yarn.

PRESENT
Have children take turns reading their illustrated sentences to the class and telling what the pictures show.

LISTENING, SPEAKING, AND VIEWING
- Remind children to speak audibly and to be good listeners by facing the presenter when a classmate is speaking.
- Place the finished book in the Reading Workstation for everyone to enjoy. Children may wish to add a copy of their work to their Writing Portfolio.

Write About It
Have children draw a picture of their favorite place to go. Guide them to label their drawings.

Objective
- Publish and present a piece of writing

Materials
- children's writing from Day 4

5-Day Writing

Sentences	
DAY 1	Shared: A List
DAY 2	Interactive: Sentences
DAY 3	Independent: Prewrite and Draft Sentences
DAY 4	Independent: Revise and Edit Sentences
DAY 5	Independent: Publish and Present

Transitions That Teach
While children are lining up, have them name things that move **rapidly**.

Approaching Level

Oral Language

Objective Preteach oral vocabulary
Materials • none

THEME WORDS: *vehicle, transportation*

- Tell children the meanings for **vehicle** and **transportation**. A vehicle *can carry or move people and things from one place to another. Cars and airplanes are two kinds of* vehicles. Transportation *is the different ways to get from where you are to where you want to go. Trucks and boats are types of* transportation.
- Discuss the words with children. *What kinds of* vehicles *might kids use to get to school? What form of* transportation *is faster: an airplane or a car? Explain.*
- Have children use the following sentence frames to generate oral sentences using the words: *The type of vehicle that I like is ________. A very fast form of transportation is ________.*

High-Frequency Words

Objective Preteach high-frequency words
Materials • **High-Frequency Word Cards:** *a, like, see, the, we*

PRETEACH WORD: *see*

- Display the **High-Frequency Word Card** for **see**.
- **Read** Point to and say the word *see. This is the word* see. *It means "to look at." I see the children.*
- **Spell** *The word* see *is spelled* s-e-e. Have children read and spell *see.*
- **Write** Finally, have children write the word *see.*
- Have children work with a partner to make up sentences using the word *see.* Ask them to talk about things they see on their way to school.

HIGH-FREQUENCY WORDS REVIEW

Tier 2

Display the High-Frequency Word Cards for **a**, **like**, **we**, **the**, and **see** from the previous three units. Display one card at a time as children chorally read and spell the word. Mix and repeat. Note words children need to review.

ELL

Partners When pairing children to make up sentences, pair English Language Learners with children who are more proficient. Write their sentences, read them together, and point out the high-frequency words.

Approaching Level

Phonemic Awareness

Objective Identify initial sound /t/

Materials
- **Photo Cards:** *table, teeth, tie, tiger, toe, top, toys*
- **Sound-Spelling Card:** *Turtle*

PHONEME ISOLATION

Model

- Display the **Photo Card** for *tiger. This is a tiger. Listen for the beginning sound in* tiger: */t/.* Tiger *begins with /t/.* Repeat for *tie.*
- Distribute the small **Sound-Spelling Cards**. Point out the articulation picture. *Look at the shape of the mouth on the card. When I say /t/, I separate my teeth and place the tip of my tongue lightly on the hard ridge behind my upper teeth. A little puff of air comes out when I say the sound.*

Guided Practice/Practice

- Display the Photo Cards. Have children select a picture, name it, and say the initial sound of the picture name: *This is a* _________. _________ *begins with /t/.*

Phonics

Objective Recognize words that begin with /t/*t*

Materials
- **Sound-Spelling Card:** *Turtle*
- **Word-Building Cards**
- **Photo Cards:** *table, teeth, tie, tiger, toe, top, toys*

PRETEACH: RECOGNIZE */t/t*

Model

- Display Photo Cards for *toe* and *tie* and the *Turtle* Sound-Spelling Card. *This is the letter* t. T *stands for the /t/ sound that you hear at the beginning of* toe. *I will place a* t *on the picture of the* toe *because* toe *begins with /t/.* Repeat with *tie.*

Guided Practice/Practice

- Display the Photo Cards. *This is a table. What sound do you hear at the beginning of* table? *What letter stands for /t/? Let's place the* t ***Word-Building Card*** *on the table because* table *begins with /t/.* Repeat with remaining Photo Cards for /t/*t*. Guide children to trace the letter *t* on their small Word-Building Cards.
- For additional practice, point out other words that begin with initial /t/. Hold the *t* card up while children repeat chorally.

SOUND-SPELLINGS REVIEW

Display Word-Building Cards for *s, p, t, m,* and *a,* one at a time. Have children chorally say the sound. Repeat and vary the pace.

Corrective Feedback

Mnemonic Display the *Turtle* Sound-Spelling Card. Say: *This is the* Turtle *Sound-Spelling Card. The sound is /t/. The /t/ sound is spelled with the letter* t. *Say /t/ with me: /t/. This is the sound at the beginning of* turtle. *What is the letter? What is the sound? What word begins with /t/?* Turtle *is the word we can use to remember the sound for* t, */t/.*

ELL

Extra Practice Provide additional practice in recognizing and naming letters for children whose native languages do not use the symbols of the Latin alphabet.

On Level

High-Frequency Words

Objective Review high-frequency words *see, a, like, the, we*

Materials • **High-Frequency Word Cards:** *a, like, see, the, we*

REVIEW: *see, a, like, the, we*

- Display the **High-Frequency Word Card** for **see**.
- **Read** Point to and say the word *see. This is the word* see. *It means "to look at." We see things with our eyes.*
- **Spell** *The word* see *is spelled* s-e-e. Have children read and spell *see.*
- **Write** Finally, have children write the word *see.*
- Repeat with **like**, **the**, **we**, and **a**. Have partners make up questions and answers using the words *see, a, like, the, we.*

Phonemic Awareness/Phonics

Objective Blend /a/*a*, /p/*p*, /s/*s*, and /t/*t*

Materials • **Photo Cards** • **Word-Building Cards** • pocket chart • **Sound-Spelling WorkBoards**

PHONEME BLENDING

- Place the **Photo Cards** facedown in front of you. Choose one at random and give a hint about it. Then say the sounds. For example, say: *This is an animal that flies at night. Here are the sounds in the word: /b/ /a/ /t/. I will blend these sounds together: /baaat/,* bat. *The word is* bat. Show the picture.
- Ask children to choose a Photo Card in secret. Have each child in turn say a clue about his or her word, then say the sounds of the word that names the photo. Have children repeat.

PHONICS

- Display **Word-Building Card** *a. The name of this letter is* a. *A stands for the /a/ sound we hear at the beginning of* apple. *What is the sound? I'll hold up the* a *card because* apple *begins with /a/.* Repeat with *p (pig), s (Sam),* and *t (top)*. Then distribute the small Word-Building Cards. Say: *ant, pan, sit, tube, anchor, sun, paper, tan.* Children hold up and name their Word-Building Card.
- Place Word-Building Cards *t, a,* and *p* in the pocket chart. Children identify each letter. Move your hand from left to right below the letters as you blend: *Now listen as I blend the sounds together: /taaap/,* tap. *What's the word?* Have children write *t, a,* and *p* several times on their **WorkBoards** as they say /t/, /a/, /p/. Repeat with the words *pat* and *sat.*

ELL

Sound-Letter Relationships Provide additional practice in pronouncing the initial sounds /a/, /p/, /s/, /t/ and naming the corresponding letters as children point to them.

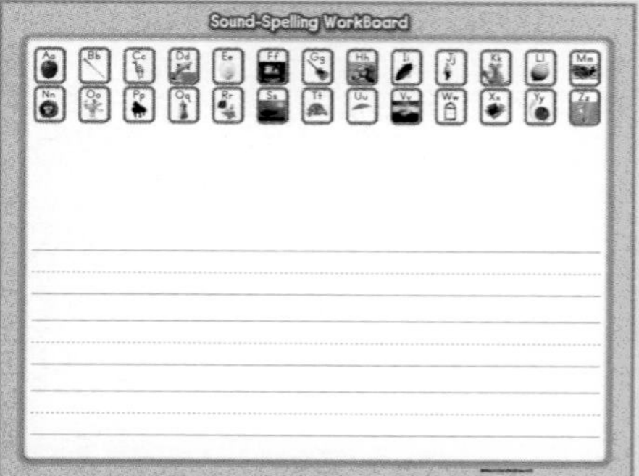

Sound-Spelling WorkBoard

Beyond Level

High-Frequency Words/Vocabulary

Objectives Review high-frequency words; introduce *on* and *that*

ACCELERATE

Write *on* and *that* on the board.

- **Read** Point to *on. This is the word* on. *I can stand on the hill. I put the book on the desk.*
- **Spell** *The word* on *is spelled* o-n. Have children read and spell *on.*
- **Write** Finally, have children write the word *on.*
- Repeat the routine with *that.* Have children work with a partner to make up oral sentences using the words *on* and *that.*

EXPAND ORAL VOCABULARY

Gifted Talented

- **Suffixes** Review the meanings of the oral vocabulary word *rapidly* with children. Then explain that a suffix is a word part added to the end of a word to form a new word.
- Say: *The suffix* -ly *at the end of* rapidly *means "in a certain way." When you do something* rapidly, *you do it in a fast way. Another word with the suffix* -ly *is* slowly. Slowly *means "in a slow way."*

- Have children take turns using the new word *slowly* in a sentence. Then tell children that they will work with a partner to name things they do slowly and things they do rapidly.

Phonics

Objectives Review /t/*t* and introduce /e/*e;* blend and read words

Materials
- **Sound-Spelling Cards**
- **Word-Building Cards**
- **Sound-Spelling WorkBoards**

ENRICH

- Display the *Turtle* **Sound-Spelling Card**. Say: *This is the* Turtle *Sound-Spelling Card.* Remind children that the /t/ sound is spelled with the letter *t.* Top *and* tax *begin with /t/. What other words begin with /t/?*
- Repeat the routine above with the *Egg* Sound-Spelling Card. Ask children to say /e/ and *egg* with you. Repeat with *c, k, g, n, t,* and *w.*
- Display **Word-Building Cards** *c, k, e, g, k, n, t,* and *w.* Have children repeat the letter name and sound as they write the letter several times on their **WorkBoards**.

ELL

Partners When pairing children to make up sentences, pair English Language Learners with children who are more proficient. Write their sentences, read them together, and point to the high-frequency words.

ELL ENGLISH LANGUAGE LEARNERS

Oral Language Warm-Up

Content Objective Learn theme vocabulary
Language Objective Sing and act out song to demonstrate understanding
Materials • **Listening Library Audio CD**

BUILD BACKGROUND KNOWLEDGE

All Language Levels

- Introduce the unit theme "Transportation" using the song "Transportation Is the Way!" Display a picture of a vehicle, such as a picture from *The Bus for Us* or one of the **Visual Vocabulary Resources**. Teach the word *ride* as you point to a picture that shows a vehicle people ride in. Have children repeat the word three times.
- Play "Transportation Is the Way!" on the **Listening Library Audio CD**. Act out each line as you sing the song.
- Then teach children the song. Emphasize the key words that name kinds of transportation, such as *bus, plane, boat, taxi, train, bike, van, motorcycle,* and *sedan*.
- Play the song several times until children begin to correctly repeat the song.
- Ask children to tell about kinds of transportation they ride in. Build on their responses to model speaking in complete sentences. For example: *You ride in a school bus.*

Academic Language

Language Objective Use academic language in classroom conversations

All Language Levels

- This week's academic words are **boldfaced** throughout the lesson. Define the word in context and provide a clear example from the selection. Then ask children to generate an example or a word with a similar meaning.

Academic Language Used in Whole Group Instruction

Oral Vocabulary Words	Vocabulary and Grammar Concepts	Strategy and Skill Words
continue **glide** **rapidly** **transportation** **vehicle**	**shape words** **action words**	**story structure** **make predictions** **confirm predictions** **action**

Cognates

Help children identify similarities and differences in pronunciation and spelling between English words and Spanish cognates:

continue	*continuar*
rapidly	*rápidamente*
transportation	*transportación*
vehicle	*vehículo*
prediction	*predicción*
confirm	*confirmar*
action	*acción*

ELL ENGLISH LANGUAGE LEARNERS

Vocabulary

Language Objective Demonstrate understanding and use of key words by describing different kinds of transportation

Materials • **Visual Vocabulary Resources**

PRETEACH KEY VOCABULARY

All Language Levels

Use the **Visual Vocabulary Resources** to preteach the weekly oral vocabulary words *continue, glide, rapidly, transportation,* and *vehicle*. Focus on one or two words per day. Use the following routine that appears in detail on the cards.

- Define the word in English and provide the example given.
- Define the word in Spanish, if appropriate, and indicate if the word is a cognate.
- Display the picture and explain how it illustrates or demonstrates the word. Engage children in structured partner-talk about the image, using the key word.
- Ask children to chorally say the word three times.
- Point out any known sound-spellings or focus on a key aspect of phonemic awareness related to the word.

PRETEACH FUNCTION WORDS AND PHRASES

All Language Levels

Use the Visual Vocabulary Resources to preteach the function words *quickly* and *slowly*. Focus on one word per day. Use the detailed routine on the cards.

- Define the word in English and, if appropriate, in Spanish. Point out if the word is a cognate.
- Refer to the picture and engage children in talk about the word. For example, children will partner-talk using sentence frames, or they will listen to sentences and replace a word or phrase with the new function word.
- Ask children to chorally repeat the word three times.

TEACH BASIC WORDS

Beginning/Intermediate

Use the Visual Vocabulary Resources to teach the basic words *garbage truck, tractor, taxi, fire engine, tow truck,* and *school bus.* Teach these "local vehicles" words using the routine provided on the card.

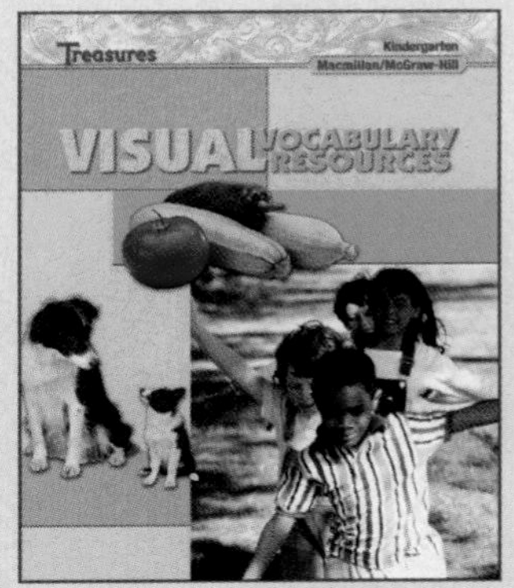

Visual Vocabulary Resources

Approaching Level

High-Frequency Words

Objective Reteach high-frequency words

Materials
- **High-Frequency Word Cards:** *a, like, see, the, we*
- **Sound-Spelling WorkBoards**

RETEACH WORD: *see*

Tier 2

- Distribute a **WorkBoard** to each child. Then display the **High-Frequency Word Card** for **see**.
- Use the **Read/Spell/Write** routine to reteach the word. Point to and say the word. *This is the word* see. *It means "to look at." I can't see if I close my eyes.* See *is spelled* s-e-e. Have children read and spell *see.* Then have them write the word on their WorkBoards.
- Have children work with a partner to make up sentences using the word *see.* Ask them to talk about things they might see at a park.

CUMULATIVE REVIEW

Display the High-Frequency Word Cards **a**, **like**, **we**, **the**, and **see** from the previous three units. Display one card at a time as children chorally read and spell the word. Mix and repeat. Note words children need to review.

Pre-decodable Reader

Objective Preteach Pre-decodable Reader *I See Sam*

Materials
- **Pre-decodable Reader:** *I See Sam*

PRETEACH *I See Sam*

- Display the cover of the book. Have children identify the cover and read the title and author's name. Open to the title page and point out the title. *What's the name of this page? Let's read the title together.* Point out the word *See. What do you think we will see in this book?*
- Page through the book. Ask children what they see in each picture. Point out that each rebus shows a form of transportation. Ask children to find the words *see, a, I,* and *like.*
- Read the book chorally with children. Have them point to each word or rebus as they read it. Provide corrective feedback as needed.
- Ask children to use *see* to name things they see in the pictures.
- After reading, ask children to recall things they read about.

ELL

Partners When pairing children to make up sentences, pair English Language Learners with children who are more proficient. Write their sentences, read them together, and point out the high-frequency word *see.*

Pre-Decodable Reader
I See Sam
by Anita Wylie • illustrated by Maribel Soares
Sight Word Practice

Pre-decodable Reader

Approaching Level

Phonemic Awareness

Objective Blend with /t/ and /p/

Materials • **Puppet**

Puppet

PHONEME BLENDING

Tier 2

Model

- *Listen as Happy says the sounds for tap: /t/ /a/ /p/. Now Happy will blend the sounds: /taaap/, /tap/,* tap. *Happy blended /t/ /a/ /p/ together to say the word* tap. *Now listen again. Happy will do another word.* Repeat the blending with the word *pat:* /p/ /a/ /t/.

Guided Practice/Practice

- Have the **Puppet** say /m/ /a/ /t/. Ask children to repeat. *Now you blend the sounds and say the word with Happy: /mmmaaat/,* mat. Repeat with the following:

/t/ /o/ /p/ /p/ /a/ /m/ /p/ /a/ /s/
/p/ /a/ /k/ /p/ /a/ /t/ /t/ /i/ /p/

Phonics

Objective Reinforce letter-sound correspondence for /t/*t*

Materials • **Sound-Spelling Card:** *Turtle* • **Sound-Spelling WorkBoards** • **Word-Building Cards** • **Photo Card:** *table*

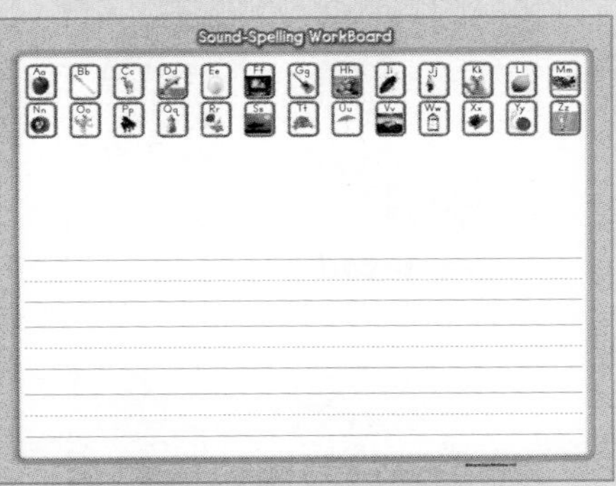

Sound-Spelling WorkBoard

RETEACH /t/*t*

Model

- Display the *Turtle* **Sound-Spelling Card.** *The letter* t *stands for the /t/ sound as in* turtle. *What is this letter? What sound does it stand for?* Repeat with the **Photo Card** for *table.*
- Trace *t* on a small **Word-Building Card.** *I will say a sentence. We will trace* t *on the cards when we hear /t/.* Say: *Tim sees ten tiny turtles.*

Guided Practice/Practice

- Distribute a **WorkBoard** to each child. Say: *tall, ten, moon, Tim, dog, tub, water, glass, tent, Tam.* Children write *t* on their WorkBoard when they hear a word with /t/. Guide them with the first two words.

SOUND-SPELLINGS REVIEW

Display Word-Building Cards for *s, p, m,* and *a,* one at a time. Point to the letters in a random order. Have children chorally say the sound. Repeat and vary the pace.

Corrective Feedback

Blending Error: *When I see the word* tap, *I blend sounds /t/ /a/ /p/. Then I say the word fast:* tap. *Listen again: /t/ /a/ /p/, /taaap/,* tap. Continue with the other words and then repeat *tap.*

On Level

Pre-decodable Reader

Objective Reread *I See Sam* to develop fluency

Materials • **Pre-decodable Reader:** *I See Sam*

REREAD FOR FLUENCY

- Ask children to look back at the illustrations in *I See Sam*. Have them use their own words to retell what the book was about. Then work with them to read with accuracy and expression. Model reading a page: *When I read, "I see a train," I grouped together the words "I see" and then I paused a little before saying "a train." Grouping words like this makes my reading sound natural, as if I were speaking normally.* Have children reread a page with expression and by speaking audibly and clearly.
- Provide time to listen as children read their page(s). Comment on their accuracy and expression and provide corrective feedback by modeling proper fluency.
- Use the same routine for **Pre-decodable Reader** *Can Tam See?* on Day 4.

Pre-decodable Reader

Pre-decodable Reader

Beyond Level

Pre-decodable Reader

Objective Reread *Can Tam See?* to reinforce fluency

Materials • **Pre-decodable Reader:** *Can Tam See?; I See Sam*

REREAD FOR FLUENCY

- Have children reread several pages of *Can Tam See?* Work with them to read with accuracy and expression. Model reading a page. Point out how you raised your voice at the end of a question: *When I read* Can Tam See? *my voice went up at the end.*
- Listen to children read. Comment on their accuracy and expression. Provide corrective feedback by modeling fluency.

INNOVATE

- Have children draw book covers for two new books that might follow *Can Tam See?* Have them choose from the titles *Can Pam See?* and *Can Sam See?*
- Use the above routine for *I See Sam* on Day 4.

Corrective Feedback

Letter-Sound Correspondence If children cannot discern medial short /e/*e*, review the letter-sound relationship. Write *e* on the board and say /eee/ together. Write *red, bed, led, fed*. Point to each word and have children echo-chant: /rrreeed/, *red;* /beeed/, *bed;* /llleeed/, *led*; /fffeeed/, *fed*.

ELL ENGLISH LANGUAGE LEARNERS

Access to Core Content

Content Objective Develop listening comprehension
Language Objective Discuss text using key words and sentence frames
Materials • **ELL Resource Book,** pp. 62–69

PRETEACH BIG BOOK/TRADE BOOK

All Language Levels

Use the Interactive Question-Response Guide on **ELL Resource Book** pages 62–69 to introduce children to *The Bus for Us*. Preteach half of the selection on Day 1 and half on Day 2.

- Use the prompts provided in the guide to develop meaning and vocabulary. Use the partner-talk and whole-class responses to engage children and increase student talk.
- When completed, revisit the selection and prompt children to talk about the illustrations. Provide sentence starters as needed and build on children's responses to develop language.

ELL Resource Book

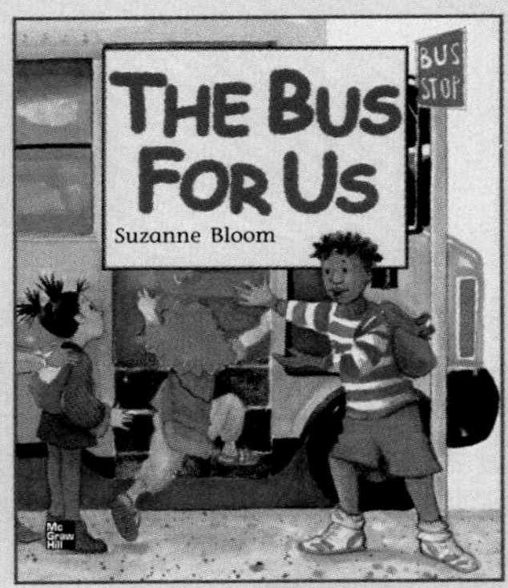

Big Book

Beginning	Intermediate	Advanced
Use Visuals During the Interactive Reading, select several pictures. Describe them and have children summarize what you said.	**Summarize** During the Interactive Reading, select a few lines of text. After you read them and explain them, have children summarize the text.	**Expand** During the Interactive Reading, select a larger portion of text. After you read it and explain it, have children summarize the text.

Approaching Level

High-Frequency Words

Objective Recognize high-frequency words *see, a, like, the, we*

Materials
- **High-Frequency Word Cards:** *a, like, see, the, we*
- **Word-Building Cards**

REVIEW WORDS: *see, a, like, the, we*

- Display the **High-Frequency Word Card** for **see**. Say the word and have children repeat it. Point to each letter and have children name it.
- Distribute small **Word-Building Cards** *s, e,* and *e*. Model putting the letters together to form *see*. Then have children form *see*.
- Repeat the above routines with the words **like**, **the**, **a**, and **we**.
- Ask a question with the word *see*: *Can you see the door?* Have children use *see* to answer the question. Continue with the other words.

HIGH-FREQUENCY WORDS REVIEW

Display the High-Frequency Word Cards for *see, a, like, the,* and *we,* one card at a time, as children chorally read and spell the word. Mix and repeat. Note words children need to review.

Phonemic Awareness

Objective Identify initial and final /t/*t*

Materials
- **Photo Cards:** *feet, hat, jet, net, nut, table, teeth, tiger, toe, top*
- **WorkBoard Sound Boxes; Teacher's Resource Book,** p. 136
- **Sound Boxes** • markers

PHONEME ISOLATION

Tier 2

Model

- Use the **Sound Boxes** and the **Photo Card** for *toe. Listen for the beginning sound in* toe. Toe *begins with /t/. I'll place a marker in the first box to show that I hear /t/ at the beginning of* toe.
- Display the Photo Card for *net. Listen for the final sound in* net: net. Net *ends with /t/. Listen again: /nnneeet/,* net. *I'll place a marker in the last box to show that I hear* t *at the end of* net.

Guided Practice/Practice

- Distribute Sound Boxes and markers. Display the Photo Cards. Children select a picture and name it. Have them listen for /t/ and place the marker in the first or last box as they say: *This is a(n) ________. I hear /t/ at the ________ of ________.*
- Repeat with each picture name. Provide guidance as needed.

ELL

Extra Practice During the Cumulative Review, pair children at different levels of proficiency and have partners take turns reading and spelling the high-frequency words to each other.

Approaching Level

Phonics

Objectives Review blending initial /t/*t*; build fluency

Materials • **Word-Building Cards** • pocket chart

REVIEW SKILLS

Tier 2

Model

- Place **Word-Building Card** *t* in the pocket chart. *The name of this letter is* t. *The letter* t *stands for the /t/ sound. Say /t/. What is the letter? What is the sound?*
- Place *a* next to *t*. *The name of this letter is* a. *The letter* a *stands for the /a/ sound. Say /a/. What is the letter? What is the sound?* Place *p* next to *a* and repeat.
- Move your hand from left to right below the letters. *Now listen as I blend the three sounds together: /taaap/,* tap. *What's the word? Let's blend the word together: /t/ /a/ /p/, /taaap/,* tap.

Guided Practice/Practice

- Give the *t, a,* and *p* cards to children. Each child says the sound for the letter on his or her card: /t/ /a/ /p/. Have children blend the sounds to say the word *tap.*

Build Fluency

- Have children blend *tap* as quickly as they can.

Pre-decodable Reader

Pre-decodable Reader

Objective Preteach Pre-decodable Reader *Can Tam See?*

Materials • **Pre-decodable Reader:** *Can Tam See?*

PRETEACH *Can Tam See?*

- Display the cover of the book and read the title. Open to the title page and point out the title. *Let's read the title together.* Have children sound out each word as you run your finger under it. Tam *is the name of the cat. What do you think Tam will see?*
- Page through the book. Ask children what they see in each picture. Point out and name each rebus. Ask children to find the words *can, the,* and *see.*
- Read the book chorally with children. Have them point to each word or rebus as they read it. Provide corrective feedback as needed.
- Ask children to use *can, the,* and *see* to talk about the pictures. *Tam can see the dog.*
- After reading, ask children to recall things they read about.

What Tam Sees

Have children draw a picture of something else Tam might see while in a boat, train, or jet. Have children label their pictures.

Corrective Feedback

Association Error If children have difficulty identifying initial and final /t/, say: *My turn: /nnnuuut/,* nut. *I hear the /t/ sound at the end of* nut: */nnnuuut/. What is the sound? What is the letter? Let's start over.* Repeat the word *nut* for children to identify the position of /t/.

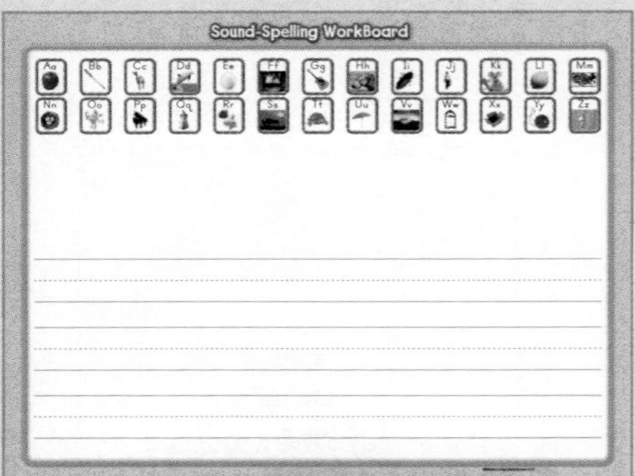

Sound-Spelling WorkBoard

On Level

Phonics

Objective Blend /a/*a*, /p/*p*, /s/*s*, and /t/*t*

Materials
- **Word-Building Cards**
- pocket chart
- **Sound-Spelling WorkBoards**

REVIEW SKILLS

- Display **Word-Building Card** *a. The name of this letter is* a. A *stands for the /a/ sound we hear at the beginning of* apple. *What is the sound? I'll hold up the* a *card because* apple *begins with /a/.* Repeat with *p (pig), s (Sam),* and *t (top).*
- Distribute the small Word-Building Cards. Say: *ant, pan, sit, tube, anchor, sun, paper, tan.* Children hold up and name their Word-Building Card that matches the initial sound in the word that you name. Guide practice with the first two words.
- **Blend Words** Place Word-Building Cards *t, a,* and *p* in the pocket chart. Have children identify each letter. Move your hand from left to right below the letters as you blend the word. *Now listen as I blend the sounds together: /taaap/,* tap. *What's the word?*
- Have children write *t, a,* and *p* several times on their **WorkBoards** as they say /t/, /a/, /p/. Repeat with *pat* and *sat.*

Beyond Level

Phonics

Objectives Review /t/*t* and introduce /e/*e;* blend and read words

Materials
- **Sound-Spelling Cards**
- **Word-Building Cards**

ACCELERATE

- Help children read words with short *e* and consonants *b, c, k, g, n, p, s, t,* and *w.* Write the following words on the board: *wet, cat, net, Ken, peg, ten, pen, get, Ben, bet, web, set.* Use **Sound-Spelling Cards** as needed to review sounds.
- Display Word-Building Cards *t, e, n. Blend the sounds to read the word. Listen: /t/ /e/ /n/, /teeennn/,* ten. *The word is* ten. Guide children to blend the sounds and read *ten.*

ELL ENGLISH LANGUAGE LEARNERS

Access to Core Content

Content Objective Develop listening comprehension
Language Objective Discuss text using key words and sentence frames
Materials • **ELL Resource Book**, pp. 70–71

PRETEACH BIG BOOK OF EXPLORATIONS

All Language Levels

Use the Interactive Question-Response Guide on **ELL Resource Book** pages 70–71 to preview the **Big Book of Explorations** selection "Signs in the Park." Preteach half of the selection on Day 3 and half on Day 4.

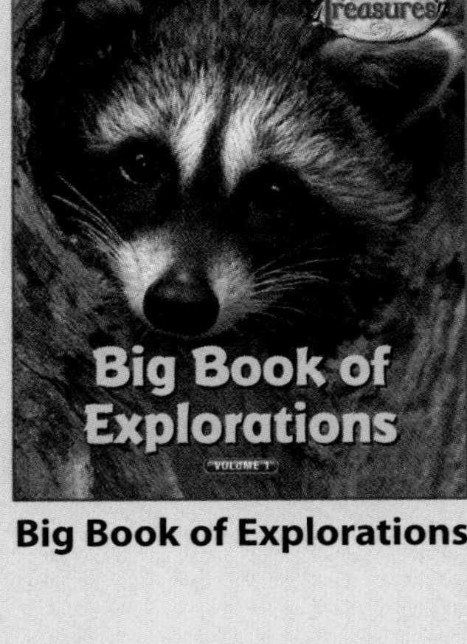

Big Book of Explorations

Grammar

Content Objective Identify action words
Language Objective Speak in complete sentences, using sentence frames
Materials • **Listening Library Audio CD** • **Photo Cards**

ACTION WORDS (VERBS)

All Language Levels

- Review verbs. Tell children that verbs are action words. Say: *The planes fly.* Have children repeat and act out the action of being a plane. Ask children to name and act out actions they do.
- Play "Let's Ride" from the **Listening Library Audio CD**. Tell children to listen for action words, which tell about things they can do.

Let's Ride
Time to take a little ride.
Open the door and get inside.
Open door and sit.
Now the engine starts to hum.
Shakes a bit, goes brr . . . brrum!
Hum, shake.
Then the tires go around.
Rolling faster on the ground.
Make circles in air with arms.
Turn the steering wheel just so.
Turn steering wheel.
To take us where we want to go.

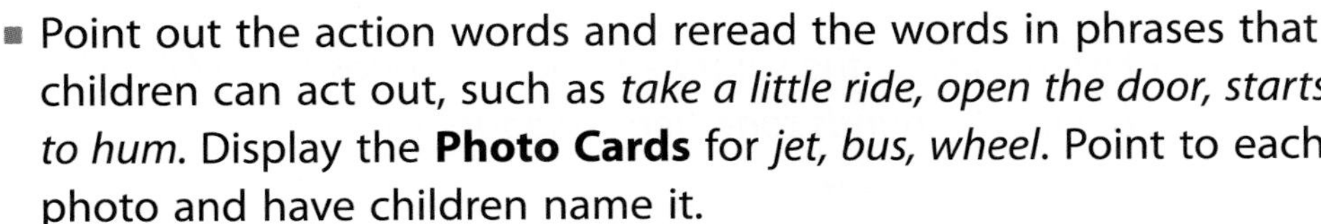

- Point out the action words and reread the words in phrases that children can act out, such as *take a little ride, open the door, starts to hum*. Display the **Photo Cards** for *jet, bus, wheel*. Point to each photo and have children name it.

PEER DISCUSSION STARTERS

All Language Levels

- Distribute Photo Cards of vehicles children discussed this week, such as *bus, car, jet,* and *bike*.
- Pair children and have them complete the sentence frame: *This is a* ________. Ask them to expand on their sentences by providing as many details as they can. Circulate, listen in, and take note of each child's language use and proficiency.

Puppet

Approaching Level

Phonemic Awareness

Objective Blend sounds to form words with /t/*t*

Materials • **Puppet** • **Photo Cards:** *bat, hat, jet, net, nut, top* • pocket chart

PHONEME BLENDING

Tier 2

Model

- Display the **Photo Cards** in the pocket chart and hold up the **Puppet**. *Happy is going to say the sounds in a word: /n/ /u/ /t/. Now Happy will blend these sounds together: /nnnuuut/. Let's say the sounds with Happy: /n/ /u/ /t/. Now let's blend them together: /nnnuuut/. Let's say the word with Happy:* nut. Point to the *nut* photo.

Guided Practice/Practice

- *Happy will say three sounds: /b/ /a/ /t/.* Guide children in blending the sounds with the Puppet: /baaat/, *bat*. Have children point to the picture for *bat* and say the word again. Continue with the remaining photo names and cards.

Phonics

Objective Blend /a/*a*, /p/*p*, /s/*s*, and /t/*t* to read words

Materials • **Word-Building Cards** • pocket chart

REVIEW SKILLS

Tier 2

Model

- Place **Word-Building Cards** *s, a,* and *t* in the pocket chart. *The name of this letter is* s. *The letter* s *stands for the /s/ sound. Say /s/. The name of this letter is* a. *The letter* a *stands for the /a/ sound. Say /a/. The name of this letter is* t. *The letter* t *stands for the /t/ sound. Say /t/.*
- *Listen as I say the sound each letter stands for: /s/ /a/ /t/. Now I will blend the sounds together: /sssaaat/,* sat.

Guided Practice/Practice

- Keep the Word-Building Cards in the pocket chart. Have children take turns pointing to the cards and saying the letter sounds. Guide children in blending the sounds and saying the word: /s/ /a/ /t/, /sssaaat/, *sat*. Repeat, building and having children blend the words *pat, tap, Tam,* and *mat*.

Corrective Feedback

Sound Error If children miss making the letter-sound correspondence, say: *My turn:* tie. *I hear /t/ at the beginning of* tie. *I'll hold up my* t *card because* tie *begins with /t/. What is the sound? What letter stands for that sound? Let's start again.*

ELL

Extra Practice Provide additional practice in recognizing and naming letters for children whose native languages do not use the symbols of the Latin alphabet.

Approaching Level

Leveled Reader Lesson 1

Objective Read *Bear Goes to Town* to apply skills and strategies

Materials • **Leveled Reader:** *Bear Goes to Town*

BEFORE READING

- **Preview** Read the title and the names of the author and illustrator. Talk about the title and illustration. Have children make a prediction. Ask: *Where do you think the bear is going? Have you ever gone on a trip?* Explain to children that using their background knowledge, such as knowledge about traveling, helps them to monitor and adjust their understanding of the story.
- **Review High-Frequency Words** Write **I**, **see**, and **a**, and read the words aloud. Guide children as they name the letters in each word. Have them find each word and read it in the book.
- **Page Through the Book** Name unfamiliar items and identify the rebus pictures.
- **Model Concepts About Print** Demonstrate book handling for children. Guide them as they follow along with their books. Display pages 2–3. *This is the top of the page. This is the bottom of the page. When I read the words on the page, I start at the left and read from left to right. Follow my finger as I read.*
- **Set a Purpose for Reading** *Let's find out how Bear gets around town.*

DURING READING

- Remind children to use the rebuses and illustrations and to look for the high-frequency words *I, see,* and *a*. Show children how to self-correct if a word doesn't sound right or doesn't make sense. *I see the first rebus on page 3 and I think, "car." But then I notice that the vehicle is yellow with checkers on the door and has a sign on top of it. The word in the sign starts with a* t *and* taxi *starts with* t. *I think the vehicle is a taxi, not just any car. Bear wants the taxi to stop and give him a ride. That makes sense.*
- Monitor children's reading and provide help as needed.

AFTER READING

- Ask children to point out words that they had trouble reading and to share strategies they used to help them. Reinforce good behaviors. For example, say: *Michelle, I noticed that you pointed to each rebus picture and then said the word aloud.*

- Have children work in pairs to reread the story aloud. Ask them to then take turns to ask and answer each other's questions about the story.

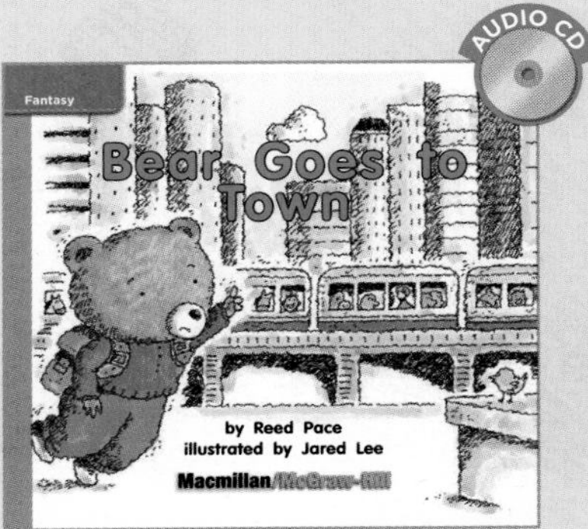

Leveled Reader

Digital Learning

Use the **Leveled Reader Audio CD** for fluency building *after* children read the book with your support during Small Group time.

Bear in a Taxi

Have children draw pictures to show Bear riding in the taxi. Have them write the letters *Tt* for *taxi* below the picture.

Leveled Reader

ELL

Retell Use the Interactive Question-Response Guide Technique to help English Language Learners understand *Tig Can See*. As you read, make meaning clear by pointing to pictures, demonstrating word meaning, paraphrasing text, and asking children questions.

What Tig Sees

Have children draw one thing that they see in the book. Have them write *I see* below their pictures.

On Level

Leveled Reader Lesson 1

Objective Read *Tig Can See* to apply skills and strategies

Materials • **Leveled Reader:** *Tig Can See*

BEFORE READING

- **Preview** Read the title and the names of the author and illustrator. Ask children to describe the cover. *What other vehicles fly?* Explain to children that using their background knowledge, such as knowledge about vehicles, helps them to monitor and adjust their understanding of the story. *What do you think the book is about? Do you think it is a real or made-up story?* Point out that the title page also has the title and author's name.
- **Model Concepts About Print** Demonstrate book handling. *I hold the book so that the cover is on the front and the words are not upside down. I open the book, read each page, and turn it. I start with the first page and end with the last.*
- **Review High-Frequency Words** Write **can**, **see**, and **the** on chart paper. Have children find each word in the book and point to the word as they read it.
- **Set a Purpose for Reading** *Let's find out what Tig sees around town.*

DURING READING

- Have children turn to page 2 and begin by whisper-reading the first two pages.
- Remind children to look for the new high-frequency word *see* and to use the rebus pictures and illustrations.
- Monitor children's reading and provide help as needed. Stop during the reading and ask open-ended questions to facilitate discussion, such as: *What is Tig riding? Why is riding in an airplane a good way to see things?* Build on children's responses to develop deeper understanding of the text.

AFTER READING

- Ask children to point out words they had trouble reading and to share strategies they used. Reinforce good behaviors. For example: *Rosa, I noticed that you put your finger under each word. After you read it, you looked carefully at the picture.*
- **Retell** Tell children to retell the story in their own words. Help them share ideas in complete sentences. As necessary, recast children's responses in complete sentences for them to repeat.

Beyond Level

Leveled Reader Lesson 1

Objective Read *How They Go* to apply skills and strategies

Materials • **Leveled Reader:** *How They Go*

BEFORE READING

- **Preview** Read the title and the names of the author and illustrator. Have children identify the back cover and the front cover with you. Explain to children that using their background knowledge, such as knowledge about transportation, helps them to monitor and adjust their understaning of the story. *What do you see on the cover? Where do you think the animals are going?* Explain that this story is about two cats—Tom and Kit. Page through the book with children. Pause to name unfamiliar items.
- **Introduce Story Words** Point to the word *country* on page 10. Read the sentence and ask children to use the picture clues to explain what *country* means.
- **Set a Purpose for Reading** *Let's find out how the two cats travel.*

DURING READING

- Remind children that when they come to an unfamiliar word, they can look for familiar chunks in the word, break the word into syllables and sound out each part, or think about what the word might mean. If the word does not sound right or make sense in the sentence, children can self-correct.
- Monitor children's reading and provide help as needed.

AFTER READING

- Ask children to point out words they had trouble reading and to share the strategies they used to figure them out.
- Tell children to retell the story and to share ideas in complete sentences. Guide children to ask and respond to questions, referring to the words and illustrations in the book.

Gifted and Talented

- **Analyze** *Why do you think Tom wants to visit the country and Kit wants to see the city? Which place would you like to visit? Why?*
- PARTNERS: Have children work in pairs to study photographs of the city and the country. Have them list words that describe each kind of area.
- **Model** Draw a Venn diagram on a large piece of paper with the labels *City*, *Country*, and *Both*. Tell children to use their lists to tell about the city, the country, and both. For example, *apartment buildings*, *houses*, and *library*. When finished, use the Venn diagram to compare and contrast city and country life.

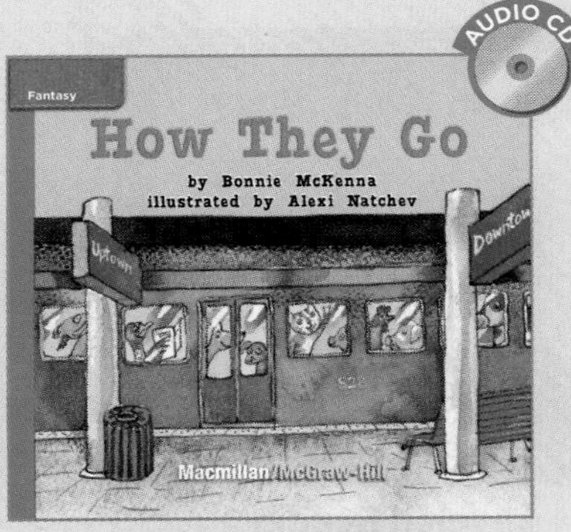

Leveled Reader

Ride Sentences

Have children write sentences about vehicles they would like to ride, and draw pictures of the vehicles.

Leveled Reader

Vocabulary

Preteach Vocabulary Use the routine in the **Visual Vocabulary Resources**, pages 313–314, to preteach the ELL Vocabulary listed on the inside front cover of the Leveled Reader.

ELL ENGLISH LANGUAGE LEARNERS

Leveled Reader Library

Leveled Reader

Content Objective Read to apply skills and strategies
Language Objective Retell information using complete sentences
Materials • **Leveled Reader:** *Tiger Can See*

BEFORE READING

All Language Levels

- **Preview** Read the title *Tiger Can See*. Ask: *What's the title? Say it again.* Repeat with the author's name. Point to the cover illustration and say: *I see a tiger in a plane.* Point to the tiger and plane as you name them. *The tiger is flying in the plane. Now turn to a partner and tell more about what you see in this picture.*
- **Page Through the Book** Use simple language to tell about the photo on each page. Immediately follow up with questions, such as: *Can Tiger see a clock or a truck? Can Tiger see the bridge?*
- **Review Skills** Use the inside front cover to review the phonics skill and high-frequency words.
- **Set a Purpose** Say: *Let's read to find out about what Tiger can see from the plane.*

DURING READING

All Language Levels

- Have children whisper-read each page, or use the differentiated suggestions below. Circulate, listen in, and provide corrective feedback, such as modeling how to make and confirm predictions.
- **Retell** Stop after every two pages and ask children to state what they have learned so far. Reinforce language by restating children's comments when they have difficulty using story-specific words. Provide differentiated sentence frames to support children's responses and engage children in partner-talk.

Beginning

Echo-Read Have children echo-read after you.

Check Comprehension Point to pictures and ask questions such as: *Does Tiger see a cat? Point to the cat. Does Tiger see a bus or a truck?*

Intermediate

Choral-Read Have children choral-read with you.

Check Comprehension Ask questions/prompts such as: *Describe what Tiger can see in this picture. What other things can Tiger see in this picture?*

Advanced

Choral-Read Have children choral-read.

Check Comprehension Ask: *Where did Tiger see the tree? What else did Tiger see in the park? Would you like to fly in the plane with Tiger? Why or why not?*

ELL ENGLISH LANGUAGE LEARNERS

AFTER READING

All Language Levels

Book Talk Children will work with peers of varying language abilities to discuss their books for this week. Display the four **Leveled Readers** read this week: *How They Go* (Beyond Level), *Tig Can See* (On Level), *Bear Goes to Town* (Approaching Level), and *Tiger Can See* (English Language Learners).

Ask the questions and provide the prompts below. Call on children who read each book to answer the questions or respond to the prompt. If appropriate, ask children to find the pages in the book that illustrate their answers.

- **Who is your book about?**
- **What vehicles did you see in the book?**
- **What did the character in your book see?**
- **Did you ever ride in any of the vehicles you read about? Which ones?**
- **What did you see in the book that you like best? Tell about it.**

Develop Listening and Speaking Skills Tell children to remember the following:

- Share information in cooperative learning interactions. Remind children to work with their partners to retell the story and complete any activities. Ask: *What happened next in the story?*
- Employ self-corrective techniques and monitor their own and other children's language production. Children should ask themselves: *What parts of this passage were confusing to me? Can my classmates help me clarify a word or sentence that I don't understand?*
- Use high-frequency English words to describe people, places, and objects.
- Narrate, describe, and explain with specificity and detail. Ask: *Where did the story take place? Can you describe the setting? What else did you notice?*
- Express opinions, ideas, and feelings on a variety of social and academic topics. Ask: *What do you think about the characters in the story?*

Approaching Level

Phonemic Awareness

Objective Categorize words with initial /t/

Materials
- **Photo Cards:** *comb, deer, elbow, rose, teeth, tie, tiger, toe, toothbrush, toys, turkey, turtle*
- pocket chart

PHONEME CATEGORIZATION

Tier 2

Model

- Display the **Photo Cards** for *turkey, rose,* and *toys. I am going to name the pictures. Two of the words begin with /t/. One does not. Listen:* turkey, rose, toys. Turkey *and* toys *begin with the /t/ sound.* Rose *does not begin with /t/.* Rose *does not belong.*

Guided Practice/Practice

- Display the Photo Cards for *deer, turtle,* and *tiger* in the pocket chart. Have children name each photo with you. Repeat each name, emphasizing the initial sound. Ask children which word does not belong because it does not begin with /t/. Repeat with the cards for *toe, teeth, elbow* and *toothbrush, comb, tie.*

ELL

Sound-Letter Relationships Provide additional practice in pronouncing the /t/, /s/, /p/ sounds and naming the corresponding letters, as children point to them.

Phonics

Objective Identify initial /t/t, /s/s, /p/p and build fluency

Materials
- **Photo Cards:** *pea, peach, penny, pie, six, soap, sock, sun, table, tiger, toe, turtle*
- **Word-Building Cards**
- pocket chart
- **Sound-Spelling WorkBoards**

BUILD FLUENCY: LETTER-SOUND CORRESPONDENCE

Tier 2

Model

- Place **Word-Building Cards** *p, s,* and *t* in the top row of the pocket chart. Review the sound each letter stands for. Hold up the Photo Card for *pea*. Name the picture and identify its initial sound: *This is a picture of a pea.* Pea *begins with /p/: /p/, /p/,* pea. *The letter* p *stands for the /p/ sound, so I will place the pea below the letter* p. Place the Photo Card under the letter *p*.

Guided Practice/Practice

- Place the remaining Photo Cards facedown in a stack. Have children take turns choosing the top card and naming the picture. Guide them to identify the initial sound and to place the card in the pocket chart under the correct letter.

Build Fluency

- Display the Word-Building Cards. Have children name each letter as quickly as they can. Then have them write the letters on their **WorkBoards** several times as they say the sounds.

Approaching Level

Leveled Reader Lesson 2

Objective Reread *Bear Goes to Town* to reinforce fluency, phonics, and making predictions

Materials • **Leveled Reader:** *Bear Goes to Town*

Leveled Reader

FOCUS ON FLUENCY

- Tell children that you will read one page of the book and they should read that page right after you. They should follow along in their books and try to read at the same speed and with the same expression that you use.

SKILL MAKE AND CONFIRM PREDICTIONS

- *Look at the cover. Before we read the book, did you think Bear would buy a scooter at the scooter store? What made you think that? What forms of transportation did you think Bear would use? Were your predictions correct?*

REREAD PREVIOUSLY READ BOOKS

- Distribute copies of the past several **Leveled Readers**. Tell children that rereading the books will help them develop their reading skills.
- Circulate and listen in as children read. Stop them periodically and ask them how they are figuring out words or checking their understanding. Tell children to read other previously read Leveled Readers during independent reading time.

High-Frequency Words

Objective Review high-frequency words *see, a, like, the,* and *we*

Materials • **High-Frequency Word Cards:** *a, like, see, the, we*

BUILD WORD AUTOMATICITY: *see, a, like, the, we*

- Distribute copies of the **High-Frequency Word Card** for **see**. Say the word and have children repeat it. Have children name each letter in the word. Repeat with the words **a**, **like**, **the**, and **we**.
- **Build Fluency** Use the High-Frequency Word Cards to review previously taught words. Repeat, guiding children to read more rapidly.

Meet Grade-Level Expectations

As an alternative to this day's lesson, guide children through a reading of the On Level Leveled Reader. See page 586. Because both books contain the same vocabulary, phonics, and comprehension skills, the scaffolding you provided will help most children gain access to this more challenging text.

Corrective Feedback

Throughout the lessons, provide feedback based on children's responses. If the answer is correct, ask another question. If the answer is tentative, restate key information to assist the child. If the answer is wrong, provide corrective feedback, such as hints or clues, refer to a visual such as a **Sound-Spelling Card** or story illustration, or probe with questions to help the child clarify any misunderstanding.

On Level

Leveled Reader Lesson 2

Objective Reread to apply skills and strategies to retell a story

Materials • **Leveled Reader:** *Tig Can See*

BEFORE READING

- Ask children to look through *Tig Can See* and recall what the book is about. Reinforce vocabulary by repeating children's sentences using more sophisticated language in complete sentences. For example: *Yes, Tig can see the bus and the car. He can see a variety of vehicles from above.* Have children repeat in complete sentences.

DURING READING

- Have children join you in a choral-reading of the story. Model reading with expression. *When I read page 2, I emphasized what Tig can see by saying the word* clock *a little stronger. I used the same strong emphasis when I read* bridge *on page 3.* Ask children to use the same kind of expression when they read.
- Assign each child a page. Have children practice by whisper-reading. *Follow along as other children read, and be ready to come in when it is your turn. Remember to use lots of expression.*

AFTER READING

- Have children use their own words to retell a main event from the selection.
- *Look at the picture on page 8. If the story continued on page 9, what do you think the page would tell? What else might Tig see? Where would he be? Would Tig be happy to see it?*

Extend the Book

Have children draw pictures showing where they think Tig will fly to next. Have them include one or more items in their picture that begin with /t/. Children can label the /t/ items.

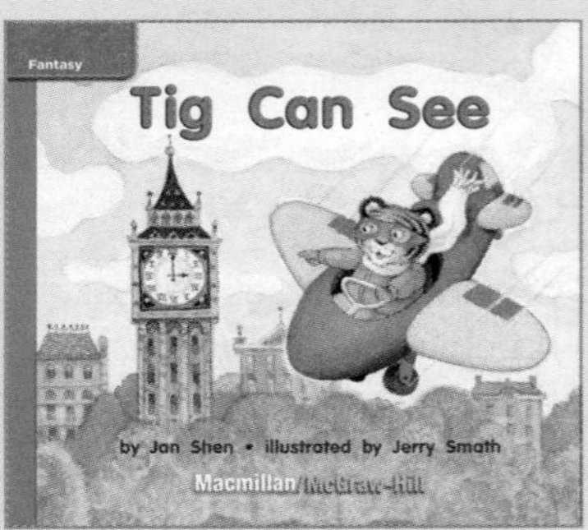

Leveled Reader

Beyond Level

Leveled Reader Lesson 2

Objective Reread to apply skills and strategies to retell a story

Materials • **Leveled Reader:** *How They Go*

BEFORE READING

- Ask children to look back at *How They Go* and recall what the book is about. Remind them of the predictions they made yesterday before reading the book. Ask: *Were your predictions right? How was the book like you thought it would be? How was it different?*

DURING READING

- Assign each child a page of the book to read aloud. Have children practice by whisper-reading. *Follow along as each child reads, and be ready to come in when it is your turn. Remember to use lots of expression.*

AFTER READING

- Explain that if we look at how a story is organized, we can understand it better. Model the strategy: *I thought that the story would be about different ways to travel. I was right, because the cats use many different vehicles. It goes back and forth between the vehicles the cat in the city rides on and the vehicles the cat in the country travels in.* Guide children to share predictions they made about the story. *What did you think would happen? Why did you think so? How did the story structure help you? What did you do if your prediction was not right?*

ON YOUR OWN

Write a Story

Children can write a story about a place they would like to visit and how they would get there. Have them illustrate their stories.

Leveled Reader

ELL

Partners When children write and illustrate stories, pair English Language Learners with children who are more proficient.

Expand Vocabulary

Objective Learn and apply the meaning of the new words and phrases *rides, goes,* and *gets on* and brainstorm words that tell how to get places

Materials • **Leveled Reader:** *How They Go*

ENRICH: *rides, goes, gets on*

Gifted Talented

- Have children reread pages 4 and 5 in *How They Go.* Have them point to *rides* on each page. Ask questions: *What does Tom ride on?* Have children demonstrate the meaning of *rides* on a bus and *rides* on a bike. Ask: *What else do you ride on?*
- Repeat with *goes* (pages 6 and 7) and *gets on* (pages 12 and 13).
- Have children brainstorm other words that tell how they go places. *(walk, skip, jump, hop, run, jog)* Record their responses in a web with "How We Go" in the center.

ELL ENGLISH LANGUAGE LEARNERS

Fluency

Content Objectives Reread Pre-decodable Readers to develop fluency; develop speaking skills

Language Objective Tell a partner what a selection is about

Materials • **Pre-decodable Readers:** *I See Sam; Can Tam See?*

REREAD FOR FLUENCY

Beginning

- Review the high-frequency words **see**, **a**, **we**, and **the** using the **Read/Spell/Write** routine.

Intermediate/Advanced

- Use each word in a sentence that illustrates its use, such as: *I see a book.* Point to a book. *We see the door.* Have the whole group point to the door.

All Language Levels

- Guide children through a choral-reading of *I See Sam* and *Can Tam See?* Model reading with appropriate phrasing to make the reading sound natural. For example, point out that when you read *I see a train*, you group the words *I see* and then pause a little before you say *a train*. Model reading several sentences using appropriate phrasing and have children chorally repeat.

DEVELOP SPEAKING/LISTENING SKILLS

All Language Levels

- Have children reread *I See Sam* and *Can Tam See?* to a partner. Remind them to listen carefully and follow along in their book as their partner is reading. Work with children to read with accuracy and appropriate phrasing.
- Ask children to tell their partner about the pictures on each page. Then have the other partner describe the pictures.

Beginning	Intermediate	Advanced
Confirm Understanding Point to the pictures for partners to identify. Ask: *What do you see?* Restate the correct answer in a complete sentence.	**Express Opinions** Ask partners to tell you which is their favorite picture in the book. Prompt them to explain why it is their favorite picture.	**Compare and Contrast** Have partners compare two different pictures and describe them. Prompt them to explain how they are alike and different.

ELL ENGLISH LANGUAGE LEARNERS

High-Frequency Words

Content Objective Spell high-frequency words correctly
Language Objective Write in complete sentences, using sentence frames
Materials • **Sound-Spelling WorkBoards** • **Sound-Spelling Cards** • **Photo Cards**

Beginning/Intermediate

- Write the high-frequency word *see* on the board. Have children copy the word on their **WorkBoards**. Then help them say, then write, a sentence for the word. Provide the sentence starter *I see* ________.

Advanced

- Children should first orally state their sentence. Correct as needed. Then they can draw a picture to complete the sentence. For children who are ready, help them spell words using their growing knowledge of English sound-spelling relationships. Model how to segment the word children are trying to spell and attach a spelling to each sound. Use the **Sound-Spelling Cards** to reinforce the spellings for each English sound.

Writing

All Language Levels

- Dictate the following sound and ask children to write the letter: /t/. Have them write the letter five times as they say /t/. Demonstrate correct letter formation, as needed.
- Then display a set of **Photo Cards**. Select at least five cards whose picture names begin with /t/ (tiger, table, teeth, turtle, toe) and three whose picture names begin with /p/ (pen, penny, pizza).
- Say the name of each card, stretching the initial sound to emphasize it. You may also need to reinforce the meaning of the word and model correct mouth formation when forming the sound. Use the articulation pictures and prompts on the back of the small Sound-Spelling Cards for support. Tell children that if the picture name begins with /t/, you want them to write the letter *t* on their WorkBoards.

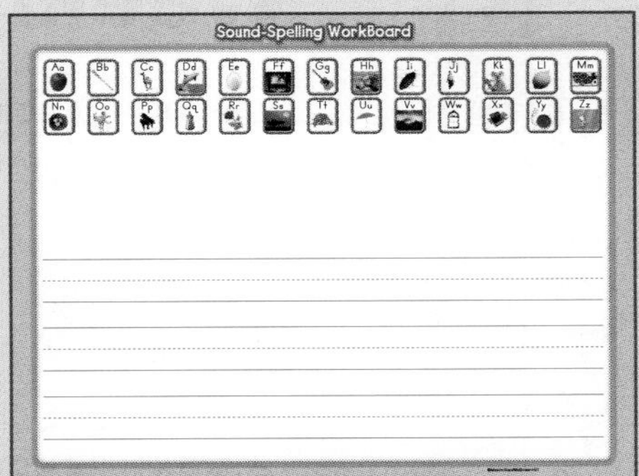

Sound-Spelling WorkBoard

Phonemic Awareness/ Phonics

For English Language Learners who need more practice with this week's phonemic awareness and phonics skills, see the Approaching Level lessons. Focus on minimal contrasts, articulation, and those sounds that do not transfer from the child's first language to English. For a complete listing of transfer sounds, see pages T10–T31.

Weekly Assessment

Use your Quick Check observations and the assessment opportunities identified below to evaluate children's progress in key skill areas.

Skills	Quick Check Observations	Pencil and Paper Assessment
PHONEMIC AWARENESS/ PHONICS /t/t	535	Activity Book, pp. 4, 9, 12 Practice Book, pp. 61, 65
HIGH-FREQUENCY WORDS *see*	556	Activity Book, pp. 7–8 Practice Book, pp. 63–64
COMPREHENSION Make and Confirm Predictions	546	Activity Book, pp. 5–6, 11 Practice Book, p. 62

Quick Check Rubric

Skills	1	2	3
PHONEMIC AWARENESS/ PHONICS	Does not connect the /t/ sound with the letter *Tt* and has difficulty blending the CVC words *tap, pat,* and *sat*.	Usually connects the /t/ sound with the letter *Tt* and blends the CVC words *tap, pat,* and *sat* with occasional support.	Consistently connects the /t/ sound with the letter *Tt* and blends the CVC words *tap, pat,* and *sat*.
HIGH-FREQUENCY WORDS	Does not identify the high-frequency words.	Usually recognizes the high-frequency words with accuracy, but not speed.	Consistently recognizes the high-frequency words with speed and accuracy.
COMPREHENSION	Does not make or confirm predictions using the pictures and text.	Usually makes and confirms predictions using the pictures and text.	Consistently makes and confirms predictions using the pictures and text.

DIBELS LINK

PROGRESS MONITORING

Use your DIBELS results to inform instruction.

IF...

Initial **S**ound **F**luency (**ISF**) 0–7

THEN...

Evaluate for Intervention

TPRI LINK

PROGRESS MONITORING

Use your TPRI scores to inform instruction.

IF...

Phonemic Awareness — Still Developing
Graphophonemic Knowledge — Still Developing
Listening Comprehension — Still Developing

THEN...

Evaluate for Intervention

Diagnose		Prescribe
Review the assessment answers with children. Have them correct their errors. Then provide additional instruction as needed.		
PHONEMIC AWARENESS/ PHONICS /t/*t*	**IF...** **Quick Check Rubric:** Children consistently score 1 or **Pencil and Paper Assessment:** Children get 0–2 items correct	**THEN...** Reteach Phonemic Awareness and Phonics Skills using the **Phonemic Awareness** and **Phonics Intervention Teacher's Editions**. SPIRAL REVIEW Use the Build Fluency lesson in upcoming weeks to provide children practice reading words with /t/*t*.
HIGH-FREQUENCY WORDS *see*	**Quick Check Rubric:** Children consistently score 1 or **Pencil and Paper Assessment:** Children get 0–2 items correct	Reteach High-Frequency Words using the **Phonics Intervention Teacher's Edition**. SPIRAL REVIEW Use the High-Frequency Words lesson in upcoming weeks to provide children practice reading the word *see*.
COMPREHENSION Skill: Make and Confirm Predictions	**Quick Check Rubric:** Children consistently score 1 or **Pencil and Paper Assessment:** Children get 0–2 items correct	Reteach Comprehension Skill using the **Comprehension Intervention Teacher's Edition**.

Response to Intervention

To place children in Tier 2 or Tier 3 Intervention use the *Diagnostic Assessment.*

- Phonemic Awareness
- Phonics
- Vocabulary
- Comprehension
- Fluency

Week 2 ★ At a Glance

Priority Skills and Concepts

Comprehension

- **Genre:** Nonfiction, Folktale
- **Strategy:** Recognize Text Structure
- **Skill:** Classify and Categorize

- **Skill:** Make and Confirm Predictions

High-Frequency Word

- *go*

Oral Vocabulary

- **Build Robust Vocabulary:** *familiar*, *journey*, *prepare*, *relax*, *travel*

Fluency

- **Word Automaticity**
- **Sound-Spellings**

Phonemic Awareness

- **Phoneme Isolation**
- **Phoneme Blending**
- **Phoneme Categorization**

Phonics

- *Ii*

Grammar

- **Action Words (Verbs)**

Writing

- **Posters**

Key

 Tested in Program

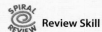

 Review Skill

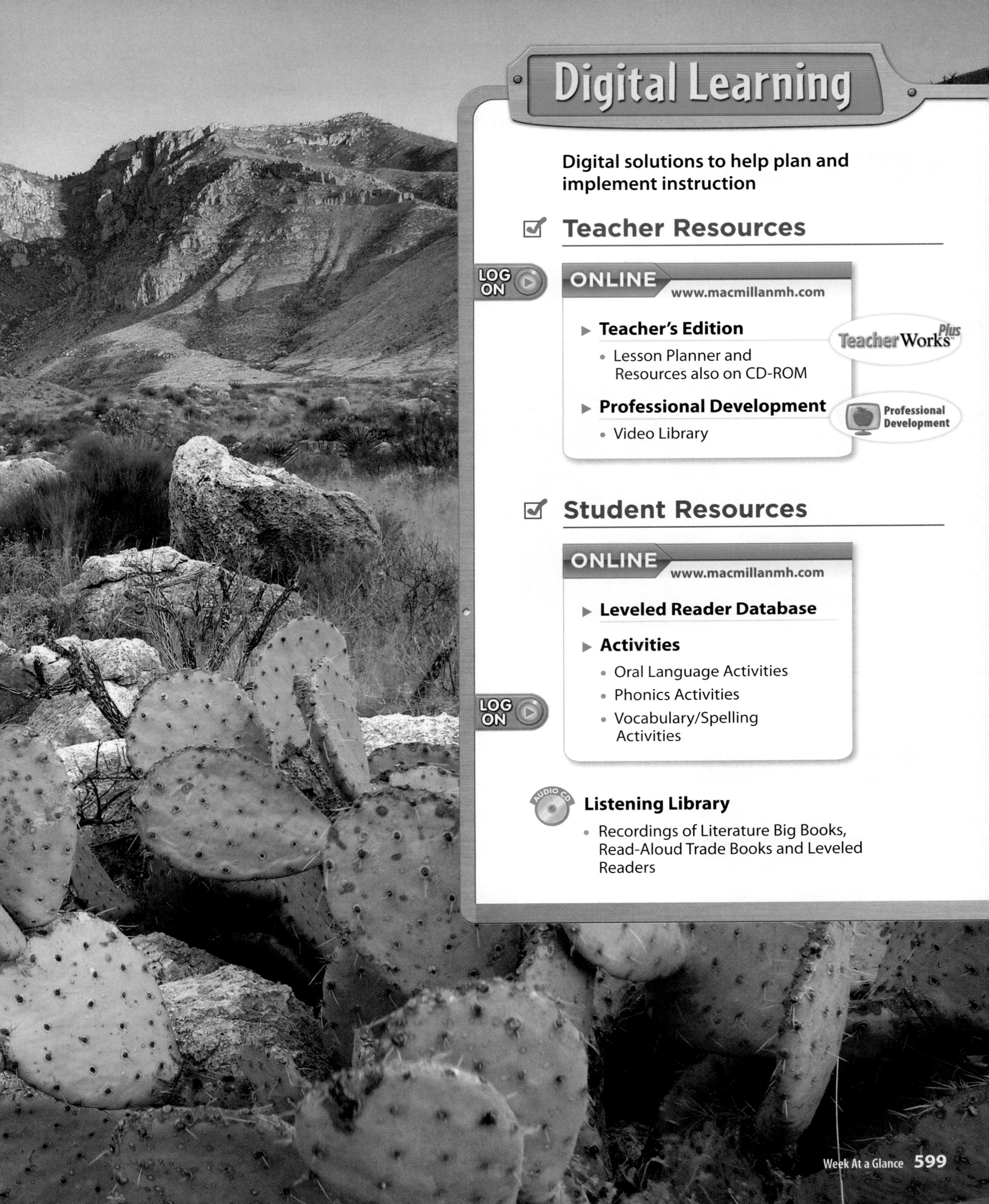

Digital Learning

Digital solutions to help plan and implement instruction

Teacher Resources

LOG ON

ONLINE www.macmillanmh.com

- **Teacher's Edition**
  - Lesson Planner and Resources also on CD-ROM
- **Professional Development**
  - Video Library

TeacherWorks Plus

Professional Development

Student Resources

ONLINE www.macmillanmh.com

- **Leveled Reader Database**
- **Activities**
  - Oral Language Activities
  - Phonics Activities
  - Vocabulary/Spelling Activities

LOG ON

AUDIO CD

Listening Library

- Recordings of Literature Big Books, Read-Aloud Trade Books and Leveled Readers

Weekly Literature

Theme: Traveling Far and Near

Student Literature

A mix of fiction and nonfiction

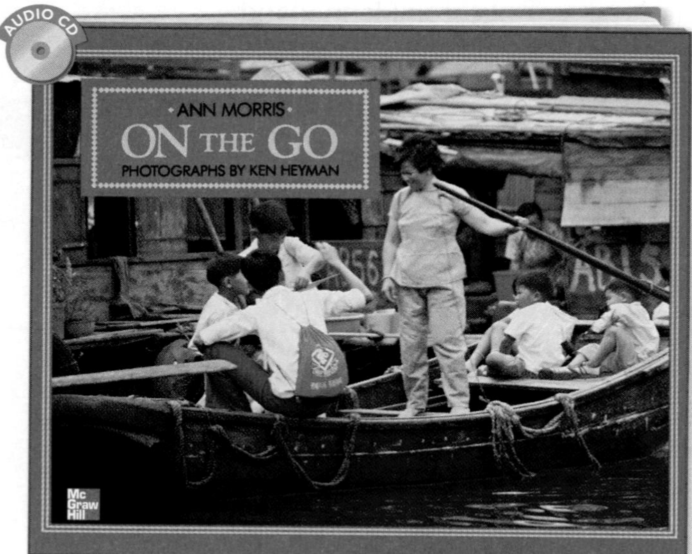

Big Book

Genre Expository

Big Book of Explorations

Genre Expository

Support Literature

Interactive Read-Aloud Anthology

Genre Folktale

Oral Vocabulary Cards

- Listening Comprehension
- Build Robust Vocabulary

Pre-decodable Readers

Resources for Differentiated Instruction

Leveled Readers

AUDIO CD

GR Levels Rebus-D

Genre	Fiction

- **Same Theme**
- **Same Vocabulary/Phonics**
- **Same Comprehension Skills**

Approaching Level

On Level

Beyond Level

ELL

Leveled Reader Database
Go to **www.macmillanmh.com.**

Practice

Activity Book

Practice Book

ELL Practice Book

Response to Intervention

Tier 2

- Phonemic Awareness
- Phonics
- Vocabulary
- Comprehension
- Fluency

Unit Assessment

Assess Unit Skills

- Phonemic Awareness
- Phonics
- High-Frequency Words
- Listening Comprehension

HOME-SCHOOL CONNECTION

- Family letters in English and Spanish
- Take-home stories and activities

Suggested Lesson Plan

Go to www.macmillanmh.com for Online Lesson Planner

Big Book

WHOLE GROUP	DAY 1	DAY 2
ORAL LANGUAGE • Oral Vocabulary • Phonemic Awareness	**Focus Question** Where do you like to go when you travel? Build Background, 610 **Oral Vocabulary** *familiar, journey, prepare, relax, travel*, 610 **Phonemic Awareness** Phoneme Isolation, 613	**Focus Question** What do people use to go from place to place? **Oral Vocabulary** *familiar, journey, prepare, relax, travel*, 618 Sound Words, 625 **Phonemic Awareness** Phoneme Blending, 626
WORD STUDY • Phonics • High-Frequency Words	**Phonics** Introduce /i/*i*, 614 Handwriting: Write *Ii*, 615 Activity Book, 14 Practice Book, 67 **High-Frequency Words** *go*, 612	**Phonics** Review /i/*i*, /t/*t*, 626 Blend with /i/*i*, 627 **Review High-Frequency Words**, 628
READING • Listening Comprehension • Apply Phonics and High-Frequency Words • Fluency	**Share the Big Book** *On the Go*  Big Book **Strategy:** Recognize Text Structure **Skill:** Classify and Categorize, 611	**Reread the Big Book** *On the Go*  Big Book **Strategy:** Recognize Text Structure, 620 **Skill:** Classify and Categorize, 620 Retell, 624 **Pre-decodable Reader:** *Go, Go, Go*, 628 Activity Book, 15–16 Practice Book, 68 **Fluency** Echo-Read, 624
LANGUAGE ARTS • Writing • Grammar	**Shared Writing** Lists, 617 **Grammar** Action Words (Verbs), 616	**Interactive Writing** Posters, 629
ASSESSMENT • Informal/Formal	Quick Check Phonemic Awareness, 613	Quick Check Comprehension, 624

SMALL GROUP Lesson Plan — **Differentiated Instruction 604–605**

Priority Skills

Phonemic Awareness/Phonics	High-Frequency Words	Oral Vocabulary	Comprehension
/i/i	*go*	Sound Words	**Strategy:** Recognize Text Structure **Skill:** Classify and Categorize

Half-Day Kindergarten

Teach Core Skills

Focus on tested skill lessons, other lessons, and small group options as your time allows.

DAY 3

Focus Question Do you go far or near when you ride a bike?

Oral Vocabulary *familiar, journey, prepare, relax, travel*, 630

Oral Vocabulary Cards: "The Two Frogs"

Phonemic Awareness
Phoneme Isolation, 635

Phonics
Picture Sort: /i/i, 636

Blend with /i/i, 637

Read Words, 637

High-Frequency Words
go, 634

Activity Book: "We Can Go!" 17–18

Practice Book, 69–70

Read for Fluency, 634

Read the Big Book of Explorations
"My Bike" and "Riding the Subway Train," 37–38

Text Feature:
Use Labels, 632

Big Book of Explorations

Independent Writing
Prewrite and Draft Posters, 639

Grammar
Action Words (Verbs), 638

Quick Check High-Frequency Words, 634

DAY 4

Focus Question Why is it fun to go to new places?

Oral Vocabulary *familiar, journey, prepare, relax, travel*, 640

Sound Words, 643

Phonemic Awareness
Phoneme Blending, 644

Phonics
Picture Sort, 644

Blend Words, 645

Activity Book, 19

Practice Book, 71

Review High-Frequency Words, 646

Interactive Read Aloud
Listening Comprehension, 642

Read Aloud: "Timimoto"

Pre-decodable Reader:
It Can Go, Go, Go!, 646

Read Aloud

Independent Writing
Revise and Edit Posters, 647

Quick Check Phonics, 645

DAY 5 Review and Assess

Focus Question Where would you tell a friend to go traveling?

Oral Vocabulary *familiar, journey, prepare, relax, travel*, 648

Sound Words, 650

Phonemic Awareness
Phoneme Categorization, 651

Phonics
Read Words, 652

Dictation, 652

Activity Book, 22

High-Frequency Words
a, *go*, *like*, *see*, *the*, 650

Read Across Texts
Strategy: Recognize Text Structure, 655

Skill: Classify and Categorize, 655

Activity Book, 21

Fluency Word Automaticity, 650

Independent Writing
Publish and Present Posters, 653

Weekly Assessment, 680–681

Differentiated Instruction

What do I do in small groups?

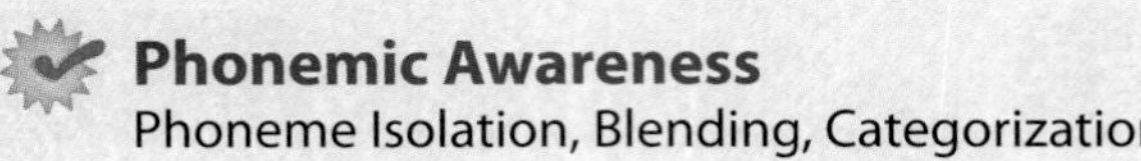

IF... **children need additional instruction, practice, or extension based on your Quick Check observations for the following priority skills**

Phonemic Awareness
Phoneme Isolation, Blending, Categorization

Phonics
Ii

High-Frequency Words
go

Comprehension
Strategy: Recognize Text Structure
Skill: Classify and Categorize

THEN...

Approaching	Preteach and
ELL	Reteach Skills
On Level	Practice
Beyond	Enrich and Accelerate Learning

LOG ON Suggested Small Group Lesson Plan

	DAY 1	DAY 2
Approaching Level • **Preteach/Reteach** Tier 2 **Tier 2 Instruction**	• Oral Language, 654 • High-Frequency Words, 654 ELL High-Frequency Words Review, 654 • Phonemic Awareness, 655 • Phonics, 655 ELL Sound-Spellings Review, 655	• High-Frequency Words, 660 ELL • Pre-decodable Reader, 660 • Phonemic Awareness, 661 • Phonics, 661
On Level • **Practice**	• High-Frequency Words, 656 • Phonemic Awareness/Phonics, 656 ELL	• Pre-decodable Reader, 662
Beyond Level • **Extend/Accelerate** Gifted Talented **Gifted and Talented**	• High-Frequency Words/Vocabulary, 657 ELL Expand Oral Vocabulary, 657 • Phonics, 657	• Pre-decodable Reader, 662
ELL • **Build English Language Proficiency** • **See ELL in other levels.**	• Oral Language Warm-Up, 658 • Academic Language, 658 • Vocabulary, 659	• Access to Core Content, 663

Small Group

Focus on Leveled Readers

Levels Rebus–D

Approaching

On Level

Beyond

ELL

Manipulatives

Sound-Spelling WorkBoards

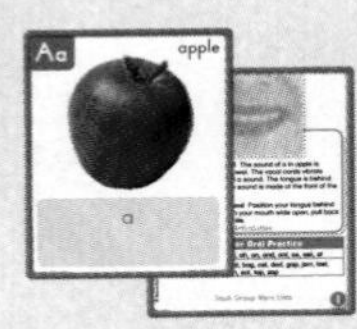
Sound-Spelling Cards

Photo Cards

High-Frequency Word Cards

Visual Vocabulary Resources

Additional Leveled Readers

Leveled Reader Database
www.macmillanmh.com

Search by

- Comprehension Skill
- Content Area
- Genre
- Text Feature
- Guided Reading Level
- Reading Recovery Level
- Lexile Score
- Benchmark Level

Subscription also available

DAY 3	DAY 4	DAY 5
• High-Frequency Words, 664 ELL • Phonemic Awareness, 664 • Phonics, 665 • Pre-decodable Reader, 665	• Phonemic Awareness, 668 • Phonics, 668 ELL • Leveled Reader Lesson 1, 669	• Phonemic Awareness, 674 • Phonics, 674 ELL • Leveled Reader Lesson 2, 675 • High-Frequency Words, 675
• Phonics, 666	• Leveled Reader Lesson 1, 670 ELL	• Leveled Reader Lesson 2, 676
• Phonics, 666	• Leveled Reader Lesson 1, 671 Synthesize, 671	• Leveled Reader Lesson 2, 677 ELL • Expand Vocabulary, 677
• Access to Core Content, 667 • Grammar, 667	• Leveled Reader, 672–673	• Fluency, 678 • High-Frequency Words, 679 • Writing, 679

What do I do with the rest of my class?

- Activity Book
- Practice Book
- ELL Practice Book
- Leveled Reader Activities
- Literacy Workstations
- Online Activities
- Buggles and Beezy

Classroom Management Tools

Weekly Contract

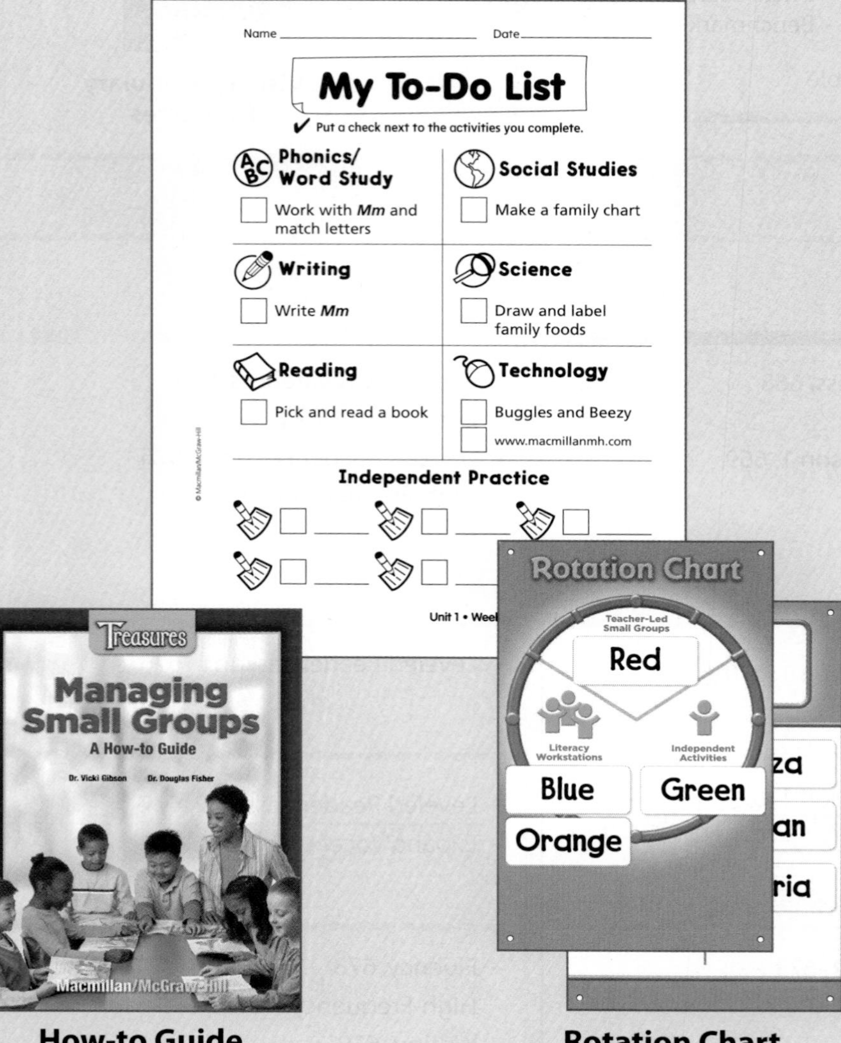

How-to Guide

Rotation Chart

Digital Learning

- Match Letters
- Match Letters to Sounds
- Blend Words

- Read Other Books by the Author or Illustrator

Practice

Activity Book

Practice Book

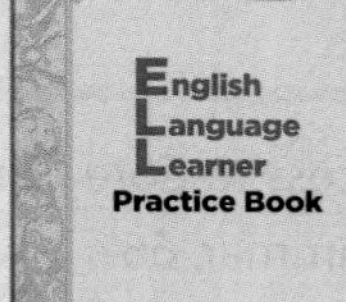

ELL Practice Book

Independent Activities

ONLINE INSTRUCTION www.macmillanmh.com

Oral Language Activities

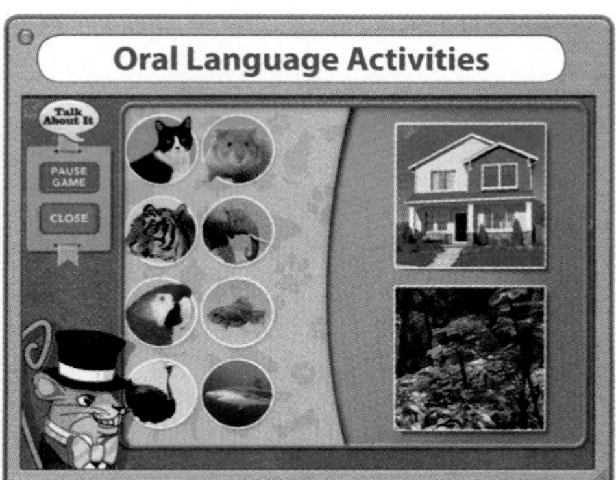

- Focus on Unit Vocabulary and Concepts
- English Language Learner Support

Vocabulary/Spelling Activities

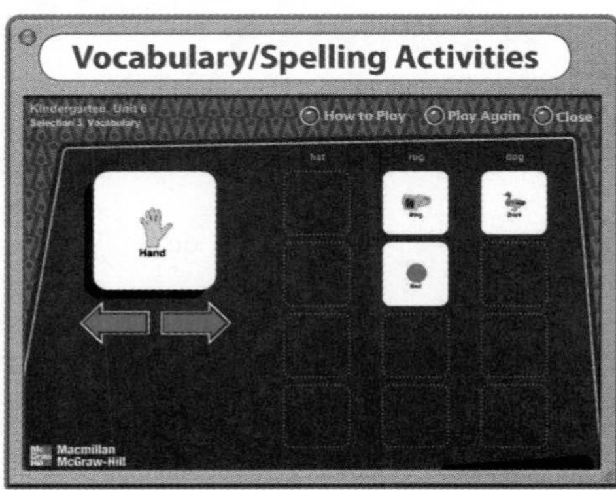

- Differentiated Lists and Activities

Leveled Reader Database

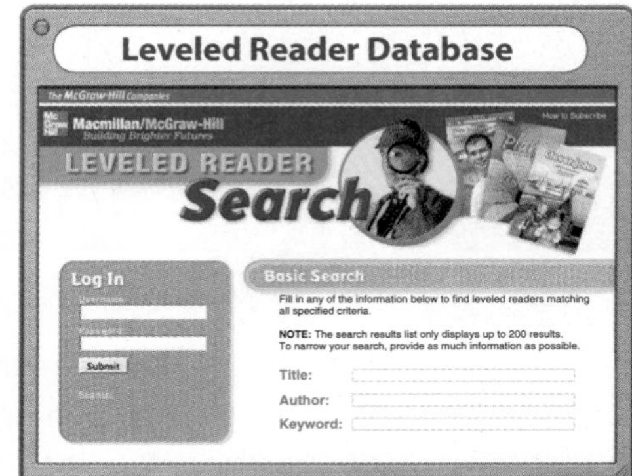

- Leveled Reader Database
- Search titles by level, skill, content area, and more

Available on CD

LISTENING LIBRARY
Recordings of selections
- Literature Big Books
- Read-Aloud Trade Books
- Leveled Readers
- ELL Readers

NEW ADVENTURES WITH BUGGLES AND BEEZY
Phonemic awareness and phonics activities

CD-ROM
Treasures
New Adventures with Buggles and Beezy

Leveled Reader Activities

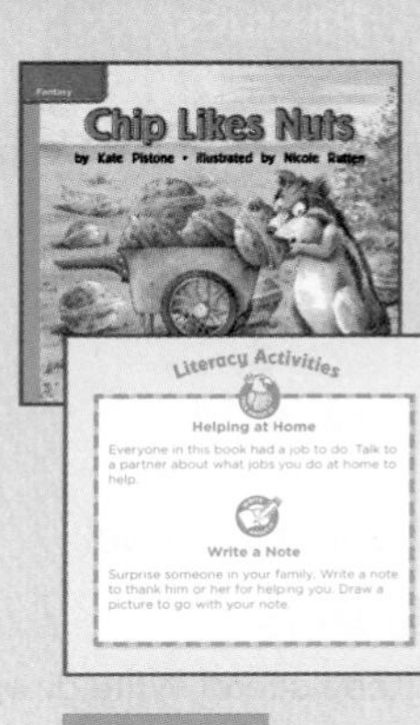

Approaching | On Level | Beyond | ELL

See inside cover of all Leveled Readers.

Literacy Workstations

See lessons on pages 608–609.

Managing the Class

What do I do with the rest of my class?

Reading

Objectives

- Read and discuss a book in a group
- Read a book aloud

Phonics/Word Study

Objectives

- Build sentences using high-frequency words
- Play a game and identify words that end in *-it*, *-im*, *-ip*, *-at*, *-am*, and *-ap*

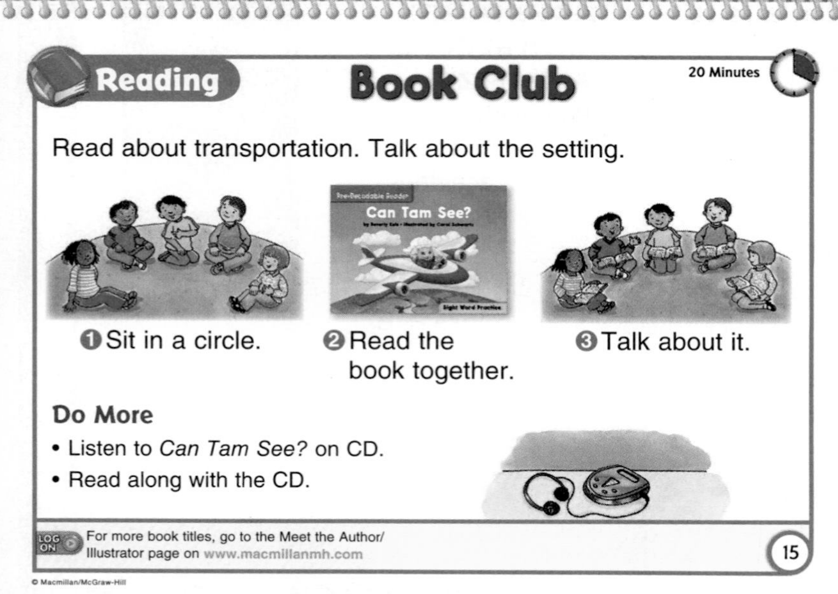

Reading
Book Club
20 Minutes
Read about transportation. Talk about the setting.
Can Tam See?
1 Sit in a circle.
2 Read the book together.
3 Talk about it.
Do More
• Listen to Can Tam See? on CD.
• Read along with the CD.
For more book titles, go to the Meet the Author/Illustrator page on www.macmillanmh.com
15
© Macmillan/McGraw-Hill

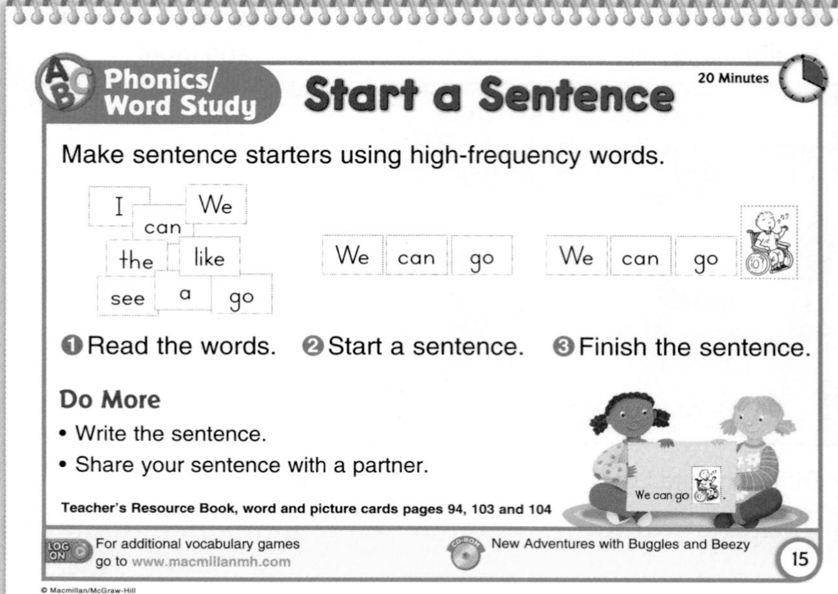

Phonics/Word Study
Start a Sentence
20 Minutes
Make sentence starters using high-frequency words.
I
We
can
the
like
see
a
go
We can go
We can go
1 Read the words.
2 Start a sentence.
3 Finish the sentence.
Do More
• Write the sentence.
• Share your sentence with a partner.
Teacher's Resource Book, word and picture cards pages 94, 103 and 104
We can go
For additional vocabulary games go to www.macmillanmh.com
New Adventures with Buggles and Beezy
15
© Macmillan/McGraw-Hill

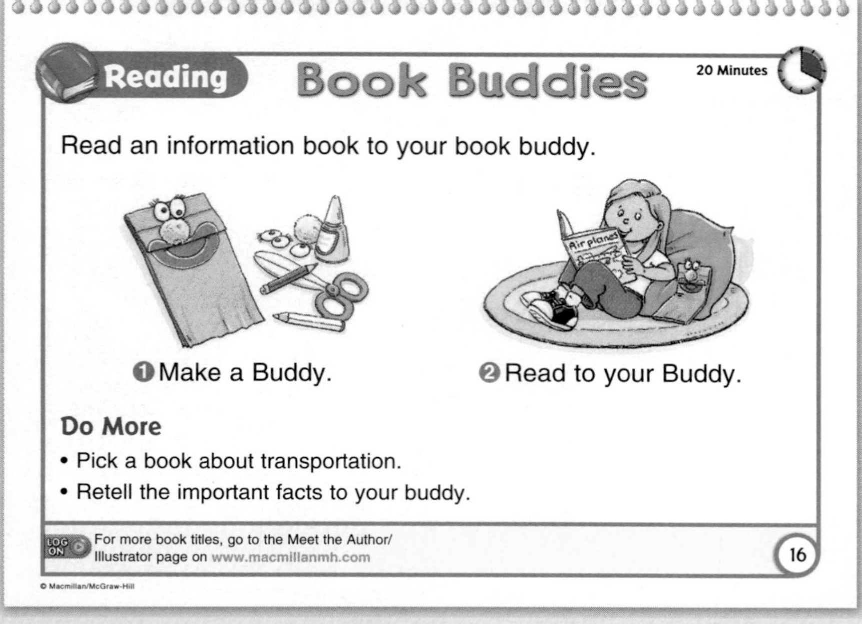

Reading
Book Buddies
20 Minutes
Read an information book to your book buddy.
Airplanes
1 Make a Buddy.
2 Read to your Buddy.
Do More
• Pick a book about transportation.
• Retell the important facts to your buddy.
For more book titles, go to the Meet the Author/Illustrator page on www.macmillanmh.com
16
© Macmillan/McGraw-Hill

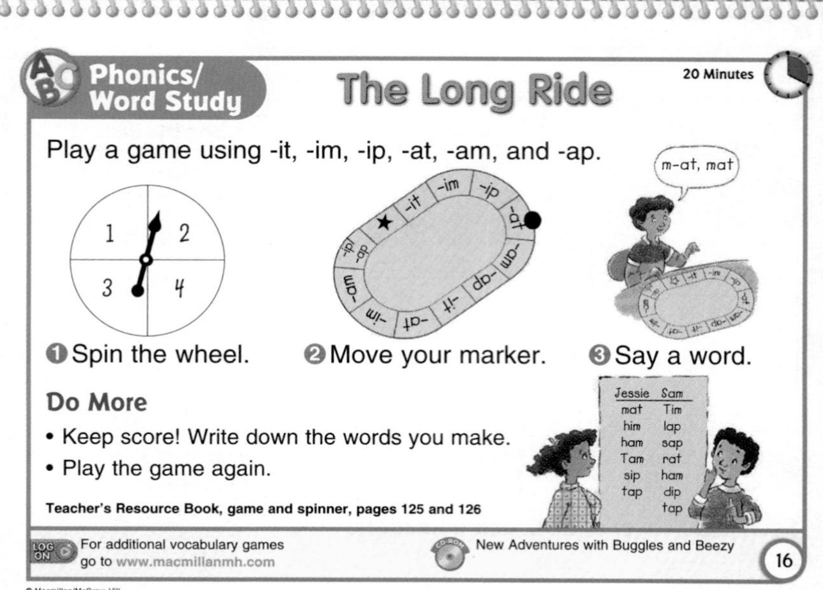

Phonics/Word Study
The Long Ride
20 Minutes
Play a game using -it, -im, -ip, -at, -am, and -ap.
m-at, mat
1
2
3
4
1 Spin the wheel.
2 Move your marker.
3 Say a word.
Do More
• Keep score! Write down the words you make.
• Play the game again.
Teacher's Resource Book, game and spinner, pages 125 and 126
Jessie Sam
mat Tim
him lap
ham sap
Tam rat
sip ham
tap dip
tap
For additional vocabulary games go to www.macmillanmh.com
New Adventures with Buggles and Beezy
16
© Macmillan/McGraw-Hill

Literacy Workstations

Literacy Workstation Flip Charts

Writing

Objectives

- Write a list of words that contains *Ii*
- Write a sentence with the words *go* and *see*

Content Literacy

Objectives

- Use clay to investigate floating and sinking
- Compare and contrast different ways to travel

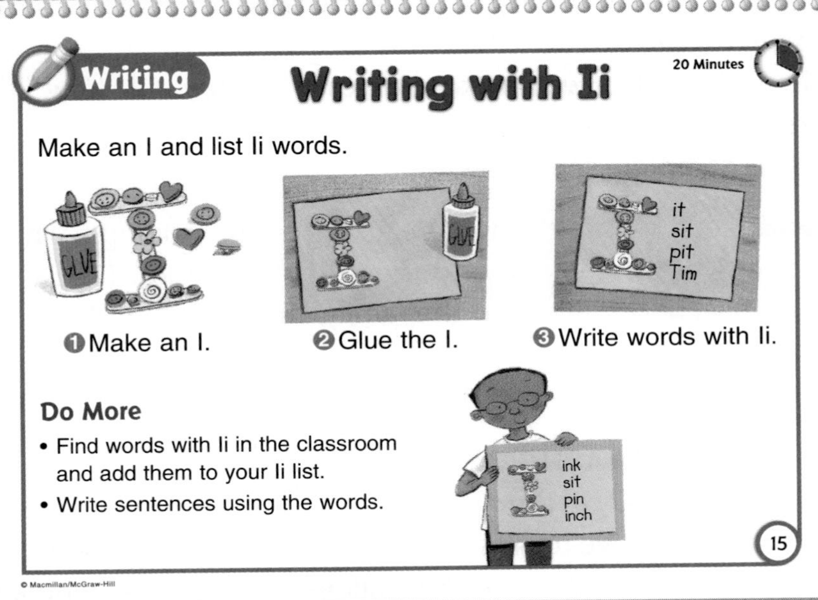

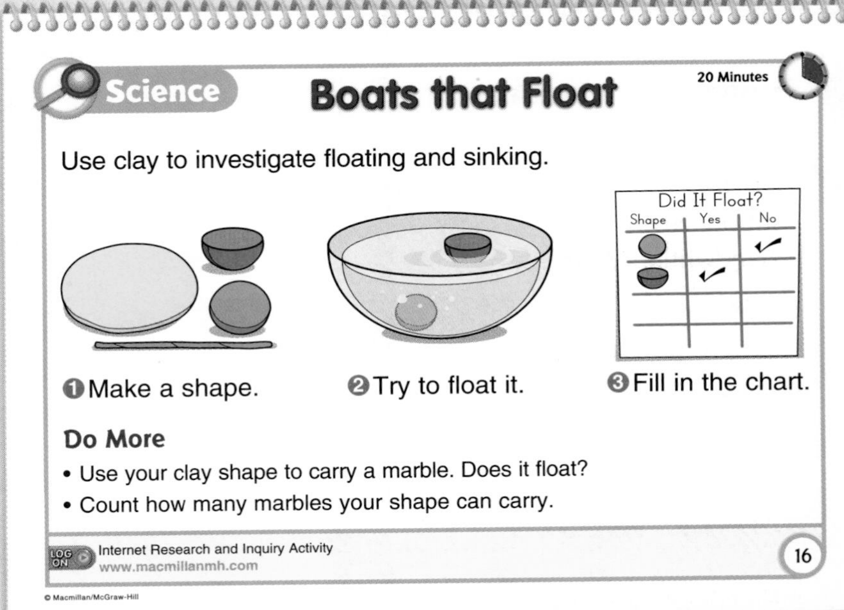

Science
Boats that Float
20 Minutes
Use clay to investigate floating and sinking.
Did It Float?
Shape
Yes
No
❶Make a shape.
❷Try to float it.
❸Fill in the chart.
Do More
• Use your clay shape to carry a marble. Does it float?
• Count how many marbles your shape can carry.
Internet Research and Inquiry Activity
www.macmillanmh.com
16
© Macmillan/McGraw-Hill

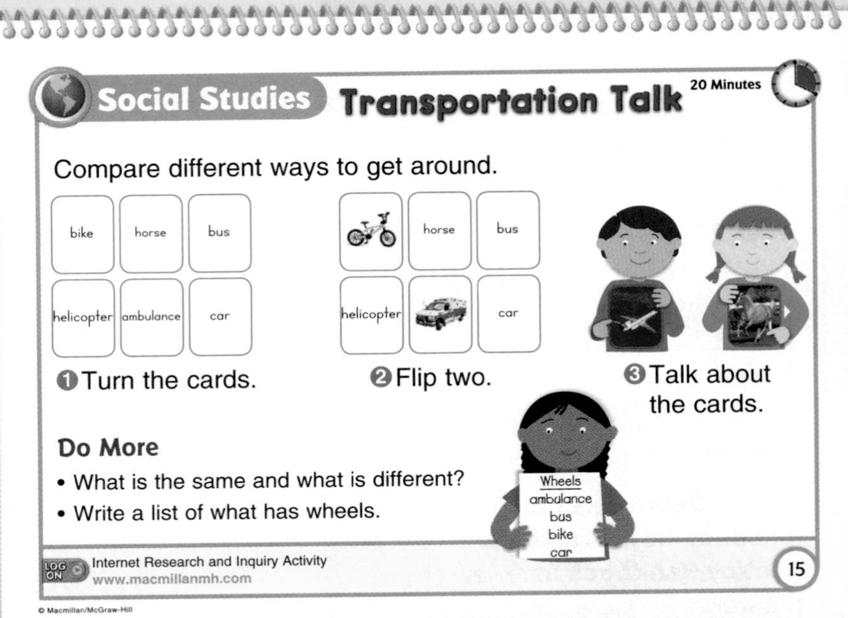

Social Studies
Transportation Talk
20 Minutes
Compare different ways to get around.
bike
horse
bus
helicopter
ambulance
car
horse
bus
helicopter
car
❶Turn the cards.
❷Flip two.
❸Talk about the cards.
Do More
• What is the same and what is different?
• Write a list of what has wheels.
Wheels
ambulance
bus
bike
car
Internet Research and Inquiry Activity
www.macmillanmh.com
15
© Macmillan/McGraw-Hill

Day 1 At a Glance

WHOLE GROUP

Oral Language
- Build Background

Comprehension
- Read *On the Go*
- Strategy: Recognize Text Structure
- Skill: Classify and Categorize

High-Frequency Words
- Introduce *go*

Phonemic Awareness
- Phoneme Isolation: /i/

Phonics
- Introduce /i/*i*
- Handwriting: Write *Ii*

Grammar
- Action Words (Verbs)

Writing
- Shared Writing: Lists

SMALL GROUP

- Differentiated Instruction, pages 654–679

Oral Vocabulary

Week 2

familiar journey prepare
relax travel

Review

continue glide rapidly
transportation vehicle

Use the **Define/Example/Ask** routine in the **Instructional Routine Handbook** to review the words.

Oral Language

Build Background: *Traveling Far and Near*

INTRODUCE THE THEME

Tell children that this week they will be talking and reading about places they have **traveled** to and **journeys**, or long trips, they have taken, such as going to a lake or visiting family that lives far away.

Write the following question on the board: *Where do you like to go when you travel?* Point out the capital letter at the beginning of the question and the punctuation at the end. Track the print as you read aloud the question. Then prompt children to answer the question.

ACCESS PRIOR KNOWLEDGE

- Ask children where they would like to go on a journey. Ask: *How will you travel to this place? What will you do there?* Have children answer using complete sentences.

Think Aloud Let's look at this picture. It is a family helping each other cross a river by stepping on rocks. They are hiking. They are wearing backpacks. (Point to the family, river, rocks, and backpacks as you describe the picture.) Where do you think would be a nice place to go on a hike?

DISCUSS THE PHOTOGRAPH

Talk about what the family in the photograph is doing, how they are dressed, and why they have to cross the river on rocks. Discuss other ways they could get across the river. Ask children about places where they could walk or hike, such as a city park or national park.

Teaching Chart 22

Share the Big Book

Listening Comprehension

PREVIEW Display the cover. *I see children and a grown-up **traveling** on a boat.* Have children discuss different ways people travel in order to monitor comprehension by building background.

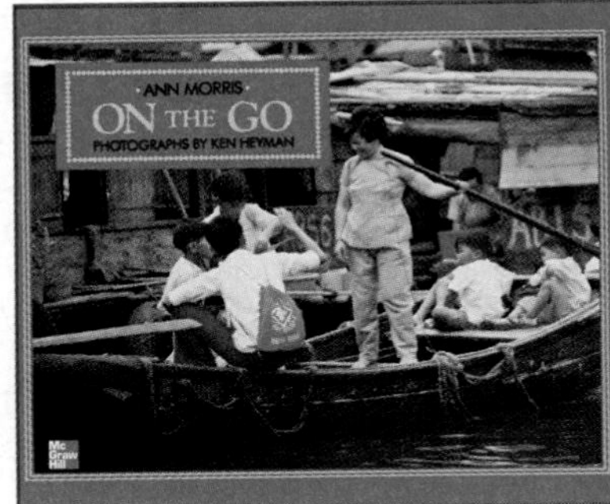

Big Book

Read the title and the names of the author and photographer. *What do you think this book will be about?*

GENRE: INFORMATIONAL TEXT/ EXPOSITORY Tell children that this book is **expository**. It tells facts about real people and places. It is also called nonfiction.

STRATEGY **Recognize Text Structure**

EXPLAIN/MODEL Remind children that thinking about how authors group information can help them understand it. Display pages 5–10.

Think Aloud All of these photographs show some ways that people get around. I wonder if the structure of the book will be to tell about different ways that people travel, one way at a time.

SKILL **Classify and Categorize**

EXPLAIN/MODEL Display an array of objects, such as colored blocks. *All of these are blocks, but they can be put into different groups, based on things such as their color.* Display pages 6–7 and 10–11.

Think Aloud These photos all show people traveling, but I can put them into different groups, based on how they are traveling. Some are walking and others are using vehicles with wheels.

Read the Big Book

SET PURPOSE Tell children to pay attention to the structure of the book to figure out what will come next. Use the **Define/Example/Ask** routine to teach the story words on the inside back cover.

Respond to Literature

MAKE CONNECTIONS Discuss the book. Help children retell important facts from the book. *What are some of the ways people travel in your community? How do you travel?*

Objectives

- Discuss the theme
- Discuss the way authors group information
- Listen and respond to a story
- Recognize text structure/ classify and categorize
- Retell important facts heard in a text

Materials

- Teaching Chart 22
- Big Book: *On the Go*

ELL

Use the **Interactive Question-Response Guide** for *On the Go*, **ELL Resource Book** pages 72–79, to guide children through a reading of the book. As you read, make meaning clear by pointing to the pictures, demonstrating word meanings, paraphrasing text, and asking children questions.

Digital Learning

Story on **Listening Library Audio CD**

Objectives

- Read the high-frequency word *go*
- Identify the word *go* in text and speech
- Review the high-frequency words *a, like, see, the*

Materials

- High-Frequency Word Cards: *a, go, like, see, the*
- Teaching Chart 23

ELL

Reinforce Meaning Hold up the **High-Frequency Word Card** *go* and walk to the door saying, *I go to the door.* Then ask children individually and in groups to go to other parts of the room. For example, *Mitali and Oscar, go to the board.* Have children say where they go. (We go to the board.) Use **Teaching Chart 23** to review prior high-frequency words. *Do you see a turtle? What animal do you like?*

High-Frequency Words

go

go

INTRODUCE Display the **High-Frequency Word Card** for **go**. Use the **Read/Spell/Write** routine to teach the word.

- **Read** Point to and say *go. This is the word* go. *Let's* go *to the park.*
- **Spell** *The word* go *is spelled* g-o. *What's the first sound in* go? *That's right. The first sound in* go *is /g/. That's why the first letter is* g. *After the* g, *I see one* o. *Let's read and spell* go *together.*
- **Write** *Now let's write the word* go *on our papers. Let's spell aloud the word as we write it:* go, g-o.

REVIEW *a, like, see, the* Display each card and have children read the word.

see | a | like | the

READ THE RHYME AND CHIME Tell children to point to *go* each time they see it. Repeat the rhyme together for fluency. Then add *go* to the class Word Wall.

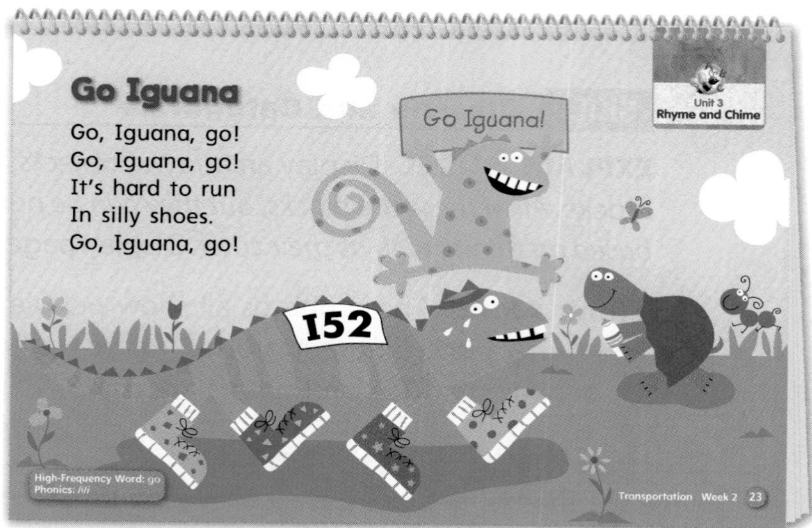

Go Iguana
Go, Iguana, go!
Go, Iguana, go!
It's hard to run
In silly shoes.
Go, Iguana, go!
Go Iguana!
152
Unit 3
Rhyme and Chime
High-Frequency Word: go
Phonics: /g/
Transportation Week 2 23

Teaching Chart 23

For Tier 2 instruction, see page 654.

TIME TO MOVE!

Using shape words and *go,* instruct children to go to different places in the classroom. For example: *Go to the square block. Go to a triangle.*

Phonemic Awareness

Phoneme Isolation

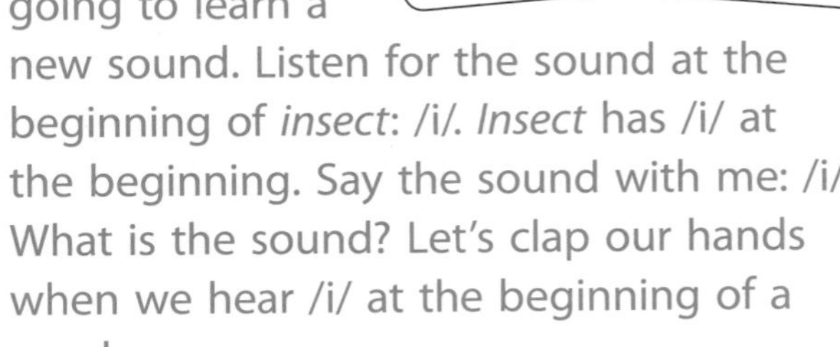

Model

Display the **Photo Card** for *insect*.

Today we are going to learn a new sound. Listen for the sound at the beginning of *insect*: /i/. *Insect* has /i/ at the beginning. Say the sound with me: /i/. What is the sound? Let's clap our hands when we hear /i/ at the beginning of a word.

Repeat with the Photo Card for *inch*.

Read the "Go Iguana" Rhyme and Chime again. Have children clap every time they hear /i/.

Go, Iguana, go!
Go, Iguana, go!
It's hard to run
In silly shoes.
Go, Iguana, go!

Review /t/, /p/

Display the Photo Card for *table*.

This is a *table*. The beginning sound in *table* is /t/. Listen: *table*. What is the beginning sound?

Repeat for *pizza*.

Guided Practice/Practice

Display and name each Photo Card.

Say each picture name with me. Tell me the sound at the beginning of the word.

Children identify the initial sound. Guide practice with the first card.

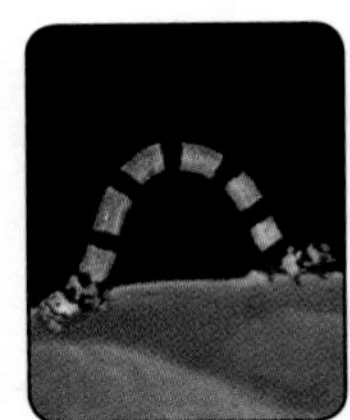

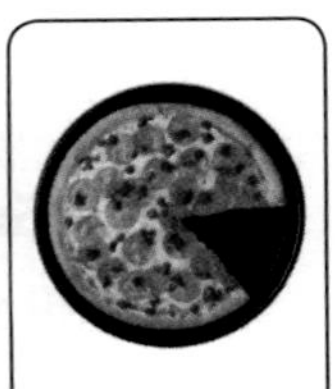

Quick Check

Can children identify initial sound /i/?

During **Small Group Instruction**

If No → **Approaching Level** Provide additional practice, page 655.

If Yes → **On Level** Children blend words with initial, medial /i/, page 656.

Beyond Level Children categorize words with /i/, page 657.

Objectives

- Identify initial /i/
- Review initial /t/ and /p/

Materials

- Photo Cards: *inch, inchworm, ink, insect, invitation, pear, pen, pie, pizza, table, teeth, tie, top*

ELL

Pronunciation Display and have children name **Photo Cards** from this and prior lessons to reinforce phonemic awareness and word meanings. Point to the card for *insect* and ask: *What do you see?* (an insect) What is the sound at the beginning of the word *insect*? (/i/) Repeat with other cards to practice /t/, /p/, and other sounds introduced in prior lessons.

Objectives

- Match the letter *i* to the /i/ sound
- Handwriting: write *Ii*

Materials

- Sound-Spelling Card: *Insect*
- Teaching Chart 23
- Word-Building Cards
- Handwriting
- Handwriting Teacher's Edition
- Activity Book, p. 14
- Practice Book, p. 67

ELL

Variations in Language
Speakers of Spanish, Vietnamese, Hmong, Cantonese, Haitian Creole, and Korean may have difficulty perceiving and pronouncing /i/. Use the Approaching Level phonics lessons for additional pronunciation and decoding practice.

Sound Pronunciation

See **Sound Pronunciation CD** for a model of the /i/ sound. Play this for children needing additional models.

Corrective Feedback

Linguistic Differences
When the /i/ and /e/ sounds appear before the consonants *m* or *n* in words, such as *pin/pen* and *him/hem,* many speakers of African American Vernacular English won't pronounce or hear the difference. Focus on articulation, such as mouth position for each vowel sound, during the lesson.

Phonics

Introduce /i/*i*

Ii

Model

Display the *Insect* **Sound-Spelling Card**.

This is the *Insect* card. The sound is /i/.

The /i/ sound is spelled with the letter *i*. Say it with me: /i/. This is the sound at the beginning of the word *insect*. Listen: /i/, /i/ *nsect, insect*.
What is the name of this letter? What sound does this letter stand for?

Read the "Go Iguana" Rhyme and Chime. Show children the difference between a letter and a word. Repeat the title. Ask children to point to the second word in the title. Tell children that *Iguana* begins with *I*. Model placing a self-stick note below the *I* in *Iguana*.

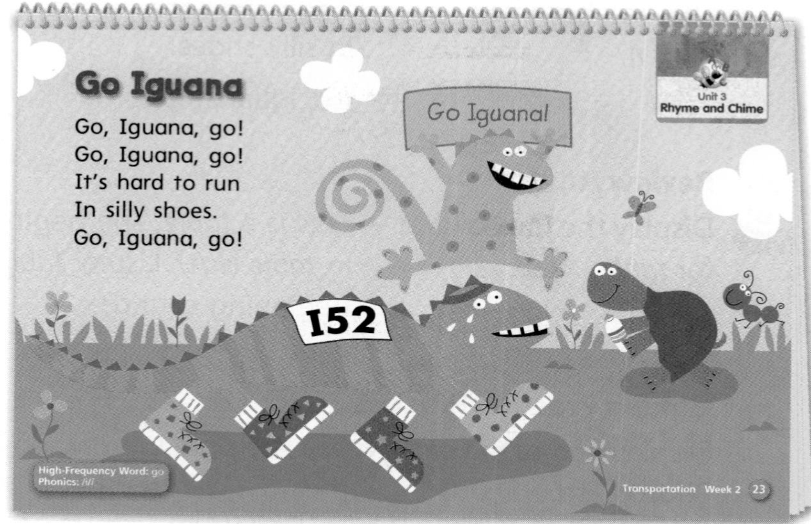

Teaching Chart 23

Guided Practice/Practice

Read the rest of the rhyme. Stop after each line. Children place self-stick notes below words that begin with *i*. Guide practice with *Iguana* in line 1.

Let's put a sticky note below the word in the line that begins with the letter *i*. The word *iguana* begins with the letter *i*.

Corrective Feedback

If children have difficulty with words with short /i/, say: *The letter* i *stands for the /i/ sound at the beginning of* it: */i/ /t/,* it. *Let's blend it together: /iiit/,* it. *Now it's your turn. Blend* it.

Build Fluency: Sound-Spellings

Display the following **Word-Building Cards**: *a, i, m, p, s, t*. Have children chorally say each sound. Repeat and vary the pace.

Handwriting: Write *Ii*

MODEL Model holding up your writing hand. Say the handwriting cues below as you write the capital and lowercase forms of *Ii* on the board. Then trace the letters on the board and in the air.

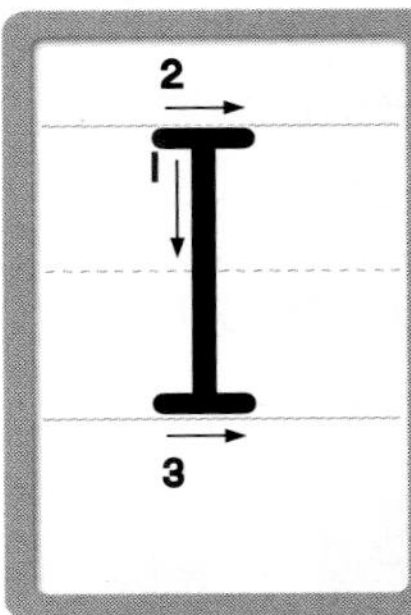

Straight down. Go back to the top. Straight across. Go to the bottom line. Straight across.

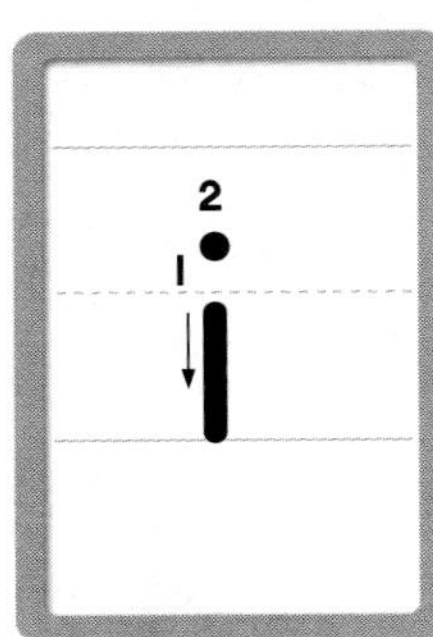

Straight down, dot above.

PRACTICE Ask children to hold up their writing hand.

- Say the cues together as children trace with their index finger the letters you wrote on the board.
- Have children write *I* and *i* in the air as they say /i/.
- Distribute handwriting practice pages. Observe children's pencil grip and paper position, and correct as necessary. Have children say /i/ every time they write the letter *i*.

For Tier 2 instruction, see page 655.

Daily Handwriting

Check that children form letters starting at the top and moving to the bottom. See **Handwriting Teacher's Edition** for ball-and-stick and slant models.

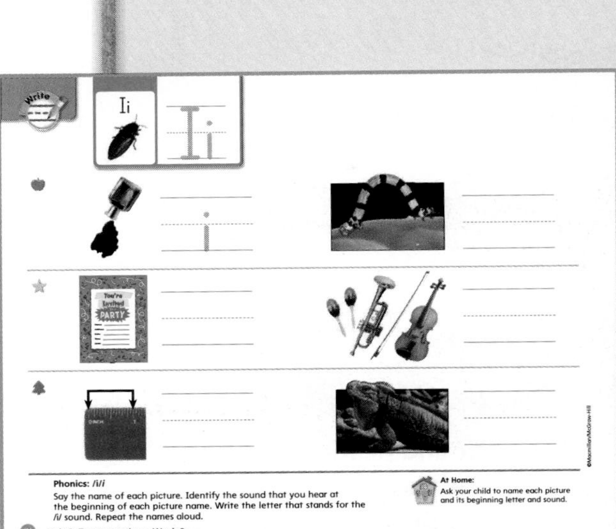

Activity Book, page 14
Practice Book, page 67

Objective

- Recognize and use action words (verbs)

Materials

- Photo Cards: *boil, mix, sing, write*
- Big Book: *On the Go*

Grammar

Action Words (Verbs)

MODEL Use the **Big Book** *On the Go* to discuss action words. Remind children that an action word tells what someone or something does. Point to the photos on pages 8–9 as you read the second sentence: *They ride on horses and donkeys and camels.* Ask children which word tells what the people do. (*ride*)

- Repeat with the sentences on pages 16–17: *A fire engine hurries to put out the fire. Buses carry people all over town.* Explain that the words *ride, hurries,* and *carry* are action words. *Action words explain what someone or something does.*

PRACTICE Show children the **Photo Cards** for *sing, write, boil,* and *mix.*

- Have children make a sentence using the action word pictured on the Photo Card. Model saying sentences, such as:

John will write *his name.*

Karen sings *in the choir.*

I boiled *water to make spaghetti.*

- After saying each sentence, guide children to identify the action word. Tell children that when *-ed* is added to the end of a word, it means it happened in the past, as in the word *boiled*.
- Have children make up their own sentences using action words. Encourage them to practice using the past tense with the following words: *banged, rushed, opened*. Guide them to name the action word in each sentence.

ELL

Basic and Academic Language Display the **Photo Cards** from the lesson and pair English Language Learners with fluent speakers. Have partners make up sentences using the action words pictured on the cards. Write their sentences, read them with children, and say: *Tell me the action word, or verb, in your sentence.*

Writing

Shared Writing: Lists

BRAINSTORM

Remind children that in *On the Go,* they learned that people use different kinds of vehicles to **travel** from place to place.

WRITE

- Create three lists as shown below. Read the headings aloud as you track the print. Have children repeat.
- *We can sort the vehicles in the book according to where we use them: on land, on water, or in the air.*
- Read page 15. *I see two vehicles that travel on land, so I will write* car *and* bus *in the list of vehicles that go on land.*
- Continue by reading pages 18–19, 20, 22, and 24–27. Have children tell you which category each vehicle belongs in. Add their ideas to the lists. Tell them to add illustrations.
- Point out how the words are written one under the other. *A list helps us remember information and ideas.*
- Save the lists to refer to in other writing activities this week.
- You may wish to add the words from the list to the Word Wall.

On Land	On Water	In the Air
car	rowboat	jet plane
bus	sailboat	helicopter
train		rocket

Write About It

Have children draw and label a picture. Suggest that they draw a picture of a vehicle that travels on land.

Objective

- List and sort types of transportation

Materials

- Big Book: *On the Go*

5-Day Writing

Lists	
DAY 1	Shared: Lists
DAY 2	Interactive: Posters
DAY 3	Independent: Prewrite and Draft Posters
DAY 4	Independent: Revise and Edit Posters
DAY 5	Independent: Publish and Present

ELL

Prewriting Planning
Provide the **Big Book** for children to use. Help them point to and name the different ways to travel. Have them say which way they like to travel.

Transitions That Teach

While getting ready for dismissal, have children tell about places they might **travel** to when school is out.

Day 2 At a Glance

WHOLE GROUP

Oral Language
- Build Robust Vocabulary

Comprehension
- Reread *On the Go*
- Strategy: Recognize Text Structure
- Skill: Classify and Categorize
- Fluency: Echo-Read

Vocabulary
- Sound Words
- Story Words: *oxen, tugboat*

Phonemic Awareness
- Phoneme Blending

Phonics
- Review /i/*i*, /t/*t*, /p/*p*, /s/*s*
- Blend with /i/*i*
- Pre-decodable Reader: *Go, Go, Go*

Writing
- Interactive Writing: Posters

SMALL GROUP

- Differentiated Instruction, pages 654–679

Oral Vocabulary

Week 2

familiar journey prepare
relax travel

Review

continue glide rapidly
vehicle transportation

Use the **Define/Example/Ask** routine in the **Instructional Routine Handbook** to review the words.

Oral Language

Build Robust Vocabulary

INTRODUCE WORDS

Tell children that today they are going to talk about the **Big Book** *On the Go.* Display pages 5–17. *This book shows people traveling to many places. Some people are traveling by foot to places that are near. Other people are on long trips, or journeys. How do some people travel to places that are far? What are ways that you have traveled?* Remind children to use complete sentences when speaking.

Vocabulary Routine

Use the routine below to discuss the meaning of each word.

Define: When you **travel**, you go from one place to another. Say the word with me.
Example: The children in our class travel to school by bus, car, and subway.
Ask: What is your favorite way to travel?

Define: A **journey** is a trip, usually a long one. Say the word with me.
Example: The astronauts spent months planning their journey to Mars.
Ask: If you could go on a journey to any place in the world, where would you go?

CREATE A CHART

Make a chart, or use **Teaching Chart G3**. Write the heads as shown. Read the chart together as you track the print. *Traveling around town and to the store are examples of traveling to places that are near. I will write those words under* Near. *I also see people on journeys to places that are far away. Where do you think they are going?* Add children's ideas to the chart.

Places to Travel

Near	Far
to market	to another city
around town	to another country
down the road	to another continent

Listen for Rhyme

IDENTIFY RHYME
Explain that rhyming words have the same sound at the end. For example, *sit* and *fit* rhyme because both words end with /it/.

I will say two words at a time. When you hear two rhyming words, raise your hand. Listen: sit/fit, car/bus, pig/cat, big/pig, can/fan, sack/sick, call/fall, send/sand, go/slow.

TRAVELING RHYME
Let's say a fun rhyme about some of the different ways to travel or the ways people go from one place to another. Play the rhyme "Take a Trip," using the **Listening Library Audio CD**. Then teach children the words and say the rhyme together.

Recite the rhyme again and ask: *Which word rhymes with* train? (*plane*) *Which word rhymes with* car? (*far*) *Which word rhymes with* moon? (*soon*)

Take a Trip

Take a bus or take a train,
Take a boat or take a plane.
Take a taxi, take a car,
May-be near or may-be far.
Take a spaceship to the moon,
But be sure to come back soon.

ELL ENGLISH LANGUAGE LEARNERS

Beginning

Confirm Understanding Review vocabulary from prior lessons by asking about things that are far or near. For example, *Am I near or far from the board?* (near) Elaborate: *Yes, I am near the board. Are we near or far from the moon?* (far) Elaborate: *Yes, we are far from the moon.*

Intermediate

Enhance Understanding Brainstorm places that are far or near and list them on a chart. Have children complete sentence frames with the words *far from* or *near* and one of the words from the chart. We are _______ the _______.

Advanced

Share Information Have children name ways to go to places on the chart, such as walking, or riding in a car, plane, or train. *Which ways are best for going places that are* near? *Which are best for going* far? Have pairs dictate answers to the questions in complete sentences for you to write down.

Objectives

- Use oral vocabulary words *travel* and *journey*
- Complete a chart
- Distinguish rhyming pairs of words from non-rhyming pairs
- Recognize rhyme

Materials

- Big Book: *On the Go*
- Graphic Organizer; Teaching Chart G3
- Listening Library Audio CD

Digital Learning

Rhyme on Listening Library Audio CD

Objectives

- Recognize text structure to classify and categorize
- Recognize how authors group information in text
- Respond to a book
- Retell important facts from a text
- Develop fluency

Materials

- Big Book: *On the Go*
- Activity Book, pp. 15–16
- Practice Book, p. 68

Big Book

Digital Learning

Story on **Listening Library Audio CD**

ELL

Gesture and Talk Use gestures and other strategies to help make the text comprehensible.

p. 5
carrying: Point to the baby in the picture. Gesture the act of carrying something. Tell children to act out carrying with you, describing the action.

Reread the Big Book

Listening Comprehension

CONCEPTS ABOUT PRINT Display the cover and read the title aloud as you track the print. Ask children to tell what they remember about the book.

STRATEGY Recognize Text Structure

Explain to children that they have been learning to recognize the pattern and structure of words in books. Ask them how the different forms of transportation in *On the Go* are organized.

SKILL Classify and Categorize

Tell children that today they are going to read the **Big Book** again and sort the different ways people can **travel** from place to place.

Think Aloud The people on the cover are taking a **journey** in a boat. The lady carrying the baby on page 5 is walking. Riding in a boat and walking are two different ways for people to travel.

Read the Big Book and use the prompts on the inside covers.

page 5

CONCEPTS ABOUT PRINT

- *Who can point to the first letter of the first word?*

All over the world
people move from place to place
carrying babies on their backs, 5

pages 6–7

CLASSIFY AND CATEGORIZE

Think Aloud Walking is one way to go from place to place. These pages show two different ways to carry things—on your head and in baskets on your shoulder.

6 baskets over their shoulders,

and almost anything on their heads. 7

Develop Comprehension

pages 8–9

CLASSIFY AND CATEGORIZE

Think Aloud People can **travel** on foot or on animals. Those are two ways for people and things to go from place to place.

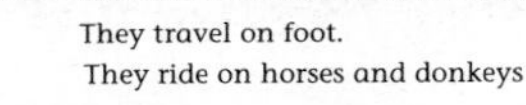
They travel on foot.
They ride on horses and donkeys

and camels.

pages 10–11

TEXT STRUCTURE

Think Aloud The first pages were about traveling by foot. The next were about traveling on animals. These are about traveling on wheels. The author tells about one way to travel at a time.

Wheels make things go easier and faster.

They can be pedaled or pushed...

pages 12–13

TEXT STRUCTURE

- *How do the different ways to travel on this page go together?* (They are all ways to travel with wheels.)

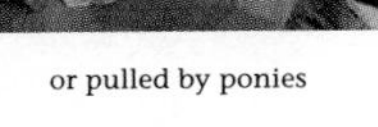
or pulled by ponies

or oxen...

page 14

CULTURAL PERSPECTIVES

Think Aloud The picture is of a city in India. The man is pulling a rickshaw, which has wheels but no pedals or motor. Rickshaws are a good way to travel through narrow alleys and around tight corners.

or people.

Some wheels are powered by motors.

Comprehension

Recognize Text Structure

- (all pages) The words and pictures follow a pattern: The page with a picture of a baby animal always asks a question and the next page, with the picture of the baby and its mother, always answers the question.

Make Predictions

- (page 12) I see that the baby seal has fluffy white fur but that the mommy has short gray fur. I think the baby's fluffy fur will change as it grows up.
- (page 18) I see that the baby penguin has fluffy brown feathers but that the mommy has short white and black feathers. What do you think will happen to the baby's fluffy fur as it grows up?

Story Word

(page 24) cub joey pup

About the Author/Illustrator: John Butler

John Butler was born in Kent, England. He studied to be an art teacher but instead worked as a designer and illustrator of educational wall charts. He then traveled throughout West Africa. He has illustrated more than thirty children's books, and has written six, many of which reflect his interest in the natural environment.

Big Book Inside Back Cover

ELL

pp. 8–9
ride: Use toys to demonstrate riding on an animal or show a picture of someone riding on an animal. Lead children in pretending to gallop around the room on horses as they say *ride*.

pp. 10–11
pedaled: Point to the people on the bicycles on page 10. Point to the wheels. Have children pedal and say: *Pedal the bike.*

pp. 14–15
powered by motors: Point to the car on page 15. Say: *A car moves with a motor,* while making an engine sound. Then point to the vehicles on page 14 and say: *A _____ is not powered with a motor.* Point to the bus on page 15. *Is a bus powered by a motor?*

Develop Comprehension

Text Evidence

Classify and Categorize

Explain Children often need to find text evidence to support their answers. *When figuring out how the author puts information into groups, I look through the pages to find things that are similar, or the same. For example, all boats travel on water.*

Discuss Reread pages 11–15. Ask: *What are the different ways that help vehicles go from place to place?* (animals, people, motors) *Where in the book did you find your answer?*

ELL

pp. 18–19
tracks: Point to each example of tracks on these pages. Say: *A train goes on tracks.* Revisit page 15. Point to the street under the vehicles. *Does a car go on tracks?*

pp. 20–21
travel on water: Point out the boat and indicate with your finger how it moves across the water. Say: *A boat goes on the water.* Flip back through previous pictures of vehicles. *Does a* ___________ *go on water?*

pages 16–17

CLASSIFY AND CATEGORIZE

- *What do all of the vehicles on this page have?* (They all have wheels and motors.) *What other way to go could the author have put on this page?*

pages 18–19

COMPARE AND CONTRAST

- *How are these three vehicles the same? How are they different?* (They are all vehicles that travel on tracks. Unlike the others, a trolley travels on a city street.)

All aboard! Trains switch from track to track.
A trolley moves on rails along the city street.
Zoom! You can go 150 miles an hour on a monorail.
18
19

pages 20–21

PHONICS

- *What word begins with the /b/ sound?* (boats)

People travel on water, too.
Some row their boats.
Others push then along with poles.
20

Some people sell refreshments from their boats.
21

pages 22–23

TEXT STRUCTURE

- *The words on the left-hand page tell about sailboats. What do you think the right page will be about?* (tugboats)

Sailors hope for a good wind.
22

Tugboats guide ships from all over the world into the harbor.
23

pages 24–25

REREAD

Think Aloud There is a word that I don't know. What do you think *cargo* is? People send things to other places. *Cargo* must be things people send.

24

Jet planes carry people and cargo across continents.

25

pages 26–27

CLASSIFY AND CATEGORIZE

- *Why are a helicopter and a rocket in the same group of things that go?* (Possible answers: They are both ways to travel in the air. They can both go straight up.)

You can go straight up in a helicopter

26

or a rocket.... Liftoff!

27

pages 28–29

AUTHOR'S PURPOSE

- *Why do you think the author wrote this book?* (She wanted to teach us about different ways to go from one place to another.)

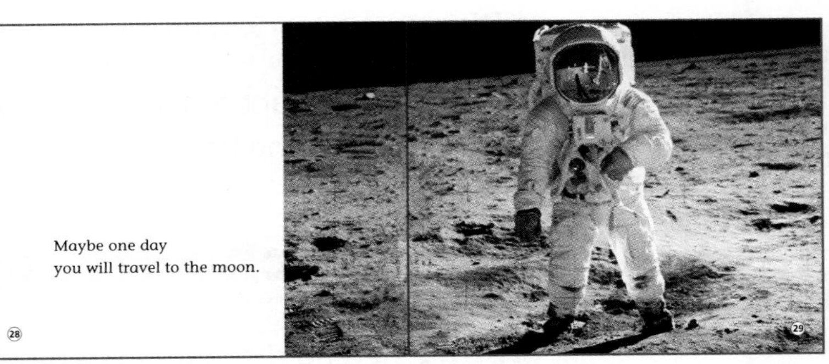

Maybe one day you will travel to the moon.

28 29

pages 30–31

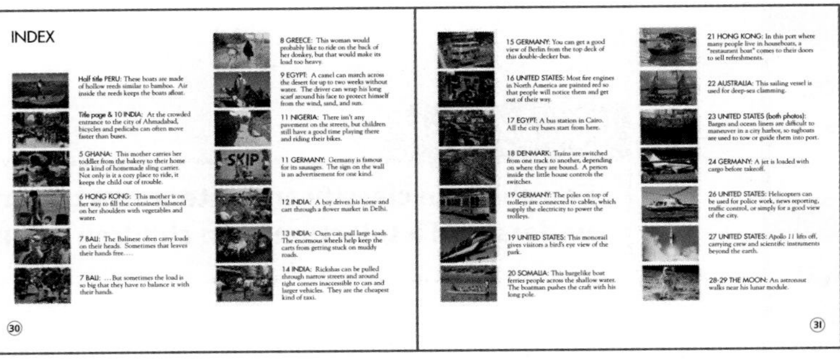

INDEX

Half title PERU: These boats are made of hollow reeds similar to bamboo. Air inside the reeds keeps the boats afloat.

Title page & 10 INDIA: At the crowded entrance to the city of Ahmadabad, bicycles and pedicabs can often move faster than buses.

5 GHANA: This mother carries her toddler from the bakery to their home in a kind of homemade sling carrier. Not only is it a cozy place to ride, it keeps the child out of trouble.

6 HONG KONG: This mother is on her way to fill the containers balanced on her shoulders with vegetables and water.

7 BALI: The Balinese often carry loads on their heads. Sometimes that leaves their hands free....

7 BALI: ...But sometimes the load is so big that they have to balance it with their hands.

8 GREECE: This woman would probably like to ride on the back of her donkey, but that would make its load too heavy.

9 EGYPT: A camel can march across the desert for up to two weeks without water. The driver can wrap his long scarf around his face to protect himself from the wind, sand, and sun.

11 NIGERIA: There isn't any pavement on the streets, but children still have a good time playing there and riding their bikes.

11 GERMANY: Germany is famous for its sausages. The sign on the wall is an advertisement for one kind.

12 INDIA: A boy drives his horse and cart through a flower market in Delhi.

13 INDIA: Oxen can pull large loads. The enormous wheels help keep the carts from getting stuck on muddy roads.

14 INDIA: Rickshas can be pulled through narrow streets and around tight corners inaccessible to cars and larger vehicles. They are the cheapest kind of taxi.

30

15 GERMANY: You can get a good view of Berlin from the top deck of this double-decker bus.

16 UNITED STATES: Most fire engines in North America are painted red so that people will notice them and get out of their way.

17 EGYPT: A bus station in Cairo. All the city buses start from here.

18 DENMARK: Trains are switched from one track to another, depending on where they are bound. A person inside the little house controls the switches.

19 GERMANY: The poles on top of trolleys are connected to cables, which supply the electricity to power the trolleys.

19 UNITED STATES: This monorail gives visitors a bird's eye view of the park.

20 SOMALIA: This bargelike boat ferries people across the shallow water. The boatman pushes the craft with his long pole.

21 HONG KONG: In this port where many people live in houseboats, a "restaurant boat" comes to their doors to sell refreshments.

22 AUSTRALIA: This sailing vessel is used for deep-sea clamming.

23 UNITED STATES (both photos): Barges and ocean liners are difficult to maneuver in a city harbor, so tugboats are used to tow or guide them into port.

24 GERMANY: A jet is loaded with cargo before takeoff.

26 UNITED STATES: Helicopters can be used for police work, news reporting, traffic control, or simply for a good view of the city.

27 UNITED STATES: Apollo *11* lifts off, carrying crew and scientific instruments beyond the earth.

28-29 THE MOON: An astronaut walks near his lunar module.

31

ELL

pp. 24–25
jet planes: Gesture flying by stretching your arms out and moving side to side. Ask children to use their hands as pretend planes.

pp. 26–27
helicopter, rocket: Repeat your simulation of a jet flying. Show a gradual takeoff and landing. Then point to the helicopter and use your hand to demonstrate how it goes straight up. Point to the rocket. Use a pencil to simulate its straight ascent. Tell children to copy your actions and say the words.

pp. 28–29
moon: Show a landscape that includes the moon. Point to the moon and say the word. Then point to where the astronaut is standing and say: *He's on the moon.*

Respond to Literature

TALK ABOUT IT Have children talk about the words and photographs that they liked and refer to the book as they answer the questions.

- *Which type of train can go 150 miles per hour?* (monorail) LOCATE
- *What is the topic of this book; what is it about?* COMBINE (different ways to travel)
- *What groups can you make to show the different ways people **travel**?* CONNECT (Possible answers: People that travel on the ground, water, or air. People that use animals. Vehicles powered by motors or powered by people.)

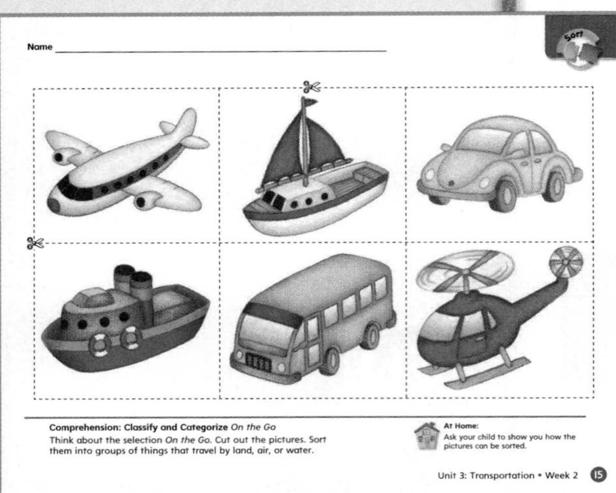
Name ______

Sort

Comprehension: Classify and Categorize *On the Go*
Think about the selection *On the Go*. Cut out the pictures. Sort them into groups of things that travel by land, air, or water.

At Home:
Ask your child to show you how the pictures can be sorted.

Unit 3: Transportation • Week 2 15

Activity Book, pages 15–16
Practice Book, page 68

Retell

GUIDED RETELLING
Remind children that as they listened to *On the Go,* they used words and photographs to help them understand the book. Now they will retell the important facts by looking at the photographs. Page through the book, asking children to tell you about each page.

- Display pages 5–7 and ask children to describe the different ways to travel shown and to retell important facts about each one.
- Repeat the above with each group of pages in the book.
- Discuss the story. *What did you learn from reading this book?*
- Have children act out a way to travel on water, wheels, and animals from the book.

Retelling Rubric

4 Excellent
Retells the selection without prompting, using detailed information, and referring to text structure and features. Clearly describes the main idea.

3 Good
Retells the selection with little guidance, using some details, and occasionally referring to text structure and features. Generally describes the main idea.

2 Fair
Retells the selection with some guidance, using limited details. Partially describes the main idea.

1 Unsatisfactory
Retells the selection only when prompted, using limited details. Does not describe the main idea.

Fluency: Echo-Read

MODEL Reread the sentences on pages 18 and 19. Read the exclamatory sentences with excitement and energy. Then reread the pages again and have children echo-read as you track the print.

Quick Check

Can children classify and categorize by sorting information into groups to understand a selection? Can children retell important facts from a text?

Vocabulary

Sound Words

Chant the following jingle:

Hear the telephone, "ring, ring,"

Hear the bike bell, "ding, ding,"

Hear the car horn, "honk, honk,"

Hear the clock, "tick-tock!"

- Repeat the first line and ask children which words name a sound. Repeat the routine with each line.
- Display the **Photo Cards** for *ambulance, car, dog, kitten,* and *watch*. Ask children to name a sound that goes with each picture.
- Discuss the information some sounds provide. For example, a siren tells other drivers that an ambulance or fire truck is close by.

NAME SOUND WORDS Tell children you are going to name some things that make different sounds. For example: *drum, bell, cow, horn.* Have children say a sound word.

Story Words: *oxen, tugboat*

Display page 13 of *On the Go* and point out the picture of *oxen*.

Explain that oxen are strong animals frequently used by farmers. Point out that when there is more than one *ox*, the plural is *oxen*.

COMPOUND WORDS Display page 23 of *On the Go* and read the text. When I read the word *tugboat*, I heard two words: *tug* and *boat*. Explain that when two shorter words make one longer word, such as *tugboat*, it is called a compound word. Point to the picture of the tugboat.

Explain that a tugboat is a small, very powerful boat that tugs and pushes larger boats.

Have children use gestures while reciting the jingle. They can pretend to answer the telephone for the first line, ring a bike bell for the second line, drive a car for the third line, and move their arms like a clock for the last line.

Objectives

- Use sound words
- Learn the story words *oxen* and *tugboat*
- Recognize that compound words are made of shorter words

Materials

- Photo Cards: *ambulance, car, dog, kitten, watch*

Digital Learning

LOG ON For children who need additional language support and oral vocabulary development, use the activities found at **www.macmillanmh.com.**

ELL

Reinforce Meaning Point to the **Photo Cards** for *ambulance, car, dog, kitten* and *watch*. Help children identify the sound in English that goes with each picture. Then ask children for the equivalent sound in their native language. For example: *What sound does an ambulance make in your language? Is the sound the ambulance makes similar or different in both languages?*

Objectives

- Orally blend sounds to form words with /i/, /t/
- Identify and write letters for initial /i/, /t/, /p/, /s/ sounds
- Blend sounds in words with /i/i

Materials

- Puppet
- Word-Building Cards
- pocket chart

Teacher's Note

Isolating medial sounds is difficult for most children early in the year. Children can generally isolate initial sounds first, then ending sounds, and finally medial sounds. Therefore, do not expect mastery of this skill. These lessons are designed to get children ready to blend CVC words in upcoming lessons.

Phonemic Awareness

Phoneme Blending

Model

Use the **Puppet** to model how to blend sounds in the word *tip*.

Repeat the routine with the word *sip*.

Happy is going to say the sounds in a word. Listen to Happy as he says each sound: /t/ /i/ /p/. Happy can blend these sounds together: /tiiip/, *tip*. Say the sounds with Happy: /t/ /i/ /p/, /tiiip/, *tip*. Now say the word with Happy: *tip*

Guided Practice/Practice

Say the sounds. Children blend the sounds to form words. Guide practice with the first word, using the same routine.

Happy is going to say the sounds in a word. Listen carefully to Happy as he says each sound. You will repeat the sounds then blend them to say the word.

/i/ /f/   /t/ /a/ /p/   /s/ /i/ /t/
/i/ /t/   /p/ /a/ /t/   /i/ /n/

Phonics

Review /i/*i*, /t/*t*

Model

Hold up **Word-Building Card** *i*.

Repeat the routine for the letters *t, p, s*.

This is the letter *i*. The letter *i* stands for /i/ at the beginning of *iguana*. What is the letter? What sound does this letter stand for?

Say the word *inch*. Write the letter *i*.

Repeat for *tan*.

The beginning sound in the word *inch* is /i/. The letter *i* stands for the /i/ sound. I'll write *i*.

Guided Practice/Practice

Say each word. Children write the letter that stands for the initial sound. Guide practice with the first word.

Listen as I say each word. Write the letter that stands for the beginning sound.

is   toy   sun   if
pick   it   in   take

Build Fluency: Sound-Spellings

Display the following **Word-Building Cards**: *a, i, m, p, s, t.* Have children chorally say each sound. Repeat and vary the pace.

Blend with /i/*i*

Model

Place Word-Building Card *s* in the pocket chart.

This is the letter *s.* The letter *s* stands for the /s/ sound. Say /sss/.

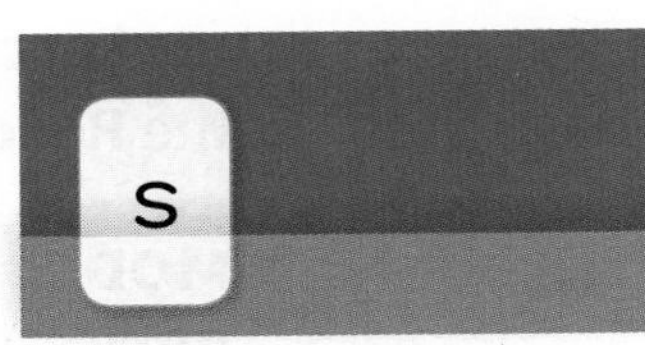

Place Word-Building Card *i* next to *s*. Move your hand from left to right.

This is the letter *i.* The letter *i* stands for the /i/ sound. Listen as I blend the two sounds together: /sssiii/. Now you say it. (/sssiii/)

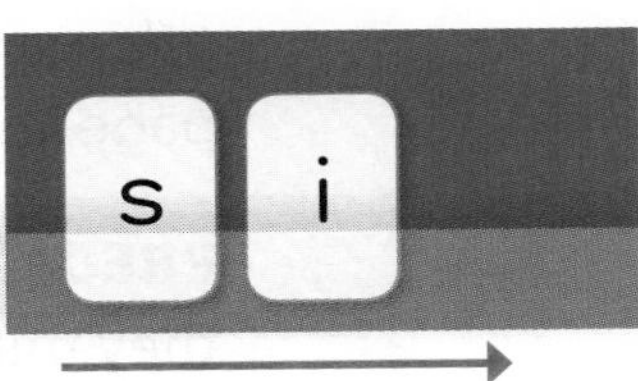

Place Word-Building Card *t* next to *si*. Move your hand from left to right.

This is the letter *t.* The letter *t* stands for the /t/ sound. Listen as I blend the three sounds together: /sssiiit/. Now you say it. (/sssiiit/, *sit*)

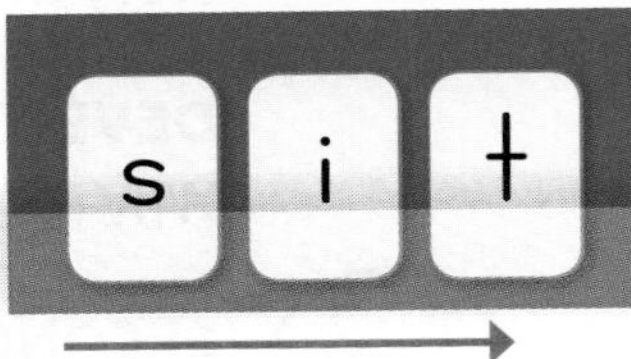

Repeat with *pit*.

Guided Practice/Practice

Children blend sounds to form words. Guide practice with the first word.

Tim	tip	pat
it	tap	sat
map	sit	mat

For Tier 2 instruction, see page 661.

ELL

Reinforce Meaning Review the meanings of words in the Guided Practice portion of the lesson by demonstrating or pointing to pictures. For example, show the tip of a pencil, then say: *The tip needs to be sharpened.* Demonstrate *sit* and *sat* by asking a child to perform the action.

Objectives

- Read the word *go*
- Identify parts of a book
- Reread for fluency

Materials

- Pre-decodable Reader: *Go, Go, Go*
- High-Frequency Word Cards: *a, go*
- pocket chart

Pre-decodable Reader

Read *Go, Go, Go*

Go, Go, Go

REVIEW HIGH-FREQUENCY WORDS Display **High-Frequency Word Cards** for **a** and **go** in the pocket chart. Review words using the **Read/Spell/Write** routine.

MODEL CONCEPTS ABOUT PRINT Demonstrate book handling. Guide children to follow along. *This is the front cover, back cover, and title page.* Ask children to identify the front cover, back cover, and title page. Instruct children to read from right to left.

PREDICT Read the title and point to the boat. Ask children what they think the boat will do.

FIRST READ Point out the rebus and discuss what it stands for. Have children point to each word, sounding out the decodable words and saying the sight words quickly. Children should chorally read the story the first time through.

DEVELOP COMPREHENSION Ask: *What kinds of vehicles can go? Why would it be hard for the boat to travel on the racetrack?*

SECOND READ Have partners reread the book together. Circulate, listen in, and provide corrective feedback.

A car can go.
2

Go car go!
3

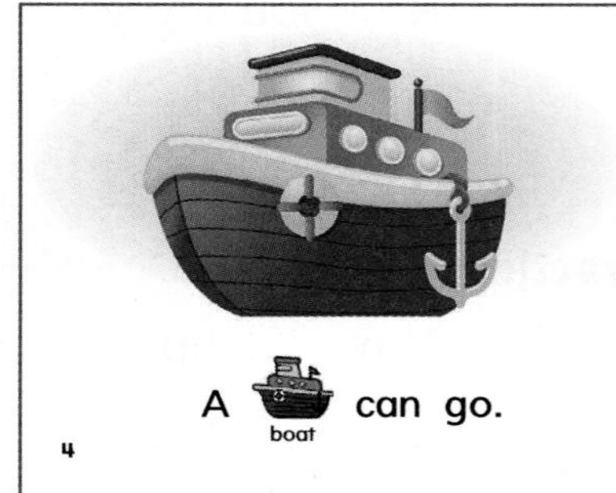

A boat can go.
4

Go boat go!
5

A plane can go.
6

Go plane go!
7

Go, go, go!
8

Pre-decodable Reader

Writing

Interactive Writing: Posters

REVIEW

- Display and read aloud the lists from the Shared Writing activity.

WRITE

- *We are going to write a travel poster for a special **journey**. First we'll write a title.* Write the title *Away We Go!*
- Collaborate with children to write the sentence frame *We can go by ________.* Read the words together as you track the print. Guide children to suggest a vehicle to complete the sentence. Write the word, asking children to write all the letters they know. Direct children to look at the Word Wall for help.
- Write the sentence frame *We can go to ________.* Read the words together as you track the print. *Where should we **travel** to?* Guide children to suggest a place name to complete the sentence. Write the words, having children write all the letters they know.

Away We Go!
We can go by rocket!
We can go to the moon!

- Read the completed poster with children as you track the print.
- To extend the activity, work with children to write about things you might do during the trip, such as: *Take a walk in space.*

Write About It

Have children draw a picture of themselves traveling by air. Help them write a caption using the high-frequency word *see.*

Objectives

- Write sentences for a travel poster
- Use letter knowledge to write letters in a word

Materials

- Shared Writing lists from Day 1

5-Day Writing

Posters	
DAY 1	Shared: Lists
DAY 2	Interactive: Posters
DAY 3	Independent: Prewrite and Draft Posters
DAY 4	Independent: Revise and Edit Posters
DAY 5	Independent: Publish and Present

ELL

Use Personal Experience Ask children what ways people travel from their homes to different places. Have children say the name of the vehicle their family uses the most.

Transitions That Teach

While packing up, have children tell about a **journey** they would like to take to a faraway place.

DAY 3 At a Glance

WHOLE GROUP

Oral Language
- Build Robust Vocabulary
- Oral Vocabulary Cards: "The Two Frogs"

Comprehension
- Read "My Bike" and "Riding the Subway Train"

High-Frequency Words
- Review *go*

Phonemic Awareness
- Phoneme Isolation

Phonics
- Picture Sort
- Blend with /i/*i*

Grammar
- Action Words (Verbs)

Writing
- Independent Writing: Prewrite and Draft Posters

SMALL GROUP

- Differentiated Instruction, pages 654–679

Additional Vocabulary

To provide 15–20 minutes of additional vocabulary instruction, see Oral Vocabulary Cards 5-Day Plan. The pre- and posttest can be found in the **Teacher's Resource Book**, pages 218–219.

Oral Language

Build Robust Vocabulary

BUILD BACKGROUND

Display the story "The Two Frogs" using **Oral Vocabulary Card 1** and read the title aloud. *Have you ever gone on a journey to a new place?* Based on the title and illustrations, ask children to predict what they think will happen in the story.

- Read the story on the back of the cards. Pause at each oral vocabulary word and read the definition. Check children's understanding using the Identify Story Elements, Use Illustrations, and Repeat Modeled Language prompts.

Oral Vocabulary Cards

Vocabulary Routine

Use the routine below to discuss the meaning of each word.

Define: When you **prepare**, you get ready to do something or to go someplace. Say the word with me.
Example: We like to prepare our picnic baskets the night before a picnic.
Ask: What did you do this morning to prepare for school?

Define: If you are taking time to **relax**, you are taking a rest or a break. Say the word with me.
Example: After getting home from school, I like to relax in my living room.
Ask: How do you relax after school?

Define: Something that is **familiar** is something that you already know. Say the word with me.
Example: Our class is very familiar with the story *The Three Bears*.
Ask: Who are some story characters that are familiar to our class?

- Use the routine on Cards 1 and 2 to review the words **travel** and **journey**.

- Review last week's words: *continue, glide, rapidly, transportation,* and *vehicle*.

Listen for Repetition

IDENTIFY REPETITION
Tell children that repetition is when a word or group of words is said more than once. Have children listen and identify words or groups of words that are repeated.

Tell children that they will sing a song about traveling on a bus. Play the song and ask children to join in. Ask: *Why do some children travel to school on a bus?*

Discuss that some types of buses, such as a school bus, take people to places that are near and that other kinds of buses take people to places that are far. Ask: *How is a bus that takes people to places that are far different from a school bus?* Remind children to speak audibly and clearly.

AUDIO CD

The Wheels on the Bus

The wheels on the bus go round and round,
Round and round, round and round.
The wheels on the bus go round and round.
All through the town.

The driver on the bus says move on back!
Move on back! Move on back!
The driver on the bus says move on back!
All through the town.

Objectives

- **Discuss the theme**
- **Use oral vocabulary words *familiar, journey, prepare, relax,* and *travel***
- **Listen and respond to a folktale**

Materials

- **Oral Vocabulary Cards: "The Two Frogs"**

Digital Learning

Song on **Listening Library Audio CD**

Objectives

- Read and respond to a poem
- Identify rhyme and alliteration
- Create a diagram

Materials

- Big Book of Explorations, Vol. 1: "My Bike," "Riding the Subway Train," pp. 37–38
- drawing paper

Vocabulary

subway a railroad that is below the ground

hurtle to move very, very fast

approach to come near

Poetry

Genre

Big Book of Explorations

LITERARY TEXT: POETRY Tell children that today they will listen to two poems. Explain that poems help us say things in a special way. These two poems are about two ways to travel.

LITERARY ELEMENT: RHYME AND ALLITERATION

Explain/Model Tell children that some poems use words that rhyme. Remind them that rhyming words, such as *snow* and *grow*, have the same sound at the end. *Listen for the rhyming words in both poems.* Next, explain that some poems use groups of words that have the same beginning sound. *Listen to these words:* ship, show, shell. *The words* ship, show, *and* shell *have the same beginning sound. They all begin with /sh/. Listen for groups of words that have the same beginning sound in the poem "Riding the Subway Train."*

Think Aloud As I read, I will pay attention to the rhyming words I hear. I will also listen for groups of words that have the same beginning sound. These words can help me better enjoy the poem.

READ "MY BIKE" AND "RIDING THE SUBWAY TRAIN"

- **Preview and Predict** Display page 37 and read the title "My Bike." *What are the animals doing? Are they having fun? What do you think this poem will be about?* Turn to page 38 and preview "Riding the Subway Train" by reading the title and tracking the print. *What do you think this poem will be about?*
- **Vocabulary** Introduce and discuss the vocabulary words.
- **Set Purpose** Tell children to listen for words that rhyme in both poems and words that have the same beginning sound in "Riding the Subway Train." Read the poems aloud as you track the print. Emphasize the alliterative words in "Riding the Subway Train."

page 37

My Bike

One wheel, two wheels,
on the ground,
My feet make the pedals
go 'round and 'round.
The handlebars help me
steer so straight,
Down the sidewalk
and through the gate.

page 38

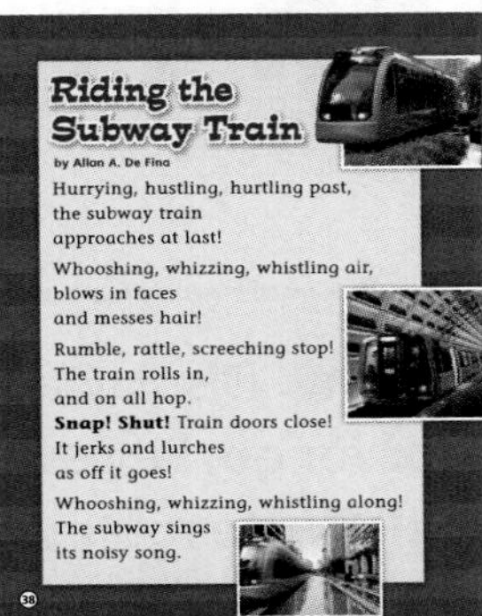

Riding the Subway Train

by Allan A. De Fina

Hurrying, hustling, hurtling past,
the subway train
approaches at last!
Whooshing, whizzing, whistling air,
blows in faces
and messes hair!
Rumble, rattle, screeching stop!
The train rolls in,
and on all hop.
Snap! Shut! Train doors close!
It jerks and lurches
as off it goes!
Whooshing, whizzing, whistling along!
The subway sings
its noisy song.

Retell and Respond

- *Which words rhyme in "My Bike"? What other words rhyme with* straight *and* gate*?*
- *What do handlebars help you do?*
- *What do you notice about the words* whooshing, whizzing, *and* whistling*? Say the sound that begins each word.*
- *Is a subway train quiet or noisy? How do you know?*

Connect to Content

Social Studies: Parts of a Bike

- Review the parts of a bike mentioned in "My Bike" (wheels, pedals, handlebars) and their functions. Help children identify other parts of a bike, such as the seat and the spokes.
- Have children draw and label the parts of a one-, two-, or three-wheeled bicycle.
- Have them write "My bike" on their drawings.

ELL

Beginning

Use Pictures Point to the different parts of the pictures as you ask questions. *Is this a wheel or a sidewalk? Is this a subway train or a bike? Are these handlebars or pedals?*

Intermediate

Ask Questions Ask questions about the different ways people travel. *Which goes faster, a bike or a subway train? What has handlebars and pedals?* Provide sentence frames: A ______ goes faster than a ______. A ______ has handlebars and pedals.

Advanced

Make Comparisons Have children talk about the modes of transportation on pages 37 and 38. Guide partners to write and answer compare and contrast questions. *How is a bike different from a subway train? How is a bike similar to a subway train?*

Objective

- Read the high-frequency word *go*

Materials

- High-Frequency Word Cards: *can, go, the, we*
- Photo Cards: *bike, bus, car, helicopter, jet, train*
- pocket chart
- Activity Book, pp. 17–18
- Practice Book, pp. 69–70

Activity Book, pages 17–18
Practice Book, pages 69–70

High-Frequency Words

go

go

REVIEW Display the **High-Frequency Word Card** for **go**. Review the word using the **Read/Spell/Write** routine.

Repeat the routine for the words **can**, **the**, **we**.

APPLY Build sentences in the pocket chart using High-Frequency Word Cards and **Photo Cards**. Read each sentence aloud, then have children chorally read it as you track the print with your finger. Use the sentence below and the following: *The car can go. The helicopter can go. The bike can go. The jet can go. The train can go.*

READ FOR FLUENCY Chorally read the Take-Home Book with children. Then have them reread the book to review high-frequency words and build fluency.

Quick Check

Can children read the word *go*?

During **Small Group Instruction**

If No → **Approaching Level** Provide additional practice with high-frequency words, page 664.

If Yes → **On Level** Children are ready to read the Take-Home Book.

Beyond Level Children are ready to read the Take-Home Book.

TIME TO MOVE!

Play "One-two-three Go!" Ask children to stand still. When you say *One-two-three Go!*, they should do a quick movement, such as running in place or touching their toes, until you say *One-two-three Stop!* Have children describe their movement.

Phonemic Awareness

Phoneme Isolation

Model

Display the **Photo Card** for *inch* and the **Sound Box**.

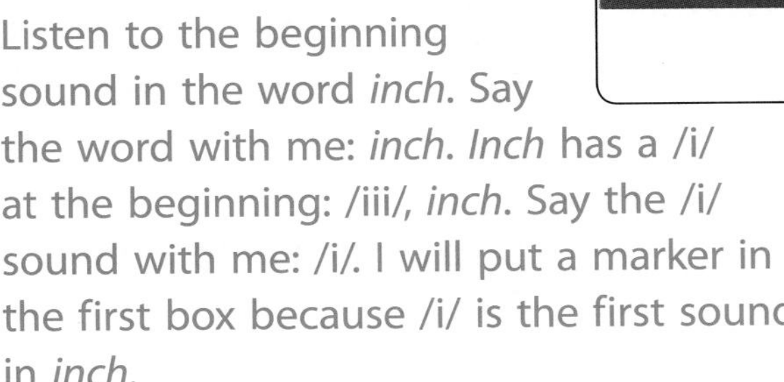

Listen to the beginning sound in the word *inch*. Say the word with me: *inch*. *Inch* has a /i/ at the beginning: /iii/, *inch*. Say the /i/ sound with me: /i/. I will put a marker in the first box because /i/ is the first sound in *inch*.

Display the Photo Card for *six*.

Say the name of the picture with me: *six*. The word *six* has /i/ in the middle. I'll put a marker in the middle box because /i/ is the middle sound of *six*.

Guided Practice/Practice

Distribute Sound Boxes and markers. Children identify the position of /i/ in words. Guide practice with the first row, using the routine.

Listen to each word. Put a marker in a box to show where you hear /i/.

in	big	did	Tim	is
it	miss	if	pig	mix

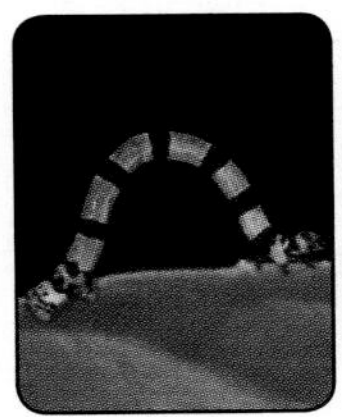

For Tier 2 instruction, see page 664.

Objective

- Listen for initial and medial /i/

Materials

- Photo Cards: *inch, inchworm, ink, mix, pig, six*
- Sound Box
- markers
- WorkBoard Sound Boxes; Teacher's Resource Book, p. 136

Objectives

- Identify initial and medial /i/*i*
- Blend with /i/
- Read simple one-syllable words

Materials

- Photo Cards: *fish, inch, ink, insect, invitation, six, mix, pig*
- pocket chart
- Word-Building Cards

Phonics

Picture Sort: /i/*i*

Model

Display the **Photo Card** for *insect* in the pocket chart.

This is an *insect*. Say it with me: *insect*. The letter *i* stands for the /i/ sound you hear at the beginning of *insect*.

Display the Photo Card for *pig*.

Say this picture name with me: *pig*. The letter *i* stands for the /i/ sound you hear in the middle of *pig*.

Display the Photo Card for *inch*.

Say the picture name with me: *inch*. I will place the picture of the *inch* under *insect* because *inch* has /i/ at the beginning.

Repeat for *six*.

Guided Practice/Practice

Children sort the Photo Cards. Guide practice with the next card.

Build Fluency: Sound-Spellings

Display the following **Word-Building Cards**: *a, i, m, p, s, t*. Have children chorally say each sound. Repeat and vary the pace.

For Tier 2 instruction, see page 665.

Blend with /i/*i*

Model

Place **Word-Building Card** *s* in the pocket chart.

This letter is *s*. It stands for /s/. Say /s/.

Place Word-Building Card *i* next to *s*. Move your hand from left to right.

This letter is *i*. It stands for /i/. Listen as I blend the two sounds: /sssiii/. Now you say it. (/sssiii/)

Place Word-Building Card *p* next to *si*. Move your hand from left to right.

This letter is *p*. It stands for /p/. Listen as I blend the three sounds: /sssiiip/, *sip*. Now you say it. (/sssiiip/, *sip*)

Repeat with *sit*.

Guided Practice/Practice

Children blend with /i/*i*.

tip Tim pit
tap pit mat

Read Words

Apply
Write the words and sentences. Guide practice blending the first word, using the **Sound-by-Sound Blending Routine**.

Read the sentences with children.

it
tip
We see Tim.
Go sit, Tim.

Corrective Feedback

Blending If needed, model blending words with short *i*. *The /i/ sound is in the middle of* sip*: /s/ /i/ /p/,* sip. *Let's blend* sip *together: /sssiiip/,* sip. *Now it's your turn. Blend* sip. Repeat with *it, pin,* and *hip*.

ELL

Variations in Language
Because there is no sound-symbol match for /i/ in Spanish, Vietnamese, Hmong, Cantonese, Haitian Creole, and Korean, children who speak one of these languages may need additional practice with pronouncing the /i/ sound. List simple words with the /i/ sound on the board. Say the words, emphasizing the /i/sound. Have children repeat each word after you.

Objectives

- Recognize action words (verbs)
- Understand past and future tenses

Materials

- Photo Cards: *alligator, boat, bridge, bike, dolphin, football, fox, jet, kitten, knight, lamp, octopus, queen, umpire, volcano, whistle, yo-yo*
- Big Book: *On the Go*

ELL

Basic and Academic Language Display **Photo Cards** from the lesson and pair English Language Learners with fluent speakers. Have partners make up sentences with the Photo Card words and the verb *play* in the present, past, and future. Write their sentences, read them chorally, and ask: *Does the verb* play *in your sentence shows that you are playing now, played before, or will play later?* Sort the sentences accordingly.

Grammar

Action Words (Verbs)

MODEL Use the **Big Book** *On the Go* to review action words. Remind children that an action word, or verb, tells what someone or something does. Point to the photo on page 8 and read the sentence. *They travel on foot.* Explain to children that *travel* is an action word. It means to go from one place to another.

- Show the **Photo Cards** for *jet, bike,* and *bridge*. Say: *We will travel to my grandparents on a jet. I travel to school on my bike. The train traveled over the bridge.* Tell children that the word *traveled* tells what something or someone did. *What did the train do?* (It traveled over a bridge.) Travel *is an action word.*
- Point out the future and past tenses of the verb, *travel*. Tell children that when the word *will* is used in front of a verb, it means that the action is going to happen in the future. When the suffix *-ed* is used with a verb, it means that the action already happened.

PRACTICE Show children the Photo Card for *kitten*. Model making a sentence with action words. Include past and future tenses. *The kitten will play with the yarn. The kitten played with the yarn. What is the action word?* (will play/played)

- Show children Photo Cards and have them make sentences using the pictures on the Photo Cards. Have them identify the action words and act out each one.

Writing

Independent Writing: Posters

Display the poster that children created for the Interactive Writing activity.

BRAINSTORM
Tell children that today they will make their own **travel** poster. Have them look at the list of vehicles from the Shared Writing activity. Add a small drawing next to each vehicle. Display the list as a reference.

PREWRITE
Write the title *Away We Go!* Read the title aloud as you track the print.

- Write the sentence frames *We can go by* ________ and *We can go to* ________ and complete each sentence. Then add a drawing of the vehicle and the destination.
- Share your poster with children and track the print as you read it.
- Have children choose a vehicle and a place they will write about.

DRAFT
Distribute poster paper, pencils, and crayons.

- Have children write their names on the top of the paper. Then ask them to write the title *Away We Go!* Assist children as necessary.
- Have children write the sentences *We can go by* ________. and *We can go to* ________. Tell them to complete the sentences with a favorite vehicle and place. Have children look at the Word Wall for help. Have them add a picture of the vehicle and the destination.
- Collect and save children's work to use tomorrow.

Away We Go!
We can go by boat.
We can go to the beach.

Write About It
Have children draw in their Writer's Notebooks. Guide them as they draw and label a picture of a place where they would like to take a **journey**.

Objectives
- Write labels
- Use letter knowledge to write letters in a word
- Draw a picture

Materials
- list and poster from Shared and Interactive Writing (Day 2)

5-Day Writing

Posters	
DAY 1	Shared: Lists
DAY 2	Interactive: Posters
DAY 3	Independent: Prewrite and Draft Posters
DAY 4	Independent: Revise and Edit Posters
DAY 5	Independent: Publish and Present

ELL
Prewriting Planning
Display and name **Photo Cards** of vehicles. Call out places to travel to and ask children to choose the appropriate Photo Card word to get there. Help children complete the sentence frames.

Transitions That Teach
While packing up, have children tell about a way they like to **relax** at home.

Day 4 At a Glance

WHOLE GROUP

Oral Language
- Build Robust Vocabulary

Comprehension
- Read Aloud: "Timimoto"

Vocabulary
- Sound Words
- Story Words: *oxen, tugboat*

Phonemic Awareness
- Phoneme Blending

Phonics
- Picture Sort
- Blend with /i/*i*
- Pre-decodable Reader: *It Can Go, Go, Go!*

Writing
- Independent Writing: Revise and Edit Posters

SMALL GROUP

- Differentiated Instruction, pages 654–679

Oral Language

Build Robust Vocabulary

GOING ON JOURNEYS

Discuss **journeys** children have taken or would like to take and things they might do on a journey. Remind them to speak clearly.

- *What new things might you see and do on a journey? What* **familiar** *things might you see and do? How might you* **relax** *on a journey?*

CREATE A WORD WEB Draw a word web, or use **Teaching Chart G1**.5 Write the heading as shown and read the words aloud as you track the print.

Think Aloud When we travel on journeys, we can sometimes see interesting people and places and do exciting new things.

Ask children to share journeys they have taken or would like to take. Have them name the things they might see and do on a journey. Add their ideas to the web. Read the words as you track the print. Work together to write a summary of the information in the web.

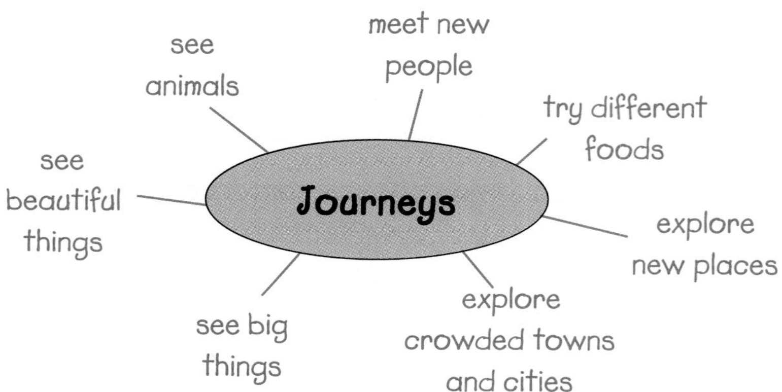

ELL ENGLISH LANGUAGE LEARNERS

Beginning

Use Illustrations Ask children to draw things they might see or do on a trip or journey. Put their drawings around the word web, and prompt each child to explain his or her drawing. For example: *Rosa, did you draw a house? Where is it? Who lives there?*

Intermediate

Complete Sentences Have children complete sentences as they talk about things they want to see or do on a trip or journey to a place of their choice: *I want to go to* ______. *I want to see* ______.

Advanced

Share Information Have partners plan a trip or journey to a place of their choice. Prompt them to discuss how they would get there, how long they would stay, and what they would do at their destination. Write their plan on the board as it is discussed.

Listen for Rhyme

IDENTIFY RHYME
Tell children that you will say a word and they will say a word that rhymes with it. Remind them that rhyming words have the same endings sounds. What rhymes with *dip, mad, cat, bit*?

TRAVELING RHYME
Tell children that they will say the rhyme about traveling that they learned on Day 2. Play the rhyme and ask children to join in.

Ask children to name and describe all the ways to **travel** they have learned.

Ask the following: *What do you think is the most **relaxing** way to travel? How would you **prepare** to take a long **journey**? Name a way to travel with which you are **familiar**.*

AUDIO CD
Take a Trip
Take a bus or take a train,
Take a boat or take a plane.
Take a taxi, take a car,
May-be near or may-be far.
Take a spaceship to the moon,
But be sure to come back soon.

Objectives

- Complete a word web
- Generate rhyme
- Use oral vocabulary words *familiar, journey, prepare, relax,* and *travel*

Materials

- Graphic Organizer; Teaching Chart G1

Oral Vocabulary

Have children use each word in a sentence about this week's stories.

familiar
journey
prepare
relax
travel

Review Work with children to review last week's words. Provide sentence starters, such as: *My favorite kind of transportation is ______. I will continue to ______.*

continue
glide
rapidly
transportation
vehicle

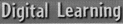

Digital Learning

Rhyme on **Listening Library Audio CD**

Objective

- Listen and respond to a folktale

Materials

- Read-Aloud Anthology: "Timimoto," pp. 49–52
- Reader Response Sheets; Teacher's Resource Book, pp. 203–204

ELL

Develop Vocabulary
Wiggle your thumbs and say: *These are my thumbs.* Then wiggle your fingers and say: *These are my fingers*. Have children repeat the sentences and actions with you.

Readers Theater

BUILDING LISTENING AND SPEAKING SKILLS
Distribute copies of "Catch a Little Rhyme," Read-Aloud Anthology pages 163–164. Have children practice performing the play throughout the unit. Assign parts and have children present the play or perform it as a dramatic reading at the end of the unit.

Interactive Read Aloud

Listening Comprehension

GENRE: LITERARY TEXT/FOLKTALE
Tell children that this story is a **folktale**. Folktales are very old stories that people have been telling for many years. See the information about folktales found in the **Read-Aloud Anthology**.

Read Aloud

CULTURAL PERSPECTIVES
Tell children that "Timimoto" is a folktale from Japan. Explain that a rice bowl is a small round bowl used to hold rice and that chopsticks are two sticks that people in many Asian countries use to pick up food.

READ "TIMIMOTO"

- **MODEL ASKING QUESTIONS ABOUT STORY STRUCTURE** Use the Think Alouds provided at point of use in the folktale.
- **MODEL FLUENT READING** Read the folktale aloud with fluent expression. Stop occasionally so that children can predict what will happen next.
- **EXPAND VOCABULARY** See page 49 of the Read-Aloud Anthology to teach new words using the **Define/Example/Ask** routine.

Respond to Literature

TALK ABOUT IT Ask children to retell the main event, identifying the characters and settings.

- *What did the old woman find at the beginning of the story?*
- *What happened when Timimoto met the giant?*
- *How are Timimoto and the mouse in "The Lion and the Mouse" alike?* (Both are small and defeat or help animals/creatures much bigger.)
- *What is the big idea, or theme, of the folktale?* (size does not matter)

Write About It

Ask children to draw a picture of something very, very small and help them label it.

Vocabulary

Sound Words

REVIEW WORDS

Distribute the **Photo Cards** *ambulance, car, watch, dog*, and *kitten* to children. Tell children you will say a sound word. *If your picture goes with the sound, hold it up*. Say words such as: *beep, honk, woof, meow*, and *tick*.

Tell children to clap when they hear a sound word as you read the following story:

> *One morning Lani woke up to the* beeping *of her alarm clock. She got up and went to the kitchen. She heard the telephone* ring. *"I'll get it!" said her brother. She walked to the sink. The kitchen timer* dinged. *"Breakfast is ready," said her father. Outside she heard a car* honk. *The dog said,* "Woof!" *Lani said, "It's a noisy morning!"*

Story Words: *oxen, tugboat*

Display page 13 of *On the Go* and point out the picture of oxen. Ask a child to point to and name the animals. *What sound do you think an ox might make?*

Display page 23 of *On the Go* and point out the picture of the tugboat. Ask a child to name the boat. Remind children that *tugboat* is a compound word because it has two words, *tug* and *boat*. *I'm going to say some words. Put your hand up if it is a compound word: inside, tiger, football, upstairs, banana.*

TIME TO MOVE!

Have a parade. Have children stand in a line. Lead them in marching around the classroom. Have children say sound words as they march.

Objectives

- Use sound words
- Review story words *oxen* and *tugboat*
- Recognize that compound words are made up of shorter words

Materials

- Photo Cards: *ambulance, car, dog, kitten, watch*
- Big Book: *On the Go*

ELL

Reinforce Vocabulary
Have children make sentences using the **Photo Cards** and the sound words. Model sentences such as: *A car goes "beep." A dog goes "woof."* Have children repeat after you.

Objectives

- Orally blend sounds to form words with /i/
- Sort picture names with initial /i/i, /t/t, /p/p
- Review letter-sound correspondence for /i/i, /t/t, /p/p
- Blend sounds in words with /i/i, /t/t, /p/p

Materials

- Puppet
- Word-Building Cards
- pocket chart
- Photo Cards: *inch, ink, invitation, pear, penguin, pizza, tiger, toe, top*
- Activity Book, p. 19
- Practice Book, p. 71

ELL

Minimal Pairs Focus on articulation. Make the /t/ and /p/ sounds. Have children repeat, noticing the small differences in articulation. Continue by having children repeat minimal contrast word pairs such as *top/pot, tap/pat, tip/pit.*

Phonemic Awareness

Phoneme Blending

Model

Use the **Puppet** to model how to blend sounds in the word *it*.

Happy is going to say the sounds in a word. Listen to Happy as he says each sound: /i/ /t/. Happy can blend these sounds together: /iiit/, *it*. Say the sounds with Happy: /i/ /t/, /iiit/, *it*. Now say the word with Happy: *it*.

Repeat the routine with *tip*.

Guided Practice/Practice

Say the sounds. Children blend the sounds to say the words. Guide practice with the first word.

Happy is going to say the sounds in a word. Listen to Happy as he says each sound. Blend the sounds together to make a word.

/i/ /n/	/s/ /i/ /ks/	/s/ /i/ /t/
/i/ /f/	/p/ /i/ /g/	/t/ /i/ /p/

Phonics

Picture Sort

i p t

Model

Place **Word-Building Card** *i* in the pocket chart.

This is the letter *i*. The sound for this letter is /i/. Say the sound with me: /i/.

Follow the routine for *t* and *p*.

This is the letter *t*. The sound for this letter is /t/. Say the sound with me: /t/.

Hold up the **Photo Card** for *inch*.

Here is the picture of an *inch*. *Inch* begins with /i/. I will place *inch* under the letter *i*.

Follow the routine for *top*.

Guided Practice/Practice

Children sort the Photo Cards. Guide practice with the next card, using the routine.

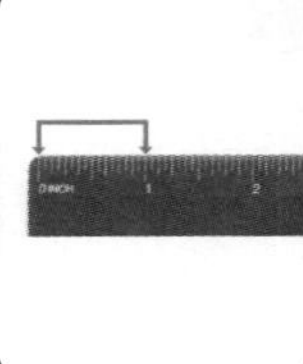

Build Fluency: Sound-Spellings

Display the following **Word-Building Cards**: *a, i, m, p, s, t*. Have children chorally say each sound. Repeat and vary the pace.

Blend with /i/*i*

Model

Place **Word-Building Card** *i* in the pocket chart.

This letter is *i*. The letter *i* stands for the /i/ sound. Say /i/.

i

Place Word-Building Card *t* next to *i*. Move your hand from left to right below the letters.

This letter is *t*. The letter *t* stands for the /t/ sound. Listen as I blend the two sounds together: /iiit/, *it*. Now you blend the sounds with me. (/iiit/)

i
t

Repeat the routine with *tip*.

Guided Practice/Practice

Children blend the sounds. Guide practice with the first word.

sat	sit	tap	Tim
pat	pit	at	sip

For Tier 2 instruction, see page 668.

Name
Phonemic Awareness: /i/
Look at the picture. Say the name of each item. Circle the item if its name begins with the same sound you hear at the beginning of *iguana*.
At Home:
Ask your child to point to and name all the items in the picture that begin with the same sound as *iguana*.
Unit 3: Transportation • Week 2 19

Activity Book, page 19
Practice Book, page 71

Corrective Feedback

Blending: Sound Error Model blending words with short *i*. *This is the /i/ sound in the middle of* sip: */s/ /i/ /p/,* sip. *Let's blend* sip *together: /sssiiip/,* sip. *Now it's your turn.* Point to each letter and ask: *What's the sound?* Then move your hand from left to right as children blend the sounds.

Objectives

- Read decodable words with /i/*i*
- Read the word *go*
- Review the high-frequency words *can, go, I, see, the*
- Reread for fluency

Materials

- Pre-decodable Reader: *It Can Go, Go, Go!*
- High-Frequency Word Cards: *can, go, I, see, the*
- pocket chart

Pre-decodable Reader

Read *It Can Go, Go, Go!*

REVIEW Display **High-Frequency Word Cards** for **can**, **go**, **I**, **see**, and **the** in the pocket chart. Use the **Read/ Spell/Write** routine for each word.

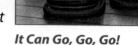

It Can Go, Go, Go!

MODEL CONCEPTS ABOUT PRINT Guide children to follow along. *I hold the book so that the cover is on the front and the words are not upside down.* Read the title and point out the one-to-one correspondence between a spoken word and a printed word.

PREDICT Ask children to describe the picture. Ask if they think the book will be about something that could really happen.

FIRST READ Turn to page 2. Point out the rebus and discuss what it stands for. Have children point to each word, sounding out the decodable words and saying the sight words quickly. Children should chorally read the story the first time through.

DEVELOP COMPREHENSION Ask the following: *Which things go on the ground?* (car, wagon, dogsled) *Which thing goes on the water?* (boat)

SECOND READ Have partners reread the book together. Have children stop their partner and reread if the text does not make sense to them.

I can see the car.

2

It can go, go, go!

3

I can see the boat.

4

It can go, go, go!

5

I can see the wagon.

6

It can go, go, go!

7

We can go, go, go!

8

Pre-decodable Reader

Writing

Independent Writing: Posters

REVISE AND EDIT

Distribute children's **travel** posters from yesterday. Have them reread their work and check for the following:

- Did I write the title at the top?
- Did I write a sentence about a vehicle?
- Did I pay attention to the spacing between words?
- Did I write a sentence about a place?
- Did I draw a picture of the vehicle and the place?

Circulate and help children as they review and self-correct their work. Have children share their posters with a partner.

Write About It

Ask children to draw in their Writer's Notebook. Have them draw a picture of a tugboat or other boat they could use for a **journey**. Help them label their drawings.

Objectives

- Revise and edit their posters
- Use letter knowledge to write letters in a word

Materials

- children's posters from Day 3
- Writer's Checklist; Teacher's Resource Book, p. 205

5-Day Writing

Posters	
DAY 1	Shared: Lists
DAY 2	Interactive: Posters
DAY 3	Independent: Prewrite and Draft Posters
DAY 4	Independent: Revise and Edit Posters
DAY 5	Independent: Publish and Present

ELL

Use New Language Point to and read the sentences on several posters. Ask children whether each sentence is about a vehicle or a place. List the names of the vehicles and the places, sorting them on a two-column chart.

Transitions That Teach

While children wait in line, have them talk about a **familiar** place that they have been to many times.

Day 5 At a Glance

WHOLE GROUP

Oral Language
- Build Robust Vocabulary

Comprehension
- Strategy: Recognize Text Structure
- Skill: Classify and Categorize
- Read Across Texts

Vocabulary
- High-Frequency Word *go*
- Build Fluency
- Sound Words

Phonemic Awareness
- Phoneme Categorization

Phonics
- Read Words
- Dictation

Writing
- Independent Writing: Publish and Present

SMALL GROUP

- Differentiated Instruction, pages 654–679

Review and Assess

Oral Language

Build Robust Vocabulary

REVIEW WORDS

Review this week's oral vocabulary words with children. Explain that all of the words will be used to discuss taking a trip on a vacation. Talk about what traveling means to them. Have children use complete sentences when speaking.

Use the following questions to check children's understanding:

- What do you do to **relax** on vacation?
- How might you **travel** to get there?
- What might you pack to **prepare** for your vacation?
- Where might you go if you took a long **journey**?
- Why would visiting the same family members each year be something that is **familiar**?

REVIEW SONGS AND RHYMES ABOUT TRAVELING

Say the rhyme "Take a Trip" and ask children to join in. Have children name and describe each form of transportation in the rhyme.

Sing "The Wheels on the Bus" with children. Point out the pattern in the song. Then have children add verses and follow the pattern, for example: *The horn on the bus goes beep, beep, beep. Beep, beep, beep*, etc.

Review and Assess

Comprehension

STRATEGY Recognize Text Structure

REFLECT ON THE STRATEGY Remind children that they have learned how to use the way a text is put together, or organized, to help them remember and understand what they read.

Think Aloud Nonfiction texts can be organized in different ways. Some nonfiction books group together things that are alike in some way and tell about each group one at a time.

SKILL Classify and Categorize

Have children recall how the nonfiction **Big Book** *On the Go* is organized.

- First, it tells about ways people can carry things as they **journey** on land. It talks about how people **travel** on foot, on animals, and on bicycles. Then, it discusses some of the vehicles that travel on land. *What are some of these vehicles?*
- The next thing the book tells about are vehicles that travel on tracks. *Which vehicles are in this part?*
- Vehicles that travel on water come next. *Are tugboats or helicopters in this part? What other vehicles travel on water?*
- The last group of vehicles the book describes are ones that travel in the air. *What vehicles travel in the air?*

Reading Across Texts

Remind children that good readers think about how texts are like—or not like—another one. Create a chart to compare and contrast *On the Go* and "Timimoto."

On the Go	Timimoto
expository	folktale
real people, things	fictional journey
ways to travel	make-believe people, things
tells about each group of vehicles one at a time	has a beginning, middle, and end

Objectives

- Use oral vocabulary words *travel, journey, familiar, prepare,* and *relax*
- Determine what words mean from how they are used
- Listen and share information
- Review the strategy and skill
- Compare and contrast texts

Materials

- Big Book: *On the Go*
- Read-Aloud Anthology: "Timimoto," pp. 49–52
- Activity Book, p. 21

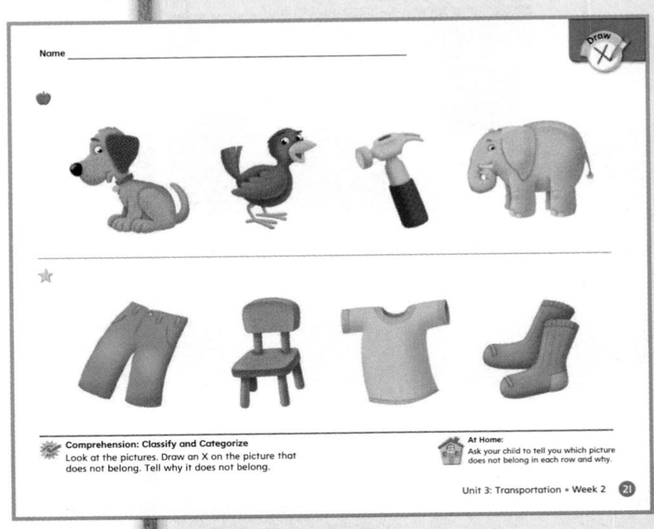

Activity Book, page 21

Objectives

- Review the high-frequency words *a, go, like, see, the*
- Build fluency
- Review sound words

Materials

- High-Frequency Word Cards: *a, go, like, see, the*
- High-Frequency Word Cards; Teacher's Resource Book, pp. 103–110
- Big Book: *On the Go*

Fluency

Connected Text Have children reread this week's **Pre-decodable Readers** with a partner. Circulate, listen in, and note those children who need additional instruction and practice reading this week's decodable and sight words.

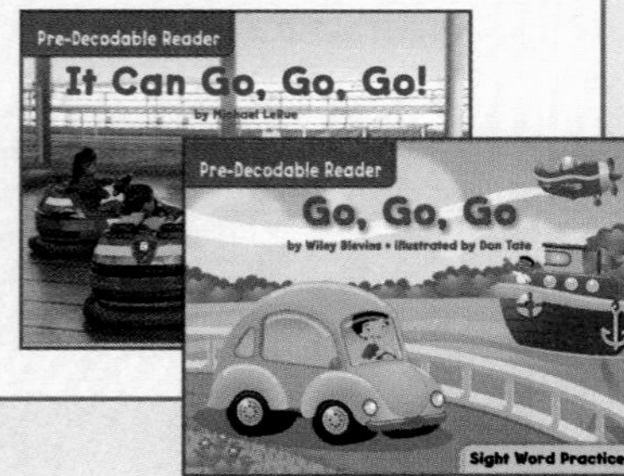

Review and Assess

Vocabulary

High-Frequency Words

Distribute one of the following **High-Frequency Word Cards** to children: **a**, **go**, **like**, **see**, **the**. Say: *When you hear the word that is on your card, stand and hold up your Word Card.*

- *On Saturdays we all* go *shopping.*
- *Sometimes we* see a *movie.*
- *We* like *fishing together every summer.*
- The *weekends are very special.*
- *My family is* a *lot of fun.*

Build Fluency: Word Automaticity

Rapid Naming Display the High-Frequency Word Cards *go, see, a, like*, and *the*. Point quickly to each card, at random, and have children read the word as fast as they can.

go	see	a	like	the

Sound Words

Let's look through On the Go *and imagine what sound words we might hear. I see a woman carrying metal pots.* Clang, clang! *I see a fire engine. How would a siren sound? In what picture might you hear the sound* toot! toot!*?*

TIME TO MOVE!

Ask children to gesture and talk about an action for the following phrase: *We go on a* ______. (Example: *We go on a bike, on a horse, on a plane.*)

Review and Assess

Phonemic Awareness

Phoneme Categorization

Guided Practice

Display the **Photo Cards** for *ink, invitation*, and *teeth*. Repeat with *top, teeth*, and *sock*.

I will say three picture names. Which picture names begin with the same sound? *Ink, invitation, teeth. Ink* and *invitation* begin with the same sound, /i/. *Teeth* does not begin with the /i/ sound. It does not belong.

Practice

Display and name each set of cards: *tiger, top, pen; sock, pumpkin, penguin; saw, insect, seal.*

Children identify the picture name that does not begin with the same sound.

I will show you three cards. Tell me which picture does not belong.

Objective

- Categorize words with the same initial sound

Materials

- Photo Cards: *ink, insect, invitation, pen, penguin, pumpkin, saw, seal, sock, teeth, tiger, top*

Objectives

- Match sounds to letters
- Read decodable and other simple one-syllable words
- Write CVC words

Materials

- Word-Building Cards
- pocket chart
- 5 index cards: *Go, see, the, map,* period mark
- 6 index cards: *We, sit, at, the, mat,* period mark
- Sound Box
- WorkBoard Sound Boxes; Teacher's Resource Book, p. 136
- Activity Book, p. 22

Phonics: /i/
Say the name of each picture. Identify the sound that you hear at the beginning of each picture name. Write the letter below the picture if its name begins with the /i/ sound.

At Home:
Ask your child to name each picture that begins with the same sound as iguana.

22 Unit 3: Transportation • Week 2

Activity Book, page 22

Review and Assess
Phonics

Build Fluency: Sound-Spellings

Rapid Naming Display these **Word-Building Cards**: *a, i, m, p, s, t*. Have children chorally say each sound. Repeat and vary the pace.

Read Words

Apply

Distribute the first set of cards. Have children stand in sequence.

Let's read the sentence together.
Go see the map.

Repeat, using the other set of cards.

Let's read the sentence together.
We sit at the mat.

Dictation

Dictate sounds for children to spell.

Have children write the letters.

Listen as I say a sound. Repeat the sound, then write the letter that stands for the sound.

/a/ /m/ /s/ /p/ /t/ /i/

Then dictate words for children to spell. Model for children how to use the **Sound Box** to segment the word. Have them repeat.

Now let's write some words. I will say a word. I want you to repeat the word, then think about how many sounds are in the word. Use your Sound Box to count the sounds. Then write one letter for each sound you hear.

mat it sit sip map pit
tip tap pat at sat Tim

Write the letters and words on the board for children to self-correct.

Review and Assess

Writing

Independent Writing: Posters

PUBLISH

Explain to children that you will gather their posters to make a class display.

- Brainstorm ideas for a title, such as "Take a Trip."
- Have a few children work on a label for the display. Write the title.
- Help children add their posters to the class bulletin board.

PRESENT

Have children take turns reading their **travel** posters to the class and telling what the pictures show. Ask them to use sound effects to describe their vehicles.

LISTENING, SPEAKING, AND VIEWING

- Remind children to speak clearly and to be good listeners when a classmate is speaking.
- Display children's posters for all to enjoy. Children may wish to add a copy of their work to their Writing Portfolios.

Write About It

Have children draw in their Writer's Notebook. Guide them to draw a picture of someone they would like to visit. Help them label their drawings.

Objective

- Publish and present a piece of writing

Materials

- children's posters from Day 4

5-Day Writing

Posters	
DAY 1	Shared: Lists
DAY 2	Interactive: Posters
DAY 3	Independent: Prewrite and Draft Posters
DAY 4	Independent: Revise and Edit Posters
DAY 5	Independent: Publish and Present

Transitions That Teach

While lining up, have children name things they do to **prepare** for school.

It Can Go Up

Children can draw themselves riding in a vehicle that goes up in the air. Have them write the caption *I can go up*.

ELL

Partners When pairing children to make up sentences, pair English Language Learners with children who are more proficient. Write their sentences, read them together, and point to the high-frequency word *go*.

Approaching Level

Oral Language

Objective Preteach oral vocabulary
Materials • none

THEME WORDS: *travel, journey*

- Tell children the meanings for **travel** and **journey**. *To* travel *is to go from one place to another. Every summer I* travel *to a new country. A* journey *is a trip, usually a long one. This summer my* journey *will take 12 hours by plane.*
- Discuss the words with children. Ask: *Do you like to* travel *by car or by plane? What* journeys *have you taken or would like to take?*
- Have children use the following sentence frames to generate complete sentences using the words: *I would like to travel to ________. I would like to take a journey to ________.*

High-Frequency Words

Objective Preteach high-frequency words
Materials • **High-Frequency Word Cards:** *a, go, like, see, the, we*

PRETEACH WORD: *go*

- Display the **High-Frequency Word Card** for **go**.
- **Read** Point to and say the word *go. This is the word* go. *It means "to move along." I go to the store.*
- **Spell** *The word* go *is spelled* g-o. Have children read and spell *go*.
- **Write** Finally, have children write the word *go*.
- Have children work with a partner to make up sentences using the word *go*. Ask them to talk about places they travel to in their neighborhood and beyond.

HIGH-FREQUENCY WORDS REVIEW Tier 2

- Display the High-Frequency Word Cards **see**, **a**, **like**, **the**, and **we** from the previous three units.
- Display one card at a time as children chorally read and spell the word. Mix and repeat. Note words children need to review.

Approaching Level

Phonemic Awareness

Objective Identify initial sound /i/

Materials
- **Photo Cards:** *ink, inch, inchworm, insect, invitation*
- **Sound-Spelling Card:** *Insect*

PHONEME ISOLATION

Model

- Display the **Photo Card** for *inch. This is an inch. Listen for the beginning sound in* inch: */iiinnnch/.* Inch *begins with /i/.*
- Display the *Insect* **Sound-Spelling Card**. Point to the articulation picture. *See how I relax my face and let the front part of my tongue rise in my mouth. My lips are slightly apart.*

Guided Practice/Practice

- Display the Photo Cards. Have children take turns selecting a picture, naming it, and saying the initial sound of the picture name: *This is an* ________. ________ *begins with /i/.*

Phonics

Objective Recognize words that begin with /i/*i*

Materials
- **Sound-Spelling Card:** *Insect*
- **Word-Building Cards**
- **Photo Cards:** *inch, inchworm, insect, invitation*

PRETEACH: RECOGNIZE /i/*i*

Model

- Display the Photo Card for *inch* and the *Insect* Sound-Spelling Card. *The name of this letter is* i. I *stands for the /i/ sound you hear at the beginning of* inch. *I will place an* i *on the picture of the inch because* inch *begins with /i/. Listen: /iiinnnch/.* Repeat with *insect*.

Guided Practice/Practice

- Display the Photo Cards on a table. Say: *This is the picture of an* invitation. *What sound do you hear at the beginning of* invitation? *What letter stands for /i/? Let's place an* i *on the invitation because* invitation *begins with /i/.* Repeat with the remaining Photo Cards. Guide children to trace the letter *i* on their **Word-Building Cards**.
- For additional practice, share other words that begin with initial /i/ (*if, it, is, illustration, inside, important, Internet*). Hold the *i* card up while children repeat each word chorally.

SOUND-SPELLINGS REVIEW

Tier 2

Display Word-Building Cards *a, m, p, s,* and *t,* one at a time. Have children chorally say the sound. Repeat and vary the pace.

Corrective Feedback

Mnemonic Display the *Insect* Sound-Spelling Card. Say: *This is the* Insect *Sound-Spelling Card. The sound is /i/. The /i/ sound is spelled with the letter* i. *Say /i/ with me: /iii/. This is the sound at the beginning of* insect. *What is the letter? What is the sound? What word begins with /i/?* Insect *is the word we can use to remember the sound for* i, */i/.*

ELL

Extra Practice Provide additional practice in recognizing and naming letters for children whose native languages do not use the symbols of the Latin alphabet.

On Level

High-Frequency Words

Objective Review high-frequency words *go, see, a, like,* and *the*

Materials • **High-Frequency Word Cards:** *a, go, like, see, the*

REVIEW: *go*

- Display the **High-Frequency Word Card** for **go**.
- **Read** Point to and say the word *go. This is the word* go. *It means "to move along." We go to the grocery store on Sundays.*
- **Spell** *The word* go *is spelled* g-o. Have children read and spell *go.*
- **Write** Finally, have children write the word *go.*
- Repeat with **see**, **a**, **like**, and **the**.

- Have partners make up questions and answers using the words *see, a, like,* and *the*. Partners will answer questions using the word. *What can you see outside? I see a tree.*

Phonemic Awareness/Phonics

Objective Blend sounds to form words and review /i/*i*, /t/*t*, and /p/*p*

Materials • **Word-Building Cards** • pocket chart

PHONEME BLENDING

Model

- Tell children that you will say the sounds in a word. Say: */i/ /n/ /ch/. Now listen as I blend the sounds together to say the word: /iiinnnch/,* inch. *The word is* inch. Repeat with *mix.*

Practice

- Say the sounds in the words below and have children blend the sounds and say each word.

/s/ /i/ /t/	/i/ /n/	/s/ /i/ /ks/	/t/ /i/ /p/
/p/ /i/ /t/	/i/ /t/	/s/ /i/ /p/	/m/ /i/ /t/

REVIEW /i/*i*, /t/*t*, /p/*p*

- Display **Word-Building Card** *i. The name of this letter is* i. I *stands for the /i/ sound we hear at the beginning of* insect. *What is the sound?* (/i/) *I'll hold up the* i *card because* insect *begins with /i/.* Repeat with *t* and *p.*
- Distribute Word-Building Cards *t, p,* and *i* to children. Say the following words, one at a time: *pan, ten, include, illustrate, pony, pen,* and *ton.* Have children hold up the respective Word-Building Card and say /i/ for words that begin with *i,* /t/ for words that begin with *t,* and /p/ for words that begin with *p.*

ELL

Sound-Letter Relationships Provide additional practice in pronouncing the initial /i/, /t/, /p/ sounds and naming the corresponding letters as children point to them.

Beyond Level

High-Frequency Words/Vocabulary

Objectives Review high-frequency words; introduce *down* and *many*

Materials • none

ACCELERATE

Write *down* and *many* on the board.

- **Read** Point to and say the word *down. This is the word* down. *It means "toward or at a lower position." The sun goes down at night.*
- **Spell** *Down is spelled* d-o-w-n. Have them read and spell *down.*
- **Write** Finally, have children write the word *down.*
- Repeat the routine with *many.*
- Have children work with a partner to make up oral sentences using the words *down* and *many.*

EXPAND ORAL VOCABULARY

Gifted Talented

- **Synonyms** Review the meaning of the oral vocabulary word *journey* with children. Then explain that a *synonym* is a word that means the same thing as another word.
- Say: *A* synonym *for the word* journey *is* trip. *When you go away someplace, you take a* trip. *Some* trips, *like going to the grocery store, are short. Other* trips, *like visiting another country, are long. These long* trips *are sometimes called* journeys.

- Have children take turns using the new word *trip* in a sentence. Then tell partners to discuss trips they would like to take.

Phonics

Objectives Categorize words with medial /i/; introduce /th/*th* and /sh/*sh*

Materials • **Word-Building Cards** • **Puppet** • pocket chart

ENRICH

- *Happy will say three words: /biiig/, /piiit/, /kaaat/. I hear /i/ in the middle of* big *and* pit. *I hear /a/ in the middle of* cat. Cat *does not belong.* Say groups of words and have children identify which word does not belong: *fig, bed, kit; dog, miss, sit; big, pull, sick.*
- Display **Word-Building Cards** *sh.* Say: *When the letters* s *and* h *appear together, they stand for the /sh/ sound at the beginning of* shell. Ask children to say /sh/, *shell, show,* and *she* with you.
- Repeat with *th,* using the words *thick, thin,* and *thank* for the voiceless /th/ and *the, this,* and *then* for the voiced /th/.

ELL

Partners When partners make up sentences with the high-frequency words, pair English Language Learners with children who are more proficient. Write their sentences, read them together, and point to the high-frequency words.

Puppet

ELL ENGLISH LANGUAGE LEARNERS

Oral Language Warm-Up

Content Objective Learn theme vocabulary
Language Objective Repeat and sing song to demonstrate understanding
Materials • **Listening Library Audio CD**

BUILD BACKGROUND KNOWLEDGE

All Language Levels

- Continue developing vocabulary around the unit theme "Transportation" using the song "Take a Trip." Display a picture of a vehicle with wheels. Teach the word *wheels* as you point to the wheels on the vehicle. Have children repeat the word.
- Play "Take a Trip" on the **Listening Library Audio CD**. Display pictures of some of the vehicles named in the song and have children tell if each does or does not have wheels.
- Then teach children the rhythm of the song by playing the song several times and having them clap to the rhythm. Emphasize the key words that name vehicles, such as *bus, train,* and *car.*
- Play the song several times until children begin to correctly repeat the song and sing along.
- Ask children to tell about vehicles they have been in. Build on their responses to model speaking in complete sentences. For example: *You ride in a car. The car has wheels called tires.*

Academic Language

Language Objective Use academic language in classroom conversations

All Language Levels

- This week's academic words are **boldfaced** throughout the lesson. Define the word in context and provide a clear example from the selection. Then ask children to generate an example or a word with a similar meaning.

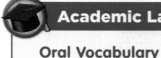

Academic Language Used in Whole Group Instruction

Oral Vocabulary Words	Vocabulary and Grammar Concepts	Strategy and Skill Words
familiar	**sound words**	**recognize**
journey	**action words**	**text structure**
prepare		**classify**
relax		**categorize**
travel		**action**

Cognates

Help children identify similarities and differences in pronunciation and spelling between English words and Spanish cognates:

prepare	*preparar*
recognize	*reconocer*
structure	*estructura*
classify	*clasificar*
prediction	*predicción*
categorize	*categorizar*
action	*acción*

ELL ENGLISH LANGUAGE LEARNERS

Vocabulary

Language Objective Demonstrate understanding and use of key words by describing traveling to places

Materials • **Visual Vocabulary Resources**

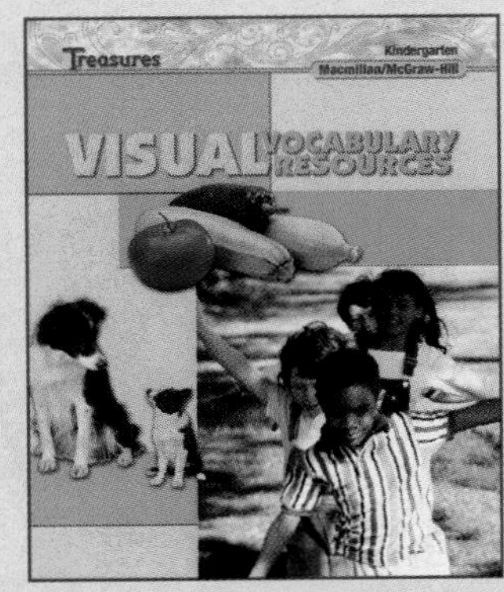

Visual Vocabulary Resources

PRETEACH KEY VOCABULARY

All Language Levels

Use the **Visual Vocabulary Resources** to preteach the weekly oral vocabulary words *familiar, journey, prepare, relax,* and *travel*. Focus on one or two words per day. Use the following routine that appears in detail on the cards.

- Define the word in English and provide the example given.
- Define the word in Spanish, if appropriate, and indicate if the word is a cognate.
- Display the picture and explain how it illustrates or demonstrates the word. Engage children in structured partner-talk about the image, using the key word.
- Ask children to chorally say the word three times.
- Point out any known sound-spellings or focus on a key aspect of phonemic awareness related to the word.

PRETEACH FUNCTION WORDS AND PHRASES

All Language Levels

Use the Visual Vocabulary Resources to preteach the function phrases *on foot* and *by train*. Focus on one phrase per day. Use the detailed routine on the cards.

- Define the phrase in English and, if appropriate, in Spanish. Point out if the phrase is a cognate.
- Refer to the picture and engage children in talk about the phrase. For example, children will partner-talk using sentence frames, or they will listen to sentences and replace a word or phrase with the new function phrase.
- Ask children to chorally repeat the phrase three times.

TEACH BASIC WORDS

Beginning/Intermediate

Use the Visual Vocabulary Resources to teach the basic words *boat, jet, trolley, rocket, wagon,* and *helicopter.* Teach these "traveling distances" words using the routine provided on the card.

Approaching Level

High-Frequency Words

Objective Reteach high-frequency words

Materials
- **High-Frequency Word Cards:** *a, go, like, see, the, we*
- **Sound-Spelling WorkBoards**

RETEACH WORDS: *go*

Tier 2

- Distribute a **WorkBoard** to each child. Then display the **High-Frequency Word Card** for **go**.
- Use the **Read/Spell/Write** routine to reteach the word. Point to and say the word. *This is the word* go. *It means "to move along." I go to school.* Go *is spelled* g-o. Have children read and spell *go.* Then have them write the word on their WorkBoards.
- Have children work with a partner to make up sentences using the word *go.* Ask them to talk about they ways they go to school.

CUMULATIVE REVIEW

Display the High-Frequency Word Cards **see**, **a**, **like**, **the**, and **we** from the previous three units. Display one card at a time as children chorally read and spell the word. Mix and repeat. Note words children need to review.

Pre-decodable Reader

Objective Preteach Pre-decodable Reader *Go, Go, Go*

Materials
- **Pre-decodable Reader:** *Go, Go, Go*

PRETEACH *Go, Go, Go*

- Display the cover of the book and read the title. Open to the title page and point out the title. *Let's read the title together.* Have children sound out each word as you run your finger under it. *What vehicles help you go where you need to go? What do you think you will read about in this book?*
- Page through the book. Ask children what they see in each picture. Point out each rebus. Ask children to find the words *a* and *can.*
- Read the book chorally with children. Have them point to each word or rebus as they read it. Provide corrective feedback as needed.
- Ask children to use *a* and *can* to talk about the pictures. *A different vehicle can go on each page.*
- After reading, ask children to recall things they read about.

ELL

Partners When pairing children to make up sentences, pair English Language Learners with children who are more proficient. Write their sentences, read them together, and point out the high-frequency word *go.*

Pre-decodable Reader

Extend *Go, Go, Go*

Have children write an additional page for *Go, Go, Go* by drawing a picture of another vehicle that "goes." Below their pictures have them complete this sentence with a rebus: *A* __________ *can go.*

Approaching Level

Phonemic Awareness

Objective Identify and blend with initial /i/

Materials • **Puppet**

PHONEME BLENDING

Tier 2

Model

- *Listen as Happy says the sounds for* pit*: /p/ /i/ /t/. Now Happy will blend the sounds: /piiit/, /pit/,* pit. *Happy blended /p/ /i/ /t/ together to say the word* pit. *Listen again. I'll do another word.* Repeat the blending with the word *it*: /i/ /t/.

Guided Practice/Practice

- Have Happy say /f/ /i/ /t/. Ask children to repeat. *Now you blend the sounds and say the word with Happy: /fffiiit/,* fit. Repeat with the following:

/t/ /i/ /n/	/h/ /i/ /t/	/i/ /n/
/m/ /i/ /t/	/i/ /z/	/s/ /i/ /t/

Puppet

Corrective Feedback

Blending Error: *When I see the word* pit, *I blend sounds /p/ /i/ /t/. Then I say the word fast. Listen again: /p/ /i/ /t/, /piiit/,* pit. Continue with the other words and then repeat *pit.*

Phonics

Objective Reinforce letter-sound correspondence for /i/*i*

Materials • **Sound-Spelling Card:** *Insect* • **Sound-Spelling WorkBoards** • **Word-Building Cards**

RECOGNIZE /i/*i*

Model

- Display the *Insect* **Sound-Spelling Card**. *The letter* i *stands for the /i/ sound as in* insect. *What is this letter? What sound does it stand for?* Repeat with *inch.*
- Trace *i* on a **Word-Building Card**. *I will say a sentence. We will trace* i *on the cards when we hear /i/.* Say: *Izzy the insect is one inch long.*

Guided Practice/Practice

- Distribute a **WorkBoard** to each child. Say: *in, top, instant, ill, moon, itself, pot, inch.* Children write *i* on their **WorkBoard** when they hear a word that begins with /i/. Guide them with the first two words.

CUMULATIVE REVIEW

Display Word-Building Cards for *a, i, m, p, s,* and *t,* one at a time. Have children chorally say the sound. Repeat and vary the pace.

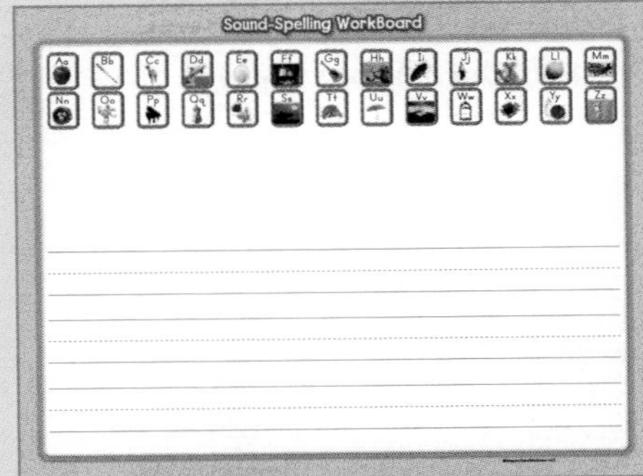

Sound-Spelling WorkBoard

Corrective Feedback

Linguistic Differences
When the /i/ and /e/ sounds appear before the consonants *m* or *n* in words, such as *pen/pin* and *him/hem*, many speakers of African American Vernacular English won't pronounce or hear the difference. Focus on articulation, such as mouth position for each vowel sound, during the lesson.

Go!

Have children draw themselves riding their favorite vehicle. Have them write their names in the caption *Go* __________ *go!*

Pre-decodable Reader

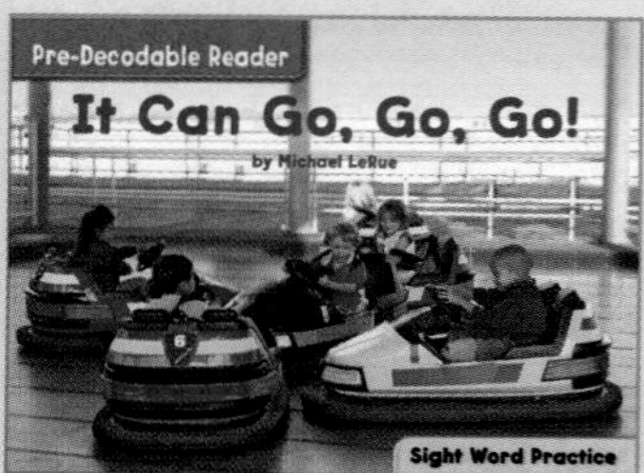

Pre-decodable Reader

Write Captions

Have children cut out pictures of vehicles from old magazines. Help children write captions, such as: *A bike can go.*

On Level

Pre-decodable Reader

Objective Reread *Go, Go, Go* to develop fluency

Materials • **Pre-decodable Reader:** *Go, Go, Go; It Can Go, Go, Go!*

REREAD FOR FLUENCY

- Ask children to look back at the illustrations in *Go, Go, Go*. Have them use their own words to retell what the book was about.
- Have children reread a page or two from *Go, Go, Go*. Work with them to read with accuracy and expression. Model reading a page. Point out how you read the exclamations with more emotion than the rest of the sentences: *When I read, "Go car go!" I said that sentence with more excitement. I wanted to show my excitement about the car going so fast.*
- Provide time to listen as children read their page(s). Comment on their accuracy and expression and provide corrective feedback by modeling proper fluency.
- Use the same routine for **Pre-decodable Reader** *It Can Go, Go, Go!* on Day 4.

Beyond Level

Pre-decodable Reader

Objective Reread *Go, Go, Go* to reinforce fluency

Materials • **Pre-decodable Readers:** *Go, Go, Go; It Can Go, Go, Go!*

REREAD FOR FLUENCY

- Have children reread *Go, Go, Go* and *It Can Go, Go, Go!*
- Provide time to listen as children read. Provide corrective feedback by modeling proper fluency.

INNOVATE

- For *Go, Go, Go,* have children add pages to the book by drawing pictures of other things that can go, go, go: *A bike can go. Go bike go!* Help them write sentence captions for their drawings.
- For *It Can Go, Go, Go!*, tell children to think of an animal that can go fast or slow. Have them draw a picture and write a sentence that can go with the picture. For example: *A dog can go fast!*

ELL ENGLISH LANGUAGE LEARNERS

Access to Core Content

Content Objective Develop listening comprehension
Language Objective Discuss text using key words and sentence frames
Materials • **ELL Resource Book,** pp. 72–79

PRETEACH BIG BOOK/TRADE BOOK

All Language Levels

Use the Interactive Question-Response Guide on **ELL Resource Book** pages 72–79 to introduce children to *On the Go*. Preteach half of the selection on Day 1 and half on Day 2.

- Use the prompts provided in the guide to develop meaning and vocabulary. Use the partner-talk and whole-class responses to engage children and increase student talk.
- When completed, revisit the selection and prompt children to talk about the photos. Provide sentence starters as needed and build on children's responses to develop language.

ELL Resource Book

Big Book

Beginning

Use Visuals During the Interactive Reading, select several pictures. Describe them and have children summarize what you said.

Intermediate

Summarize During the Interactive Reading, select a few lines of text. After you read them and explain them, have children summarize the text.

Advanced

Expand During the Interactive Reading, select a larger portion of text. After you read it and explain it, have children summarize the text.

Approaching Level

High-Frequency Words

Objective Recognize high-frequency words *a, go, like, see*

Materials
- **High-Frequency Word Cards:** *a, go, like, see*
- **Word-Building Cards**

REVIEW WORDS: *a, go, like, see*

- Display the **High-Frequency Word Card** for **go**. Say the word and have children repeat it. Point to each letter and have children name it.
- Distribute **Word-Building Cards** *g, o*. Model putting the letters together to form the word *go*. Then have children form *go*.
- Repeat the above routines with the words **a**, **like**, and **see**.
- Ask a question with *see*: *What things do you see?* Have children use *see* to answer the question. Continue with *a, go,* and *like*.

CUMULATIVE REVIEW

Display the High-Frequency Word Cards for *a, go, like,* and *see,* one card at a time, as children chorally read and spell the word. Mix and repeat. Note words children need to review.

Phonemic Awareness

Objective Identify initial and medial /i/*i*

Materials
- **Photo Cards:** *chin, inch, inchworm, insect, mix, pig, six*
- **Sound Boxes** • markers
- **WorkBoard Sound Boxes; Teacher's Resource Book,** p. 136

PHONEME ISOLATION

Tier 2

Model

- Display **Sound Boxes** and the **Photo Card** for *inch. Listen for the beginning sound in* inch. Inch *begins with /i/. I'll place a marker in the first box to show that I hear /i/ at the beginning of* inch.
- Display the Photo Card for *six. Listen for the middle sound in* six, */sssiiiks/,* six. Six *has /i/ in the middle. I'll place a marker in the middle box to show that I hear /i/ in the middle of* six.

Guided Practice/Practice

- Distribute Sound Boxes and markers. Display the Photo Cards. Children take turns selecting a picture and naming it. Have them listen for /i/ and place the marker in the first or middle box as they say: *This is a(n) ________. I hear /i/ at the ________ of ________.*
- Repeat with each picture name. Provide guidance as needed.

ELL

Extra Practice During the Cumulative Review, pair children at different levels of proficiency and have partners take turns reading and spelling the high-frequency words to each other.

Approaching Level

Phonics

Objectives Review blending medial /i/; build fluency

Materials • **Word-Building Cards** • pocket chart

REVIEW SKILLS: BLEND SOUNDS

Tier 2

Model

- Place **Word-Building Card** *s* in the pocket chart. *The name of this letter is* s. *The letter* s *stands for the /s/ sound. Say /s/. What is the letter? What is the sound?*
- Place *i* next to *s*. *The name of this letter is* i. *The letter* i *stands for /i/. Say /i/. What is the letter? What is the sound?* Repeat with *t*.
- Move your hand from left to right below the letters. *Now listen as I blend the three sounds together: /sssiiit/,* sit. *What's the word? Let's blend the word together: /s/ /i/ /t/, /sssiiit/,* sit.

Guided Practice/Practice

- Give the *i, s,* and *t* cards to children. Each child says the sound for the letter on his or her card: /s/ /i/ /t/. Have children blend the sounds to say the word *sit*. Give out the appropriate cards and repeat with *sip, pit,* and *tip*.

Build Fluency

- Have children blend the sounds to say *sit, sip, pit,* and *tip* as quickly as they can.

Pre-decodable Reader

Objective Preteach Pre-decodable Reader *It Can Go, Go, Go!*

Materials • **Pre-decodable Reader:** *It Can Go, Go, Go!*

PRETEACH *It Can Go, Go, Go!*

- Display the book cover and read the title. Show the title page and point out the title. *Let's read the title together.* Run your finger under the words as you read the title. *Look at the picture. What can go? What else do you think can go?*
- Page through the book. Ask children what they see in each picture. Point out and name each rebus. Ask children to find the words *go, a, can, I, like, see,* and *the.*
- Read the book chorally with children. Have them point to each word or rebus as they read it. Provide corrective feedback.
- Ask children to use *can* and *go* to talk about the pictures. *The boat can go, go, go.*
- After reading, ask children to recall things they read about.

Corrective Feedback

Association Error If children have difficulty identifying initial and medial /i/, say: *My turn: /sssiiit/,* sit. *I hear the /i/ sound in the middle of* sit: */sssiiit/. What is the sound? What is the letter? Let's start over.* Repeat the word *sit* for children to identify the position of /i/.

Pre-decodable Reader

Draw and Go!

Have children draw a vehicle that goes on the ground, on the water, or in the air. Have children label their pictures *It can go!*

On Level

Phonics

Objective Blend and write words with /i/*i*, /t/*t*, and /p/*p*

Materials • **Word-Building Cards** • pocket chart • **Sound-Spelling WorkBoards**

REVIEW: /i/*i*, /t/*t*, /p/*p*

- Display **Word-Building Card** *i. The name of this letter is* i. *I stands for the /i/ sound we hear at the beginning of* insect. *What is the sound?* Repeat with *t* and *p*.
- **Blend Words** Place Word-Building Cards *t, i,* and *p* in the pocket chart. Point to each letter for children to identify.
- Move your hand from left to right below the letters as you blend the word. *Now listen as I blend the sounds together: /tiiip/,* tip. *What is the word?*
- Have children write *t, i, p* several times on their **WorkBoards** as they say /t/, /i/, /p/.
- Repeat with the words *sit* and *pit*.

Sound-Spelling WorkBoard

Beyond Level

Phonics

Objectives Review /th/*th* and /sh/*sh;* blend and read words

Materials • **Word-Building Cards** • **Sound-Spelling WorkBoards** • pocket chart

ACCELERATE

- Display Word-Building Cards *sh*. Say: *When the letters* s *and* h *are together, they stand for the /sh/ sound at the end of* fresh. Repeat with both voiceless and voiced *th* using *bath* and *smooth*.
- Display Word-Building Cards for *d, i, s, h*. Point to each letter for children to identify. Say: *I can blend the sounds for these letters to read the word. Listen: /d/ /i/ /sh/, /diiish/,* dish. *The word is* dish. Guide children in blending the sounds and reading *dish*.
- Help children blend and read the following words: *fish, wish, dish, shin, thin, fin, pin, think, thank, this, that, math, bathe.* Write words in the WorkBoard boxes and guide in blending the sounds to read the words.

Corrective Feedback

Letter-Sound Discrimination If children say /ch/ instead of /sh/, point to the letters *sh*. Say: *The letters* s *and* h *together stand for /sh/. Listen to the difference: /ch/, /sh/. Say /sh/ with me. Now let's sound out the words again.* Then sound out *ship* /shiiip/ *and shop* /shooop/.

ELL ENGLISH LANGUAGE LEARNERS

Access to Core Content

Content Objective Develop listening comprehension
Language Objective Discuss text using key words and sentence frames
Materials • **ELL Resource Book,** pp. 80–81

PRETEACH BIG BOOK OF EXPLORATIONS

All Language Levels

Use the Interactive Question-Response Guide on **ELL Resource Book** pages 80–81 to preview the **Big Book of Explorations** selections "Riding the Subway Train" and "My Bike." Preteach half of the selection on Day 3 and half on Day 4.

Big Book of Explorations

Grammar

Content Objective Identify action words
Language Objective Speak in complete sentences, using sentence frames
Materials • **Listening Library Audio CD** • **Photo Cards**

ACTION WORDS (VERBS)

All Language Levels

- Review verbs. Tell children that verbs are action words. Say: *The wheels go round.* Have children repeat and act out the action. Ask children to name and act out other actions they can do.
- Play "The Wheels on the Bus" from the **Listening Library Audio CD**. Tell children to listen for action words. Remind them that action words tell about what someone or something does.
- Point out the action words *go, says,* and *move*. Reread the words in phrases that children can act out, such as *go round, says move on back*. Display the **Photo Cards** for *kite, helicopter, boat,* and *car*. Point to the photo and have children name it.

The Wheels on the Bus

The wheels on the bus go round and round,
Round and round, round and round.
The wheels on the bus go round and round.
All through the town.
The driver on the bus says move on back!
Move on back! Move on back!
The driver on the bus says move on back!
All through the town.

PEER DISCUSSION STARTERS

All Language Levels

- Distribute Photo Cards of words that name people, animals, or things that can move, such as *helicopter, boat, tiger, boy,* and *girl*.
- Pair children and have them complete the sentence frame *This is a* __________. Ask them to expand on their sentences by providing as many details as they can.

Puppet

Approaching Level

Phonemic Awareness

Objective Blend sounds to form words with /i/*i*

Materials • **Puppet** • **Photo Cards:** *inch, ink, pig, six* • pocket chart

PHONEME BLENDING

Tier 2

Model

- Hold up the **Puppet**. Display the **Photo Card** for *pig*. Say: *Happy is going to say the sounds in a word: /p/ /i/ /g/. Happy can blend these sounds together: /piiig/. Now you can say the sounds: /p/ /i/ /g/. Say the word with Happy:* pig.

Guided Practice/Practice

- Display the Photo Cards in a pocket chart. Have children name each card with you.
- *Happy will say the sounds in another word: /s/ /i/ /ks/. I will blend the sounds with Happy: /sssiiiks/,* six. Point to the picture for *six* and say the word again. I hear /i/ in the middle of *six*.

Phonics

Objective Blend /i/*i*, /t/*t*, /p/*p* to read words

Materials • **Word-Building Cards** • pocket chart

REVIEW: BLEND SOUNDS

Tier 2

Model

- Place **Word-Building Cards** *i* and *t* in the pocket chart. Point to the letter *i. This is the letter* i. *I can stand for the sound /i/: /iii/.* Point to the letter *t* and repeat.
- Walk by the word and say the sound each letter stands for: /i/ /t/. *Listen as I blend the sounds together: /iiit/,* it.

Guided Practice/Practice

- **Blend Words** Add the Word-Building Card for *p* to the pocket chart to build the word *pit*. Point to each letter and have children say the letter name and the sound it stands for. Guide them as they blend the sounds together to say the word: */p/ /i/ /t/, /piiit/,* pit. Repeat with *tip*.

Corrective Feedback

Sound Error If children miss making the letter-sound correspondence, say: *My turn:* mix, */mmmiiiks/. I hear /i/ in the middle of* mix, */mmmiiiks/. I'll hold up my* i *card because I hear /i/ in the middle of /mmmiiiks/. What is the sound? What letter stands for that sound? Let's start again.*

ELL

Extra Practice Provide additional practice in pronouncing and blending sounds that do not transfer directly to the native language of some children, such as the short vowel /i/.

Approaching Level

Leveled Reader Lesson 1

Objective Read *Pig's Trip* to apply skills and strategies

Materials • **Leveled Reader:** *Pig's Trip*

BEFORE READING

- **Preview** Read the title and the names of the author and illustrator. Ask children to name the book title, author, or illustrator in a full sentence. For example: *The author of this book is Sarah Newman.* Ask: *What animal do you see on the cover? What things are around her? Where is she? What is she doing? Have you ever gone on a trip?* Explain to children that using their background knowledge, such as knowledge about traveling, helps them to monitor and adjust their understanding of the story. *What do you think this book is about?* Open and page through the book. Name unfamiliar items and identify the rebus.
- **Model Concepts About Print** Demonstrate book handling. *I hold the book so that the cover is on the front and the words are not upside down. I open the book by turning the front cover. Then I turn each page after I read it. When I am finished and I close the book, I see the back cover of the book.*
- **Review High-Frequency Words** Write **we**, **see**, **the**, and **go** on chart paper. Have children find each word in the book and point to the word as they read it.
- **Set a Purpose for Reading** *Let's find out how Pig gets around.*

DURING READING

- Have children turn to page 2 and begin by whisper-reading the first two pages.
- Remind children to look for the new high-frequency word and to use the rebus picture and illustrations.
- Monitor children's reading and provide help. Stop during the reading and ask open-ended questions to facilitate discussion, such as: *Why does Pig have to sit so much? What vehicles does Pig ride in?*

AFTER READING

- Ask children about words they had trouble reading and to share strategies they used to figure them out. Reinforce good behaviors.
- **Retell** Ask children to retell the story. Have them share their travel experiences. *Have you ever had to wait for a train, bus, or plane? Where did you wait? What did you do while you waited? Was it easy or difficult to wait? Why?*

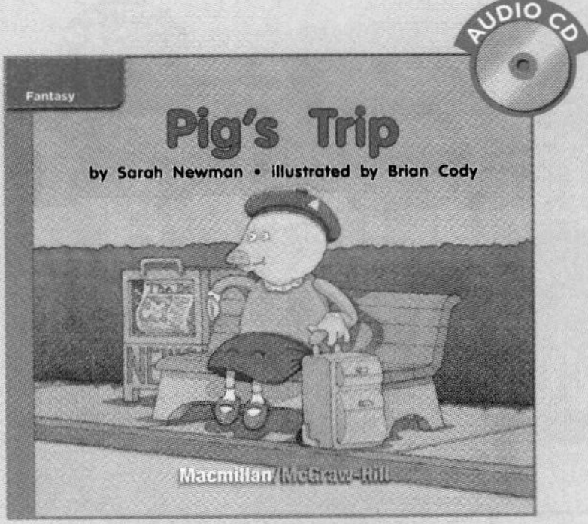

Leveled Reader

AUDIO CD

Use the **Leveled Reader Audio CD** for fluency building *after* children read the book with your support during Small Group time.

Draw a Vehicle

Have children draw pictures of a vehicle from the story that they would like to ride. Help them write about their pictures.

Leveled Reader

ELL

Retell Use the Interactive Question-Response Guide Technique to help English Language Learners understand *Pigs On Wheels*. As you read, make meaning clear by pointing to pictures, demonstrating word meaning, paraphrasing text, and asking children questions.

Draw the Wolf

Have children draw the wolf riding in some kind of vehicle. The vehicle can be the same as or different from those in the book. Have children write *Go!* below their pictures, display them, and tell where the wolf is going.

On Level

Leveled Reader Lesson 1

Objective Read *Pigs on Wheels* to apply skills and strategies

Materials • **Leveled Reader:** *Pigs on Wheels*

BEFORE READING

- **Preview** Read the title and the author's and illustrator's names. *What do you see on the cover? Who is behind the truck? What is shown on the cover that has wheels? What other vehicles have wheels?* Explain to children that using their background knowledge, such as knowledge about vehicles, helps them to monitor and adjust their understanding of the story. *What do you think this story is about?* Turn to the title page and point out that it also has the title and the names of the author and illustrator.
- **Model Concepts About Print** Demonstrate book handling. Guide them as they follow along with their books. Display pages 2–3. *When I read the words on the page, I start at the left and read from left to right. I start at the top of the page and read to the bottom. I run my finger below the words as I read them.*
- **Review High-Frequency Words** Write **I**, **see**, **the**, and **go**. Read the words aloud. Have children name the letters in each word. Have children find each word in the book. Ask them to point to and read the word.
- **Page Through the Book** Name unfamiliar items and terms, and identify the rebus pictures.
- **Set a Purpose for Reading** *Let's find out how the pigs go places.*

DURING READING

- Remind children to use the rebuses and illustrations to gain information. Tell them to look for the high-frequency words *I, see, the,* and *go.* Show children how to self-correct if a word doesn't make sense in a sentence. *On page 6, I see the wolf getting into the pig's car. I wondered if he is friends with the pigs. When I read on page 8 that the pigs say, "Go, Wolf!" I realized that they are not friends. The pigs want the wolf to go away.*
- Monitor children's reading and provide help as needed.

AFTER READING

- Have children identify words they had trouble reading and share strategies they used to figure them out.
- Ask children to retell the story and to share personal responses. *Did the story remind you of other stories you have read about pigs? What happens in those stories?*

Beyond Level

Leveled Reader Lesson 1

Objective Read *Chip Likes Nuts* to apply skills and strategies

Materials • **Leveled Reader:** *Chip Likes Nuts*

BEFORE READING

- **Preview** Point to and read the title and the names of the author and illustrator. *The illustrator of this book is Nicole Rutten. Say it with me: The illustrator of this book is Nicole Rutten.*
- *What do you see on the cover? What kind of animal is this? What do you know about these animals?* Explain to children that using their background knowledge, such as knowledge about animals, helps them to monitor and adjust their understanding of the story. *Where is this chipmunk? What is the chipmunk doing? What do you think the story is about?* Page through the book with children and pause to name unfamiliar items.
- **Introduce Story Words** Point to the word *chipmunk* on page 2. Read the sentence. Have children use the picture to explain what a chipmunk is. Have them describe the chipmunk.
- **Set a Purpose for Reading** *Let's find out how Chip uses wheels.*

DURING READING

- Remind children that when they come to an unfamiliar word, they can look for familiar chunks in the word, break the word into syllables and sound out each part, or think about what the word might mean.
- Monitor children's reading and provide help as needed.

AFTER READING

- Ask children to point out words they had trouble reading and to share the strategies they used to figure them out.
- Tell children to retell the story and to share personal responses. *What things on wheels have you seen people use to carry things?*

Gifted and Talented

- **Synthesize** *Chip gathers a lot of nuts. What might happen if Chip found even more nuts to collect?*

- Have children work in pairs to research foods eaten by other plant-eating animals, such as deer, mice, or rabbits. Tell children to use the information to invent a food-gathering machine.
- **Model** Draw a simple sketch of a machine that Chip could use for collecting and storing nuts. Tell children they will draw, label, and write a description of a new machine that could help Chip or another animal gather food.

Leveled Reader

Draw Chip

Have children draw pictures of Chip collecting nuts. Ask children to write sentences about their pictures.

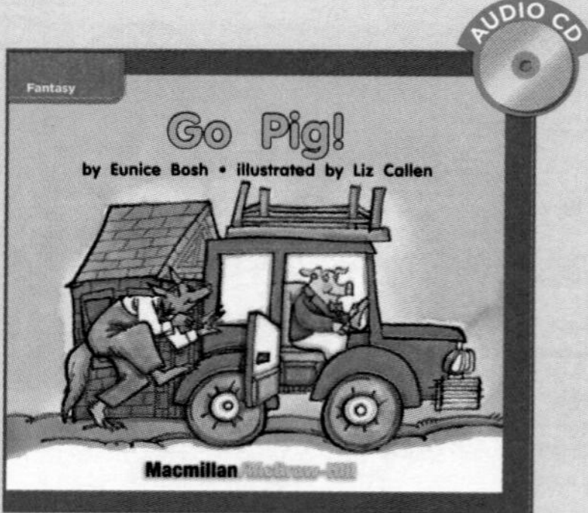

Leveled Reader

Vocabulary

Preteach Vocabulary Use the routine in the **Visual Vocabulary Resources**, pages 315–316, to preteach the ELL Vocabulary listed on the inside front cover of the Leveled Reader.

ELL ENGLISH LANGUAGE LEARNERS

Leveled Reader Library

Leveled Reader

Content Objective Read to apply skills and strategies

Language Objective Retell information using complete sentences

Materials • **Leveled Reader:** *Go Pig!*

BEFORE READING

All Language Levels

- **Preview** Read the title *Go Pig!* Ask: *What's the title? Say it again.* Repeat with the author's name. Point to the cover illustration and say: *I see a pig in a car. The car has big wheels.* Point to the pig, car, and wheels as you name each. *The pig is sitting in a car. A wolf is sneaking up behind him. Now turn to a partner and tell about this picture.*
- **Page Through the Book** Use simple language to tell about the photo on each page. Immediately follow up with questions, such as: *Is this a car? Is the pig sitting or standing?*
- **Review Skills** Use the inside front cover to review the phonics skill and high-frequency words.
- **Set a Purpose** Say: *Let's read to find out where the pig is going.*

DURING READING

All Language Levels

- Have children whisper-read each page, or use the differentiated suggestions below. Circulate, listen in, and provide corrective feedback, such as modeling how to decode words.
- **Retell** Stop after every two pages and ask children to state what they have learned so far. Reinforce language by restating children's comments when they have difficulty using story-specific words. Provide differentiated sentence frames to support children's responses and engage children in partner-talk where appropriate.

Beginning

Echo-Read Have children echo-read after you.

Check Comprehension Point to pictures and ask questions such as: *Do you see a car? Point to the pig.*

Intermediate

Choral-Read Have children choral-read with you.

Check Comprehension Ask questions/prompts such as: *What is the pig doing in this picture? Where is the wolf?*

Advanced

Choral-Read Have children choral-read.

Check Comprehension Ask: *How many pigs do you see? Where is the pig going? Why? What is the wolf doing?*

ELL ENGLISH LANGUAGE LEARNERS

AFTER READING

All Language Levels

Book Talk Children will work with peers of varying language abilities to discuss their books for this week. Display the four **Leveled Readers** read this week: *Chip Likes Nuts* (Beyond Level), *Pigs on Wheels* (On Level), *Pig's Trip* (Approaching Level), and *Go Pig!* (English Language Learners).

Ask the questions and provide the prompts below. Call on children who read each book to answer the questions or respond to the prompt. If appropriate, ask children to find the pages in the book that illustrate their answers.

- **Who is your book about?**
- **What had wheels in your book?**
- **How did wheels help?**
- **What did you go in that had wheels? How did the wheels help?**
- **Which part of the book did you like best? Tell about it.**

Develop Listening and Speaking Skills Tell children to remember the following:

- Share information in cooperative learning interactions. Remind children to work with their partners to retell the story and complete any activities. Ask: *What happened next in the story?*
- Employ self-corrective techniques and monitor their own and other children's language production. Children should ask themselves: *What parts of this passage were confusing to me? Can my classmates help me clarify a word or sentence that I don't understand?*
- Use high-frequency English words to describe people, places, and objects.
- Narrate, describe, and explain with specificity and detail. Ask: *Where did the story take place? Can you describe the setting? What else did you notice?*
- Express opinions, ideas, and feelings on a variety of social and academic topics. Ask: *What do you think about the characters in the story?*

Approaching Level

Phonemic Awareness

Objective Categorize words with initial /i/

Materials • none

PHONEME CATEGORIZATION

Tier 2

Model

- *I am going to say three words. Two words begin with /i/. One does not. Listen:* ink, inch, tap. Ink *and* inch *begin with the /i/ sound.* Tap *does not begin with /i/.* Tap *does not belong.* Repeat for *igloo, insect,* and *mail.*

Guided Practice/Practice

- Say the words *in, teeth,* and *if*, emphasizing the initial sound in each word. Have children repeat each word. Ask children which word does not belong because it does not begin with /i/. Repeat with the words *it, tap,* and *is.*

Sound-Spelling WorkBoard

Phonics

Objective Identify initial /i/*i*, /p/*p*, /t/*t* and build fluency

Materials • **Photo Cards:** *inch, insect, invitation, pea, peach, penny, pie, table, tiger, toe, turtle* • **Word-Building Cards** • pocket chart • **Sound-Spelling WorkBoards**

BUILD FLUENCY: LETTER-SOUND CORRESPONDENCE

Tier 2

Model

- Place **Word-Building Cards** *i, t, p* in the top row of the pocket chart. Review the sound that each letter stands for. Then place the **Photo Cards** facedown in a stack. Pick the first card, name the picture, and identify its initial sound. Place the Photo Card under the letter that stands for the beginning sound.

Guided Practice/Practice

- Have each child choose a Photo Card, name the picture, identify its initial sound, and place it in the pocket chart under the correct letter. Guide practice with the first Photo Card.

Build Fluency

- Display the Word-Building Cards. Have children name each letter as quickly as they can. Then ask them to write the letters on their **WorkBoards** several times as they say the sounds.

ELL

Sound-Letter Relationships Provide additional practice in pronouncing the /i/, /p/, /t/ sounds and naming the corresponding letters, as children point to them.

Approaching Level

Leveled Reader Lesson 2

Objective Reread *Pig's Trip* to reinforce fluency and identify character and plot

Materials • **Leveled Reader:** *Pig's Trip*

FOCUS ON FLUENCY

- Tell children that you will read one page of the book and they should read that page right after you. They should follow along in their books and try to read at the same speed and with the same expression that you use.

SKILL IDENTIFY CHARACTER AND PLOT

- *Look at the pictures. Who are the characters in the book? What does the pig do? How does the pig feel about traveling? How do you know? What kinds of vehicles does the pig use to travel?*

REREAD BOOKS

- Distribute copies of the past six **Leveled Readers**. Tell children that rereading the books will help them develop their reading skills.
- Circulate and listen in as children read. Stop them periodically and ask them how they are figuring out words or checking their understanding. Tell children to reread other Leveled Readers during independent reading time.

High-Frequency Words

Objective Review high-frequency words *go, see, a, like,* and *the*

Materials • **High-Frequency Word Cards:** *a, go, like, see, the*

BUILD WORD AUTOMATICITY: *go, see, a, like, the*

- Distribute copies of the **High-Frequency Word Card** for **go**. Say the word and have children repeat it. Have children name the letters in the word. Repeat with the words **see**, **a**, **like**, and **the**.
- **Build Fluency** Use the High-Frequency Word Cards to review previously taught words. Repeat, guiding children to read more rapidly.

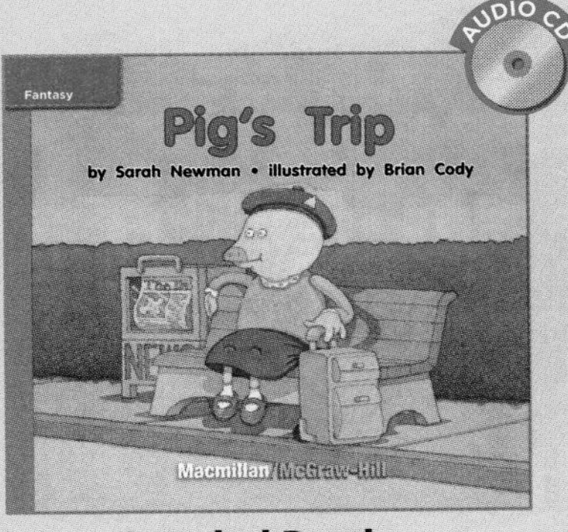

Leveled Reader

Meet Grade-Level Expectations

As an alternative to this day's lesson, guide children through a reading of the On Level Leveled Reader. See page 670. Because both books contain the same vocabulary, phonics, and comprehension skills, the scaffolding you provided will help most children gain access to this more challenging text.

ON YOUR OWN

Pig in a Car

Have children draw pictures showing the vehicle Pig will ride in after she meets her family at the airport. Help children write sentences about their pictures.

Leveled Reader

ON YOUR OWN

Extend the Story

Have children draw a picture to show what might happen next if there was another page to the story. *Does the wolf go away? Does he stay and eat with the pigs?*

On Level

Leveled Reader Lesson 2

Objective Reread to apply skills and strategies to retell a story

Materials • **Leveled Reader:** *Pigs on Wheels*

BEFORE READING

- Ask children to look through *Pigs on Wheels* and recall what the book is about. Reinforce vocabulary by repeating children's sentences using more sophisticated language. For example: *Yes, the pig in the car has a problem.*

DURING READING

- Have children join you in a choral-reading of the story. Model reading with expression. *When I read page 2, I grouped the words* I see the *together and then paused slightly before finishing the sentence. This makes my reading sound natural, as if I'm talking.* Ask children to use the same kind of expression when they read.
- Assign each child a page. Have children practice by whisper-reading. *Follow along as other children read, and be ready to come in when it is your turn. Remember, use lots of expression.*

AFTER READING

- Have children retell the story in their own words.
- *Look at the picture on page 8. What is happening in the story? Why are the pigs angry with Wolf? What do you think they are saying?*

Beyond Level

Leveled Reader Lesson 2

Objective Reread to apply skills and strategies to retell a story

Materials • **Leveled Reader:** *Chip Likes Nuts*

BEFORE READING

- Ask children to look at the pictures in *Chip Likes Nuts* and recall what the book is about. Remind them that the plot includes what happens at the beginning, middle, and end of a story. *What problem does Chip have? How is the problem solved?*

DURING READING

- Assign each child a page of the book to read aloud. Have children practice by whisper-reading. *Follow along as each child reads. Be ready to read when it is your turn.*

AFTER READING

- Explain that when you look at the structure of a story, you understand it better. Model the strategy: *When I look at the story, I notice that each new vehicle has more wheels. The cart has two wheels. The truck has four wheels. I see a pattern. The next vehicle has six wheels. The vehicles get bigger and bigger. How did the story pattern help me predict how the problem would be solved?*

Expand Vocabulary

Objectives Learn and apply the meanings of the new words *cart* and *wheel* and brainstorm names of things with wheels

Materials • **Leveled Reader:** *Chip Likes Nuts*

ENRICH: *cart, wheel*

Gifted Talented

- Have children reread page 4. *What is a cart?* (something used to carry heavy things) Have children point to the word *cart* in the **Leveled Reader**. *What else might you put in a cart?*
- *How many wheels does the cart have?* (2) Then have children find the word *wheels* on page 5. Ask them to point to the wheels in the picture.
- Have children brainstorm names of things that have wheels. Record their responses in a web with the question *What Has Wheels?* in the center circle. Challenge children to name at least one thing that has one wheel (unicycle, wheelbarrow), two wheels (bicycle, cart), three wheels (tricycle), and four wheels (skateboard, car).

Leveled Reader

Write About Chip

Have children write and illustrate stories about what Chip will do with all of the nuts he gathered.

ELL

Partners When children write and illustrate stories, pair English Language Learners with children who are more proficient.

ELL ENGLISH LANGUAGE LEARNERS

Fluency

Content Objectives Reread Pre-decodable Readers to develop fluency; develop speaking skills

Language Objective Tell a partner what a selection is about

Materials • **Pre-decodable Readers:** *Go, Go, Go; It Can Go, Go, Go!* • **Photo Cards**

REREAD FOR FLUENCY

Beginning

- Review the high-frequency words **go**, **see**, **a**, **like**, and **the** using the **Read/Spell/Write** routine.

Intermediate/Advanced

- Use each word in a sentence that illustrates its use, such as *I see a car*. Show the **Photo Card** for *car* and point to it. *I like to go on the bus.* Act out riding on a bus and show the Photo Card.
- Then provide sentence starters for children to complete. Where appropriate, act out children's responses.

All Language Levels

- Guide children through a choral-reading of *Go, Go, Go* and *It Can Go, Go, Go!* Model reading the sentence "Go car go!" Point out how you used your voice to show expression. Point out the exclamation mark. Explain that this mark means that the sentence shows excitement. Model reading the sentence again.

DEVELOP SPEAKING/LISTENING SKILLS

All Language Levels

- Have children reread *Go, Go, Go* and *It Can Go, Go, Go!* to a partner. Remind them to listen carefully and follow along in their book as their partner is reading. Work with children to read with accuracy and appropriate expression.
- Ask children to tell their partner about the pictures on each page. Then have the other partner describe the pictures. Circulate, listen in, and provide additional language as needed.

Beginning

Confirm Understanding Point to the pictures for partners to identify. Ask: *What do you see?* Restate the correct answer in a complete sentence.

Intermediate

Express Opinions Ask partners to tell you which is their favorite picture in the book. Prompt them to explain why it is their favorite picture.

Advanced

Compare and Contrast Have partners compare two different pictures and describe them. Prompt them to explain how they are alike and different.

ELL ENGLISH LANGUAGE LEARNERS

High-Frequency Words

Content Objective Spell high-frequency words correctly
Language Objective Write in complete sentences, using sentence frames
Materials • **Sound-Spelling WorkBoards** • **Sound-Spelling Cards** • **Photo Cards**

Beginning/Intermediate

- Write the high-frequency word *go* on the board. Have children copy the word on their **WorkBoards**. Then help them say, then write, a sentence for the word. Provide the sentence starter *We go to* ________.

Advanced

- Children should first orally state their sentence. Correct as needed. Then they can draw a picture to complete the sentence. For children who are ready, help them spell words using their growing knowledge of English sound-spelling relationships. Model how to segment the word children are trying to spell and attach a spelling to each sound. Use the **Sound-Spelling Cards** to reinforce the spellings for each English sound.

Writing

All Language Levels

- Dictate the following sound and ask children to write the letter: /i/. Have them write the letter five times as they say the sound. Demonstrate correct letter formation, as needed.
- Then display a set of **Photo Cards**. Select at least five cards whose picture names begin with /i/ (ink, insect, invitation, inch, inchworm) and three whose picture names begin with /t/ (tiger, table, turtle).
- Say the name of each card, stretching the initial sound to emphasize it. You may also need to reinforce the meaning of the word and model correct mouth formation when forming the sound. Use the articulation pictures and prompts on the back of the small Sound-Spelling Cards for support. Tell children that if the picture name begins with /i/, you want them to write the letter *i* on their WorkBoards.

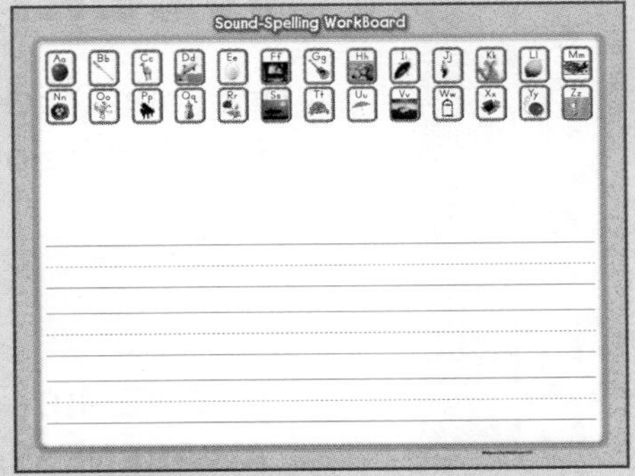

Sound-Spelling WorkBoard

Phonemic Awareness/ Phonics

For English Language Learners who need more practice with this week's phonemic awareness and phonics skills, see the Approaching Level lessons. Focus on minimal contrasts, articulation, and those sounds that do not transfer from the child's first language to English. For a complete listing of transfer sounds, see pages T10–T31.

Weekly Assessment

Use your Quick Check observations and the assessment opportunities identified below to evaluate children's progress in key skill areas.

Skills	Quick Check Observations	Pencil and Paper Assessment
PHONEMIC AWARENESS/ PHONICS /i/i — i	613	Activity Book, pp. 14, 19, 22 Practice Book, pp. 67, 71
HIGH-FREQUENCY WORDS *go* — go	634	Activity Book, pp. 17–18 Practice Book, pp. 69–70
COMPREHENSION Classify and Categorize	624	Activity Book, pp. 15–16, 21 Practice Book, p. 68

Quick Check Rubric

Skills	1	2	3
PHONEMIC AWARENESS/ PHONICS	Does not connect the /i/ sound with the letter *Ii* and has difficulty blending the CVC and VC words *sit, sip, it,* and *tip.*	Usually connects the /i/ sound with the letter *Ii* and blends the CVC and VC words *sit, sip, it,* and *tip* with occasional support.	Consistently connects the /i/ sound with the letter *Ii* and blends the CVC and VC words *sit, sip, it,* and *tip.*
HIGH-FREQUENCY WORDS	Does not identify the high-frequency words.	Usually recognizes the high-frequency words with accuracy, but not speed.	Consistently recognizes the high-frequency words with speed and accuracy.
COMPREHENSION	Does not classify and categorize using the pictures and text.	Usually classifies and categorizes using the pictures and text.	Consistently classifies and categorizes using the pictures and text.

DIBELS LINK

PROGRESS MONITORING

Use your DIBELS results to inform instruction.

IF...

Initial **S**ound **F**luency (**ISF**) 0–7

THEN...

Evaluate for Intervention

TPRI LINK

PROGRESS MONITORING

Use your TPRI scores to inform instruction.

IF...

Phonemic Awareness — Start midyear
Graphophonemic Knowledge — Start midyear
Listening Comprehension — Start midyear

THEN...

Evaluate for Intervention

Diagnose		Prescribe
Review the assessment answers with children. Have them correct their errors. Then provide additional instruction as needed.		
PHONEMIC AWARENESS/ PHONICS */i/i*	**IF...** **Quick Check Rubric:** Children consistently score 1 or **Pencil and Paper Assessment:** Children get 0–2 items correct	**THEN...** Reteach Phonemic Awareness and Phonics Skills using the **Phonemic Awareness** and **Phonics Intervention Teacher's Editions**. SPIRAL REVIEW Use the Build Fluency lesson in upcoming weeks to provide children practice reading words with /i/*i*.
HIGH-FREQUENCY WORDS *go*	**Quick Check Rubric:** Children consistently score 1 or **Pencil and Paper Assessment:** Children get 0–2 items correct	Reteach High-Frequency Words using the **Phonics Intervention Teacher's Edition**. SPIRAL REVIEW Use the High-Frequency Words lesson in upcoming weeks to provide children practice reading the word *go*.
COMPREHENSION Skill: Classify and Categorize	**Quick Check Rubric:** Children consistently score 1 or **Pencil and Paper Assessment:** Children get 0–2 items correct	Reteach Comprehension Skill using the **Comprehension Intervention Teacher's Edition**.

Response to Intervention

To place children in Tier 2 or Tier 3 Intervention use the *Diagnostic Assessment*.

- Phonemic Awareness
- Phonics
- Vocabulary
- Comprehension
- Fluency

Week 3 ★ At a Glance

Priority Skills and Concepts

Comprehension
- **Genre:** Fantasy, Nonfiction, Folktale
- **Strategy:** Recognize Story Structure
- **Skill:** Identify Character and Plot

- **Skill:** Ask Questions

High-Frequency Words
- ***go***, ***see***

Oral Vocabulary
- **Build Robust Vocabulary: *adventure*, *attach*, *haul*, *massive*, *wheels***

Fluency
- **Echo-Read**
- **Word Automaticity**
- **Sound-Spellings**

Phonemic Awareness
- **Phoneme Identity**
- **Phoneme Blending**
- **Phoneme Categorization**

Phonics
- ***Ii, Tt, Pp, Ss***

Grammar
- **Action Words (Verbs)**

Writing
- **Book Title**

Key

Tested in Program

Review Skill

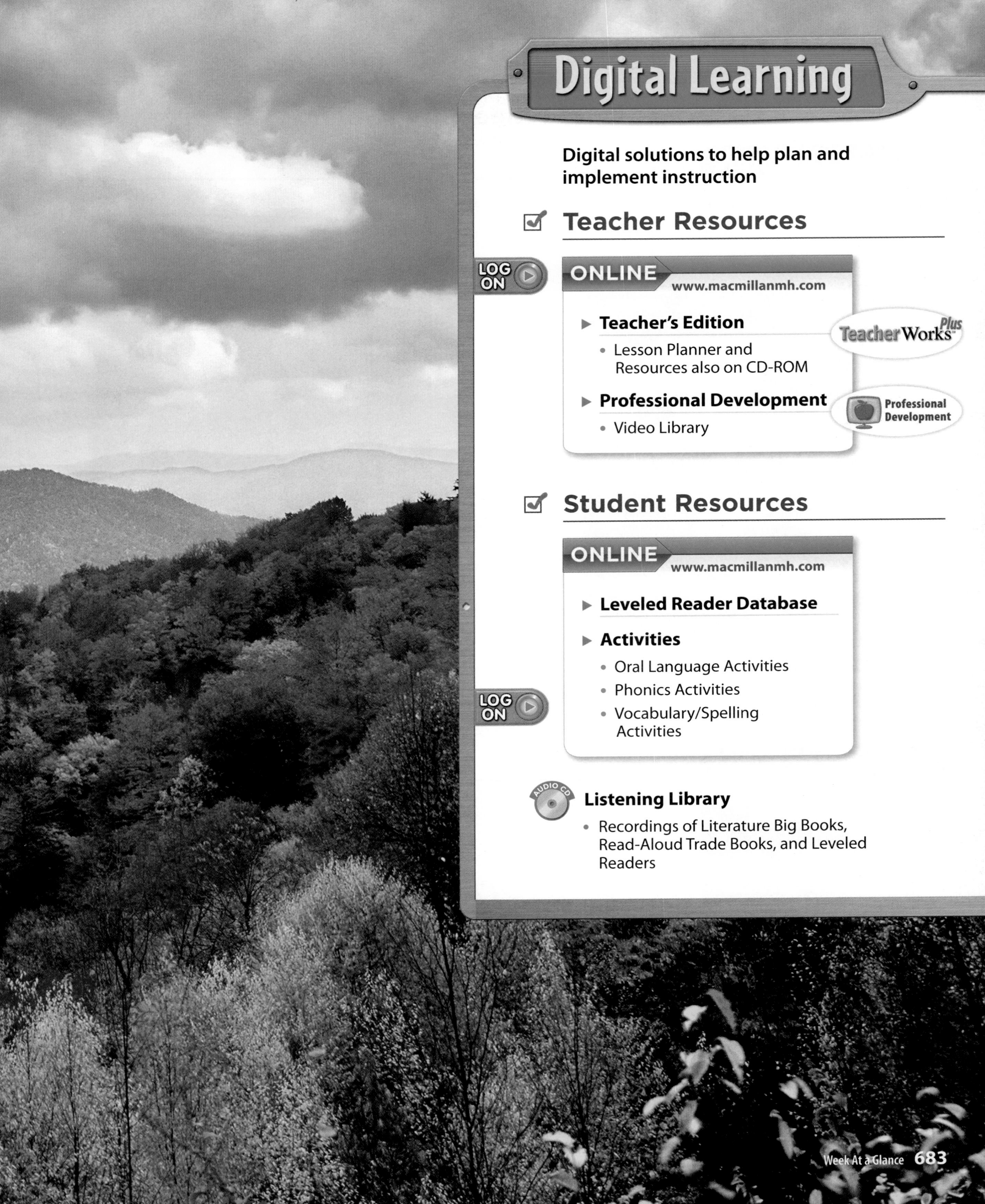

Digital Learning

Digital solutions to help plan and implement instruction

Teacher Resources

LOG ON

ONLINE
www.macmillanmh.com

- **Teacher's Edition**
  - Lesson Planner and Resources also on CD-ROM
- **Professional Development**
  - Video Library

Student Resources

LOG ON

ONLINE
www.macmillanmh.com

- **Leveled Reader Database**
- **Activities**
  - Oral Language Activities
  - Phonics Activities
  - Vocabulary/Spelling Activities

Listening Library

- Recordings of Literature Big Books, Read-Aloud Trade Books, and Leveled Readers

Weekly Literature

Theme: Wheels All Around

Student Literature

A mix of fiction and nonfiction

Trade Book

Genre Fantasy

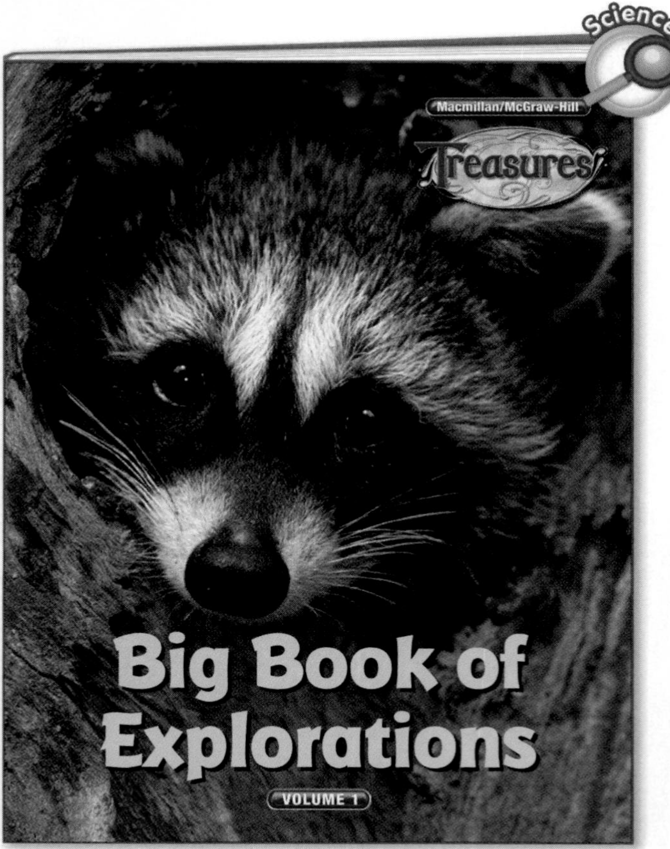

Big Book of Explorations

Genre Expository

Support Literature

Interactive Read-Aloud Anthology

Genre Folktale

Oral Vocabulary Cards

- Listening Comprehension
- Build Robust Vocabulary

Pre-decodable Readers

Resources for Differentiated Instruction

Leveled Readers: Social Studies

GR Levels Rebus–D

Genre	Expository

- Same Theme
- Same Vocabulary/Phonics
- Same Comprehension Skills

Approaching Level

On Level

Beyond Level

ELL

Leveled Reader Database
Go to www.macmillanmh.com.

Practice

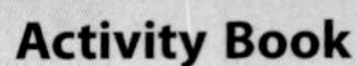
Activity Book

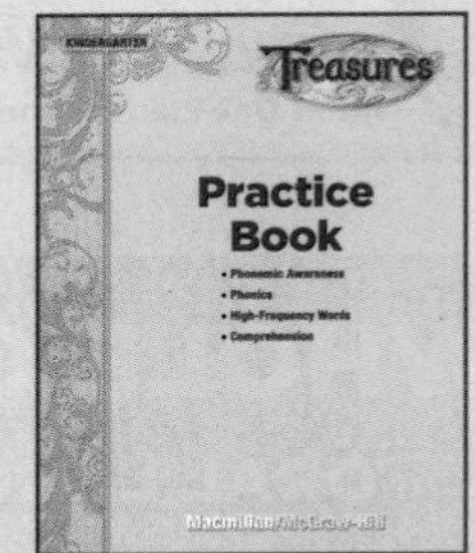

Practice Book

ELL Practice Book

Response to Intervention

- Phonemic Awareness
- Phonics
- Vocabulary
- Comprehension
- Fluency

Unit Assessment

Assess Unit Skills

- Phonemic Awareness
- Phonics
- High-Frequency Words
- Listening Comprehension

HOME-SCHOOL CONNECTION

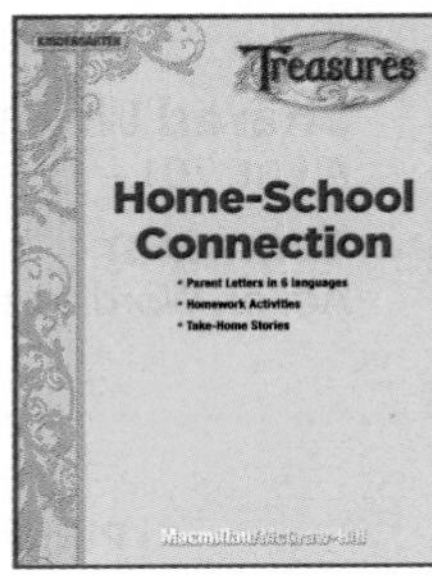

- Family letters in English and Spanish
- Take-home stories and activities

Suggested Lesson Plan

Go to www.macmillanmh.com for Online Lesson Planner

Trade Book

WHOLE GROUP	DAY 1	DAY 2
ORAL LANGUAGE • Oral Vocabulary • Phonemic Awareness	**Focus Question** Where can we go on wheels? Build Background, 694 **Oral Vocabulary** *adventure, attach, haul, massive, wheel*, 694 **Phonemic Awareness** Phoneme Identity, 697	**Focus Question** What can you see when you travel on wheels? **Oral Vocabulary** *adventure, attach, haul, massive, wheel*, 702 Shape Words, 709 **Phonemic Awareness** Phoneme Identity, 710
WORD STUDY • Phonics • High-Frequency Words	**Phonics** Review /t/*t*, /i/*i*, 698  Handwriting: Review *Tt, Ii*, 699 Activity Book, 24 Practice Book, 73 **High-Frequency Words** *see*, *go*, 696	**Phonics** Review /p/*p*, /t/*t*, /i/*i*, 710 Blend with /i/*i*, /t/*t*, /s/*s*, 711 **Review High-Frequency Words**, 712
READING • Listening Comprehension • Apply Phonics and High-Frequency Words • Fluency	**Share the Trade Book** *Duck on a Bike* **Strategy:** Recognize Story Structure, 695 **Skill:** Identify Character and Plot, 695  Trade Book	**Reread the Trade Book** *Duck on a Bike* **Strategy:** Recognize Story Structure, 704 **Skill:** Identify Character and Plot, 704 Trade Book Retell, 708 **Pre-decodable Reader:** *I See a Truck Go*, 712 Activity Book, 25–26 Practice Book, 74 **Fluency** Echo-Read, 702
LANGUAGE ARTS • Writing • Grammar	**Shared Writing** A List, 701 **Grammar** Action Words (Verbs), 700	**Interactive Writing** Book Title, 713
ASSESSMENT • Informal/Formal	Quick Check Phonemic Awareness, 697	Quick Check Comprehension, 708

SMALL GROUP Lesson Plan — **Differentiated Instruction 688–689**

Priority Skills

Phonemic Awareness/Phonics
/t/t, /i/i

High-Frequency Words
see, go

Oral Vocabulary
Shape Words, Sound Words

Comprehension
Strategy: Recognize Story Structure
Skill: Identify Character and Plot

Half-Day Kindergarten

Teach Core Skills
Focus on tested skill lessons, other lessons, and small group options as your time allows.

DAY 3

Focus Question What do you see when you go to school?

Oral Vocabulary *adventure, attach, haul, massive, wheel*, 714

Oral Vocabulary Cards: "Big, Big Trucks"

Phonemic Awareness
Phoneme Blending, 719

Phonics
Review /t/t, /p/p, /s/s, /i/i, 720
Blend with /t/t, /p/p, /s/s, /i/i, 721
Read Words, 721

High-Frequency Words
see, *go*, 718
Activity Book: "I Can Go!" 27–28
Practice Book, 75–76
Read for Fluency, 718

Read the Big Book of Explorations
"How Do You Go to School?," 39–42

Text Feature:
Use Maps, 716

Big Book of Explorations

Independent Writing
Prewrite and Draft Book Title, 723

Grammar
Action Words (Verbs), 722

Quick Check High-Frequency Words, 718

DAY 4

Focus Question Where can we go on wheels?

Oral Vocabulary *adventure, attach, haul, massive, wheel*, 724

Sound Words, 727

Phonemic Awareness
Phoneme Blending, 728

Phonics
Picture Sort, 728
Blend with /p/p, /a/a, /t/t, /i/i, 729
Activity Book, 30
Practice Book, 77

Review High-Frequency Words, 730

Interactive Read Aloud
Listening Comprehension, 726

Read Aloud: "The Singing Wagon"

Pre-decodable Reader:
Sit, Tip!, 730

Read Aloud

Independent Writing
Revise and Edit Book Title, 731

Quick Check Phonics, 729

DAY 5 Review and Assess

Focus Question Where did we see the story characters go?

Oral Vocabulary *adventure, attach, haul, massive, wheel*, 732

Shape Words, 734

Phonemic Awareness
Phoneme Categorization, 735

Phonics
Read Words, 736
Dictation, 736
Activity Book, 32

High-Frequency Words
a, *like*, *the*, *we*, *see*, *go*, 734

Read Across Texts
Strategy: Recognize Story Structure, 733
Skill: Identify Character and Plot, 733
Activity Book, 31

Fluency Word Automaticity, 734

Independent Writing
Publish and Present Book Title, 737

Weekly Assessment, 764–765

Differentiated Instruction

What do I do in small groups?

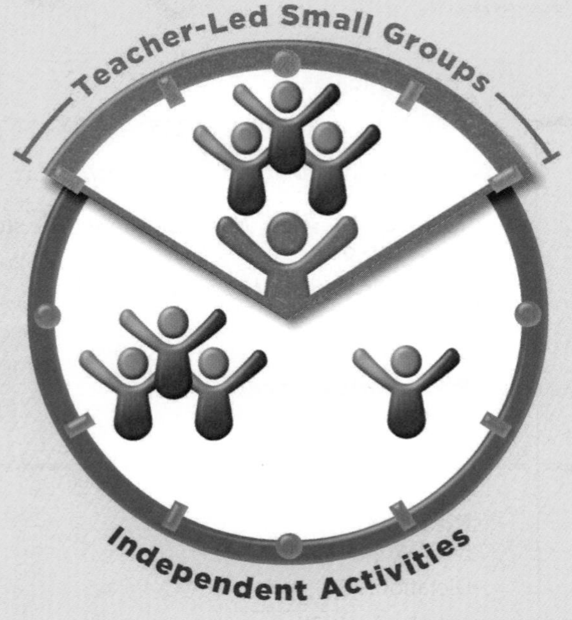

IF... **children need additional instruction, practice, or extension based on your Quick Check observations for the following priority skills**

Phonemic Awareness
Phoneme Identity, Blending, Categorization

Phonics
Ii, Tt, Pp, Ss

High-Frequency Words
see, *go*

Comprehension
Strategy: Recognize Story Structure
Skill: Identify Character and Plot

THEN...

Approaching	Preteach and
ELL	Reteach Skills
On Level	Practice
Beyond	Enrich and Accelerate Learning

Suggested Small Group Lesson Plan

	DAY 1	DAY 2
Approaching Level • **Preteach/Reteach** Tier 2 **Tier 2 Instruction**	• Oral Language, 738 • High-Frequency Words, 738 ELL High-Frequency Words Review, 738 • Phonemic Awareness, 739 • Phonics, 739 ELL Sound-Spellings Review, 739	• High-Frequency Words, 744 ELL • Pre-decodable Reader, 744 • Phonemic Awareness, 745 • Phonics, 745
On Level • **Practice**	• High-Frequency Words, 740 • Phonemic Awareness/Phonics, 740 ELL	• Pre-decodable Reader, 746
Beyond Level • **Extend/Accelerate** Gifted Talented **Gifted and Talented**	• High-Frequency Words/Vocabulary, 741 ELL Expand Oral Vocabulary, 741 • Phonics, 741	• Pre-decodable Reader, 746
ELL • **Build English Language Proficiency** • **See ELL in other levels.**	• Oral Language Warm-Up, 742 • Academic Language, 742 • Vocabulary, 743	• Access to Core Content, 747

Focus on Leveled Readers

Levels Rebus–D

Approaching

On Level

Beyond

ELL

Additional Leveled Readers

Leveled Reader Database
www.macmillanmh.com

Search by

- Comprehension Skill
- Content Area
- Genre
- Text Feature
- Guided Reading Level
- Reading Recovery Level
- Lexile Score
- Benchmark Level

Subscription also available

Manipulatives

Sound-Spelling WorkBoards

Sound-Spelling Cards

Photo Cards

High-Frequency Word Cards

Visual Vocabulary Resources

DAY 3

- High-Frequency Words, 748 ELL
- Phonemic Awareness, 748
- Phonics, 749
- Pre-decodable Reader, 749

- Phonics, 750

- Phonics, 750

- Access to Core Content, 751
- Grammar, 751

DAY 4

- Phonemic Awareness, 752
- Phonics, 752 ELL
- Leveled Reader Lesson 1, 753

- Leveled Reader Lesson 1, 754 ELL

- Leveled Reader Lesson 1, 755
  Evaluate, 755

- Leveled Reader, 756–757

DAY 5

- Phonemic Awareness, 758
- Phonics, 758 ELL
- Leveled Reader Lesson 2, 759
- High-Frequency Words, 759

- Leveled Reader Lesson 2, 760

- Leveled Reader Lesson 2, 761 ELL
- Expand Vocabulary, 761

- Fluency, 762
- High-Frequency Words, 763
- Writing, 763

What do I do with the rest of my class?

- Activity Book
- Practice Book
- ELL Practice Book
- Leveled Reader Activities
- Literacy Workstations
- Online Activities
- Buggles and Beezy

Classroom Management Tools

Weekly Contract

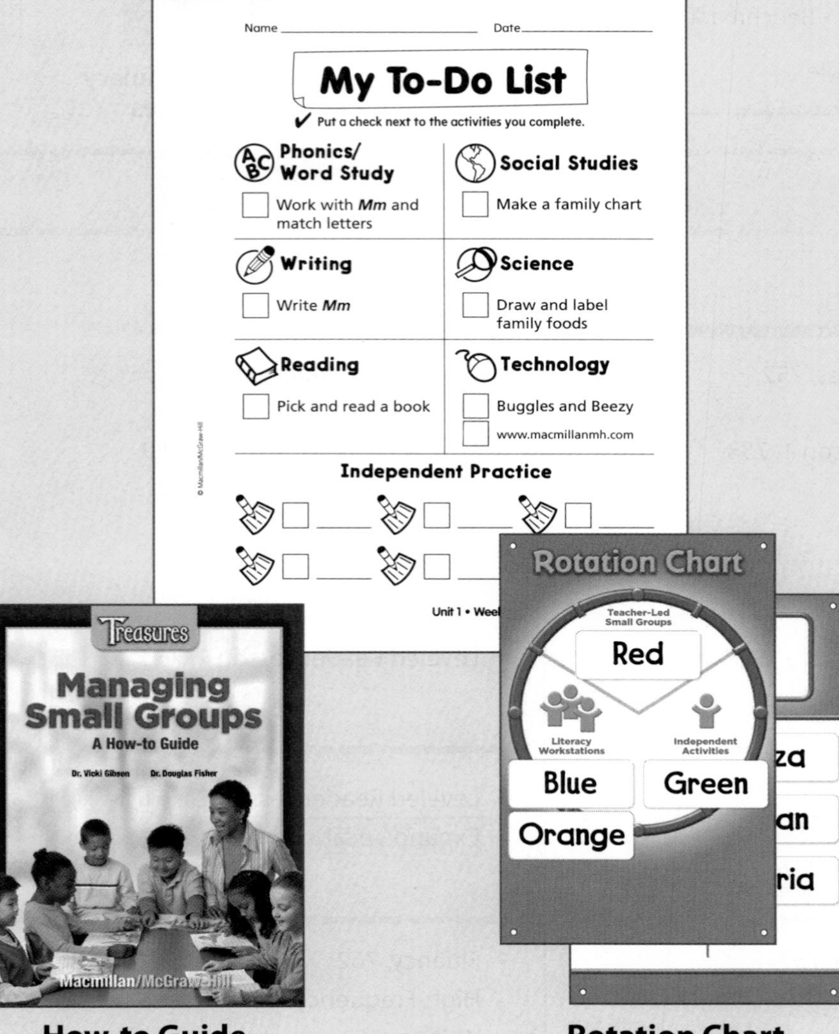

How-to Guide

Rotation Chart

Digital Learning

- Match Letters
- Match Letters to Sounds
- Blend Words

Meet the Author/Illustrator

David Shannon

- David was born in Washington, D.C. and grew up in Spokane, Washington.
- David is a huge baseball fan and loves to play softball.
- He lives with his wife in Los Angeles, California.

Other books by David Shannon

- Shannon, David. *No, David!* New York: Blue Sky Press, 1998.
- Shannon, David. *Duck on a Bike*. New York: Blue Sky Press, 2002.

- Read Other Books by the Author or Illustrator

Practice

Activity Book

Practice Book

ELL Practice Book

Independent Activities

ONLINE INSTRUCTION www.macmillanmh.com

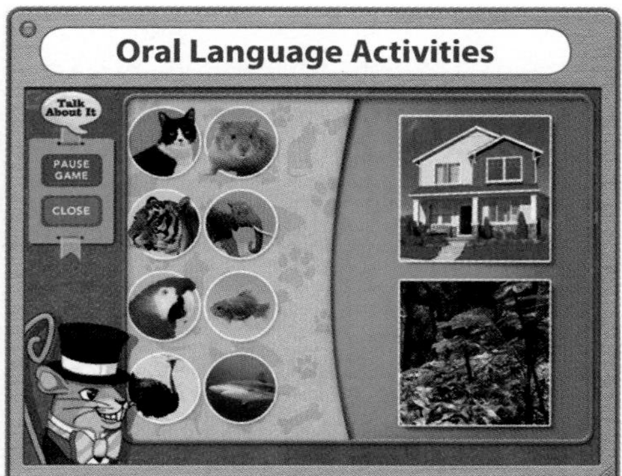

- Focus on Unit Vocabulary and Concepts
- English Language Learner Support

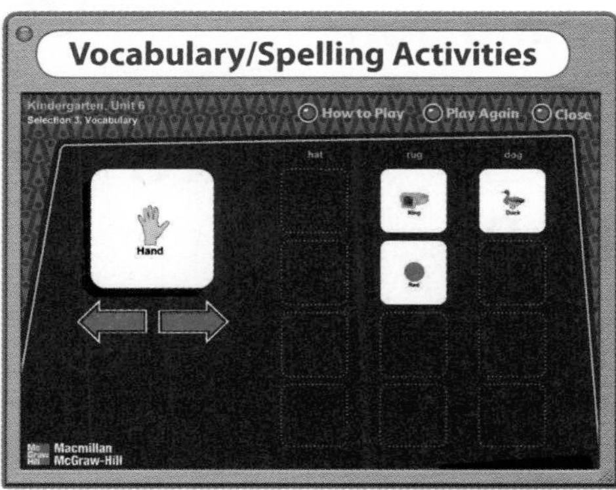

- Differentiated Lists and Activities

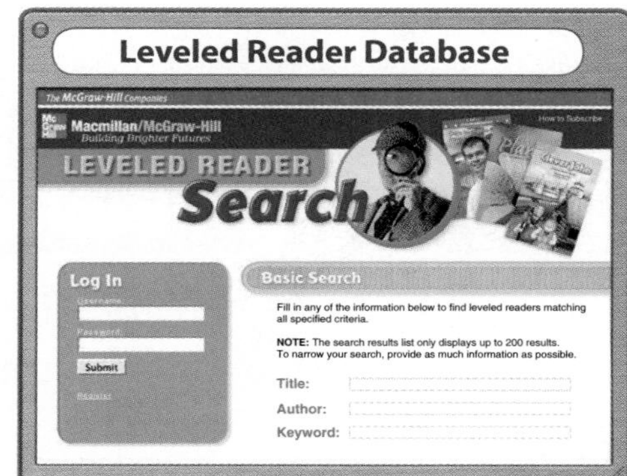

- Leveled Reader Database
- Search titles by level, skill, content area, and more

Available on CD

LISTENING LIBRARY
Recordings of selections

- Literature Big Books
- Read-Aloud Trade Books
- Leveled Readers
- ELL Readers

NEW ADVENTURES WITH BUGGLES AND BEEZY
Phonemic awareness and phonics activities

Leveled Reader Activities

Approaching

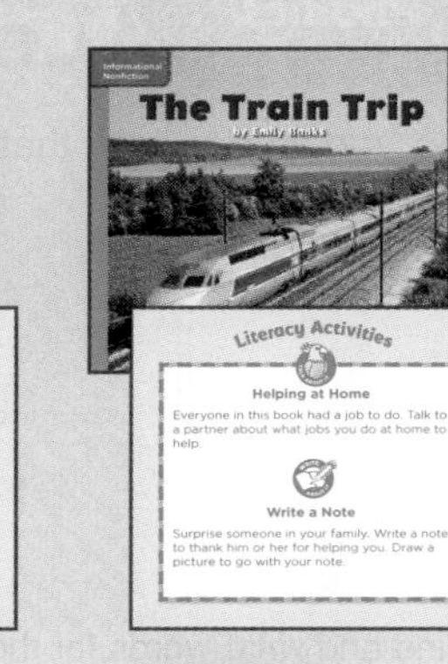

On Level

Beyond

ELL

See inside cover of all Leveled Readers.

Literacy Workstations

See lessons on pages 692–693.

What do I do with the rest of my class?

Reading

Objectives

- Read and discuss a fantasy story with a partner
- Read a book and retell the story

Phonics/Word Study

Objectives

- Sort pictures by medial vowel sounds and letters /a/*a* and /i/*i*
- Find words that begin with the letters *Ii* and *Tt*

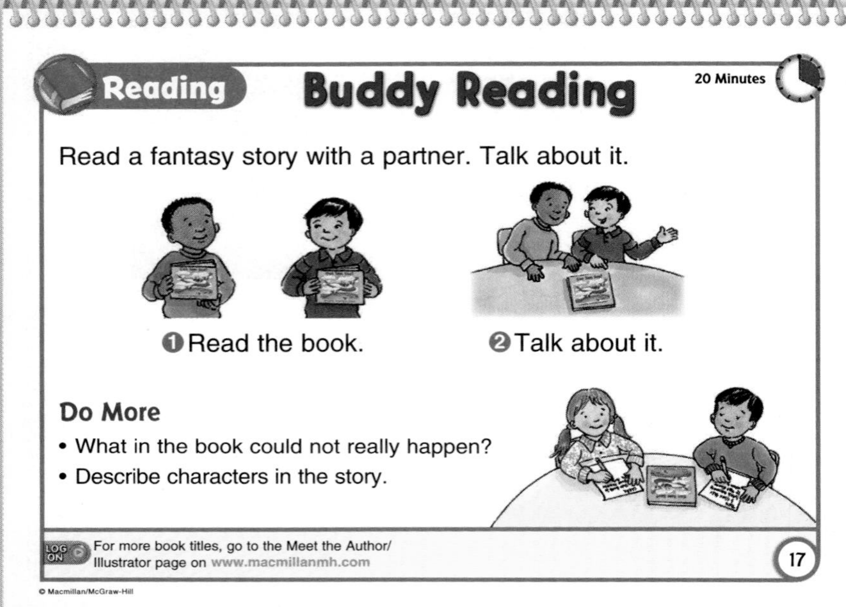

Reading
Buddy Reading
20 Minutes
Read a fantasy story with a partner. Talk about it.
❶ Read the book.
❷ Talk about it.
Do More
• What in the book could not really happen?
• Describe characters in the story.
For more book titles, go to the Meet the Author/ Illustrator page on www.macmillanmh.com
17
© Macmillan/McGraw-Hill

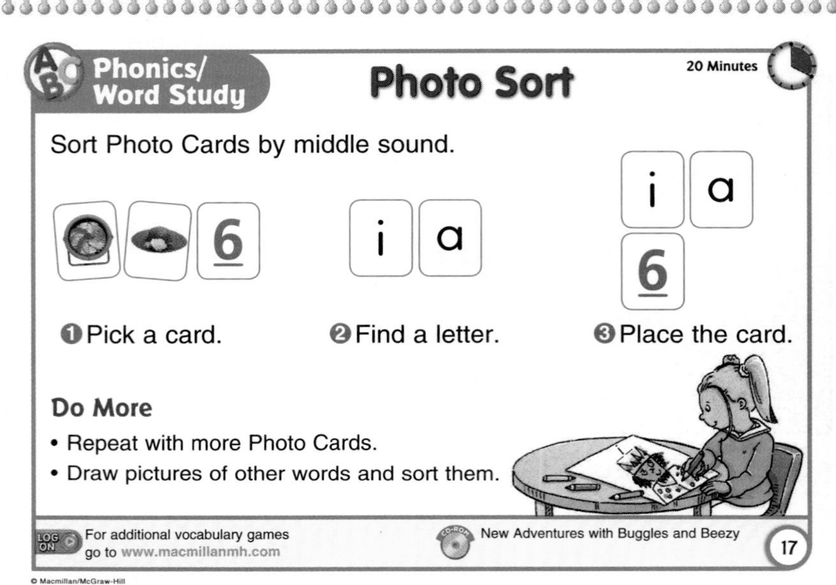

Phonics/ Word Study
Photo Sort
20 Minutes
Sort Photo Cards by middle sound.
6
i
a
❶ Pick a card.
❷ Find a letter.
❸ Place the card.
Do More
• Repeat with more Photo Cards.
• Draw pictures of other words and sort them.
For additional vocabulary games go to www.macmillanmh.com
New Adventures with Buggles and Beezy
17
© Macmillan/McGraw-Hill

Reading
Retell a Story
20 Minutes
Read and retell a story to a partner.
❶ Read a book.
❷ Retell it to a partner.
Do More
• Make your own retelling cards.
• Make a new cover for the book.
For more book titles, go to the Meet the Author/ Illustrator page on www.macmillanmh.com
18
© Macmillan/McGraw-Hill

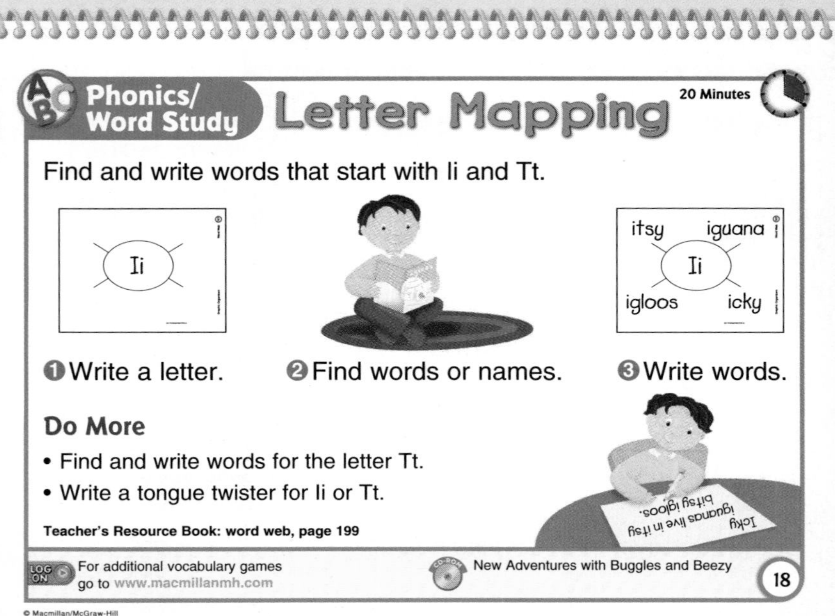

Phonics/ Word Study
Letter Mapping
20 Minutes
Find and write words that start with Ii and Tt.
Ii
itsy
iguana
igloos
icky
❶ Write a letter.
❷ Find words or names.
❸ Write words.
Do More
• Find and write words for the letter Tt.
• Write a tongue twister for Ii or Tt.
Teacher's Resource Book: word web, page 199
Icky iguanas live in itsy bitsy igloos.
For additional vocabulary games go to www.macmillanmh.com
New Adventures with Buggles and Beezy
18
© Macmillan/McGraw-Hill

Literacy Workstations

Literacy Workstation Flip Charts

Writing

Objectives

- Find, read, and make traffic signs
- Write a sentence with the words *go* and *see*

Content Literacy

Objectives

- Measure distance
- Identify and sort different ways to travel

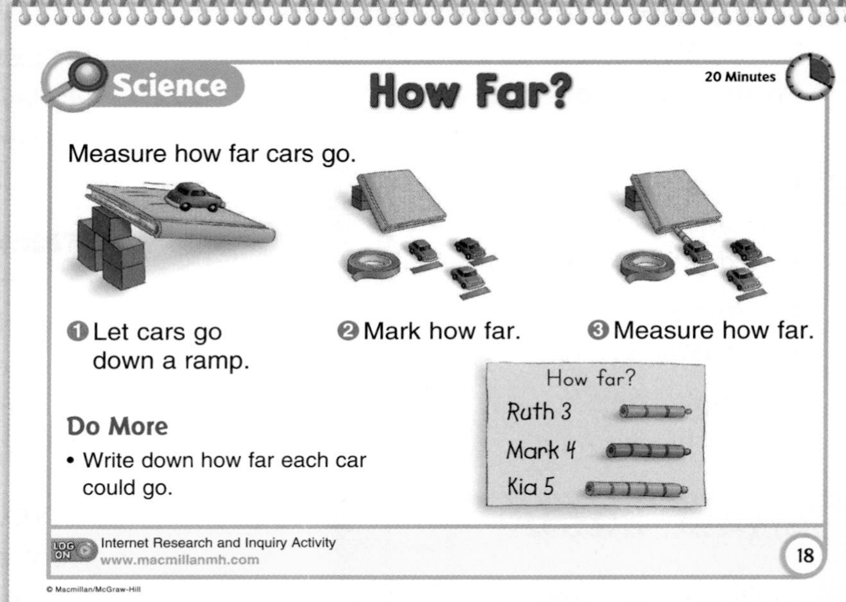

Science
How Far?
20 Minutes
Measure how far cars go.
❶ Let cars go down a ramp.
❷ Mark how far.
❸ Measure how far.
How far?
Ruth 3
Mark 4
Kia 5
Do More
• Write down how far each car could go.
Internet Research and Inquiry Activity
www.macmillanmh.com
18
© Macmillan/McGraw-Hill

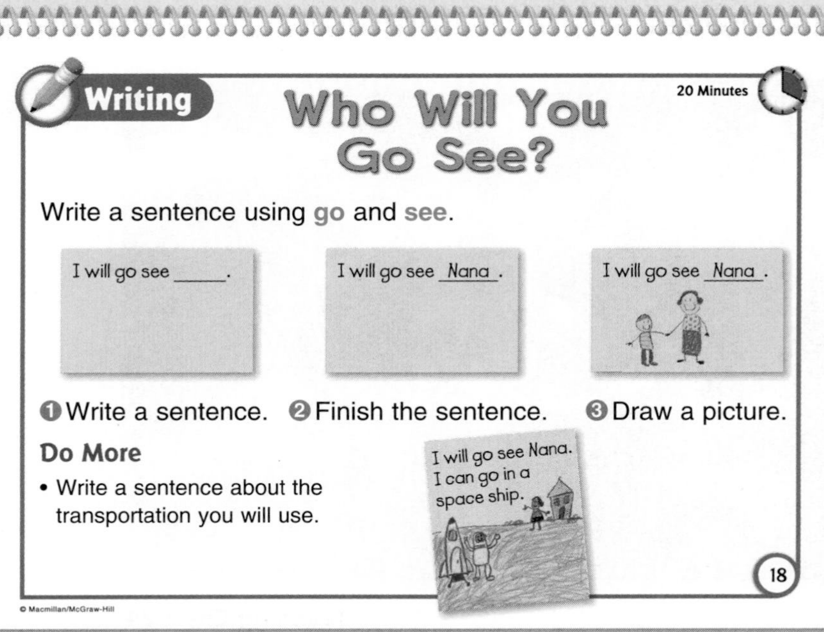

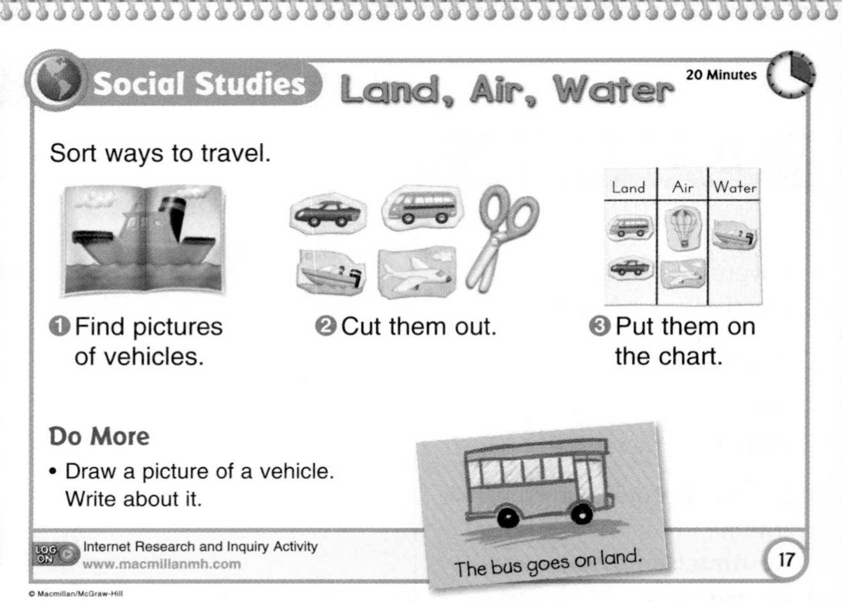

Day 1 At a Glance

WHOLE GROUP

Oral Language
- Build Background

Comprehension
- Read *Duck on a Bike*
- Strategy: Recognize Story Structure
- Skill: Identify Character and Plot

High-Frequency Words
- Introduce *go, see*

Phonemic Awareness
- Phoneme Identity

Phonics
- Review /t/*t*, /i/*i*
- Handwriting: Review *Tt, Ii*

Grammar
- Action Words (Verbs)

Writing
- Shared Writing: A List

SMALL GROUP

- Differentiated Instruction, pages 738–763

Oral Vocabulary

Week 3

adventure attach haul
massive wheels

Review

familiar journey prepare
relax travel

Use the **Define/Example/Ask** routine in the **Instructional Routine Handbook** to review the words.

Oral Language

Build Background: *Wheels All Around*

INTRODUCE THE THEME

Tell children that this week they will learn different ways **wheels** are used to move people and things around. Wheels are parts of many machines used for transportation, such as cars, scooters, and bikes.

Write the following question on two lines of the board: *Where can we go on wheels?* Point to the top and bottom of the board. Remind children that we read from top to bottom. Ask children to point to the top and bottom of the board and then answer the question.

ACCESS PRIOR KNOWLEDGE

- Have children discuss how wheels help them get around. *What things have wheels? How can wheels help you have an exciting time or go on an* **adventure***?*

Think Aloud In this picture I see a girl in a wheelchair. She is wearing a helmet and gloves. (Point to the wheelchair, helmet, and gloves as you describe the picture.) It looks like she is in a race. The ground looks like a track because it is curved and has lane lines on it. There are other children in wheelchairs behind her. (Point to these children.)

DISCUSS THE PHOTOGRAPH

Look at the photograph together. *Some people use wheelchairs to get around. Why are they called wheelchairs? How many wheels do you see in the photo? How is a wheelchair like a bike?* Guide children to answer in complete sentences.

Teaching Chart 24

Share the Trade Book

Listening Comprehension

Trade Book

PREVIEW Display the cover. *I see a duck riding a bike. Clouds are behind him.* Point to the duck, bike, and clouds as you talk. *I wonder if he is flying on the bike.* Read the title as you track the print. *What kind of* ***adventures*** *might a duck have on a bike?*

GENRE: LITERARY TEXT/FICTION Tell children that this story is **fiction**. It did not really happen.

STRATEGY Story Structure

EXPLAIN/MODEL Tell children that paying attention to the way a story is organized, such as the beginning, middle, and end, can help them understand the characters and plot. Display pages 6–13.

Think Aloud At the beginning of the story, a duck gets on a bike. Then he rides past the animals on the farm. I think the first part of the story will show the animals that the duck rides by. As I read the book, I'll figure out what happens next and last.

SKILL Identify Character and Plot

EXPLAIN/MODEL Tell children that stories have characters, or people or animals, in the story. Have children name and discuss characters in books. *What happens to the characters is called the plot.*

Think Aloud I can tell that the book is about a duck. I think the plot will be about what happens when the duck rides a bike.

Read the Trade Book

SET PURPOSE Have children pay attention to the characters in the story and what they do. Use the **Define/Example/Ask** routine to teach the story words on the inside back cover of the **Trade Book**.

Respond to Literature

MAKE CONNECTIONS Have children name their favorite part of the book. *Were you surprised that the other animals rode bikes with Duck? Could this happen in your neighborhood? Why or why not?* Have children draw an animal riding a bike.

Objectives

- Discuss the theme
- Discuss a photograph
- Listen and respond to a story
- Recognize story structure/ identify character and plot

Materials

- Teaching Chart 24
- Read-Aloud Trade Book: *Duck on a Bike*

ELL

Use the **Interactive Question-Response Guide** for *Duck on a Bike*, **ELL Resource Book** pages 82–89, to guide children through a reading of the book. As you read *Duck on a Bike*, make meaning clear by pointing to the pictures, demonstrating word meanings, paraphrasing text, and asking children questions.

Story on **Listening Library Audio CD**

Objectives

- Read the high-frequency words *go, see*
- Identify the words *go* and *see* in text and speech
- Review the high-frequency words *a, like, the, we*
- Follow oral directions involving a short sequence of actions

Materials

- High-Frequency Word Cards: *a, go, like, see, the, we*
- Teaching Chart 25

ELL

Reinforce Vocabulary
Review the high-frequency words *a, go, like, see, the,* and *we.* Display the High-Frequency Word Cards for *a, go, like, see, the,* and *we.* Gather a group of children and say: *Here we go around the room.* As you do, point to classroom objects or children and use the high-frequency words in sentences, such as *We see Maria. We see a poster. We like what the poster says.* Have children repeat.

High-Frequency Words

go, see

go | see

REVIEW Display the **High-Frequency Word Cards** for **go** and **see**. Use the **Read/Spell/Write** routine to teach the words.

- **Read** Point to and say the word *see. I* see *a book.*
- **Spell** *The word* see *is spelled* s-e-e. *What's the first sound in* see? *That's right. The first sound in* see *is /s/. That's why the first letter is* s. *After the* s, *I see two e's. Let's read and spell* see *together.*
- **Write** *Now let's write the word* see *on our papers. Let's spell aloud the word as we write it:* see, s-e-e. Repeat the routine with *go*.

REVIEW *a, like, the, we* Display each card and have children read the word. Repeat several times.

a | like | the | we

READ THE RHYME AND CHIME
Have children point to *see* and *go* each time they see them. Repeat the rhyme for fluency. Add *see* and *go* to the class Word Wall.

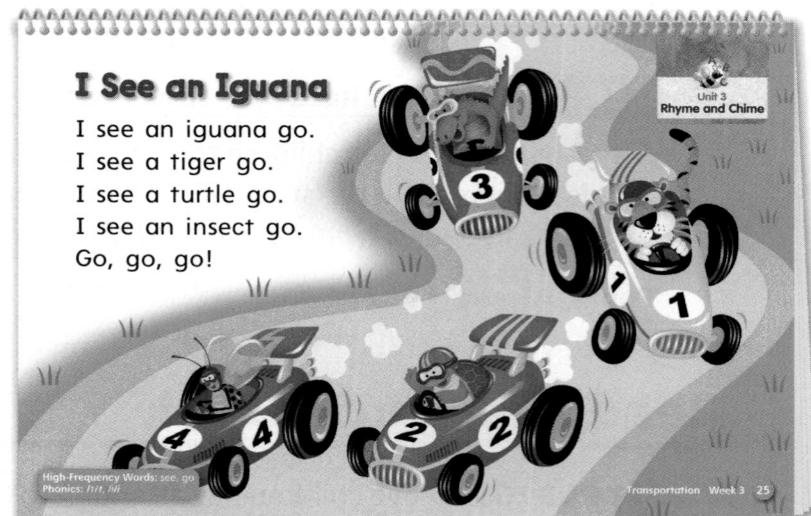

I See an Iguana
I see an iguana go.
I see a tiger go.
I see a turtle go.
I see an insect go.
Go, go, go!
Unit 3
Rhyme and Chime
High-Frequency Words: see, go
Transportation Week 3 25

Teaching Chart 25

For Tier 2 instruction, see page 738.

TIME TO MOVE!

Tell children to go and see different places and objects in the classroom. For example: *Kara, go and see the dress-ups. Tim, go and see the hamster.* Then have children take turns giving "go and see" instructions to their classmates.

Phonemic Awareness

Phoneme Identity

Model

Display **Photo Cards** for *tiger, teeth,* and *top*.

Listen to the sound at the beginning of these words: *tiger, teeth, top*. These words have the same sound, /t/, at the beginning.

Repeat with *ink, inch,* and *insect*.

Listen for words in the Rhyme and Chime that have the sound /t/ at the beginning. We'll tap the top of our heads when we hear /t/ at the beginning of a word.

Read "I See an Iguana". Have children tap every time they hear /t/.

Repeat for initial /i/.

I see an iguana go.
I see a tiger go.
I see a turtle go.
I see an insect go.
Go, go, go!

Review /p/

Display and name Photo Cards for *pie, pig,* and *pizza*.

Listen for the sound that is the same in *pie, pig,* and *pizza*.
The beginning sound, /p/, is the same.

Guided Practice/Practice

Display and name the Photo Cards. Children identify the same sound in the words. Guide practice with the first set of cards.

Say each picture name with me. Which sound is the same? (/t/)

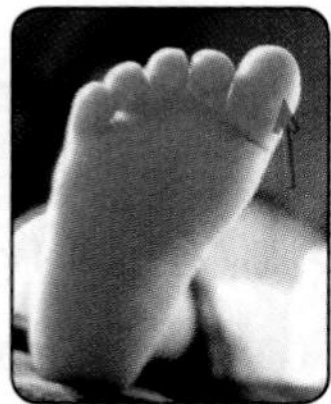

Quick Check

Can children identify the same initial sound /t/, /i/, and /p/ in words?

During **Small Group Instruction**

If No → **Approaching Level** Provide additional practice, page 739.

If Yes → **On Level** Children blend words with /t/, /i/, /p/, and /s/, page 740.

Beyond Level Children blend words with /i/, /t/, and /u/, page 741.

Objective

- **Identify and isolate the same initial sound /t/, /i/, and /p/ in words**

Materials

- **Photo Cards: *ink, inch, insect, pea, pear, pen, pie, pig, pizza, table, teeth, tie, tiger, toe, top***

ELL

Pronunciation Display and have children name Photo Cards from this and prior lessons to reinforce phonemic awareness and word meanings. Point to a card and ask: *What do you see?* (a tiger) *What is the sound at the beginning of the word* tiger? (/t/) Repeat with Photo Cards with words that begin with *p* and *i*.

Objectives

- Identify the common sounds that /t/ and vowel /i/ stand for
- Handwriting: write *Ii, Tt*

Materials

- Sound-Spelling Cards: *Insect, Turtle*
- Teaching Chart 25
- Word-Building Cards
- Handwriting Book
- Handwriting Teacher's Edition
- Activity Book, p. 24
- Practice Book, p. 73

Phonics

Review /t/*t*, /i/*i*

Model

Display the *Turtle* **Sound-Spelling Card**.

This is letter *t*. The letter stands for /t/. What is the letter? What does this letter stand for?

Repeat with the *Insect* Sound-Spelling Card.

This is letter *i*. The letter stands for /i/. What is the letter? What does this letter stand for?

Read the "I See an Iguana" Rhyme and Chime.

Reread the first two lines. Point out that *tiger* begins with *t*. Model placing a self-stick note under the letter *t* in *tiger*.

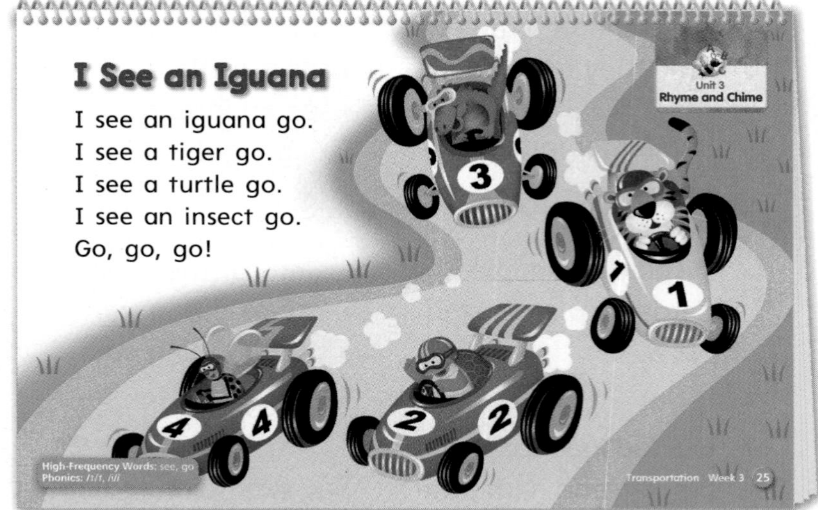

Teaching Chart 25

Guided Practice/Practice

Read the rest of the Rhyme and Chime. Stop after each line. Children place self-stick notes below words that begin with *t*. Guide practice with *turtle* in line 3. Repeat with *i*.

Let's place a sticky note below the word in the line that begins with the letter *t*. The word *turtle* begins with the letter *t*.

Which word begins with letter *i*? Yes, the word *iguana* begins with the letter *i*.

Corrective Feedback

If children cannot discern initial /i/*i*, write the word *insect* on the board. Have children say /i/, /i/, /i/ as you point to the letter *i* in *insect*.

Build Fluency: Sound-Spellings

Display the following **Word-Building Cards**: *a, m, p, s, t*. Have children chorally say each sound. Repeat and vary the pace.

Handwriting: Review *Tt, Ii*

MODEL Model holding up your writing hand. Say the handwriting cues from the **Handwriting Teacher's Edition** as you write the capital and lowercase forms of *Tt* and *Ii* on the board. Then trace the letters on the board and in the air.

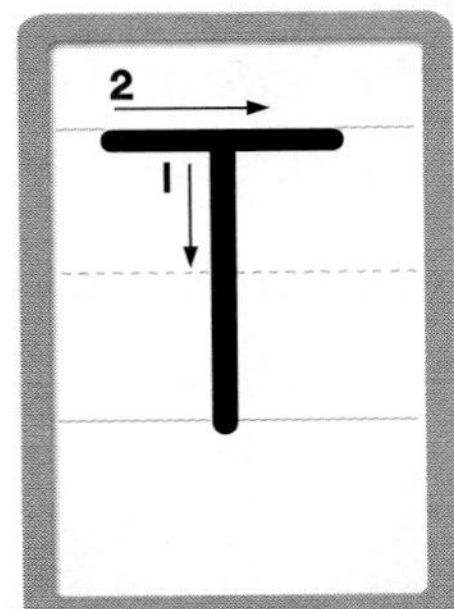

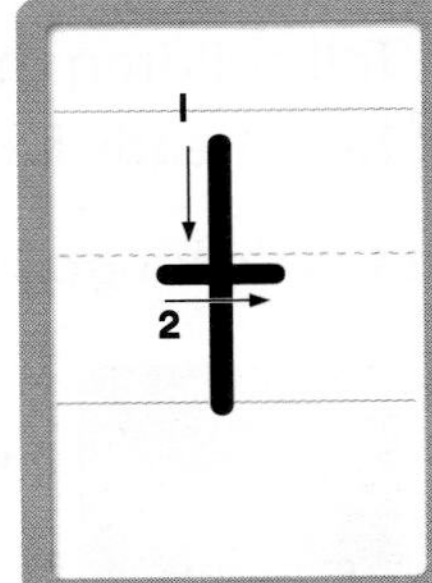

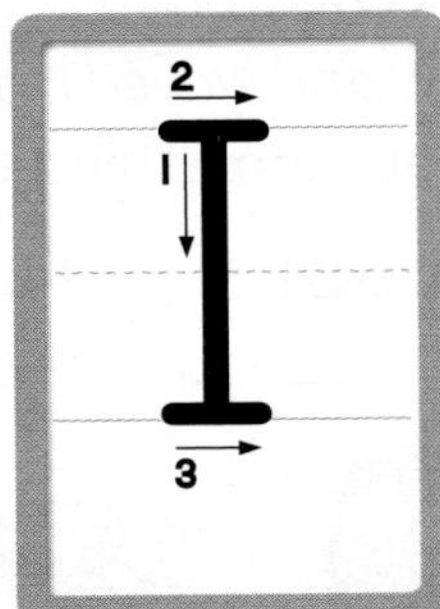

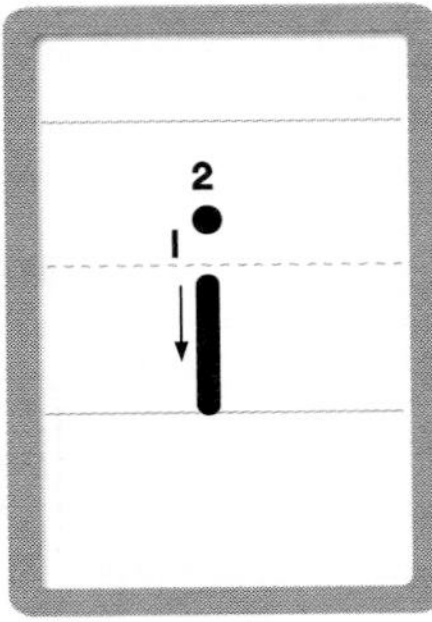

PRACTICE Ask children to hold up their writing hand.

- Say the cues together as children trace with their index finger the letters you wrote on the board.
- Have children write *T* and *t* in the air as they say /t/ multiple times. Repeat with *Ii*.
- Distribute handwriting practice pages. Observe children's pencil grips and paper positions, and correct as necessary. Have children say /t/ every time they write letter *t* and say /i/ every time they write letter *i*.

For Tier 2 instruction, see page 739.

Daily Handwriting

Check that children form letters starting at the top and moving to the bottom. See Handwriting Teacher's Edition for ball-and-stick and slant models.

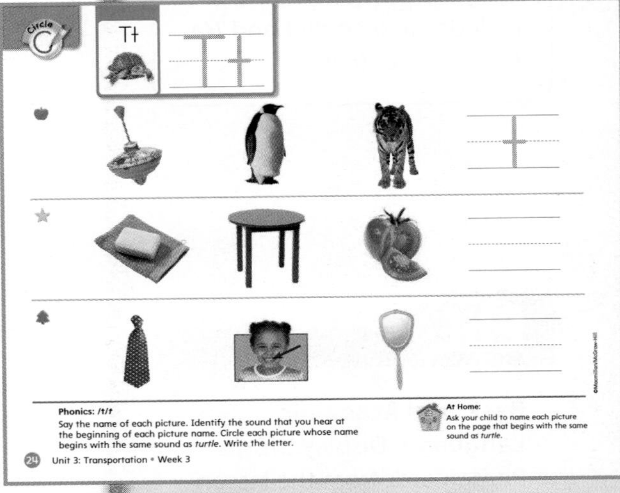

Activity Book, page 24
Practice Book, page 73

Objective

- Understand and use past-tense action words (verbs) to tell about actions

Materials

- Read-Aloud Trade Book: *Duck on a Bike*
- Photo Cards: *cow, dog, goat, horse, pig*

Corrective Feedback

Linguistic Differences Speakers of African American Vernacular English will add *had* to the simple past tense, saying: *We had picked* for *We picked*. The use of *had* indicates the past perfect tense in standard academic English. Other common nonstandard forms of irregular past-tense verbs include *He seen that* and *He had run over there*.

ELL

Basic and Academic Language Display the Photo Cards from the lesson and pair English Language Learners with fluent speakers. Have partners make up sentences about something that happened before with each animal. Write their sentences, read them with the children, and ask: *What happened before?*

Grammar

Action Words (Verbs)

MODEL Use the **Trade Book** *Duck on a Bike* to discuss action words. Remind children that an action word tells what someone or something does. Say that action words can tell about something that has already happened. Display the illustration on page 9 as you read the first sentence: *Duck rode past Cow and waved to her.* Tell children that there are two action words in that sentence—*rode* and *waved*.

- Ask children to act out and repeat the sentence *Duck rode past Cow and waved to her*. Tell children that the *rode* and *waved* tell about something that has already happened.

PRACTICE Show **Photo Cards** for *goat, cow, horse, dog,* and *pig*.

- Help children identify each picture name. Model saying sentences about actions of the animals, such as:

> *Duck* rode *past Cow.*
>
> *Goat* pushed *over the garbage.*

- After each sentence, ask children to name the action word. Then have children make up their own sentences about the action that has already happened in the *Duck on a Bike* illustration. Guide them to name the action word in each sentence. Guide children to write the action word that they identified.

Writing

Shared Writing: A List

BRAINSTORM

Remind children that in *Duck on a Bike,* they met a duck traveling on a bike. *What other things with* ***wheels*** *might Duck ride on?*

WRITE

- Create a list as shown below. Read the title aloud as you track the print. Have children repeat.
- Point to the cover of the **Trade Book** and read the title *Duck on a Bike*. Say: *Duck likes to have fun* ***adventures****. He would have fun riding on a skateboard, too, so I will write* skateboard *on the list.*
- Have children suggest other things Duck would have fun riding on. Add their suggestions to the list. Read the list together.
- Ask children to name their favorite thing that Duck could ride. Put a checkmark by the class favorite.
- Point out how the words are written one under the other. *A list helps us remember information and ideas.*
- Save the list to refer to in other writing activities this week.

Write About It

Ask each child to draw a picture of a duck or another farm animal on a bike. Help them label the drawing.

Objective

- Dictate information for a list

Materials

- Read-Aloud Trade Book: *Duck on a Bike*

5-Day Writing

Book Title	
DAY 1	Shared: A List
DAY 2	Interactive: Book Title
DAY 3	Independent: Prewrite and Draft Book Title
DAY 4	Independent: Revise and Edit Book Title
DAY 5	Independent: Publish and Present

ELL

Prewriting Planning Use the **Trade Book** to help children point to and name different kinds of farm animals before they begin working on their notebook entries. Create a list for children to refer to. Ask them to think of a word for a sound a farm animal might make. Guide them to label their pictures with the sound word.

Transitions That Teach

While children are lining up, have them name things that have **wheels**.

DAY 2 At a Glance

WHOLE GROUP

Oral Language
- Build Robust Vocabulary

Comprehension
- Reread *Duck on a Bike*
- Strategy: Recognize Story Structure
- Skill: Identify Character and Plot
- Fluency: Echo-Read

Vocabulary
- Shape Words
- Story Words: *waddled, wobbled*

Phonemic Awareness
- Phoneme Identity

Phonics
- Review /p/*p*, /t/*t*, /i/*i*
- Blend with /i/*i*, /t/*t*, /s/*s*
- Pre-decodable Reader: *I See a Truck Go*

Writing
- Interactive Writing: Book Title

SMALL GROUP
- Differentiated Instruction, pages 738–763

Oral Vocabulary

Week 3

adventure attach haul
massive wheels

Review

familiar journey prepare
relax travel

Use the **Define/Example/Ask** routine in the **Instructional Routine Handbook** to review the words.

Oral Language

Build Robust Vocabulary

INTRODUCE WORDS

Remind children that in the **Trade Book** *Duck on a Bike*, Duck has an adventure riding a bike. *When you have an adventure, you have a really exciting time. Going on a field trip can be an adventure. You can ride a bus with wheels on a field trip.* Tell children to ask each other questions about a time when they experienced an adventure. For example: *Did you ride a vehicle during your adventure? How many wheels did it have?*

Vocabulary Routine

Use the routine below to discuss the meaning of each word.

Define: **Wheels** are round objects that roll and are used to move vehicles. Say the word with me.
Example: A tricycle has three wheels, and a bicycle has two wheels.
Ask: What are some vehicles that have four wheels?

Define: When you have an **adventure**, you have a really exciting time. Say the word with me.
Example: Our trip to Mexico was an adventure for the whole family.
Ask: Can you tell about an adventure that you will never forget?

CREATE A CHART

Create a chart or use **Teaching Chart G4**. Write the title as shown. Read the chart together as you track the print. *I can use the chart to show who has adventures on bikes and what those adventures are. I'll put Duck's name in the first column. Who rides a bike next? Who rides a bike at the end of the story? Where should I put their names?* When the chart is complete, read all the words with children and have them repeat using complete sentences.

Who Rides a Bike?		
Duck	kids	Horse, Cow, Sheep Pig, Cat, Dog Chicken, Goat

Listen for Rhyme

IDENTIFY RHYME

Tell children that words rhyme when they have the same ending sounds. *The word* day *rhymes with* away. Tell children *day* and *away* end with the sounds for *-ay*. Guide children to generate new words that rhyme with *day*.

SING ABOUT TRANSPORTATION

Let's sing a song about building tracks for trains. The wheels of trains run on rails. Another word for the tracks is railroad. *It is a road made from rails. How is a railroad similar to a road used for cars? How are the wheels of a train different from the wheels of a car?*

Explain to children that railroads were built in the United States about 150 years ago and this song is almost that old.

Play the song "I've Been Working on the Railroad," using the **Listening Library Audio CD**. Then teach children the words and sing the song.

Point out that the words *day* and *away* rhyme.

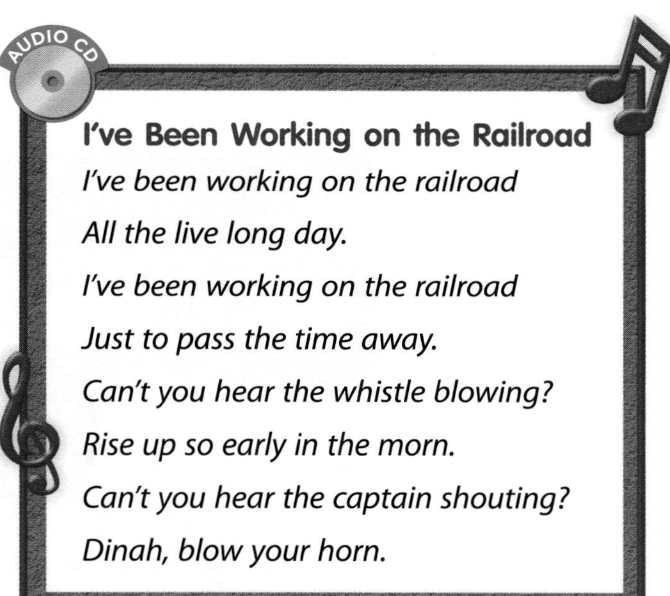

AUDIO CD
I've Been Working on the Railroad
I've been working on the railroad
All the live long day.
I've been working on the railroad
Just to pass the time away.
Can't you hear the whistle blowing?
Rise up so early in the morn.
Can't you hear the captain shouting?
Dinah, blow your horn.

ELL ENGLISH LANGUAGE LEARNERS

Beginning

Confirm Understanding Review oral vocabulary from prior lessons using the characters in *Duck on a Bike.* For example, display page 7. Say: *This is Duck. Is this Duck?* (Yes, it's Duck.) Repeat with other characters.

Intermediate

Enhance Understanding Display the same page and ask: *What is Duck riding?* (a bike) *Yes, Duck is riding a bike.* Guide children to answer in complete sentences.

Advanced

Share Preferences Have children discuss who their favorite animal character is. Ask them to dictate a sentence that tells why this character is their favorite. Write their sentences and read them together.

Objectives

- Use oral vocabulary words *wheel* and *adventure*
- Complete a chart
- Discuss the theme
- Orally generate rhymes in response to spoken words

Materials

- Read-Aloud Trade Book: *Duck on a Bike*
- Graphic Organizer; Teaching Chart G4
- Listening Library Audio CD

Digital Learning

Song on Listening Library Audio CD

Objectives

- Recognize story structure
- Identify character and plot
- Respond to a story
- Retell a story
- Develop fluency

Materials

- Read-Aloud Trade Book: *Duck on a Bike*
- Retelling Cards
- Activity Book, pp. 25–26
- Practice Book, p. 74

Trade Book

Digital Learning

AUDIO CD

Story on **Listening Library Audio CD**

ELL

Gesture and Talk
Use gestures and other strategies to help make the text comprehensible.

pp. 8–9
silliest thing: Demonstrate by being a quacking duck wobbling along on a bike while the other animals (the children) watch. Point to yourself pretending to be a duck, laugh, and say *funny, silly.* Ask children to do a silly thing, such as making a face, while saying *silly.*

Reread the Trade Book

Listening Comprehension

CONCEPTS ABOUT PRINT Display the cover and read the title aloud with children as you track the print.

STRATEGY Recognize Story Structure

Explain to children that stories usually follow a certain order (a beginning, middle, and end) in which things happen to the characters. Have them recall the plot in *Duck on a Bike.*

SKILL Identify Character and Plot

Tell children that a story's plot is what happens to the characters or people or animals. *To understand the plot, it is important to know who the characters are and what they are like.* Display pages 6–7.

Think Aloud I see Duck getting onto a bike. He looks excited. I think Duck likes to have fun **adventures** and try new things.

Read the **Trade Book** and use the prompts on the inside back cover.

pages 6–7

PLOT

Think Aloud Duck is getting on the bike. I think the story will be about what happens during Duck's adventure.

pages 8–9

CHARACTER

Think Aloud Cow thinks that a duck riding a bike is very silly. That tells me that she does not like to try to do things she isn't used to doing.

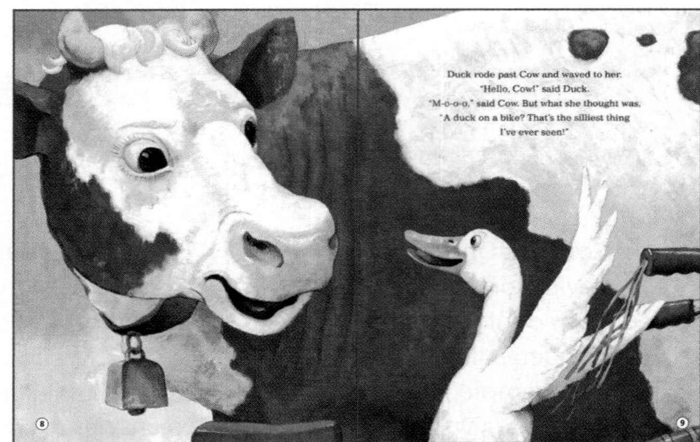

Develop Comprehension

pages 10–11

STORY STRUCTURE

Think Aloud These pages tell what Sheep thinks about Duck riding a bike. I think the next pages will tell us what other animals think about Duck's bike ride.

pages 12–13

CHARACTER

- *How can you tell that Dog would like to ride a bike?* (Possible answer: He says it is a *neat trick*.)

pages 14–15

ILLUSTRATOR'S CRAFT

- *How does the illustrator show us that Cat is not excited about Duck's ride?* (Cat is lying on her back. She is not even looking at Duck.)

pages 16–17

ASK QUESTIONS

- *What is helping Duck go faster than he usually can?* (the **wheels** on the bike)

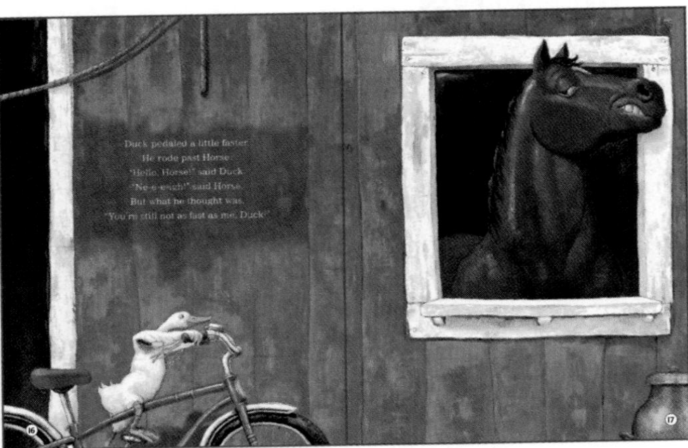

Comprehension

Recognize Story Structure

- (pages 10–11) The pages before this told us what Cow thought when Duck rode by. These pages tell what Sheep thinks about Duck riding a bike. I think the next pages will tell us what other animals think about Duck's bike ride.

Identify Character

- (pages 12–13) Do you think Dog would like to ride a bike? I think he would because he says it is a neat trick.

Identify Plot

- (pages 26–27) I see that a group of children have come to the farm and left their bikes in front of the house. This is different from what has happened on other pages. I wonder what will happen in the rest of the story?

Story Words

(page 7) **waddled** (page 7) **wobbled**

About the Author/Illustrator: David Shannon

When David Shannon illustrates a book, he sketches until he sees the character. "That's an exciting moment," he says. "Sometimes it's as if the character stands up off the paper and starts running around my drawing table." In addition to writing and drawing about wild animals on bikes, David Shannon writes about himself as a wild boy in *No, David!* and *David Goes to School.*

Trade Book Inside Back Cover

ELL

pp. 10–11
careful: Have children pretend to be Duck riding on a bike, then have them pretend to ride bikes safely. Ask children to say *careful* or *not careful* to describe what they are doing.

pp. 14–15
waste: Make a mark on a piece of paper, crumple it up, and throw it in the trash. Hold up the paper and say *waste.* Point to things in the room and things in the trash and ask children to identify whether the items are *waste* or *not waste.*

pp. 16–17
not as fast: Walk across the room with a child, but walk slowly. Tell children you were *not as fast* as the child. Ask pairs of children to walk across the room. Have children say which partner was not as fast as the other.

Text Evidence

Character and Plot

Explain Remind children that when they answer a question, they need to find evidence in the text to support their answers.

Discuss Have children look at and listen to pages 18–19. Ask: *What is happening? How do you think Duck feels?* (Duck looks scared. He looks like he's going to bump into something.)

ELL

pp. 18–19
Watch where you're going: Place objects on the floor and walk around them while thinking aloud. *I see a book, so I step around it. I see a box, so I step over it. I watch where I am going so I won't trip or fall.* Have children follow the same path. Ask them why they are looking at the floor. Have them respond: *I watch where I am going.*

pp. 22–23
show-off: Pretend to be Duck strutting away on the bike. Glance around to see who is watching, with a superior look on your face. Then stop being Duck, shake your head, and say: *Show-off!* Pretend to be Duck showing off again and ask children to say the phrase.

pp. 24–25
just like: Ask a child who shares a similarity with you to stand. Use the phrase *just like* to describe the similarity. For example: *Mario wears glasses just like me.*

Develop Comprehension

pages 18–19

PLOT

- *What problem does Chicken think Duck might have? How do you know?* (Possible answer: She thinks he might bump into something and get hurt. She tells him to watch where he is going.)

pages 20–21

CONCEPT WORDS: SOUND WORDS

- *What word tells how Goat sounds?* (m-a-a-a) *What words tell sounds other animals in this book make?* (Possible answers: *moo, b-a-a-a, cluck, woof*)

pages 22–23

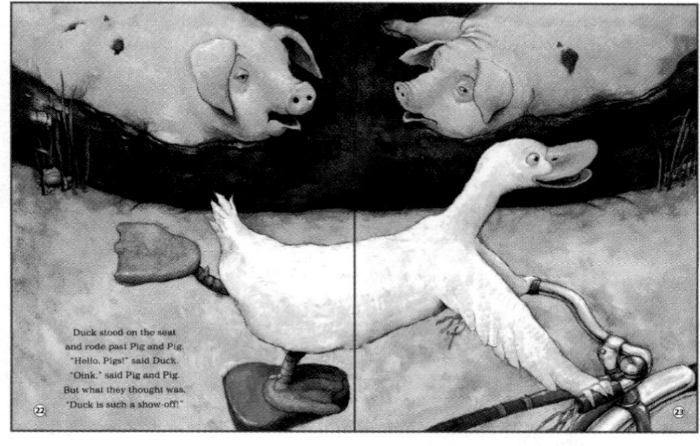

MAKE PREDICTIONS

- *Based on what is happening on this page, what do you think Duck will do next?* (Answers will vary.)

pages 24–25

CHARACTER

- *Is Duck riding safely, or is he being unsafe? Why do you think so? What does this tell us about Duck?* (He is being unsafe. He is riding with no hands. He does risky things.)

pages 26–27

PLOT

Think Aloud I see that a group of children have come to the farm and left their bikes in front of the house. I wonder how it will change what happens in the rest of the story.

pages 28–29

PLOT

- *The animals are looking at the bicycles. What might they be thinking? What might happen next?* (Possible answer: The animals are thinking about riding the bicycles. They might get on them.)

pages 30–31

CHARACTER

- *Most of the animals did not think Duck should ride a bike. How do you think they feel about riding bikes now?* (Possible answer: Now they think it is a good idea because they are having fun.)

pages 32–33

STORY STRUCTURE

- *What would you call this part of the story?* (Possible answer: the ending)

ELL

pp. 26–27
parked their bikes: Lead the class in pretending to ride and then park bikes. Have them tell what they are doing using the term *park*.

pp. 30–31
all: Ask some children to stand. *Not all of the children stand.* Ask the class to stand. *All of the children stand.* Ask each child to have all of the children do a simple task, such as putting their hands on their heads. Have the child use the phrase *all of the* when describing what the children are doing.

page 34

CHARACTER

- *Duck is looking at the tractor. What might he be thinking?* (Possible answer: He is thinking about getting on it and trying to drive it.)

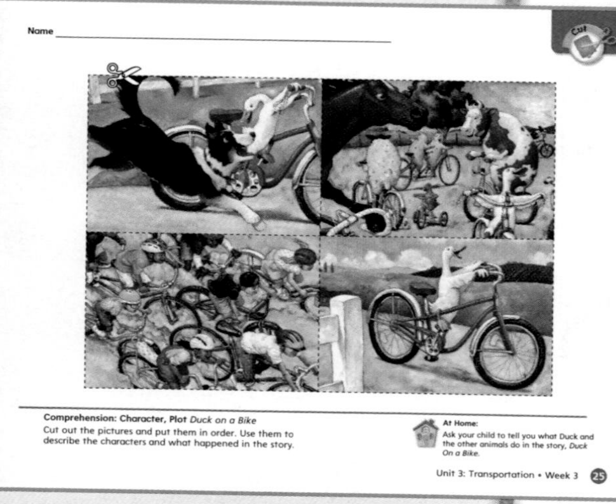

Activity Book, pages 25–26
Practice Book, page 74

Respond to Literature

TALK ABOUT IT Ask children which words and illustrations they liked and have them refer to the book as they answer these questions. Help them speak audibly and in complete sentences.

- *What vehicle is Duck riding?* (a bike) LOCATE
- *What two animals did Duck meet first?* (He met Cow and then Sheep.) COMBINE
- *Why do the animals decide to ride? Do they enjoy their **adventure**?* (They were curious to see what it felt like to ride a bike; they looked happy and said it was fun.) CONNECT

Retell

Retelling Cards

GUIDED RETELLING
Tell children that now they will use these cards to retell the story.

- Display **Retelling Card 1**. Based on children's needs, use either the Guided, Modeled, or ELL Retelling prompts. The Modeled prompts contain support for ELLs based on levels of language acquisition. Repeat with the rest of the cards, using the prompts as a guide.
- Discuss the story. *Who was your favorite character? Why?*
- Have children act out their favorite part of the story.

Fluency: Echo-Read

MODEL Reread pages 8–11, using different voices and tones for each character. Reread pages 12–19 and have children echo-read.

Quick Check

Can children identify character and plot to understand a story?
Can children begin to retell a main event from a story?

Retelling Rubric

4 Excellent

Retells the selection without prompting, in sequence, and using supporting details. Clearly describes the setting, main characters, and complete plot.

3 Good

Retells the selection with little guidance, in sequence, and using some details. Generally describes the setting, main characters, and plot.

2 Fair

Retells the selection with some guidance, mostly in sequence, and using limited details. Partially describes the setting, main characters, and plot.

1 Unsatisfactory

Retells the selection only when prompted, out of sequence, and using limited details. Does not describe the main characters or plot.

Vocabulary

Shape Words

Chant the following jingle:

I draw a circle. *It's a sun.*

I draw a square. *It's a house.*

I draw a triangle. *It's a roof.*

I draw a rectangle. *It's a door.*

I drew a picture just for you!

- Repeat the first line and tell children which word names a shape. Have them name other things that have a circle shape. Repeat with each line.
- Display the title page of the **Trade Book** *Duck on a Bike*. Have children point to and name the shapes they see in the picture.

NAME SHAPE WORDS Play "What Am I?" Give children clues such as: *I am the shape of* ***wheels****. What am I?* (circle) Then show children pictures of different shapes and ask them to sort them by shape.

Story Words: *waddled, wobbled*

- Display page 7 of *Duck on a Bike* and point out the two words *waddled* and *wobbled*. *Duck waddled when he walked, and he wobbled when he rode the bike.* Ask a child to *waddle* like a duck. Explain that *wobble* means "to move unsteadily from side to side."
- Have children repeat: *Duck waddled and wobbled.* Ask them if they think the author chose good words to describe Duck's actions.

TIME TO MOVE!

Have children follow three-step directions to move around the room like an animal: *Waddle like a duck. Trot like a horse. Hop like a rabbit.* Have children say the phrase as they make the movement.

Objectives

- Identify shape words *circle, square, triangle, rectangle*
- Sort pictures of shapes into categories
- Understand story words *waddled, wobbled*
- Identify and use words that name actions

Materials

- Read-Aloud Trade Book: *Duck on a Bike*
- pictures of different shapes

Digital Learning

For children who need additional language support and oral vocabulary development, use the activities found at **www.macmillanmh.com**.

ELL

Reinforce Meaning After children answer *What am I?* by naming a shape, have a child draw the shape on the board. Ask another child to say a sentence using the shape name and the name of an object with that shape. For example: *A wheel is the shape of a circle.*

Objectives

- Identify medial /i/, /a/ in words
- Match the letters *p*, *t*, and *i* to their sounds
- Blend sounds in words with /i/*i*, /s/*s*, /t/*t*
- Blend with /a/*a*, /m/*m*, /p/*p*

Materials

- Photo Cards: *fish, pig, six*
- Word-Building Cards
- Word-Building Cards; Teacher's Resource Book, pp. 95–102
- pocket chart

Phonemic Awareness

Phoneme Identity

Model

Display the **Photo Cards** for *fish, pig,* and *six*.

Say the words.

Repeat for medial /a/.

These picture names are *fish, pig, six*. Say the names with me: *fish, pig,* and *six*. *Fish, pig,* and *six* have /i/ in the middle.

Listen as I say three words. Listen for the sound that is the same: *hat, map, fan.*

The middle sound, /a/, is the same in *hat, map,* and *fan*.

Guided Practice/Practice

Follow the routine with these sets of words. Children identify the sound that is the same. Guide practice with the first set of words.

What sound is the same in these words?

kit, miss, lid (/i/)

cat, fan, map (/a/)

sip, Tim, big (/i/)

man, sat, had (/a/)

fix, lid, him (/i/)

pat, sad, bat (/a/)

Phonics

Review /p/*p*, /t/*t*, /i/*i*

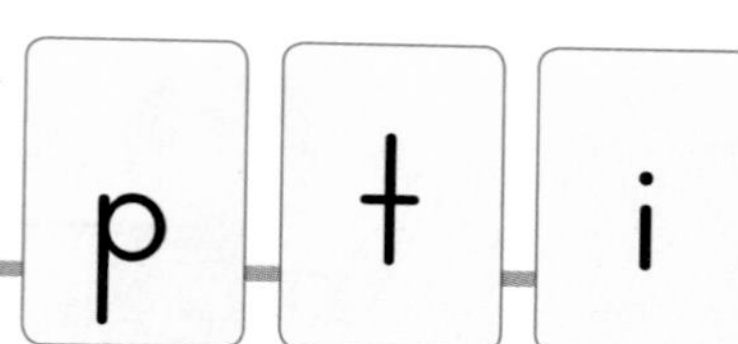

Model

Display **Word-Building Card** *p*.

Repeat for *i* and *t*.

This is letter *p*. The letter *p* stands for the sound /p/ at the beginning of *pig*.

Hold up Word-Building Card *p*.

Repeat with the word *if*.

I will say a word: *pen*. I hear the /p/ sound at the beginning of *pen*. The letter *p* stands for the /p/ sound. I hold up the *p* card.

Guided Practice/Practice

Distribute copies of **Word-Building Cards**. Children hold up the letter that stands for the beginning sound. Guide practice with the first word.

Listen as I say a word. Hold up the letter card that stands for the beginning sound.

pat	tip	in	tell
ink	pin	tan	is

Build Fluency: Sound-Spellings

Display the following Word-Building Cards: *a, i, m, p, s, t.* Have children chorally say each sound. Repeat and vary the pace.

Blend with /i/*i*, /t/*t*, /s/*s*

Model

Place Word-Building Card *s* in the pocket chart.

This letter is *s.* It stands for /s/. Say /s/.

Place Word-Building Card *i* next to *s.* Move your hand from left to right.

This letter is *i.* It stands for /i/. Listen as I blend the two sounds together: /sssiii/. Now you blend the sounds with me. (/sssiii/)

Place Word-Building Card *t* next to *si.* Move your hand from left to right.

This letter is *t.* It stands for /t/. Listen as I blend the three sounds together: /sssiiit/. What is the word? (/sssiiit/, *sit*)

Repeat with *tap.*

Guided Practice/Practice

Children blend sounds to form words. Guide practice with the first word, using the routine.

Pam	Sam	it	pat	sap
Tim	pit	sat	mat	sit

For Tier 2 instruction, see page 745.

ELL

Reinforce Meaning Review the meaning of words in the Guided Practice. Model saying each word and ask children to repeat. Pair English Language Learners with fluent speakers to make up sentences using the words. Have partners dictate their sentences. Write them on the board, read them together, and act them out. Example: *I sit on the chair.*

Objectives

- Review and read the high-frequency words *a, go, like, see*
- Know that reading moves from left to right
- Use cover, title, and illustrations to predict story events
- Reread for fluency

Materials

- Pre-decodable Reader: *I See a Truck Go*
- High-Frequency Word Cards: *a, go, like, see*

Pre-decodable Reader

Read *I See a Truck Go*

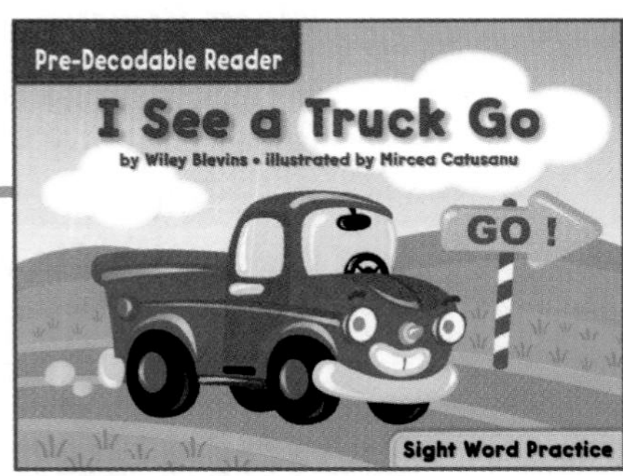

I See a Truck Go

REVIEW HIGH-FREQUENCY WORDS Display **High-Frequency Word Cards** for **go**, **see**, **a**, **like**. Review the words using the **Read/Spell/Write** routine.

MODEL CONCEPTS ABOUT PRINT
Display pages 2–3. *Read the words on the left page from left to right. Then, read the words on the right page from left to right. Use your finger as you track the print.*

PREDICT Ask children to describe the cover illustration and identify the vehicle. Ask them to read the title and predict what the story will be about.

FIRST READ Point out the rebus and discuss what it stands for. Have children point to each word and say the sight words quickly. Children should chorally read the story the first time through.

DEVELOP COMPREHENSION Ask the following: *Look at page 4. What do you think you will see on the next page? Why?*

SECOND READ Have partners reread the book together. Circulate, listen in, and provide corrective feedback.

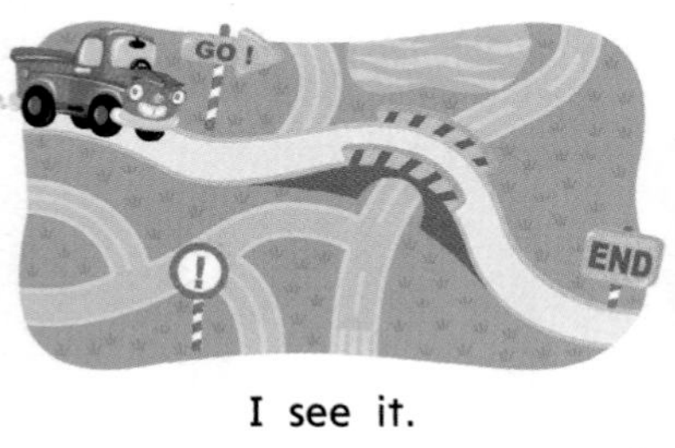

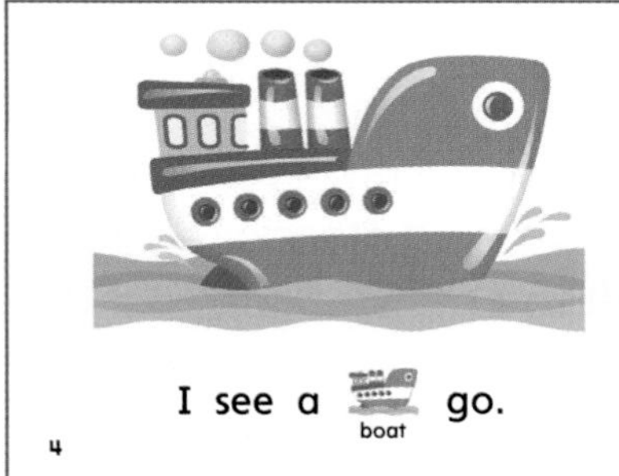

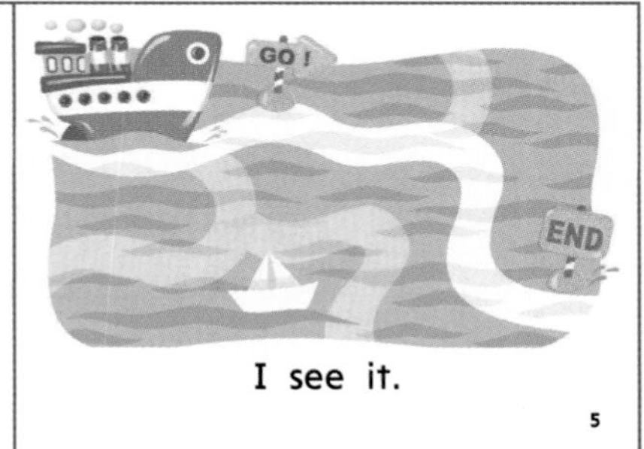

Pre-decodable Reader

Writing

Interactive Writing: Book Title

REVIEW

- Display and read the list that children created for the Shared Writing activity.

WRITE

- Tell children that you are going to write a title for a new story about another **adventure** Duck might have.
- Write the following title frame on chart paper, as it would appear on a cover. Read the title frame aloud as you track the print.

Duck on a ___________.

- Have children suggest something else Duck would have fun riding, using the list as a reference. Write the name of the item in the frame to complete the title. Tell children to help you by writing all the letters they know.
- Read the completed title aloud as you track the print. Add an illustration.
- Point out that the title they created contains information from the list.
- To extend the activity, work with children to write a story to go along with the new title or have children dictate an experience in sequence about vehicles they have used.

Write About It

Ask children to draw and label a picture of themselves on a vehicle. Help them write about the picture, using the word *go*.

Objectives

- Write a title
- Use letter knowledge to write letters in a word
- Dictate sentences to tell a story in order

Materials

- Shared Writing lists from Day 1

5-Day Writing

Book Title	
DAY 1	Shared: A List
DAY 2	Interactive: Book Title
DAY 3	Independent: Prewrite and Draft Book Title
DAY 4	Independent: Revise and Edit Book Title
DAY 5	Independent: Publish and Present

ELL

Reinforce Vocabulary Start a conversation with children about vehicles they have or wish to have. Example: *I have a scooter. My scooter is red. Do you have a scooter? It's fun to ride a scooter.*

Transitions That Teach

While packing up, have children describe an **adventure** that they would like to go on.

Day 3 At a Glance

WHOLE GROUP

Oral Language
- Build Robust Vocabulary
- Oral Vocabulary Cards: "Big, Big Trucks"

Comprehension
- Read "How Do You Go to School?"
- Text Features: Captions and Labels

High-Frequency Words
- Review *go*, *see*

Phonemic Awareness
- Phoneme Blending

Phonics
- Review /i/*i*, /t/*t*, /p/*p*, /s/*s*
- Blend with /i/*i*, /t/*t*, /p/*p*, /s/*s*

Grammar
- Action Words (Verbs)

Writing
- Independent Writing: Book Title

SMALL GROUP
- Differentiated Instruction, pages 738–763

Additional Vocabulary

To provide 15–20 minutes of additional vocabulary instruction, see Oral Vocabulary Cards 5-Day Plan. The pre- and posttests for this week can be found in the **Teacher's Resource Book**, pages 218–219.

Oral Language

Build Robust Vocabulary

BUILD BACKGROUND

Introduce the story "Big, Big Trucks" using **Oral Vocabulary Card 1** and read the title aloud. *Have you seen trucks that can haul objects? Have you seen trucks with more than four wheels?* Ask children to tell what they think this text will be about.

- Read the story on the back of the cards. Pause at each oral vocabulary word and read the definition. Check children's understanding using the Use Background Knowledge, Generate Synonyms, and Compare and Contrast prompts.

Oral Vocabulary Cards

Vocabulary Routine

Use the routine below to discuss the meaning of each word.

Define: **Haul** means "to carry a load of something." Say the word with me.
Example: The farmer will haul corn in his pickup truck.
Ask: Which of these things can haul: a wagon, a truck, a rock, a kite, a train?

Define: When you **attach** one thing to another, you fasten or join the two things. Say the word with me.
Example: I'll attach the leash to my dog's collar before I take him for a walk.
Ask: What would you use to attach a piece of yarn to a paper-bag puppet?

Define: When something is **massive**, it is large and heavy. Say the word with me.
Example: We saw a massive whale at the aquarium.
Ask: What would a massive rock look like?

- Use the routine on Cards 1 and 2 to review the words **wheel** and **adventure**.
- Review last week's words: *familiar, journey, prepare, relax,* and *travel.*

Listen for Rhyme

IDENTIFY RHYME

Tell children that they will sing a song about a way people got around long ago. Play the song and ask children to join in.

Discuss the song. Tell children that it was sung hundreds of years ago during the Revolutionary War. *How did Yankee Doodle get to town? Did he ride a vehicle with wheels? How might he get to town today?*

Model blending phonemes to form words from the song: /i/ /t/, *it*; /h/ /i/ /z/, *his*; /k/ /a/ /p/, *cap*. Then have children repeat.

Yankee Doodle

Yankee Doodle came to town
A-riding on a pony.
He stuck a feather in his cap
And called it macaroni.
Yankee Doodle, keep it up.
Yankee Doodle dandy!
Mind the music and the step.
Yankee Doodle dandy!

Objectives

- Discuss the theme
- Use oral vocabulary words *adventure, attach, haul, massive,* and *wheels*
- Listen and respond to a nonfiction selection
- Blend phonemes

Materials

- Oral Vocabulary Cards: "Big, Big Trucks"

Digital Learning

Song on **Listening Library Audio CD**

Objectives

- Retell important facts
- Use photographs, captions, and labels to find information
- Identify the topic and details in expository text
- Identify and display different kinds of transportation
- Use a picture dictionary

Materials

- Big Book of Explorations, Vol. 1: "How Do You Go to School?" pp. 39–42
- pictures of types of transportation from magazines and newspapers
- poster board

Content Vocabulary

rain forest a hot, rainy place with a lot of trees

cable a thick rope made from wires

helmet a hard covering that protects your head

Use a Picture Dictionary Guide children to find each word in a picture dictionary.

Informational Text

Genre

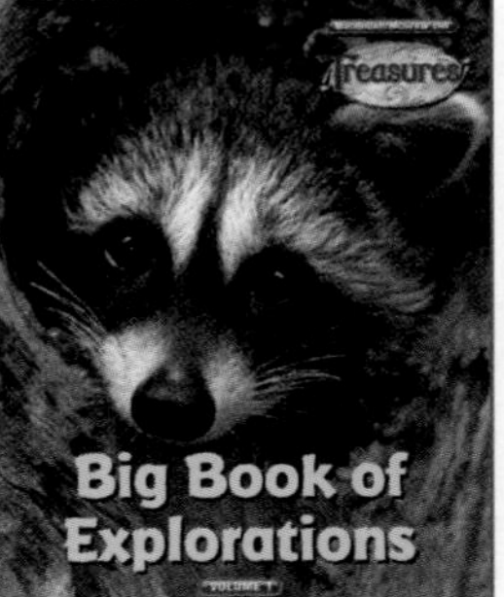

Big Book of Explorations

INFORMATIONAL TEXT: EXPOSITORY Tell children that this selection is **expository** text, a text that explains or gives information. Some expository text gives information using words and photographs. Tell children that sometimes photographs can give more information than words.

READ "HOW DO YOU GO TO SCHOOL?"

- **Preview and Predict** Display the first page and read the title as you track the print. Explain that children who live in different places in the world travel to school in different ways. *What will this selection be about? What will you learn in this selection?*
- **Content Vocabulary** Introduce and discuss the vocabulary words.
- **Text Feature: Captions and Labels** Explain the difference between captions and labels. *Captions and labels both give readers information about a picture.* Point to the girls on page 39. I *see the girls riding something that looks like a bicycle but has only one wheel. I can read the caption to see what this kind of transportation is called.* Read the caption on page 39 aloud. Point out the labels on page 42.

CONTENT FOCUS

Explain to children that kinds of transportation such as unicycles, motorcycles, scooters, boats, and cables make it faster and easier for people to get places. As you read pages 40 and 41, ask children how each child goes to school. Explain why Donna needs snow shoes to walk to school. Have children tell you how the captions help them understand how each child travels to school.

After reading page 42, ask children to name different ways that children go to school. Have children discuss similarities and differences. How are all the children in the selection alike? *Who goes to school in a rain forest?*

Use Captions and Labels Point to the photograph of Kayla and Hannah on page 39. *What are these girls riding?* (unicycles) Turn to page 40 and point to the photograph of Donna. *What are these things on Donna's feet called?* (snow shoes) Point to the boy on the scooter. *How does Jack go to school?* (on a scooter) Turn to page 41. *How does Daisy slow down?* (She uses a tree branch.) *How does Daisy carry her books?* (in a bag)

page 39

pages 40–41

Off to School!
Do you walk or ride a bus to school?

These kids go to school on a bicycle rickshaw.

Jack goes to school on a scooter.

Donna goes to school on snow shoes.

These kids go to school on a boat.

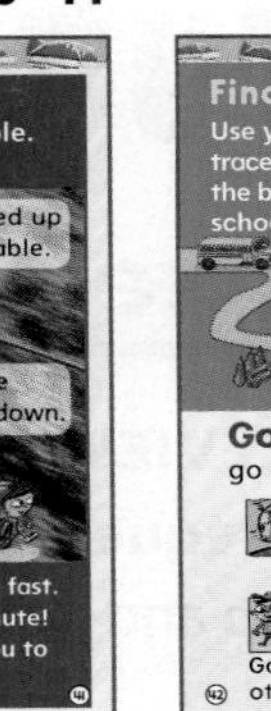

page 42

Find the Way
Use your finger to trace a path from the bus to the school.

post office
school
bank
fire station
market
park

Think Big!
How else do you think kids can get to school?

Go Safely Match the way to go to school with the safety rule.

bus
scooter
walking
Go with others.
Stay in your seat.
Wear a helmet.

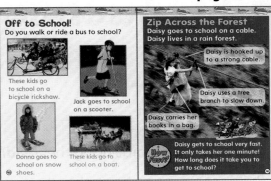

Retell and Respond

- *What is the topic, or idea, of this selection?*
- *Which kinds of transportation did you learn about?*
- *What is one rule for getting to school safely?*
- *How does transportation help people?*

Connect to Content

Social Studies: Transportation Collage

- Provide magazines, catalogs, newspapers, and poster board for each group.
- Review that there are many ways for people to get places. Have children name the ways children in the selection get to school. Have them name ways that they or children they know get to school.
- Have children work in groups to identify and cut out pictures of kinds of transportation.
- Have children write the sentence "We go to school" on their collages.

ELL

Beginning

Pantomime and Gesture Use pantomime and gestures. For example, for *unicycle* on page 39, extend your arms outward and act as if you are balancing on one wheel; for *snow shoes* on page 40, walk with big steps; for *cable* on page 41, weave a piece of yarn through a paper clip so it can slide. Demonstrate Donna's trip to school. Point to and say the words as children pantomime and echo after you.

Intermediate

Use Photographs Use photos to help children gather information. On page 40, ask: *What kind of weather is Donna dressed for? Which photo might show a warm place? How do you know?*

Advanced

Vocabulary and Key Concepts On page 41, ask: *Why does Daisy ride on a cable to travel in the rain forest? Why doesn't she take a bus? How is the way Daisy gets to school different from the way you do?*

High-Frequency Words

Objectives

- Review and read the high-frequency words *go, see*
- Follow agreed-upon rules for discussion by taking turns

Materials

- High-Frequency Word Cards: *a, can, go, I, see, the, we*
- High-Frequency Word Cards; Teacher's Resource Book, pp. 103–110
- Photo Cards: *bike, bus, train*
- pocket chart
- Activity Book, pp. 27–28
- Practice Book, pp. 75–76

Activity Book, pages 27–28
Practice Book, pages 75–76

go, see

go | see

REVIEW Display the **High-Frequency Word Cards** for **go** and **see**. Review the words using the **Read/Spell/Write** routine.

APPLY Build sentences in the pocket chart using High-Frequency Word Cards and **Photo Cards**. Read each sentence aloud, then have children chorally read it as you track the print with your finger. Use the sentence below and the following: *I see the train go. We see the bus. We can go.*

READ FOR FLUENCY Chorally read the Take-Home Book with children. Then have children reread the book to review high-frequency words and build fluency.

Quick Check

Can children read the words *go* and *see*?

During **Small Group Instruction**

If No → Approaching Level Provide additional practice with high-frequency words, page 748.

If Yes → On Level Children are ready to read the Take-Home story.

Beyond Level Children are ready to read the Take-Home story.

TIME TO MOVE!

Have children take turns repeating and dramatizing the high-frequency word sentences. As one child says *I see a bike go,* ask other children to act out riding bicycles.

Phonemic Awareness

Phoneme Blending

Model

Place a marker in each box of the **Sound Box** as you say the sounds.

Listen as I say the sounds in a word: /i/ /t/. I place a marker in a box for each sound. There are two sounds: /i/ /t/. Listen as I point to each marker and blend the sounds: /i/ /t/, /iiit/, *it*. Say the sounds with me: /i/ /t/. Now blend the sounds to say the word: *it*.

Repeat with *tip*.

Guided Practice/Practice

Distribute Sound Boxes and markers. Children place a marker in a box for each sound and then blend the sounds.

I will say the sounds in a word. Place a marker in a box for each sound you hear and then blend the sounds to say the word.

/s/ /a/ /m/ /s/ /i/ /t/ /m/ /a/ /p/

/s/ /a/ /t/ /a/ /t/ /i/ /t/

Guide practice with the first word, using the routine.

For Tier 2 instruction, see page 748.

Objectives

- Blend sounds to form one-syllable words
- Segment spoken one-syllable words into two to three phonemes

Materials

- Sound Box
- WorkBoard Sound Boxes; Teacher's Resource Book, p. 136
- markers

Objectives

- Review sound-spellings for /t/*t*, /p/*p*, /s/*s*, /i/*i*
- Blend sounds in words with /t/*t*, /p/*p*, /s/*s*, /i/*i*
- Identify the common sounds that letters represent
- Read simple one-syllable words

Materials

- Sound-Spelling Cards: *Insect, Piano, Sun, Turtle*
- Word-Building Cards
- pocket chart

Phonics

Review /t/*t*, /p/*p*, /s/*s*, /i/*i*

Model

Display the *Turtle* **Sound-Spelling Card**. Repeat for *p, s, i*.	This is the letter *t*. It stands for the /t/ sound you hear at the beginning of *turtle*. What is the letter? What sound does this letter stand for?
Say the word. Write the letter *t*. Repeat for *p, s, i*.	The beginning sound in *time* is /t/. The letter *t* stands for the /t/ sound. I'll write *t*.

Guided Practice/Practice

Children write the letter that stands for the beginning sound. Do the first word with children.	I am going to say some words. Write the letter that stands for the beginning sound. sail inch tail pick tin set pot if

Build Fluency: Sound-Spellings

Display the following **Word-Building Cards**: *a, i, m, p, s, t*. Have children chorally say each sound. Repeat and vary the pace.

For Tier 2 instruction, see page 749.

Blend with /t/t, /p/p, /s/s, /i/i

Model

Place **Word-Building Card** *P* in the pocket chart.

This letter is capital *P*. It stands for /p/. Say /p/.

Place *i* next to *P*. Move your hand from left to right.

This letter is *i*. It stands for /i/. Listen as I blend the two sounds together: /piii/. Now you blend the sounds. (/piii/)

Place *t* next to *Pi*. Move your hand from left to right.

This letter is *t*. It stands for /t/. Listen as I blend the three sounds: /piiit/, *pit*. Now you blend the sounds with me: /piiit/, *pit*.

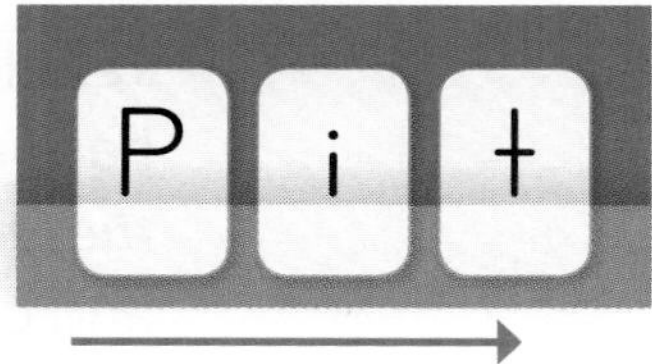

Repeat with *sip*.

Guided Practice/Practice

Children blend sounds to form words.

Tim tap tip sap
pit sip pat sit

Read Words

Apply

Write the words and sentences.

Guide practice with the first word, using the **Sound-by-Sound Blending Routine**.

Read the sentences with children.

tap
Tim
See Tim tap.
Go, Tim, go!

Corrective Feedback

Blending: Sound Error Model the sound that children missed, then have them repeat the sound. For example, for the word *pit*, say: *My turn.* Tap under the letter *t* in the word *pit* and say: *Sound? What's the sound?* Then return to the beginning of the word. Say: *Let's start over.* Blend the word with children again.

ELL

Variations in Language
Review the beginning sounds /p/, /t/, and /i/ using the *piano, turtle*, and *insect* **Sound-Spelling Cards**. Model saying the sounds and then ask children to repeat them. Because there is no sound-symbol match for /i/ in Spanish, Vietnamese, Hmong, Cantonese, Haitian Creole, and Korean, these children may need extra practice pronouncing /i/. Use the small Sound-Spelling Card articulation photos to help children pronounce the /i/ sound.

Objective

- Use past-tense and future tense action words (verbs) to tell about actions

Materials

- teacher-made chart of "Yankee Doodle"
- Photo Cards: *apple, bike, boat, book, car, dog, envelope, fish, football, game, guitar, horse, jacket, juice, jump rope, kite, ladder, newspaper, nose, piano, pizza, rose, shirt, shoe, soup, stairs, teeth, thumb, toe, tree, trumpet, umbrella*

ELL

Basic and Academic Language Display **Photo Cards** from this lesson and pair English Language Learners with fluent speakers. Help partners complete sentence frames with a Photo Card word and an action word. Read together each completed sentence. Then ask: *Did the action happened yesterday or will it happen tomorrow? How do you know?*

Grammar

Action Words (Verbs)

MODEL Use the song "Yankee Doodle" to discuss action words. Remind children that an action word tells what someone or something does. Display the words of the song on chart paper as you read the third and fourth lines: *He stuck a feather in his cap and called it macaroni.* Tell children that *stuck* and *called* are action words.

- Have children act out and say the lines *He stuck a feather in his cap and called it macaroni.* Tell children that action words can be used to tell about something that has already happened. Remind them that the actions of "Yankee Doodle" happened long, long ago. Point behind you as you say this.
- Tell children that the action words can also describe actions happening now. *If we were in the room watching Yankee Doodle put the feather in his hat, we would say:* He sticks a feather in his cap and calls it macaroni. Emphasize *sticks* and *calls.*
- Explain that action words can also tell what will happen in the future. *If we were thinking about what Yankee Doodle will be doing with his hat tomorrow, we would say:* He will stick a feather in his cap and will call it macaroni. Emphasize *will stick* and *will call.*

PRACTICE Show children the **Photo Card** for *shoe* and name the picture. Act out tying your shoe while saying: *Now I tie my shoe.* Point behind you and say: *Yesterday I tied my shoe.* Point in front of you as you say: *Tomorrow I will tie my shoe.*

- After each sentence, ask children to name the action word. Then have children say whether the action word describes something happening now or in the past. Add the sentence *Tomorrow I* __________ *my* __________.

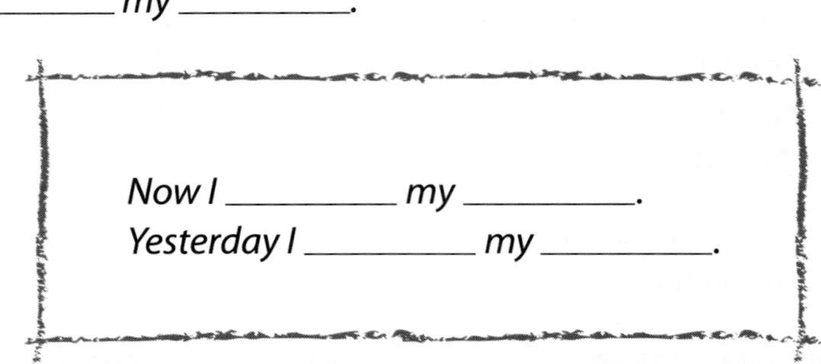

Now I __________ *my* __________.
Yesterday I __________ *my* __________.

- Guide children to use past and future tenses as they say and dramatize additional sentences using the assorted Photo Cards and sentence frames.

Writing

Independent Writing: Book Title

Display the book title that children created the day before.

BRAINSTORM
Tell children that today they will begin to create their own book covers. Have children think of other vehicles Duck might have an **adventure** riding. List all ideas and ask children to add a small drawing next to each item. Display the list as a reference.

PREWRITE
On chart paper, write the frame *Duck on a* __________. Read it aloud as you track the print. Write a vehicle name on the blank line to complete the title. Add an illustration. Share your book title with children, tracking print as you read. Have children chorally repeat.

- Have children choose a vehicle for Duck to ride.

DRAFT
Distribute paper, pencils, and crayons. Have children write their first name on the top of the paper.

- Ask children to write the sentence frame *Duck on a* __________.
- Tell children to write the name of what they want Duck to ride. Tell them to add a picture that illustrates the title.
- Collect children's work to use tomorrow.

Write About It

Ask children to draw a picture of their favorite animal in their Writer's Notebooks. Guide them to label their drawing.

Objectives

- Write a book title
- Plan a first draft for writing
- Use letter knowledge to write letters in a word
- Illustrate a book cover

Materials

- book title from Day 2 Interactive Writing

5-Day Writing

Book Title	
DAY 1	Shared: A List
DAY 2	Interactive: Book Title
DAY 3	Independent: Prewrite and Draft Book Title
DAY 4	Independent: Revise and Edit Book Title
DAY 5	Independent: Publish and Present

ELL

Use Photo Cards Display and name the **Photo Cards** for *car, bus, bike,* and *jet*. Have children complete the frame *Duck on a* __________, using one of the Photo Card names. Tell them to say new phrases using the cards and different animals.

Transitions That Teach

While children are getting ready to line up, have them name ways things can **attach** to other things.

Day 4 At a Glance

WHOLE GROUP

Oral Language
- Build Robust Vocabulary

Comprehension
- Read Aloud: "The Singing Wagon"

Vocabulary
- Sound Words
- Story Words: *waddled, wobbled*

Phonemic Awareness
- Phoneme Blending

Phonics
- Picture Sort
- Blend with /a/*a*, /i/*i*, /p/*p*, /t/*t*
- Pre-decodable Reader: *Sit, Tip!*

Writing
- Independent Writing: Book Title

SMALL GROUP

- Differentiated Instruction, pages 738–763

Oral Language

Build Robust Vocabulary

SOUNDS WHEELS MAKE

Discuss **wheels** with children. *There are many kinds of wheels. Wheels can make many different sounds.*

- Show children an object with wheels that makes noise when pushed, such as a small toy car. Have children name other things with **massive** wheels.

CREATE A CHART

Create a chart like the one below or use **Teaching Chart G3**. Ask children to name sounds that different wheels can make.

Think Aloud When I was your age, I had a little red wagon. I used to take it on all sorts of **adventures**! My wagon had wheels, and the wheels often squeaked when pulled or pushed.

Have children name other kinds of wheels and their sounds. Add their ideas to the chart. Read the words, tracking the print.

Wheels

Kind of Wheel	Sound
wagon	squeak
train	click clack
car	hum
bike	whoosh

ENGLISH LANGUAGE LEARNERS

Beginning

Confirm Understanding Show pictures of vehicles with wheels. Name each vehicle and have children repeat. Point to the wheels of the vehicle and say: These are the wheels. *Do you think these wheels squeak or hum?* Repeat with other sounds.

Intermediate

Enhance Understanding Using the same pictures, ask questions such as: *What do you see in this picture? What sound do think the wheels of this (name vehicle) make?* Prompt children to elaborate by answering in complete sentences and adding details.

Advanced

Compare and Contrast Pair children and ask each partner to describe a vehicle with wheels. Have partners compare the wheels on the vehicles and the sounds the wheels of each vehicle might make.

Listen for Rhyme

IDENTIFY RHYME
Remind children that words rhyme when they have the same ending sounds. *The word* day *rhymes with* away. Tell children *day* and *away* end with the same sound.

TRANSPORTATION SONG
Tell children that they will sing "I've Been Working on the Railroad," the song they learned about building train tracks. Play the song and ask children to join in.

Tell children that *horn* rhymes with *morn*. Ask children to name the word from the song that rhymes with *day*.

Discuss places people can visit by riding trains. Tell children that people cannot visit the island of Hawaii on a train. Show Hawaii on a map or globe. Tell children to listen attentively and ask questions if they don't understand something. *Why is it not possible to ride a train to Hawaii?* (Trains run on tracks on land or bridges, and Hawaii is surrounded by water.) *What are some other ways people could visit Hawaii?* (plane, helicopter, boat) *Which vehicles have wheels that people can use to get to Hawaii?* (plane)

AUDIO CD

I've Been Working on the Railroad

I've been working on the railroad
All the live long day.
I've been working on the railroad
Just to pass the time away.
Can't you hear the whistle blowing?
Rise up so early in the morn.
Can't you hear the captain shouting?
Dinah, blow your horn.

Objectives

- Discuss the theme
- Use oral vocabulary words *adventure, attach, haul, massive,* and *wheel*
- Complete a chart
- Orally generate rhymes in response to spoken words
- Listen attentively and ask questions

Materials

- Graphic Organizer; Teaching Chart G3

Oral Vocabulary

Have children use each word in a sentence about this week's stories.

adventure
attach
haul
massive
wheel

Review Work with children to review last week's words. *How would you* prepare *for a* journey? *What are some* familiar *places you* travel *to? What do you do to* relax?

familiar
journey
prepare
relax
travel

Digital Learning

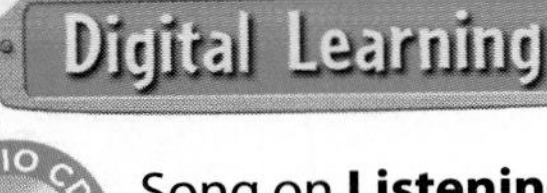

Song on **Listening Library Audio CD**

Objectives

- Listen and respond to a folktale
- Discuss the big idea of a folktale

Materials

- Read-Aloud Anthology: "The Singing Wagon," pp. 53–57
- Reader Response Sheets; Teacher's Resource Book, pp. 203–204

ELL

Use Pictures Show a picture of a wagon, such as the one in the **Big Book** *On the Go* from Week 2. Remind children that a wagon has wheels and can be pushed or pulled. Have children point to the picture and say *wagon*.

Readers Theater

BUILDING LISTENING AND SPEAKING SKILLS
Distribute copies of "Catch a Little Rhyme," Read-Aloud Anthology pages 163–164. Have children practice performing the play throughout the unit. Assign parts and have children present the play or perform it as a dramatic reading at the end of the unit.

Interactive Read Aloud

Listening Comprehension

Read Aloud

GENRE: LITERARY TEXT/FOLKTALE
Explain that "The Singing Wagon" is a **folktale**. Folktales are very old stories that people all over the world have been telling for many years. See the information about folktales found in the **Read-Aloud Anthology**.

CULTURAL PERSPECTIVES
Tell children that "The Singing Wagon" is a Pueblo tale. The Pueblo are Native Americans from the southwestern United States. Coyotes are small wolves common in the western United States.

READ "THE SINGING WAGON"

- **MODEL ASKING QUESTIONS ABOUT COMPREHENSION** Use the Think Alouds provided at point of use in the folktale.
- **MODEL FLUENT READING** Read the folktale aloud with fluent expression. Stop occasionally and ask children to predict what will happen next. Confirm or revise predictions as needed.
- **EXPAND VOCABULARY** See page 53 of the Read-Aloud Anthology to teach new words using the **Define/Example/Ask** routine.

Respond to Literature

TALK ABOUT IT Ask children to discuss the theme of this folktale.

- *What did the Black Beetle Old Man use to carry wood?*
- *What happened to the wagon **wheels** when the wagon was full?*
- *What happened to the song when the wagon was empty?*
- Have children use the Reader Response Sheets to draw or write about their opinions of the folktale. Have children add the sheets to their Writing Portfolios.

Write About It

Ask children to draw their favorite characters and parts of the story. Help them label their drawings.

Vocabulary

Sound Words

REVIEW SOUNDS
Ask the following questions and have children respond with a sound word.

What sound does a car horn make? (honk, beep)

What sound does a dog make? (woof)

What sound does a cat make? (meow)

What sound does a telephone make? (ring)

What sound does a clock make? (tick-tock)

Display the **Trade Book** *Duck on a Bike*. Continue asking questions about animal sounds.

What does a cow say? (moo)

What does a sheep say? (baa)

What does a horse say? (neigh)

What does a goat say? (maaa)

What does a pig say? (oink)

What does a mouse say? (squeak)

Story Words: *waddled, wobbled*

Ask children to name animals and things that *waddle* or *wobble* and to make sentences about them. For example: *Penguins waddle. Block buildings wobble.*

TIME TO MOVE!

Sing a version of "If You're Happy and You Know It" using sound words. Use lyrics such as: *If you're happy and you know it, honk your horn: Honk! Honk! If you're happy and you know it, be a clock: Tick-Tock!*

Objectives

- **Review sound words**
- **Recognize sensory details**
- **Review story words**

Materials

- **Read-Aloud Trade Book:** ***Duck on a Bike***

ELL

Reinforce Vocabulary
Write animal sounds in speech balloons on self-stick notes for use in the **Trade Book** *Duck on a Bike*. Say: *The cow says moo. What does the cow say?* Prompt children to answer: *The cow says moo,* and affix the corresponding note on the cow. Repeat with each animal in the book.

Objectives

- Blend sounds to form words: /p/, /t/, /i/
- Sort picture names by initial sound
- Review sound-spellings for /i/*i*, /p/*p*, /t/*t*
- Blend sounds in words with *a, i, p, t*
- Read simple one-syllable words

Materials

- Puppet
- Word-Building Cards
- pocket chart
- Photo Cards: *inch, insect, penguin, pumpkin, teeth, top*
- Activity Book, p. 30
- Practice Book, p. 77

Phonemic Awareness

Phoneme Blending

Model

Use the **Puppet** to model how to blend sounds to form *at*.

Repeat with *pat*.

Happy is going to say the sounds in a word. Listen to Happy: /a/ /t/. Happy can blend these sounds together: /aaat/. Say the sounds with Happy: /a/ /t/. Now blend the sounds to say the word *at* with Happy.

Guided Practice/Practice

Children blend sounds to form words.

Guide practice with the first word, using the same routine.

Happy is going to say the sounds in a word. Listen to Happy as he says each sound. Then blend the sounds to say the word.

/a/ /n/	/p/ /a/ /n/	/a/ /m/
/p/ /i/ /t/	/s/ /a/ /t/	/m/ /a/ /t/

Phonics

Picture Sort

Model

Place **Word-Building Card** *p* in the pocket chart.

Repeat the routine for *t* and *i*.

This is the letter *p*. The sound for this letter is /p/.

Hold up the **Photo Card** for *pumpkin*.

Follow the routine for *top*.

Here is a picture of a *pumpkin*. *Pumpkin* begins with /p/. I place *pumpkin* under the letter *p* because *pumpkin* begins with /p/.

Guided Practice/Practice

Children sort the Photo Cards. Guide practice with the first card, using the routine.

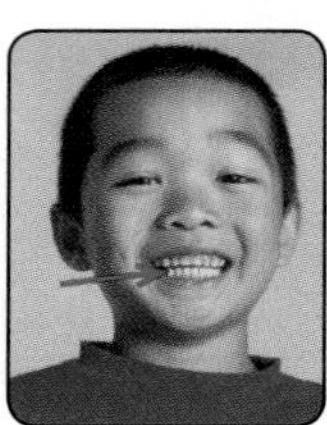

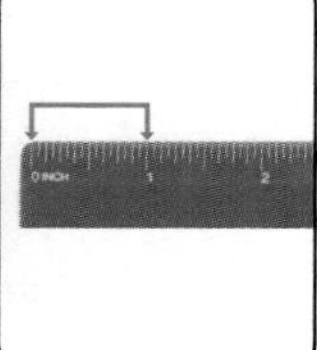

Build Fluency: Sound-Spellings

Display the following **Word-Building Cards**: *a, i, m, p, s, t*. Have children chorally say each sound. Repeat and vary the pace.

Blend with /p/*p*, /a/*a*, /t/*t*, /i/*i*

Model

Place Word-Building Card *p* in the pocket chart.

This letter is *p*. The letter *p* stands for the /p/ sound. Say /p/.

Place Word-Building Card *a* next to *p*. Move your hand from left to right below the letters.

This letter is *a*. The letter *a* stands for the /a/ sound. Listen as I blend the two sounds together: /paaa/. Now blend the sounds with me. (/paaa/)

Place Word-Building Card *t* next to *pa*. Move your hand from left to right.

This letter is *t*. The letter *t* stands for the /t/ sound. Listen as I blend the three sounds together: /paaat/, *pat*. Now you blend the sounds with me. (/paaat/, *pat*)

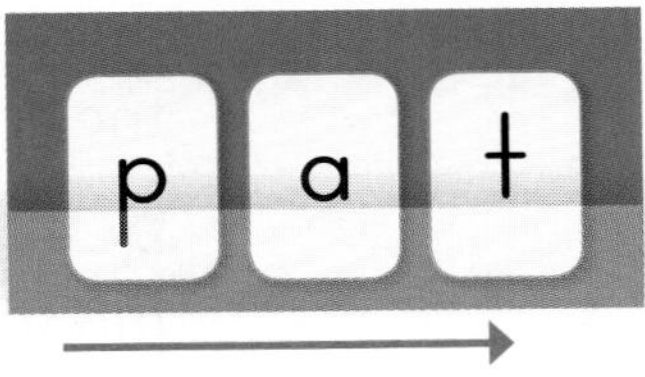

Repeat with *pit*.

Guided Practice/Practice

Children blend sounds to form words.

Guide practice with the first word.

sit	sat	Tam	Tim
Sam	Pam	map	pit

Corrective Feedback

Blending: Sound Error Model the sound that children missed, then have them repeat the sound. For example, for the word *pit*, say: *My turn.* Tap under the letter *i* in the word *pit* and say: *Sound? What's the sound?* Then return to the beginning of the word. Say: *Let's start over.* Blend the word with children again.

For Tier 2 instruction, see page 752.

Activity Book, page 30
Practice Book, page 77

Objectives

- Read decodable words with /t/t, /i/i
- Read the words *go, see*
- Review the high-frequency words *can, go, I, see, the, we*
- Know that reading moves from top to bottom
- Reread for fluency

Materials

- Pre-decodable Reader: *Sit, Tip!*
- High-Frequency Word Cards: *can, go, I, see, the, we*

Pre-decodable Reader

Read *Sit, Tip!*

REVIEW Display the **High-Frequency Word Cards** for **can**, **go**, **I**, **see**, **the**, and **we**. Use the **Read/Spell/Write** routine to review each word.

Sit, Tip!

MODEL CONCEPTS ABOUT PRINT Display pages 2–3. Point to the top and bottom of the page as you say: *This is the top of the page. This is the bottom of the page.* Have children show the top and bottom of subsequent pages. Have them track print from left to right.

PREDICT Ask children to name things in the cover illustration. *Who do you think will be a character in this book? How can you tell?*

FIRST READ Children point to each word and say the high-frequency words quickly. If needed, provide corrective feedback and guide them page by page. Children should chorally read the story the first time through.

DEVELOP COMPREHENSION Ask the following prompts: *Who is this story about?* (Pat, Pam, Tip, Dad) *What happens on page 8?* (Dad stops Tip so he won't follow the girls.)

SECOND READ Have partners reread the book together.

Can we go?
2

We can go.
3

Sit Tip.
4

We can go.
5

Sit Tip.
6

We can go.
7

Tip sat. We can go!
8

Pre-decodable Reader

Writing

Independent Writing: Book Title

REVISE AND EDIT

Distribute children's book covers. Have them check for the following:

- Did I write my name at the top?
- Did I write the title of the book?
- Did I pay attention to spacing between letters?
- Did I draw a picture that matches the title?

Circulate and help children review and revise their sentences to improve the clarity and effectiveness of their work. Have children share their sentences with partners. Guide them to evaluate their work using the Writer's Checklist.

Write About It

Ask children to draw or write a simple narrative to go along with their book titles. Have them illustrate their stories.

Objectives

- Revise and edit book titles
- Use letter knowledge to write letters in a word
- Share writing

Materials

- children's writing from Day 3
- Writer's Checklist; Teacher's Resource Book, p. 205

5-Day Writing

Book Title	
DAY 1	Shared: A List
DAY 2	Interactive: Book Title
DAY 3	Independent: Prewrite and Draft Book Title
DAY 4	Independent: Revise and Edit Book Title
DAY 5	Independent: Publish and Present

ELL

Reinforce Vocabulary
Create and illustrate a book cover showing Duck riding on a scooter. Read the book title aloud. Point out that the title tells a new story about Duck. Point to the drawing and ask what the story might be about.

Transitions That Teach

While they pack up, have children name vehicles that **haul** things to places.

Day 5 At a Glance

WHOLE GROUP

Oral Language
- Build Robust Vocabulary

Comprehension
- Strategy: Recognize Story Structure
- Skill: Identify Character and Plot
- Read Across Texts

Vocabulary
- High-Frequency Words
- Build Fluency
- Shape Words

Phonemic Awareness
- Phoneme Categorization

Phonics
- Build Fluency
- Read Words
- Dictation

Writing
- Independent Writing: Publish and Present

SMALL GROUP

- Differentiated Instruction, pages 738–763

Review and Assess

Oral Language

Build Robust Vocabulary

REVIEW WORDS

Review this week's oral vocabulary words with children. Explain that all of the words will be used to discuss a moving adventure. Talk about what happens when people move to a new apartment or house. *What kinds of thing do they take with them? Why do they put their belongings in boxes?*

Use the following questions to check children's understanding:

- How might people **haul** their belongings to a new home?
- What could they **attach** to boxes to make them easier to carry?
- What are some **massive** things that people may move to a new home?
- What are some things with **wheels** that people use to help move their belongings?
- Why would moving to a new home be an **adventure**?

REVIEW SONGS FROM THE PAST

Sing the song "Yankee Doodle" and have children sing along. Discuss with children whether or not the song describes an adventure. Then sing "I've Been Working on the Railroad" with children. Have children name the words in the song that rhyme. *How would working on a railroad be an adventure?* Ask children to respond in complete sentences.

Review and Assess

Comprehension

STRATEGY Recognize Story Structure

REFLECT ON THE STRATEGY Remind children that stories usually follow a certain structure, or order in which things happen. They have a beginning, middle, and end.

Think Aloud I can think about what happens to the characters in the beginning, middle, and end of a story to help understand and remember the whole story.

SKILL Identify Character and Plot

Create a chart to compare what happens to the characters in *Duck on a Bike* and "The Singing Wagon" in the beginning, middle, and end of each story. Remind children that characters are the people or animals in the story.

Characters and Plot

Duck on a Bike	The Singing Wagon
Duck and other farm animals	Black Beetle Old Man, Black Beetle Old Woman
(B) Duck rides a bike.	(B) Black Beetle Old Man pulls wagon down the hill.
(M) None of the other animals want to ride.	(M) Other animals try to push the wagon, but they sing and dance when **wheels** squeak.
(E) Finally, the other animals ride bikes, too.	(E) Black Beetle Old Man pulls wagon himself. He and his wife sing the wagon song.

Reading Across Texts

Ask children to retell a main event from the stories they have listened to this week.

- *Could real animals do what the animals in* Duck on a Bike *do?*
- *Could animals really do what the animals do in* "The Singing Wagon"*?*
- Ask children to draw pictures showing the difference between a real event in one story with an imaginary event in another.

Objectives

- Use oral vocabulary words *adventure, attach, haul, massive,* and *wheel*
- Listen and share information
- Speak in complete sentences
- Review the strategy and skill
- Make connections to ideas in other texts

Materials

- Read-Aloud Trade Book: *Duck on a Bike*
- Read-Aloud Anthology: "The Singing Wagon," pp. 53–57
- Activity Book, p. 31

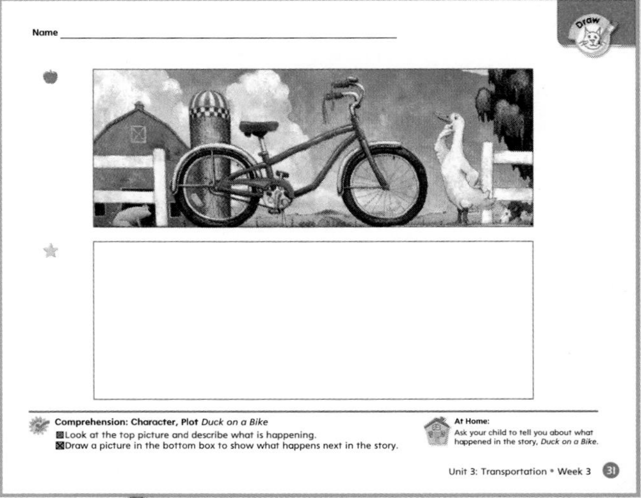

Name ____________________

Draw

Comprehension: Character, Plot *Duck on a Bike*
Look at the top picture and describe what is happening.
Draw a picture in the bottom box to show what happens next in the story.

At Home:
Ask your child to tell you about what happened in the story, *Duck on a Bike*.

Unit 3: Transportation • Week 3 31

Activity Book, page 31

Objectives

- Review high-frequency words *a, go, like, see, the, we*
- Review shape words
- Build fluency

Materials

- High-Frequency Word Cards: *a, go, like, see, the, we*
- High-Frequency Word Cards; Teacher's Resource Book, pp. 103–110
- Read-Aloud Trade Book: *Duck on a Bike*
- index cards with shapes and shape words on them
- pictures of differently shaped items

Fluency

Connected Text Have children reread this week's **Pre-decodable Readers** with a partner. Circulate, listen in, and note those children who need additional instruction and practice reading this week's decodable and sight words.

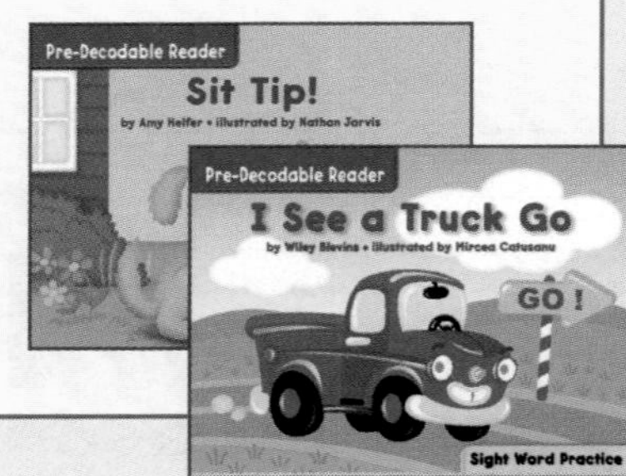

Review and Assess

Vocabulary

High-Frequency Words

Distribute one of the following **High-Frequency Word Cards** to each child: **a**, **go**, **like**, **see**, **the**, and **we**. Say: *When you hear the word that is on your card, stand and hold up your Word Card.*

- *I* like *to ride my bike.*
- We like *to* see *my friend's animals.*
- The *cat drives* a *tractor with wheels.*
- We see the *dog* go *under* the *bed.*
- *I* like *to* go *to my friend's house on* the *bus.*

Build Fluency: Word Automaticity

Rapid Naming Display the High-Frequency Word Cards *see*, *go*, *a*, *like*, *we*, and *the*. Point quickly to each card, at random, and have children read the word as fast as they can.

Shape Words

Page through the **Trade Book** *Duck on a Bike*. Have children take turns pointing out the shapes they see in the illustrations. Then have them sort pictures of objects into shape categories.

Rapid Naming Display the index cards one at a time. Have children chorally name the shapes as fast as they can.

TIME TO MOVE!

Arrange children in small groups. Give instructions, such as: *Group 1, go to the square blocks. Group 2, go to the rectangular window.* Once children move, have them tell where they are in a full sentence. For example: *I am by the square blocks.*

Review and Assess

Phonemic Awareness

Phoneme Categorization

Guided Practice

Display the **Photo Cards** for *lamp, up,* and *deer.*

I will say three picture names: *lamp, up,* and *deer.* Repeat these words with me. Which picture names end with the same sound? *Lamp* and *up* both end with the same sound, /p/. *Deer* does not end with the /p/ sound. It does not belong.

Practice

Children identify the picture name that does not end with the same sound.

Use these sets of cards: *soap, mop, dog; ink, jet, feet; farm, nail, gem; queen, nurse, bus; ant, game, bat; map, hat, rope.*

I will show you three cards. Tell me which picture does not belong.

For Tier 2 instruction, see page 758.

Objective

- Categorize words with the same final sounds

Materials

- **Photo Cards:** ***ant, bat, bus, deer, dog, farm, feet, game, gem, hat, ink, jet, lamp, map, mop, nail, nurse, queen, rope, soap, up***

Objectives

- Review sound-spellings for /m/m, /p/p, /t/t
- Use knowledge of letter-sound relationships to decode regular words in text

Materials

- Word-Building Cards
- pocket chart
- 5 index cards: *I*, *see*, *Pam*, *sit*, period mark
- 6 index cards: *Tap*, *the*, *mat*, comma mark, *Sam*, period mark
- Sound Box
- WorkBoard Sound Boxes; Teacher's Resource Book, p. 136
- markers
- Activity Book, p. 32

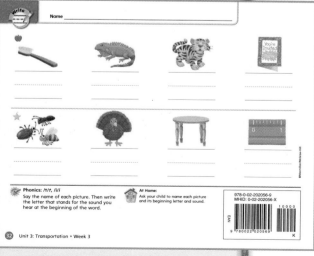

Name

Phonics: /t/t, /i/i
Say the name of each picture. Then write the letter that stands for the sound you hear at the beginning of the word.

At Home: Ask your child to name each picture and its beginning letter and sound.

32 Unit 3: Transportation • Week 3

Activity Book, page 32

Review and Assess

Phonics

Build Fluency: Sound-Spellings

Rapid Naming Display the following **Word-Building Cards**: *a, i, m, p, s, t*. Have children chorally say each sound. Repeat and vary the pace.

Read Words

Apply

Distribute the first set of cards. Have children stand in sequence.	Let's read the sentence together. I see Pam sit.
Repeat with other set.	Tap the mat, Sam.

Dictation

Dictate sounds for children to spell.	Listen as I say a sound. Repeat the sound, then write the letter that stands for the sound. /t/ /i/ /s/ /m/ /a/ /p/
Then dictate words for children to spell. Model for children how to use the **Sound Boxes** to segment the sounds in the word. Have them repeat.	Now let's write some words. I will say a word. I want you to repeat the word, then think about how many sounds are in the word. Use your Sound Boxes to count the sounds. Then write one letter for each sound you hear. it sit pit tip tap pat
Write the letters and words on the board for children to self-correct.	

For Tier 2 instruction, see page 758.

Review and Assess

Writing

Independent Writing: Book Title

PUBLISH
Explain to children that you will gather their book titles and post them on a section of the Big Question Board.

- Brainstorm ideas for the board section title, such as "Book Covers About Duck Travels."

PRESENT
Ask children to take turns reading their book covers to the class. Have children give a short summary of a story that could go with the title. For example: *Duck sleds to school but finds out school is closed.*

LISTENING, SPEAKING, AND VIEWING

- Remind children to speak audibly and clearly when they present. Remind them to be good listeners when a classmate is speaking.
- Place the finished book on the Big Question Board for everyone to enjoy. As children view the illustration, encourage them to create an imaginary story of their own in response to the picture.
- When the board is disassembled, have children add copies of their work to their Writing Portfolios. Tell them to review their portfolios and note their progress.

Write About It

Ask children to draw in their Writer's Notebooks a picture of animals traveling to school. Help them label their drawings.

Objectives

- Publish and present a piece of writing
- Share writing with others

Materials

- children's book titles from Day 4

5-Day Writing

Book Title	
DAY 1	Shared: A List
DAY 2	Interactive: Book Title
DAY 3	Independent: Prewrite and Draft Book Title
DAY 4	Independent: Revise and Edit Book Title
DAY 5	Independent: Publish and Present

Transitions That Teach

While lining up, have children name things that are **massive**.

Approaching Level

Oral Language

Objective Preteach oral vocabulary
Materials • none

THEME WORDS: *wheel, adventure*

- Tell children the meanings for **wheel** and **adventure**. *A* wheel *is a round thing that makes vehicles move. A bicycle is a vehicle with two* wheels. *An* adventure *is an exciting, fun experience. The trip to the Grand Canyon was a real* adventure.
- Discuss the words with children. *What things have* wheels*? How can* wheels *help you go on an* adventure*?*
- Have children use the following sentence frames to generate complete oral sentences using the words: *A ________ has four wheels. It would be an adventure to go to ________.*

High-Frequency Words

Objective Reinforce high-frequency words
Materials • **High-Frequency Word Cards:** *a, go, like, see, the, we*

REINFORCE WORDS: *see, go*

- Display the **High-Frequency Word Card** for **see**.
- **Read** Point to and say the word *see. This is the word* see. *It means "to look at." I see many children.*
- **Spell** *The word* see *is spelled* s-e-e. *We hear /s/ at the beginning of the word. The letter* s *makes the /s/ sound, so we write the letter* s *at the beginning of the word.* Have children read and spell *see.*
- **Write** Finally, have children write the word *see.*
- Repeat the routine for **go**.

- Have children work with a partner to make up oral sentences using the words *see* and *go.* Ask them to talk about things they have seen on an adventure.

HIGH-FREQUENCY WORDS REVIEW

Tier 2

Display the High-Frequency Word Cards **a**, **like**, **the**, and **we** from the previous units. Display one card at a time as children chorally read and spell the word. Mix and repeat. Note words children need to review.

ELL

Partners When partners make up sentences with high-frequency words, pair English Language Learners with children who are more proficient. Write their sentences, read them together, and point to the high-frequency words.

Approaching Level

Phonemic Awareness

Objective Identify words that begin with the same initial sound

Materials
- **Photo Cards:** *inch, insect, invitation, teeth, tiger, top, pen, piano, pie*
- **Sound-Spelling Cards:** *Insect, Piano, Turtle*

PHONEME IDENTITY

Model

- Display **Photo Cards** for *inch, insect,* and *invitation.* Name the cards. *What sound do you hear at the beginning of* inch, insect, *and* invitation? *The /i/ sound is at the beginning of* inch, insect, *and* invitation. Repeat for *top, teeth, tiger* and *pie, piano, pen.*
- Display the small *Insect* **Sound-Spelling Card.** Point out the articulation picture. *See how I relax my face and let the front part of my tongue rise high in my mouth. My lips do not get round.* Repeat with the *Turtle* and *Piano* small Sound-Spelling Cards.

Guided Practice/Practice

- Say *inchworm, ill, it.* Guide children as they tell what sound is the same at the beginning of all three words. Repeat with *toothbrush, table, top* and *pen, pumpkin, penguin.*

Phonics

Objective Recognize words that begin with /i/*i*, /t/*t*, and /p/*p*

Materials
- **Sound-Spelling Cards:** *Insect, Piano, Turtle*
- **Word-Building Cards**
- **Photo Cards:** *inch, insect, invitation, pen, piano, pie, teeth, toe, top*

PRETEACH: RECOGNIZE /i/*i*, /t/*t*, /p/*p*

Model

- Display Photo Cards for *inch, teeth,* and *piano* and the *Insect* Sound-Spelling Card. *The name of this letter is* i. I *stands for the /i/ sound at the beginning of* inch. *I will use the* i ***Word-Building Card*** *and place it on the* inch *picture because* inch *begins with /i/. Listen: /iiinch/.* Repeat with the *Turtle* and *Piano* Sound-Spelling Cards.

Guided Practice/Practice

- Display the Photo Cards. Have children name the picture, the beginning sound, and the letter that stands for the sound. Have them put the Word-Building Card for the letter on the Photo Card. Repeat with remaining Photo Cards.

SOUND-SPELLINGS REVIEW

Display Word-Building Cards for *i, t,* and *p,* one at a time. Have children chorally say the sound. Repeat and vary the pace.

Letter Wagon

Have children draw pictures of a red wagon filled with things that begin with /i/, /t/, and /p/, such as iguana, turtle, pig, ink, tire, or purse. Help children label their drawings.

Corrective Feedback

Mnemonic Display the *Turtle* Sound-Spelling Card. *This is a turtle. The beginning sound is /t/. The /t/ sound is spelled with the letter* t. *Say /t/ with me: /t/. This is the sound at the beginning of* turtle. *What is the letter? What is the sound? What word begins with /t/?* Turtle *is the word we can use to remember the sound for* t, */t/.*

ELL

Extra Practice Provide additional practice in recognizing and naming letters for children whose native languages do not use the symbols of the Latin alphabet.

On Level

High-Frequency Words

Objective Review high-frequency words *go, see, a,* and *like*

Materials • **High-Frequency Word Cards:** *a, go, like, see*

REVIEW

- Display the **High-Frequency Word Card** for **go**.
- **Read** Point to and say the word *go. This is the word* go. *It means "to move along." We go to school.*
- **Spell** *The word* go *is spelled* g-o. Have children read and spell *go.*
- **Write** Finally, have children write the word *go.*
- Repeat with **see**, **a**, and **like**. Then have partners make up questions and answers using the words. Ask them to talk about things they might see while on an adventure.

Phonemic Awareness/Phonics

Objective Identify and blend /i/*i*, /t/*t*, /s/*s*, and /p/*p* words

Materials • **Word Building Cards** • pocket chart • **Photo Cards:** *six, mix, chin*

PHONEME IDENTITY

Model

- Display the **Photo Cards** for *six, mix,* and *chin. Listen to the picture names:* six, mix, chin. *What sound do you hear in the middle of* six, mix, *and* chin? *The /i/ sound is in the middle of* six, mix, *and* chin. Repeat for *fan, hat,* and *map.*

Practice

- Say the following groups of words. Have children identify the middle sound in each group: *mad, tap, can; win, mill, pick; tack, dad, pass; pin, rip, sick; cat, rash, mad; fish, tick, chip.*

REVIEW: /i/*i*, /t/*t*, /s/*s*, and /p/*p*

- Display **Word-Building Card** *i. The name of this letter is* i. I *stands for the /i/ sound we hear at the beginning of* insect. *What is the sound? I'll hold up the* i *card because* insect *begins with /i/.* Repeat with *t, s,* and *p.*
- Say: *pan, ten, sun, inside, seven, if, sorry, pony, pen,* and *ton.* Have children hold up their Word-Building Cards and say /i/, /t/, /s/, or /p/ for words that begin with those initial sounds. Guide practice with the first two words.

Sound-Letter Relationships Provide additional practice in pronouncing the initial /i/, /t/ /p/ sounds and naming the corresponding letters as children point to them.

Beyond Level

High-Frequency Words/Vocabulary

Objectives Review high-frequency words *go, see, a, like;* introduce *sit*
Materials • none

ACCELERATE

- Write *sit* on the board.
- **Read** Point to and say the word *sit. This is the word* sit. *It means "to rest in a sitting position." Let's sit on the porch.*
- **Spell** *The word* sit *is spelled* s-i-t. Have children read and spell *sit.*
- **Write** Finally, have children write the word *sit.*
- Have children work with a partner to make up oral sentences using the word *sit.* Ask them to talk about their favorite places to sit.

EXPAND ORAL VOCABULARY

Gifted Talented

- **Synonyms** Review the meanings of oral vocabulary words *insects* and *interesting* with children. Then explain that a *synonym* is a word that means the same thing as another word.
- Say: *A* synonym *for the word* insect *is* bug. *A bug is a very small animal that often has wings. Most bugs fly. A bee is a kind of* bug *that flies. A* synonym *for the word* interesting *is* fascinating. *When something is* fascinating, *it is extremely exciting or attractive to see.*
- Have children take turns using the new words *bugs* and *fascinating* using complete sentences. Then tell children that they will work with a partner to ask a question using the word.

Phonics

Objectives Review /i/*i* and /t/*t* and introduce /u/*u;* blend and read words
Materials • **Sound-Spelling Cards:** *Insect, Turtle, Umbrella*
• **Word-Building Cards** • **Sound-Spelling WorkBoards**

ENRICH

- Have children listen as you blend these sounds together: /tiiip/. Ask: *What word did I say?* (tip) Repeat with /tuuub/, *tub.*
- Display the *Insect* **Sound-Spelling Card**. Remind children that the /i/ sound is spelled with the letter *i.* Inch *and* insect *begin with /i/. What other words begin with /i/?* Repeat for /t/*t* and /u/*u.*
- Display the **Word-Building Cards** for *i, p, s, t, u, b, c, n,* and *r.* Point to the letters one at a time. Say the letter name and sound. Have children repeat the sound as they write the letter several times.

ELL

Partners When pairing children to make up sentences, pair English Language Learners with children who are more proficient. Write their sentences, read them together, and point to the high-frequency words.

ELL ENGLISH LANGUAGE LEARNERS

Oral Language Warm-Up

Content Objective Learn theme vocabulary

Language Objective Repeat and sing a song to demonstrate understanding

Materials • **Listening Library Audio CD**

BUILD BACKGROUND KNOWLEDGE

All Language Levels

- Continue developing vocabulary around the unit theme "Transportation" by playing the song "I've Been Working on the Railroad" from the **Listening Library Audio CD.** Display a picture of a railroad and train, such as a picture from last week's **Big Book** *On the Go*. Teach the word *railroad* as you point to the train's wheels and the tracks they ride on. Have children repeat the word three times.
- Then teach children the song by playing the song several times and having them act out the motions and sounds. Emphasize the key words that describe sounds, such as *whistle blowing, captain shouting,* and *blow your horn.*
- Ask children to tell about any experiences they have had on a train. Build on their responses to model speaking in complete sentences. For example: *You rode a train to your cousin's house. Your cousin lives far away.*

Academic Language

Language Objective Use academic language in classroom conversations

All Language Levels

- This week's academic words are **boldfaced** throughout the lesson. Define the word in context and provide a clear example from the selection. Then ask children to generate an example or a word with a similar meaning.

Academic Language Used in Whole Group Instruction

Oral Vocabulary Words	Vocabulary and Grammar Concepts	Strategy and Skill Words
adventure	**shape words**	**recognize**
attach	**action words**	**story structure**
haul		**character**
massive		**plot**
wheel		**action**

Cognates

Help children identify similarities and differences in pronunciation and spelling between English words and Spanish cognates:

adventure	*aventura*
massive	*masivo*
recognize	*reconocer*
structure	*estructura*
action	*acción*

ELL ENGLISH LANGUAGE LEARNERS

Vocabulary

Language Objective Demonstrate understanding and use of key words by describing how wheels help

Materials • **Visual Vocabulary Resources**

PRETEACH KEY VOCABULARY

All Language Levels

Use the **Visual Vocabulary Resources** to preteach the weekly oral vocabulary words *adventure, attach, haul, massive,* and *wheel.* Focus on one or two words per day. Use the following routine that appears in detail on the cards.

- Define the word in English and provide the example given.
- Define the word in Spanish, if appropriate, and indicate if the word is a cognate.
- Display the picture and explain how it illustrates or demonstrates the word. Engage children in structured partner-talk about the image, using the key word.
- Ask children to chorally say the word three times.
- Point out any known sound-spellings or focus on a key aspect of phonemic awareness related to the word.

PRETEACH FUNCTION WORDS AND PHRASES

All Language Levels

Use the Visual Vocabulary Resources to preteach the function words *toward* and *past*. Focus on one word per day. Use the detailed routine on the cards.

- Define the word in English and, if appropriate, in Spanish. Point out if the word is a cognate.
- Refer to the picture and engage children in talk about the word. For example, children will partner-talk using sentence frames or they will listen to sentences and replace a word or phrase with the new function word.
- Ask children to chorally repeat the word three times.

TEACH BASIC WORDS

Beginning/Intermediate

Use the Visual Vocabulary Resources to teach the basic words *duck, cow, pig, horse, sheep,* and *goat.* Teach these "farm animals" words using the routine provided on the card.

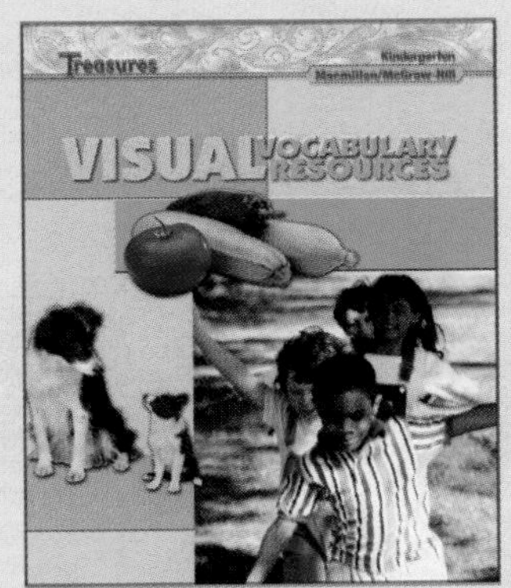

Visual Vocabulary Resources

Approaching Level

High-Frequency Words

Objective Reinforce high-frequency words

Materials
- **Sound-Spelling WorkBoards**
- **High-Frequency Word Cards:** *a, go, like, see, the, we*

REINFORCE WORDS: *see, go*

- Distribute a **WorkBoard** to each child. Then display the **High-Frequency Word Card** for **see.**
- Use the **Read/Spell/Write** routine to review *see*. Point to and say the word. *This is the word* see. *It means "to look at." I see with my eyes.* See *is spelled* s-e-e. Have children read and spell *see*. Then have them write the word on their WorkBoards. Repeat with **go**.
- Have children work with a partner to make up sentences using the words *see* and *go*. Ask them to talk about what they see as they go home. Have children use complete sentences.

CUMULATIVE REVIEW

Display the High-Frequency Word Cards **a**, **like**, **the**, and **we**. Display one card at a time as children chorally read and spell the word. Mix and repeat. Note words children need to review.

ELL

Partners When pairing children to make up sentences, pair English Language Learners with children who are more proficient. Write their sentences, read them together, and point out the high-frequency words.

Pre-decodable Reader

Objective Preteach Pre-decodable Reader *I See a Truck Go*

Materials
- **Pre-decodable Reader:** *I See a Truck Go*

PRETEACH *I See a Truck Go*

Pre-decodable Reader

- Display the cover of the book and read the title. Have children open to the title page and point out the title. *Let's read the title together.* Have children sound out each word as you run your finger under it. Tell children to use the cover illustration to predict what might happen in the story. *What do you see in the illustration? Where do you think the truck is going? What else do you think we will see in this book?*
- Page through the book. Ask children what they see in each picture. Point out each rebus. Ask children to find the words *I, see,* and *go.*
- Read the book chorally with children. Have them point to each word or rebus as they read it. Provide corrective feedback.
- Ask children to use *I, see,* and *go* to talk about the pictures. *I see a boat go. I see a train go.*
- After reading, ask children to recall what they read.

Approaching Level

Phonemic Awareness

Objective Identify and blend with initial *i* and *a*

Materials • **Photo Cards:** *alligator, ant, apple, astronaut, ax, inch, inchworm, ink, insect, invitation* • **Puppet**

Puppet

PHONEME IDENTITY

Tier 2

- Display the **Photo Cards**. *Listen for the beginning sound in these words:* ink, insect, inch. *I hear the /i/ sound at the beginning of these words.* Repeat with Photo Cards for *ant* and *ax*.

Guided Practice/Practice

- Display Photo Cards for *inchworm, invitation,* and *ink*. Name each picture. *What sound is in the beginning of each word?* (/i/) Repeat with Photo Cards for *apple and astronaut*.

PHONEME BLENDING

Model

- *Listen as Happy says the sounds for* in: */i/ /n/. Now he will blend the sounds: /iiinnn/,* in. *Happy put /i/ /n/ together to say the word* in. Repeat blending with the word *at*: /a/ /t/.

Guided Practice/Practice

- Have Happy say /i/ /t/ and have children repeat. *Blend the sounds and say the word with Happy: /iiit/,* it. Repeat with *is, an,* and *if.*

Corrective Feedback

Blending: Sound Error Model the sound that children missed. For example, for the word *sip*, say: *My turn*. Tap under the letter *i* in the word *sip* and say: *Sound? What's the sound?* Then return to the beginning of the word. Say: *Let's start over*. Blend the word with children again.

Phonics

Objective Reinforce letter-sound correspondence for /s/s, /p/p, /t/t, /i/i

Materials • **Sound-Spelling Cards:** *Insect, Piano, Sun, Turtle* • **Sound-Spelling WorkBoards** • **Word-Building Cards**

RETEACH: /s/s, /p/p, /i/i

Model

- Display the *Sun* **Sound-Spelling Card**. *The letter* s *stands for the /s/ sound as in* sun. *What is this letter? What sound does it stand for?* Repeat with *inch, pig,* and *top.*

Guided Practice/Practice

- Distribute **WorkBoards** to children. Say: *paper, song, table, pig, sun, inch, tent, it.* Children write on their WorkBoards the letter that stands for the beginning sound they heard for each word.

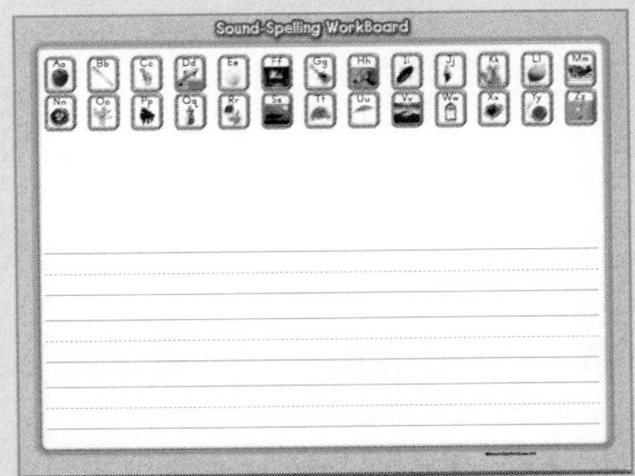

Sound-Spelling WorkBoard

CUMULATIVE REVIEW

Display **Word-Building Cards** for *i, t,* and *p,* one at a time. Have children chorally say the sound. Repeat and vary the pace.

On Level

Pre-decodable Reader

Objective Reread *I See a Truck Go* to develop fluency

Materials • **Pre-decodable Readers:** *I See a Truck Go; Sit, Tip!*

REREAD FOR FLUENCY

- Ask children to review the illustrations in *I See a Truck Go.* Have them use their own words to retell a main event from the story.
- Have children reread a page or two of *I See a Truck Go.* Work with them to read with accuracy and expression. Model reading a page. Point out how you grouped the words: *I grouped together the words "I see a truck go," and then I paused before reading the next page. Grouping words like this makes my reading sound natural, not too fast and not too slow.*
- Provide time to listen as children read their page(s). Have children identify the high-frequency words.
- Use the same routine for **Pre-decodable Reader** *Sit, Tip!*

Pre-decodable Reader

Pre-decodable Reader

Beyond Level

Pre-decodable Reader

Objective Reread *I See a Truck Go* to reinforce fluency

Materials • **Pre-decodable Readers:** *I See a Truck Go; Sit, Tip!*

REREAD FOR FLUENCY

- Have partners reread *I See a Truck Go* and *Sit, Tip!*
- Provide time to listen as children read. Comment on their accuracy and expression and provide corrective feedback.

INNOVATE

- For *I See a Truck Go,* have children suggest new vehicles that could be added to the book, such as a wheelbarrow, scooter, or bicycle. Have children draw their vehicle and then write a complete sentence, following the model of the book. For example: *I see a [rebus of wheelbarrow] go.*
- For *Sit, Tip!,* tell children to think of a different ending to the story and draw it. Have them write a sentence to go with the picture.

Corrective Feedback

Sound Error *When I say the* word in, *I hear the sounds /i/ /n/. Listen again: /i/ /n/,* in. *What sound do you hear in the beginning? What sound do you hear at the end?* Continue with *if, an, it* and then repeat *in.*

ELL ENGLISH LANGUAGE LEARNERS

Access to Core Content

Content Objective Develop listening comprehension
Language Objective Discuss text using key words and sentence frames
Materials • **ELL Resource Book,** pp. 82–89

PRETEACH BIG BOOK/TRADE BOOK

All Language Levels

Use the Interactive Question-Response Guide on **ELL Resource Book** pages 82–89 to introduce children to *Duck on a Bike*. Preteach half of the selection on Day 1 and half on Day 2.

- Use the prompts provided in the guide to develop meaning and vocabulary. Use the partner-talk and whole-class responses to engage children and increase student talk.
- When completed, revisit the selection and prompt children to talk about the illustrations. Provide sentence starters as needed and build on children's responses to develop language.

ELL Resource Book

Trade Book

Beginning

Use Visuals During the Interactive Reading, select several pictures. Describe them and have children summarize what you said.

Intermediate

Summarize During the Interactive Reading, select a few lines of text. After you read them and explain them, have children summarize the text.

Advanced

Expand During the Interactive Reading, select a larger portion of text. After you read it and explain it, have children summarize the text.

Approaching Level

High-Frequency Words

Objective Reinforce high-frequency words *go, see, a, like*

Materials • **High-Frequency Word Cards:** *a, go, like, see* • **Word-Building Cards**

REINFORCE WORDS: *go, see, a, like*

- Display the **High-Frequency Word Card** for **go**. Say the word and have children repeat it. Point to each letter and have children name it.
- Distribute **Word-Building Cards** for *g* and *o*. Model putting the letters together to form the word *go* and then have children form *go*.
- Repeat the above routines with the words **see**, **a**, and **like**.
- Ask a question with the word *go: Where do you want to go on vacation?* Have children use *go* to answer the question. Tell them to speak in complete sentences. Continue with the other words.

CUMULATIVE REVIEW

Display the High-Frequency Word Cards for *go, see, a,* and *like,* one card at a time, as children chorally read and spell the word. Mix and repeat. Note words children need to review.

ELL

Extra Practice During the Cumulative Review, pair children at different levels of proficiency and have partners take turns reading and spelling the high-frequency words to each other.

Phonemic Awareness

Objective Blend sounds to form words

Materials • **Puppet**

PHONEME BLENDING

Tier 2

Model

- *Listen as Happy says the sounds for* pin: */p/ /i/ /n/. Now Happy will blend the sounds: /piiinnn/, /pin/,* pin. *Happy put /p/, /i/, and /n/ together to say the word* pin. *Now listen again, I'll do another word.* Repeat blending with the words *lip, tab,* and *tan.*

Guided Practice/Practice

- Have three children stand side by side. Ask the first child to say the /l/ sound. Have the next child say the /i/ sound. Have the third child say the /d/ sound. Have them say the sounds in order and blend them: /llliiid/, *lid*.
- Repeat with other sound sets and children: /t/ /a/ /p/; /p/ /a/ /m/; /m/ /i/ /t/.

Puppet

Approaching Level

Phonics

Objective Review blending /i/i, /p/p, /s/s, /t/t to form words and build fluency

Materials • **Word-Building Cards** • pocket chart

REVIEW SKILLS

Tier 2

Model

- Display **Word-Building Card** *s. This letter is* s. *The letter* s *stands for the /s/ sound. Say /s/. What is the letter? What is the sound?*
- Place *i* next to *s. This letter is* i. *The letter* i *stands for the /i/ sound. Say /i/. What is the letter? What is the sound?* Move your hand from left to right below the letters. *Now listen as I blend the two sounds together: /sssiii/.*
- Place *p* next to *i* and repeat the routine. *Now listen as I blend the three sounds together: /sssiiip/,* sip. *What's the word? Let's blend the sounds together: /s/ /i/ /p/, /sssiiip/,* sip.

Guided Practice/Practice

- Give children Word-Building Cards for *p, i, t.* Have each child say the sound for their letter. Ask children to blend the sounds to say the word *pit.* Repeat with *tip.*

Build Fluency

- Have children blend *sip, pit,* and *tip* as quickly as they can.

Pre-decodable Reader

Objective Preteach Pre-decodable Reader *Sit, Tip!*

Materials • **Pre-decodable Reader:** *Sit, Tip!*

PRETEACH *Sit, Tip!*

- Display the book cover and read the title. Have children open to the title page and point out the title. *Let's read the title together.* Have children sound out each word as you run your finger under it. *The title of this book is* Sit, Tip! Tell children to use the cover illustration to help them predict what might happen. *Who is Tip? What might he do?*
- Page through the book. Ask children what they see in each picture. Ask them to find the words *go* and *see.*
- Read the book chorally with children. Have them point to each word as they read it. Provide corrective feedback as needed.
- Ask children to use *go* and *see* to talk about the pictures. *I see Pat and Pam go.* After reading, ask children to recall things they read about.

Corrective Feedback

Association Error If children have difficulty identifying medial /i/, say: *My turn: /sssiiip/,* sip. *I hear the /i/ sound in the middle of sip: /sssiiip/. What is the sound? What is the letter? Let's start over.* Repeat the word *sip* for children to identify the position of /i/.

Pre-decodable Reader

Draw a Character

Ask children to draw their favorite characters from *Sit, Tip!* and to write the characters' names below their drawings.

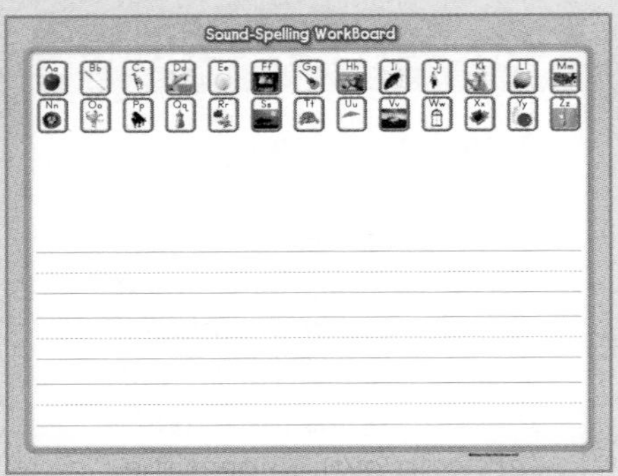
Sound-Spelling WorkBoard

On Level

Phonics

Objective Blend /i/*i*, /t/*t*, /s/*s, and* /p/*p* words

Materials
- **Word-Building Cards**
- pocket chart
- **Sound-Spelling WorkBoards**

REVIEW: /i/*i*, /t/*t*, /s/*s*, /p/*p*

- **Blend Words** Place **Word-Building Cards** *s, i,* and *p* in the pocket chart. Point to each letter for children to identify the letter name and sound. Move your hand from left to right below the letters as you blend the word.
- *Now listen as I blend the sounds together: /sssiiip/,* sip. *What's the word?* Repeat with *tip, sit,* and *pit.*
- Have children write *s, i, p* several times on their **WorkBoards** as they say /s/, /i/, /p/. Have them repeat for *t, i, p; s, i, t;* and *p, i, t.*

Beyond Level

Phonics

Objectives Review /i/*i* and /t/*t* and introduce /u/*u;* blend and read words

Materials
- **Word-Building Cards**
- **Sound-Spelling WorkBoards**

ACCELERATE

- Display the Word-Building Cards for *r, u, b.* Point to each letter for children to identify. *I can blend the sounds for these letters to read the word. Listen: /r/ /u/ /b/, /rrruuub/,* rub. *The word is* rub. Guide children to blend the sounds and read *rub.*
- Help children read simple three-letter words with short *u* and consonants *p, s, t, b, c, n,* and *r,* such as *bun, cut,* and *tub.* Ask children to write the words in the WorkBoard boxes and guide them to blend the sounds to read the words.

Corrective Feedback

Letter-Sound Discrimination If children say /e/ instead of /u/, write the letter *u* and point to it. Say: *This letter stands for /u/. Say it with me: /u/. Now let's sound out some words with /u/ again.* Build and blend the words *duck* /duuuk/, *bus* /buuus/, and *cup* /kuuup/.

ENGLISH LANGUAGE LEARNERS

Access to Core Content

Content Objective Develop listening comprehension
Language Objective Discuss text using key words and sentence frames
Materials • **ELL Resource Book**, pp. 90–91

PRETEACH BIG BOOK OF EXPLORATIONS

All Language Levels

Use the Interactive Question-Response Guide on **ELL Resource Book** pages 90–91 to preview the **Big Book of Explorations** selection "How Do You Go to School?" Preteach half of the selection on Day 3 and half on Day 4.

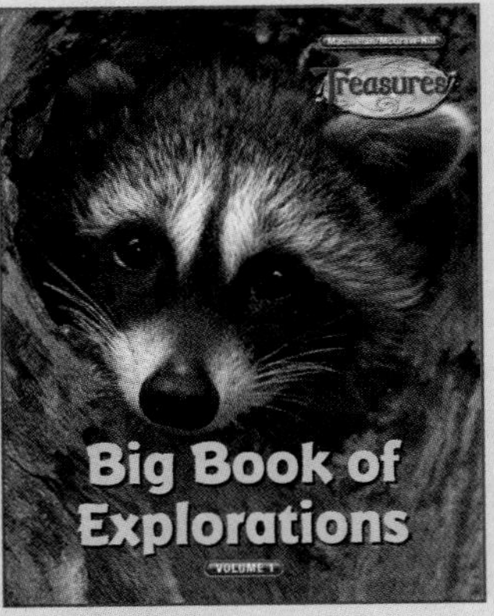

Big Book of Explorations

Grammar

Content Objective Identify action words
Language Objective Speak in complete sentences, using sentence frames
Materials • **Listening Library Audio CD** • **Photo Cards**

ACTION WORDS (VERBS)

All Language Levels

- Review verbs. Tell children that verbs are action words. Say: *I ride a bike*. Have children repeat and act out the action. Ask children to name and act out other actions they can do.
- Play "Yankee Doodle" from the **Listening Library Audio CD**. Tell children to listen for action words, which tell about things people or animals can do.
- Point out the action words *came, riding, stuck, called, keep,* and *mind*. Reread the words in phrases that children can act out. Display **Photo Cards** for *horse, dog, door*. Point to each card and have children name it and then name an action to do with it.

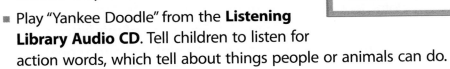

Yankee Doodle

Yankee Doodle came to town.
A-riding on a pony.
He stuck a feather in his cap.
And called it macaroni.
Yankee Doodle, keep it up.
Yankee Doodle dandy!
Mind the music and the step.
Yankee Doodle dandy!

PEER DISCUSSION STARTERS

All Language Levels

- Distribute Photo Cards of words that name animals that children have read about, such as *cow, dog, goat,* and *horse*.
- Pair children and have them complete the sentence frame *This is a* __________. Ask them to expand on their sentences by providing as many details as they can. Circulate, listen in, and take note of each child's language use and proficiency.

Puppet

Approaching Level

Phonemic Awareness

Objective Blend /s/*s*, /p/*p*, /t/*t*, /i/*i* to form words

Materials • **Puppet** • **Photo Cards:** *inch, pen, sun, teeth* • pocket chart

PHONEME BLENDING

Tier 2

Model

- Display the **Photo Card** for *sun*. Hold up the **Puppet**. *Happy is going to say the sounds in a word: /s/ /u/ /n/. Happy can blend these sounds together: /sssuuunnn/. Now you say the sounds: /s/ /u/ /n/. Say the word with Happy:* sun.

Guided Practice/Practice

- Display the Photo Cards in a pocket chart. Have children name each photo with you. Then say: *Happy will say the sounds in a word: /i/ /n/ /ch/. Blend the sounds together with Happy to say the word: /iiinnnch/,* inch. *Point to the picture for the word you named.* Repeat with the remaining Photo Cards.

Phonics

Objective Blend /i/*i*, /t/*t*, /p/*p*, /s/*s* to read words

Materials • **Word-Building Cards** • pocket chart

REVIEW SKILLS

Tier 2

Model

- Place **Word-Building Cards** *s, i,* and *t* in the pocket chart. Point to *s*. *The name of this letter is* s. *The letter* s *stands for the /s/ sound. Say /s/.* Point to *i*. *The name of this letter is* i. *The letter stands for the /i/ sound. Say /i/.* Point to *t* and repeat.
- Say the sound each letter stands for: /s/ /i/ /t/. *Now I will blend the sounds together: /sssiiit/,* sit.

Guided Practice/Practice

- Keep the Word-Building Cards in the pocket chart. Have children take turns saying the letter sounds and blending the word: /s/ /i/ /t/, /sssiiit/, *sit*. Guide practice as necessary. Repeat with the Word-Building Cards for *tip, sip,* and *pit*.

Corrective Feedback

Sound Error If children miss making the letter-sound correspondence, say: *My turn:* sit, */sssiiit/. I hear /i/ in the middle of* sit, */sssiiit/. I'll hold up my* i *card because I hear /i/ in the middle of /sssiiit/. What is the sound? What letter stands for that sound? Let's start again.*

ELL

Extra Practice Provide additional practice in pronouncing and blending sounds that do not transfer directly to the native language of some children, such as the short vowel /i/.

Approaching Level

Leveled Reader Lesson 1

Leveled Reader Library

Objective Read *See It Go Up* to apply skills and strategies

Materials • **Leveled Reader:** *See It Go Up*

BEFORE READING

- **Preview** Read the title and the name of the author. *What do you see on the cover? Does that look like fun?* Tell children to use the cover illustration and the title to help them predict what the story might be about.
- **Model Concepts About Print** Demonstrate book handling for children. Guide them as they follow along with their books. *This is the top of the page. This is the bottom of the page. When I read the words on the page, I start at the left and read from left to right. Follow my finger as I read.*
- **Review High-Frequency Words** Write **see** and **go** and read the words aloud. Guide children as they name the letters in each word. Have children find each word in the book and point to it as they read it.
- **Page Through the Book** Name unfamiliar terms and identify the rebus pictures.
- **Set a Purpose for Reading** *Let's find out what can go up.*

DURING READING

- Remind children to use the rebuses and photographs to gain information and to look for the high-frequency words *see* and *go*. Show children how to self-correct if a word doesn't sound right or doesn't make sense in the sentence. *I see the first rebus on page 2 and I think, "arrow," but* It can go arrow *doesn't make sense. The arrow must represent the word* up. It can go up *makes much more sense.*
- Monitor children's reading and provide help as needed.

AFTER READING

- Ask children to point out words that they had trouble reading and to share strategies they used to help them. Reinforce good behaviors. For example, say: *Mina, I noticed that you followed each word you read aloud with your finger. Good job!*
- Ask children to retell the story and to share personal responses. *Did the story show all the vehicles that can go up? Which vehicles look like fun to ride in?*

Leveled Reader

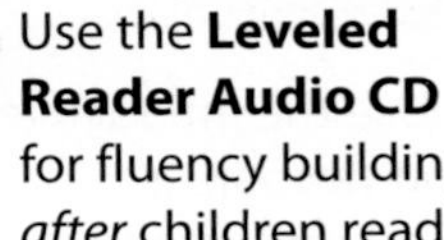

AUDIO CD

Use the **Leveled Reader Audio CD** for fluency building *after* children read the book with your support during Small Group time.

Draw a Vehicle

Have children draw different ways to travel. Suggest that they write *Go!* below their pictures.

Leveled Reader

ELL

Retell Use the Interactive Question-Response Guide Technique to help English Language Learners understand *Fast or Slow*. As you read, make meaning clear by pointing to pictures, demonstrating word meaning, paraphrasing text, and asking children questions.

Draw Fast or Slow

Have children draw pictures of things that go fast or slow. Help them label their pictures with the word *fast* or *slow*.

On Level

Leveled Reader Lesson 1

Leveled Reader Library

Objective Read *Fast or Slow?* to apply skills and strategies

Materials
- **Leveled Reader:** *Fast or Slow?*

BEFORE READING

- **Preview** Have children point to the title page as you read the title and the name of the author. Ask children to point to and describe the cover and note that it is a photograph. Point out the words *fast* and *slow* in the title. *What do you think the book is about?* Point out that the title page also has the title and author's name.
- **Model Concepts About Print** Demonstrate book handling. *I hold the book so that the cover is on the front and the words are not upside down. I open the book by turning the cover. Then I turn each page as I read it.*
- **Review High-Frequency Words** Write **see** and **go** on chart paper. Have children find each word in the book and point to the word as they read it.
- **Set a Purpose for Reading** *Let's find out what can travel fast or slow.*

DURING READING

- Have children turn to page 2 and begin by whisper-reading the first two pages.
- Remind children to look for the new high-frequency word and to use the photographs to gain information.
- Monitor children's reading and provide help. Stop during the reading and ask open-ended questions to facilitate discussion, such as: *What can go fast? What can go slow? What do you think each vehicle sounds like when it goes fast or slow?* Build on children's responses to develop deeper understanding of the text.

AFTER READING

- Ask children to point out words they had trouble reading and to share strategies they used to figure them out. Reinforce good behaviors. For example: *Bess, I noticed that you put your finger on each line. After you read it, you looked carefully at the photograph.*
- **Retell** Tell children to retell important facts in the selection. Help them make a personal connection. *What vehicles have you ridden in or would like to ride in? Have you ever floated a toy boat in a pond?*

Beyond Level

Leveled Reader Lesson 1

Objective Read *The Train Trip* to apply skills and strategies

Materials • **Leveled Reader:** *The Train Trip*

Leveled Reader

BEFORE READING

- **Preview** Ask children to point to and read the title as you name the author. Have them point out the front cover and the back cover. *What vehicle do you see on the front cover? Where do you think the train is going? What do you think this book is about?* Page through the book with children and pause to name unfamiliar items.
- **Introduce Story Words** Point to the word *tracks* on page 4. Read the sentence. Have children use the picture to explain what tracks are. Repeat with *bridge* on page 14.
- **Page Through the Book** Pause to name unfamiliar actions or items.
- **Set a Purpose for Reading** *Let's find out about traveling on a train.*

DURING READING

- Remind children that when they come to an unfamiliar word, they can look for familiar chunks in the word, break the word into syllables and sound out each part, or think about what the word might mean. If the word does not sound right or make sense in the sentence, children can self-correct.
- Monitor children's reading and provide help as needed.

AFTER READING

- Ask children to point out words they had trouble reading and to share the strategies they used to figure them out.
- Ask children to retell the story and to share personal responses. *Have you ever taken a trip on a train? What can you tell us about your train trip?*

Gifted Talented

- **Evaluate** *Why you think a train trip is a good or bad way to travel?*
- **Model** On the board, draw a T chart with the heading *Train* and the column labels *Pro* and *Con*. Solicit pros and cons of traveling by train. Tell children to create a chart for another form of transportation, and then have them write a complete sentence that completes this frame: *I want/do not want to travel by* ________ *because* ________ *and* ________.

Draw a Scene

Tell children to imagine they are traveling on a train. Have them draw a scene that they might see out the window. Have them write *The Train Trip* below their pictures. Ask partners to describe their scenes.

Leveled Reader

Vocabulary

Preteach Vocabulary Use the routine in the **Visual Vocabulary Resources**, pages 317–318, to preteach the ELL Vocabulary listed on the inside front cover of the Leveled Reader.

ELL ENGLISH LANGUAGE LEARNERS

Leveled Reader Library

Leveled Reader

Content Objective Read to apply skills and strategies
Language Objective Retell information using complete sentences
Materials • **Leveled Reader:** *See It Go*

BEFORE READING

All Language Levels

- **Preview** Read the title *See It Go*. Ask: *What's the title? Say it again.* Repeat with the author's name. Point to the cover photo and say: *I see an airplane.* Point to the airplane as you name it. *It can fly. Now turn to a partner and tell about this picture.*
- **Page Through the Book** Use simple language to tell about the photo on each page. Immediately follow up with questions, such as: *Is this an airplane? Is this a boat or a balloon?*
- **Review Skills** Use the inside front cover to review the phonics skill and high-frequency words.
- **Set a Purpose** Say: *Let's read to find out about what goes fast and what goes slow.*

DURING READING

All Language Levels

- Have children whisper-read each page, or use the differentiated suggestions below. Circulate, listen in, and provide corrective feedback, such as modeling how to use photos to help understand words.
- **Retell** Stop after every two pages and ask children to state what they have learned so far. Reinforce language by restating children's comments when they have difficulty using story-specific words. Provide differentiated sentence frames to support children's responses and engage children in partner-talk where appropriate.

Beginning

Echo-Read Have children echo-read after you.

Check Comprehension Point to pictures and ask questions such as: *Do you see an airplane? Point to a boat that goes fast.*

Intermediate

Choral-Read Have children choral-read with you.

Check Comprehension Ask questions/prompts such as: *What is the child doing in this photo? Describe the car that goes slow.*

Advanced

Choral-Read Have children choral-read.

Check Comprehension Ask: *How is the plane like the balloon? How is it different? Which photos show things you have been on? Tell about them.*

ELL ENGLISH LANGUAGE LEARNERS

AFTER READING

All Language Levels

Book Talk Children will work with peers of varying language abilities to discuss their books for this week. Display the four **Leveled Readers** read this week: *The Train Trip* (Beyond Level), *Fast or Slow?* (On Level), *See It Go Up* (Approaching Level), and *See It Go* (English Language Learners).

Ask the questions and provide the prompts below. Call on children who read each book to answer the questions or respond to the prompt. If appropriate, ask children to find the pages in the book that illustrate their answers.

- **What is the title of your book?**
- **What vehicles do the photos show?**
- **What did you learn about the vehicles?**
- **Have you ever been on any of the vehicles in your book? What was it like? Did you go fast or slow?**
- **Did you like this book? Tell why or why not.**

Develop Listening and Speaking Skills Tell children to remember the following:

- Share information in cooperative learning interactions. Remind children to work with their partners to retell the story and complete any activities. Ask: *What happened next in the story?*
- Employ self-corrective techniques and monitor their own and other children's language production. Children should ask themselves: *What parts of this passage were confusing to me? Can my classmates help me clarify a word or sentence that I don't understand?*
- Use high-frequency English words to describe people, places, and objects.
- Narrate, describe, and explain with specificity and detail. Ask: *Where did the story take place? Can you describe the setting? What else did you notice?*
- Express opinions, ideas, and feelings on a variety of social and academic topics. Ask: *What do you think about the characters in the story?*

Approaching Level

Phonemic Awareness

Objective Categorize words with the same final sounds

Materials
- **Photo Cards:** *bat, bike, bus, hat, house, map, net, nut, top*
- pocket chart

PHONEME CATEGORIZATION

Tier 2

Model

- Display the **Photo Cards** for *net, hat,* and *bike.* Say: *Listen to the ending sound as I name each picture. Two of the words end in the same sound. One does not. Listen:* net, hat, bike. Net *and* hat *end with the /t/ sound.* Bike *does not end with /t/.* Bike *does not belong.*

Guided Practice/Practice

- Display the Photo Cards for *top, map,* and *nut* in a pocket chart. Have children name each Photo Card with you. Repeat each name, emphasizing the final sound. Ask children which word does not belong because it does not end in /p/. Repeat with the cards for *bat, bus,* and *house.*

ELL

Sound-Letter Relationships Provide additional practice in pronouncing the /s/, /p/, /t/, /i/ sounds and naming the corresponding letters, as children point to them.

Phonics

Objective Identify initial sounds /s/*s*, /p/*p*, /t/*t*, /i/*i* and build fluency

Materials
- **Photo Cards:** *inch, insect, invitation, pen, pie, pizza, soap, sock, sun, teeth, tiger, top*
- **Word-Building Cards**
- pocket chart
- **Sound-Spelling WorkBoards**

BUILD FLUENCY: LETTER-SOUND CORRESPONDENCE

Tier 2

Model

- Place **Word-Building Cards** *s, p, t,* and *i* in the top row of the pocket chart. Review the sound that each letter stands for.
- Shuffle the Photo Cards and place them facedown in a stack. Pick the first card, name the picture, and identify its beginning sound. Place the Photo Card under the letter in the pocket chart that stands for the initial sound.

Guided Practice/Practice

- Have children choose a Photo Card, name the picture, identify its beginning sound, and place it in the pocket chart under the correct letter. Guide practice with the first Photo Card.

Build Fluency

- Display the Word-Building Cards. Have children name each letter as quickly as they can. Then ask them to write the letters on their **WorkBoards** several times as they say the sounds.

Approaching Level

Leveled Reader Lesson 2

Leveled Reader Library

Objective Reread *See It Go Up* to reinforce fluency and phonics, and to classify and categorize

Materials • **Leveled Reader:** *See It Go Up*

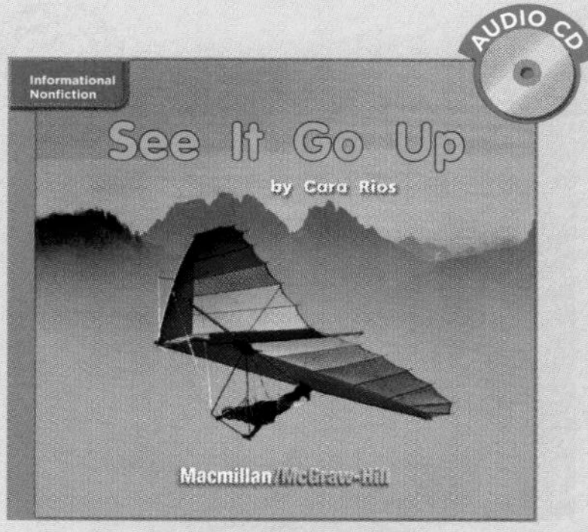

Leveled Reader

FOCUS ON FLUENCY

- Tell children that you will read one page of the book and they should read that page right after you. They should follow along in their books and try to read at the same speed and with the same expression that you use.

SKILL CLASSIFY AND CATEGORIZE

- *Think of all the vehicles in the book. How are all the vehicles alike? How are they different? Which vehicles can take you far? Which can take you only a short distance?*

REREAD BOOKS

- Distribute copies of the past six **Leveled Readers**. Tell children that rereading the books will help them develop their skills.
- Circulate and listen in as children read. Stop them periodically and ask them how they are figuring out words or checking their understanding. Tell children to read other previously read Leveled Readers during independent reading time.

High-Frequency Words

Objective Review high-frequency words *go, a, see,* and *like*

Materials • **High-Frequency Word Cards:** *a, go, like, see*

BUILD WORD AUTOMATICITY: *go, a, see, like*

- Distribute copies of the **High-Frequency Word Card** for **go**. Say the word and have children repeat it. Have children name the letters in the word. Repeat with the words **a**, **see**, and **like**.
- **Build Fluency** Use the High-Frequency Word Cards to review previously taught words. Display the words and point to them in random order. Have children read them as quickly as possible.

Meet Grade-Level Expectations

As an alternative to this day's lesson, guide children through a reading of the On Level Leveled Reader. See page 754. Since both books contain the same vocabulary, phonics, and comprehension skills, the scaffolding you provided will help most children gain access to this more challenging text.

Add a Page

Children can add a page to *See It Go Up* by drawing pictures of other things that go up.

Leveled Reader

On Level

Leveled Reader Library

Leveled Reader Lesson 2

Objective Reread to apply skills and strategies to retell a story

Materials • **Leveled Reader:** *Fast or Slow?*

BEFORE READING

- Ask children to look through *Fast or Slow?* and recall what the selection was about. Reinforce vocabulary by repeating children's sentences using more sophisticated language. For example: *Yes, the race car can go fast. It is very speedy.*

DURING READING

- Have children join you in a choral-reading of the selection. Model reading with expression. *When I read page 2, I said* fast *with strong emphasis. I used the same strong emphasis when I read* slow *on page 3. I wanted to emphasize the difference between how the two vehicles move.* Ask children to use the same kind of expression when they read.
- Assign each child a page. Have children practice by whisper-reading. *Follow along as other children read, and be ready to come in when it is your turn. Remember to use lots of expression.*

AFTER READING

- Have children retell important facts from the selection in their own words.
- *Look at the pictures of vehicles in the book. Which things can you ride in? Which things go fast? Which things go slow?*

Extend the Book

Extend the selection by having children draw something that they would like to ride in. Have them write a caption telling whether *It can go fast* or *It can go slow.*

Beyond Level

Leveled Reader Lesson 2

Objective Reread to apply skills and strategies to retell a story

Materials • **Leveled Reader:** *The Train Trip*

BEFORE READING

- Ask children to look back at *The Train Trip* and recall important facts in the selection. *Where are some of the places you can go on a train? What can you can see while riding on a train?*

DURING READING

- Assign each child a page of the book to read aloud. Have children practice by whisper-reading. *Follow along as each child reads, and be ready to come in when it is your turn.*

AFTER READING

- Explain that if we look at how an author has grouped information in a book, we can understand it better. Model the strategy: *When I read the book, I notice that many of the pages begin with* You can *or* You go. *Knowing this makes it easier for me to read the book. How else are the pages of the book alike?* (Each page has a sentence that tells about the photo.)

ON YOUR OWN

Write a Story

Children can write and illustrate stories about other things people can see while riding in a train.

Practice Reader

Expand Vocabulary

Objective Learn and apply the multiple meanings of the new words *trip* and *past* and brainstorm other multiple-meaning words

Materials • **Leveled Reader:** *The Train Trip*

ENRICH: *trip, past*

Gifted Talented

- Have children reread page 2. Ask them to point to *trip* and read aloud the sentence. Say: *In this sentence,* trip *means "a journey from one place to another."* Then explain that *trip* can have more than one meaning. Walk across the room and "trip." Say: *I have to be careful so I don't trip and fall.* Ask: *What does* trip *mean in this sentence?* (to fall, stumble)
- Repeat with *past* (pages 6 and 10). Demonstrate walking *past* the window and talk about something that happened in the *past.*
- Use *trip* and *past* to begin a list of multiple-meaning words and their meanings. Then have children find other words in the book that have more than one meaning. (*can, train, tracks*)
- Together, brainstorm other words with more than one meaning. Add them to the list.

ELL

Partners When children write and illustrate stories, pair English Language Learners with children who are more proficient.

ELL ENGLISH LANGUAGE LEARNERS

Fluency

Content Objectives Reread Pre-decodable Readers to develop fluency; develop speaking skills

Language Objective Tell a partner what a selection is about

Materials • **Pre-decodable Readers:** *I See a Truck Go; Sit, Tip!* • **Photo Cards**

REREAD FOR FLUENCY

Beginning

- Review the high-frequency words **go**, **see**, **the**, and **we** using the **Read/Spell/Write** routine.

Intermediate/Advanced

- Use each word in a sentence that illustrates its use. For example: *We see the car go*. Show the **Photo Card** for *car* and point to it.

All Language Levels

- Guide children through a choral-reading of *I See a Truck Go* and *Sit, Tip!* Model reading a page, such as: *I see a truck go*. Point out how you paused before reading the next page to look at the picture first. Explain that pausing helps make the reading sound natural. Model reading the page again and have children chorally repeat.

DEVELOP SPEAKING/LISTENING SKILLS

All Language Levels

- Have children reread *I See a Truck Go* and *Sit, Tip!* to a partner. Remind them to listen carefully and follow along in their book as their partner is reading. Work with children to read with accuracy and appropriate pausing.
- Ask children to tell their partner about the pictures on each page. Then have the other partner describe the pictures. Circulate, listen in, and provide additional language as needed.

Beginning

Confirm Understanding Point to the pictures for partners to identify. Ask: What do you see? Restate the correct answer in a complete sentence.

Intermediate

Express Opinions Ask partners to tell you which is their favorite picture in the book. Prompt them to explain why it is their favorite picture.

Advanced

Compare and Contrast Have partners compare two different pictures and describe them. Prompt them to explain how they are alike and different.

ELL ENGLISH LANGUAGE LEARNERS

High-Frequency Words

Content Objective Spell high-frequency words correctly

Language Objective Write in complete sentences, using sentence frames

Materials • **Sound-Spelling WorkBoards** • **Sound-Spelling Cards** • **Photo Cards**

Beginning/Intermediate

- Write the high-frequency words **go** and **see** on the board. Have children copy the words on their **WorkBoards**. Then help them say, then write, a sentence for each word. Provide the sentence starter *We go to* ________; *I see a* ________.

Advanced

- Children should first orally state their sentence. Correct as needed. Then they can draw a picture to complete the sentence. For children who are ready, help them spell words using their growing knowledge of English sound-spelling relationships. Model how to segment the word children are trying to spell and attach a spelling to each sound. Use the **Sound-Spelling Cards** to reinforce the spellings for each English sound.

Writing

All Language Levels

- Dictate the following sounds and ask children to write the letters: /t/, /i/. Have them write each letter five times as they say /t/ and then /i/. Demonstrate correct letter formation, as needed.
- Then display a set of **Photo Cards**. Select at least five cards whose picture names begin with /i/ (ink, insect, invitation, inch, inchworm) and five whose picture names begin with /t/ (tiger, table, turtle, teeth, top).
- Say the name of each card, stretching the initial sound to emphasize it. You may also need to reinforce the meaning of the word and model correct mouth formation when forming the sound. Use the articulation pictures and prompts on the back of the small Sound-Spelling Cards for support. Tell children that you want them to write the first letter in each picture's name on their WorkBoards.

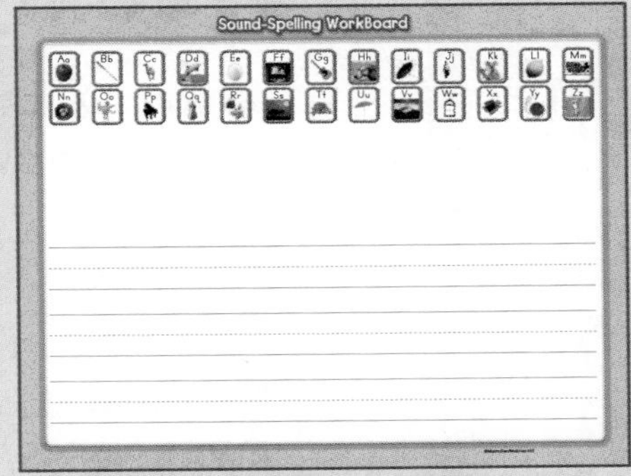

Sound-Spelling WorkBoard

Phonemic Awareness/ Phonics

For English Language Learners who need more practice with this week's phonemic awareness and phonics skills, see the Approaching Level lessons. Focus on minimal contrasts, articulation, and those sounds that do not transfer from the child's first language to English. For a complete listing of transfer sounds, see pages T10–T31.

Progress Monitoring

Weekly Assessment

Use your Quick Check observations and the assessment opportunities identified below to evaluate children's progress in key skill areas.

Skills	Quick Check Observations	Pencil and Paper Assessment
PHONEMIC AWARENESS/ PHONICS /i/i, /t/t (i, t)	703	Activity Book, pp. 24, 30, 32 Practice Book, pp. 73, 77
HIGH-FREQUENCY WORDS *go, see* (go, see)	724	Activity Book, pp. 27–28 Practice Book, pp. 75–76
COMPREHENSION Identify Character and Plot	714	Activity Book, pp. 25–26, 31 Practice Book, p. 74

Quick Check Rubric

Skills	1	2	3
PHONEMIC AWARENESS/ PHONICS	Does not connect the /i/, /t/ sounds with the letters *Ii, Tt* and has difficulty blending the CVC words *sit, pit, pat,* and *sip.*	Usually connects the /i/, /t/ sounds with the letters *Ii, Tt* and blends the CVC words *sit, pit, pat,* and *sip* with only occasional support.	Consistently connects the /i/, /t/ sounds with the letters *Ii, Tt* and blends the CVC words *sit, pit, pat,* and *sip.*
HIGH-FREQUENCY WORDS	Does not identify the high-frequency words.	Usually recognizes the high-frequency words with accuracy, but not speed.	Consistently recognizes the high-frequency words with speed and accuracy.
COMPREHENSION	Does not identify character or plot using the pictures and text.	Usually identifies character and plot using the pictures and text.	Consistently identifies character and plot using the pictures and text.

DIBELS LINK

PROGRESS MONITORING

Use your DIBELS results to inform instruction.

IF...

Initial **S**ound **F**luency (**ISF**) 0–7

THEN...

Evaluate for Intervention

TPRI LINK

PROGRESS MONITORING

Use your TPRI scores to inform instruction.

IF...

Phonemic Awareness Start midyear
Graphophonemic Awareness Start midyear
Listening Comprehension Start midyear

THEN...

Evaluate for Intervention

Diagnose		Prescribe
Review the assessment answers with children. Have them correct their errors. Then provide additional instruction as needed.		
PHONEMIC AWARENESS/ PHONICS /i/i, /t/t	**IF...** **Quick Check Rubric:** Children consistently score 1 or **Pencil and Paper Assessment:** Children get 0–2 items correct	**THEN...** Reteach Phonemic Awareness and Phonics Skills using the **Phonemic Awareness** and **Phonics Intervention Teacher's Editions**. SPIRAL REVIEW Use the Build Fluency lesson in upcoming weeks to provide children practice reading words with /i/*i* and /t/*t*.
HIGH-FREQUENCY WORDS *go, see*	**Quick Check Rubric:** Children consistently score 1 or **Pencil and Paper Assessment:** Children get 0–2 items correct	Reteach High-Frequency Words using the **Phonics Intervention Teacher's Edition**. SPIRAL REVIEW Use the High-Frequency Words lesson in upcoming weeks to provide children practice reading words with *go* and *see*.
COMPREHENSION Skill: Identify Character and Plot	**Quick Check Rubric:** Children consistently score 1 or **Pencil and Paper Assessment:** Children get 0–2 items correct	Reteach Comprehension Skill using the **Comprehension Intervention Teacher's Edition**.

Response to Intervention

To place children in Tier 2 or Tier 3 Intervention use the *Diagnostic Assessment.*

- Phonemic Awareness
- Phonics
- Vocabulary
- Comprehension
- Fluency

End-of-Week Assessment

Teacher Notes

Use this page to record lessons that work well or need to be adapted for future reference.

Lessons that work well

Lessons that need adjustments

Use this page to record lessons that work well or need to be adapted for future reference.

Lessons that work well

Lessons that need adjustments

Computer Literacy

Computer Basics

Objectives

- Learn the basic parts of a computer
- Identify proper handling of floppy disks and CD-ROMs
- Practice responsible use and care of computers

Materials

- www.macmillanmh.com
- floppy disks
- CD-ROMs

Vocabulary

monitor looks like a TV screen

keyboard has letters and numbers on buttons called keys

mouse allows you to point and click with an arrow called a cursor

disk drive a device that reads data off a floppy disk or CD-ROM

floppy disk a disk made of plastic and metal that stores data

CD-ROM a circular disk that stores data

Computer Literacy
Focus on Keyboard and Internet Skills and Media Literacy
www.macmillanmh.com

Remind children never to have liquid near electrical appliances.

ACCESS PRIOR KNOWLEDGE

Discuss with children:

- *What can you do with a computer?*

EXPLAIN

- Talk with children to find out how many use computers. Brainstorm reasons why people use computers. Have children take turns speaking one at a time.
- Tell children that computers have different parts. The **monitor** displays information. The **keyboard** and **mouse** are used to enter information into the computer.

MODEL

- Using a computer as a model, show children the following parts of a computer: monitor, keyboard, mouse, and **disk drive**. Point to each part as you say its name and have children repeat.
- Have children look at a keyboard. Explain to them that the long button on the bottom of the keyboard is the space bar. Tell children that the top row contains numbers and the three middle rows are where the letters are found. Have them find the letters with which their names begin.
- Have children locate the disk drive. Model how to insert a **floppy disk**, followed by how to eject it. Show them how to insert and remove a **CD-ROM**.

Technology Makes a Difference

Explain that children should act responsibly when using a computer. Some safety tips include

- no drinks or food around the computer;
- do not bang on the keyboard, mouse, or monitor;
- do not place your fingers or pencils in disk drives;
- do not pull on any cables.

Media Literacy

Advertisements

ACCESS PRIOR KNOWLEDGE

Discuss with children:

- *What is the purpose of advertising?*
- *Where do you see advertisements?*
- *Do advertisements ever lie or mislead us?*
- *How do advertisements work?*

EXPLAIN

Introduce the lesson vocabulary by discussing each word and its definition with children.

- Explain that **advertising** is a form of **communication** that attempts to **persuade** potential customers to purchase a particular **brand** of product or service.
- All types of **media** are used to deliver advertising **messages**, including television, radio, movies, magazines, newspapers, video games, the Internet, and billboards.

MODEL

- Show children examples of advertisements for popular, age-appropriate products. Discuss the elements of the advertisements.
- Tell children that they will be running for a position as your class representative to the student council. As the representative, they will help share ideas, interests, and concerns with adults in the school. They will also help raise money for school activities.
- Explain to children that in order to get votes, they must create an advertisement to persuade their classmates that they are the best person for the job. The advertisement should include the qualities that will make them a good representative.
- Provide children with poster board and markers. Instruct children to create an advertisement poster using words, pictures, or both.
- Hang children's advertising posters around the classroom. If you wish, you may have children vote for their class representative based on which advertisement is most persuasive.

Objectives

- Identify advertisements
- Understand that advertisements try to persuade consumers to buy a particular product or service

Materials

- examples of advertisements
- poster board and markers

Media Literacy Activities
Lessons that help children identify and explore the use of advertisements in different forms of media

Theme Project Wrap-Up

Research/Organizing and Presenting Ideas

After children complete their projects, they can present what they have learned.

Review and Evaluate

How do I share what I have learned?

Help children decide what materials they will need.

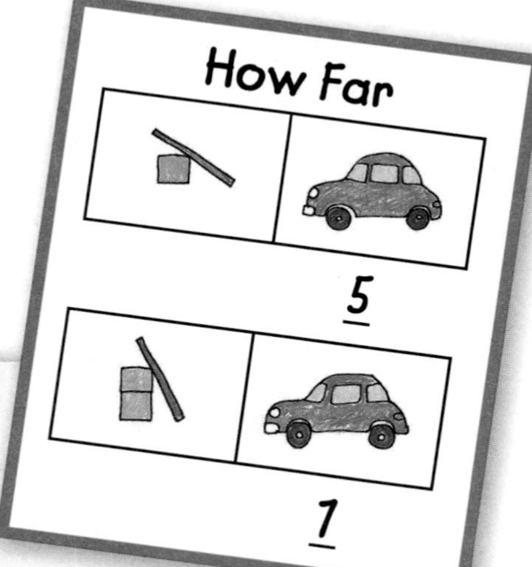

Teacher Checklist

Assess the Research Project

Plan the Project

✔ Participated in identifying types of transportation.
✔ Used the picture dictionary.
✔ Used multiple resources to gather information.

Do the Project

✔ Explained which sources were useful and why.
✔ Chose an appropriate form to present information.
✔ Gathered information and used materials effectively.

Assess the Presentation

Speaking

✔ Presented material in an organized way.
✔ Spoke in a clear voice that everyone could hear.
✔ Spoke in complete sentences.

Representing

✔ Used visuals in conjunction with writing to add details and help illustrate facts and information.
✔ Used pictures and photos appropriate for the topic.

Assess the Listener

Listening

✔ Set a purpose for listening.
✔ Listened for the main idea and identified details.
✔ Waited until the speaker finished before asking questions.

Children's Checklist

Research Process

✔ Where did you find the best project ideas?
✔ Did you use the picture dictionary?
✔ Did you use other provided texts?

Presenting

Speaking

✔ Did you practice your presentation?
✔ Did you speak in a clear voice and use complete sentences?
✔ Did you relax and smile at your audience?

Representing

✔ Did you show pictures or photos to go with your report?
✔ Did you pass around your visuals for everyone to see?
✔ Did your visuals help your audience understand what you were telling about?

SCORING RUBRIC FOR THEME PROJECT			
4 Excellent	3 Good	2 Fair	1 Unsatisfactory
The child • presents the main idea with supporting details; • may make sophisticated observations; • presents accurate, well-produced visuals that enhance the topic.	The child • clearly fulfills all the steps of the project; • provides adequate details; • makes several relevant observations.	The child • attempts to present some of the required steps; • demonstrates some difficulty with research; • may make somewhat unclear observations.	The child • does not appear to grasp the task in its entirety; • has great difficulty with organizational skills; • presents unnecessary or inaccurate information.

Home-School Connection

Transportation Day provides an excellent opportunity for home and community involvement.

- Have family members, other children, and members of the community come to the presentations of the projects.
- Videotape the presentations for family members to borrow.

Big Question Wrap-Up

Review the Big Question for this unit with the children. Discuss what they learned about travel. Help them respond to the following questions: *What are the different ways people travel? How do you like to travel?* Remind children to take turns when speaking.

Administer the Test

Unit 3 TEST
TESTED SKILLS AND STRATEGIES
COMPREHENSION STRATEGIES AND SKILLS
• Strategies: Recognize text/story structure
• Skills: Make predictions, classify and categorize, character and plot
HIGH-FREQUENCY WORDS
• *see, go*
PHONEMIC AWARENESS
• Phoneme isolation (/t/)
• Phoneme blending (/t/, /i/)
PHONICS
• /t/*t*, /i/*i*
CONCEPT WORDS
• Shape words

Use Multiple Assessments for Instructional Planning

To create instructional profiles for your children, look for patterns in the results from any of the following assessments.

Running Records

Use the instructional reading level determined by the Running Record calculations for regrouping decisions.

Benchmark Assessments

Administer tests three times a year as an additional measure of both children's progress and the effectiveness of the instructional program.

Analyze the Data

Use information from a variety of informal and formal assessments, as well as your own judgment, to assist in your instructional planning. Children who consistently score at the lowest end of each range should be evaluated for Intervention. Use the **Diagnostic Assessment** for guidelines in the **Intervention Teacher's Editions**.

Diagnose		Prescribe
ASSESSMENTS	**IF...**	**THEN...**
UNIT TEST	0–15 Correct	Reteach skills using the **Intervention Teacher's Editions**.

For users of DIBELS

Use the results from the DIBELS Progress Monitoring tests to confirm instructional decisions.

DIBELS LINK

PROGRESS MONITORING

Use your DIBELS results to inform instruction.

IF...

Initial **S**ound **F**luency (**ISF**)	0–7
Phoneme **S**egmentation **F**luency (**PSF**)	Start midyear

THEN...

Evaluate for Intervention

For users of TPRI

Use the scores from the TPRI as a progress monitoring tool to confirm instructional decisions.

TPRI LINK

PROGRESS MONITORING

Use your TPRI scores to inform instruction.

IF...

Phonemic Awareness	Still Developing
Graphophonemic Knowledge	Still Developing
Listening Comprehension	Still Developing

THEN...

Evaluate for Intervention

Response to Intervention

To place children in Tier 2 or Tier 3 Intervention use the *Diagnostic Assessment.*

- Phonemic Awareness
- Phonics
- Vocabulary
- Comprehension
- Fluency

Additional Resources

Contents

Instructional Routines

Professional Development

- Read the routine prior to using *Treasures.* Use the Routine QuickNotes as a reminder of key routine steps throughout Unit 1, or as needed.
- View the online classroom video clip through **TeacherWorks Plus**. Watch master teachers use these routines.

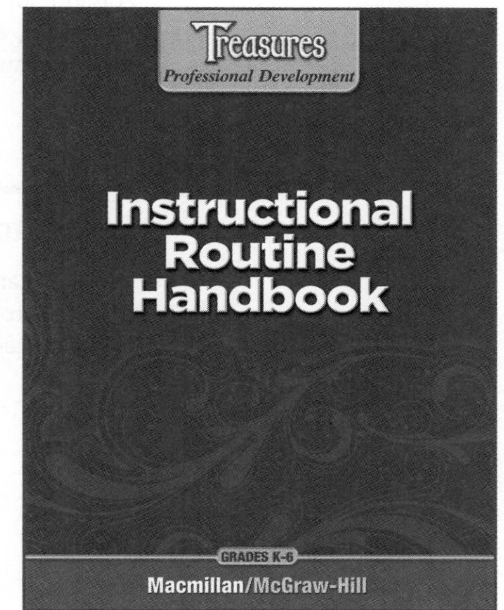

1. **Phonological Awareness/ Phonemic Awareness**
   Rhyme
   Oddity Tasks
   Sound Categorization
   Oral Blending
   Oral Segmentation
   Manipulation
2. **Phonics**
   Blending
   Introducing Sound-Spelling Cards
   Letter Recognition
   Building Words
   Building Fluency
   Reading Decodables
   Multisyllabic Words Routine
3. **Fluency**
   Strategies
4. **Vocabulary**
   Define/Example/Ask Routine
   Strategies
5. **High-Frequency Words**
   Read/Spell/Write Routine
   Reading Pre-decodables
6. **Spelling**
   Dictation
7. **Comprehension**
   Strategies
   Skills
   Reading Big Books
   Reading Student Book
8. **Writing**
   Conferences
   Revision Assignments
   Writing Process
   Using Rubrics
   Using Anchor Papers
   Writers' Express Sequence
9. **Research Process**
   Big Question Board
10. **Classroom Management**
    Workstation Flip Charts
    Contracts
    Centers
    Small Groups
11. **Listening/Speaking/Viewing**
12. **Assessment**

Instructional Routines

Additional Readings

WEEK 1

By the Authors and Illustrators

For additional information on authors, illustrators, and selection content, go to www.macmillanmh.com.

Bloom, Suzanne. *A Splendid Friend, Indeed.* Boyds Mills, 2005. Children will recognize certain things about themselves and others in this story of cooperative and annoying behaviors.

Related to the Theme

Use these and other classroom or library resources to provide additional read alouds to build academic language.

Burleigh, Robert. *Messenger, Messenger.* Atheneum, 2000. Calvin, a messenger, gets around the city on his bicycle, in all kinds of weather; told in rhyme and colorfully illustrated.

Crews, Donald. *School Bus.* Greenwillow, 1984. Readers can follow the path as the school bus makes its way to school and back.

Jacobs, Paul Dubois. *My Subway Ride.* Gibbs Smith, 2004. The different sights and sounds of the subway, as it travels through New York City.

Pearson, Debora. *Alphabeep.* Holiday House, 2003. This describes a vehicle or street sign for every letter of the alphabet from Ambulance to Zamboni.

Raffi, Sylvie Wickstrom. *The Wheels on the Bus.* HarperTrophy, 1984. An old bus collects an odd assortment of passengers and then travels around town making a series of sounds.

Willems, Mo. *Don't Let the Pigeon Drive the Bus!* Hyperion, 2004. An amusing story of a pigeon who will not take no for an answer when he asks to drive the bus.

WEEK 2	WEEK 3
Morris, Ann. *Work*. HarperCollins, 1998. In this photo essay, take a journey around the world to see what other people do for work.	**Shannon, David. *David Goes to School*. Blue Sky Press, 1999.** David wreaks havoc in his classroom, but the day ends peacefully as he washes all of the desks and receives a gold star from his teacher.

Ayers, Katherine. *A Long Way*. Candlewick Press, 2003. A young girl has a present for her grandmother, and as she delivers it, her imagination turns the package into a car, a plane, a boat, and a train.	**Barton, Byron. *My Car*. Greenwillow, 2001.** Simple sentences and bold, colorful illustrations tell all about the things Sam enjoys doing in his little car.
Baer, Edith. *This Is the Way We Go to School*. Scholastic, 1990. Children around the world are shown traveling to school using different modes of transportation.	**Blackstone, Sheila. *Bear on a Bike*. Barefoot Books, 2001.** A bear takes off to see the world on a variety of vehicles, including a bike, covered wagon, steamboat, and hot-air balloon.
Harshman, Marc. *Roads*. Marshall Cavendish, 2002. A child describes all of the sights on the way in a car to Grandma and Grandpa's house.	**Brown, Margaret Wise. *Two Little Trains*. HarperCollins, 2001.** Two trains are on parallel journeys heading west. One is new and streamlined; the other is small and old. Get a closer look and you'll see that one is the real thing and the other is a toy.
Johnson, D. B. *Henry Hikes to Fitchburg*. Houghton Mifflin, 2000. Henry chooses to walk leisurely to Fitchburg and enjoy nature, while his friend is busy earning the money to take a train.	**Hubbell, Patricia. *Trucks. Whizz! Zoom! Rumble!* Marshall Cavendish, 2003.** All kinds of trucks are presented in rhyme, and in full color, with a brief description of their functions.
McDonnell, Flora. *I Love Boats*. Candlewick, 1995. Boats for play, boats for work, boats for racing, and boats for fishing are all on display with lively acrylic and gouache illustrations.	**Milich, Zoran. *City Signs*. Kids Can Press, 2002.** Thirty photographs demonstrate that children who can't read can still understand many of the words they see around them in the form of stop signs, exit and enter signs, and the word *pizza* on a storefront.
Spence, Amy and Rob. *Clickety Clack*. Viking, 1999. A train has a collection of very noisy and unusual passengers, who are described in rhyming verse.	

Selection Honors, Prizes, and Awards

The Bus For Us

by ***Suzanne Bloom***

Pennsylvania Young Reader's Choice Award Nominee (2003)

Duck on a Bike

by ***David Shannon***

Author: *David Shannon*, winner of the Caldecott Honor Book Award (1999), *New York Times Book Review* Best Illustrated Children's Books (1998), Missouri Building Block Picture Book Award (1999), Georgia Children's Book Award, and North Dakota's Flicker Tale Children's Book Award (2000) for *No David!*; Montana Treasure State Award Winning Book Award (1999), Maryland Black-Eyed Susan Book Award, Children's Literature Association of Utah's Beehive Award, and the Wisconsin Educational Media Association's Golden Archer Award (2000) for *A Bad Case of Stripes*; Golden Kite Award for Picture Book Illustration (2000) for *The Rain Came Down; New York Times Book Review* Best Illustrated Children's Books (1994) for *How Georgie Radbourn Saved Baseball*; George G. Stone Center for Children's Books Recognition of Merit Award (2003)

Resources

Audio Bookshelf
44 Ocean View Drive
Middletown, RI 02842
800-234-1713
www.audiobookshelf.com

Discovery Communications
4540 Preslyn Drive
Raleigh, NC 27616
888-892-3484

Dorling Kindersley
375 Hudson Street
New York, NY 10014
Tel: 800-631-8571
Fax: 201-256-0000
http://us.dk.com

Great Plains National Instructional Television Library
GPN Educational Media
1407 Fleet Street
Baltimore, MD 21231
800-228-4630
http://shopgpn.com

Innovative Educators
P.O. Box 520
Montezuma, GA 31063
888-252-KIDS
Fax: 888-536-8553
www.innovative-educators.com

Library Video Co.
P.O. Box 580
Wynnewood, PA 19096
800-843-3620
www.libraryvideo.com

Listening Library
400 Hahn Road
Westminster, MD 21157
800-243-4504

Live Oak Media
P.O. Box 652
Pine Plains, NY 12567
800-788-1121
www.liveoakmedia.com

Macmillan/McGraw-Hill
220 East Danieldale Road
DeSoto, TX 75115-9960
Tel: 800-442-9685
Fax: 972-228-1982
www.macmillanmh.com

MCA Video
MCA Records/Universal Studios
100 Universal City Plaza
Universal City, CA 91608
818-777-1000

Microsoft Corp.
One Microsoft Way
Redmond, WA 98052
800-426-9000
www.microsoft.com

National Geographic Society
1145 17th Street N.W.
Washington, DC 20036
800-647-5463
www.nationalgeographic.com

Recorded Books
270 Skipjack Road
Prince Frederick, MD 20678
800-636-3399
www.recordedbooks.com

Sunburst Communications
Sunburst Technology
1550 Executive Drive
Elgin, IL 60123
888-492-8817
www.sunburst.com

SVE & Churchill Media
6465 North Avondale Avenue
Chicago, IL 60631
800-253-2788

Tom Snyder Productions
100 Talcott Avenue
Watertown, MA 02472
800-342-0236
www.tomsnyder.com

Weston Woods
143 Main Street
Norwalk, CT 06851
800-243-5020
www.teacher.scholastic.com/products/westonwoods/

Go to www.macmillanmh.com.
Use the zip code finder to locate other resources in your area.

Web Sites

The Academy of Natural Sciences
http://www.ansp.org/

Acadia National Park
http://www.nps.gov/acad

Agriculture in the Classroom
http://www.agclassroom.org/

Arches National Park
http://www.nps.gov/arch

Asian American History Resources Online - CET
http://www.cetel.org/res.html

Association of Zoos and Aquariums
http://www.aza.org/

Bronx Zoo
http://www.bronxzoo.com/

Cincinnati Zoo
http://www.cincinnatizoo.org/

Colonial Williamsburg
http://www.history.org/

Denali National Park and Preserve
http://www.nps.gov/dena

Ellis Island
http://www.ellisisland.org/

Glacier National Park
http://www.nps.gov/glac

Grand Canyon National Park
http://www.nps.gov/grca

Grand Teton National Park
http://www.nps.gov/grte

High Museum of Art, Atlanta
http://www.high.org/

International Civil Rights Center and Museum
http://www.sitinmovement.org/

Japanese American National Museum
http://www.janm.org/

K12Station – Library of K–12 Education Links
http://www.k12station.com/k12link_library.html

Kids.gov
http://www.kids.gov/

KidsHealth in the Classroom
http://classroom.kidshealth.org/

Meteorology
http://www.wxdude.com/

The Metropolitan Museum of Art, New York
http://www.metmuseum.org/

Minneapolis Institute of Arts
http://www.artsmia.org/

Minnesota Zoo
http://www.mnzoo.com/

MoMA | The Museum of Modern Art
http://www.moma.org/

Monterey Bay Aquarium
www.montereybayaquarium.org

Mount Rushmore National Memorial
http://www.nps.gov/moru

Museum of Fine Arts, Boston
http://www.mfa.org/

Museum of Science, Boston
http://www.mos.org/

Museum of Science and Industry, Chicago
http://www.msichicago.org/

NASA
http://www.nasa.gov/

NASA Kids' Club
http://www.nasa.gov/audience/forkids/kidsclub/flash/index.html

National Air and Space Museum
http://www.nasm.si.edu/

National Civil Rights Museum
http://www.civilrightsmuseum.org/home.htm

National Museum of African American History and Culture
http://nmaahc.si.edu/

National Museum of American History
http://americanhistory.si.edu/

National Museum of the American Indian
http://www.nmai.si.edu/

National Museum of Women in the Arts
http://www.nmwa.org/

National Music Museum
http://www.usd.edu/smm/

National Park Service
http://www.nps.gov/

National Weather Service Education Resources
http://www.nws.noaa.gov/om/edures.shtml

National Women's History Museum
http://www.nwhm.org/

National Zoo
http://nationalzoo.si.edu/

Native American Facts for Kids: Resources on American Indians for Children and Teachers
http://www.native-languages.org/kids.htm

New England Aquarium
http://www.neaq.org/index.php

New York Aquarium
http://www.nyaquarium.com/

Newseum
http://www.newseum.org/

Omaha's Henry Doorly Zoo
http://www.omahazoo.com/

Philadelphia Museum of Art
http://www.philamuseum.org/

Philadelphia Zoo
http://www2.philadelphiazoo.org/

Plimoth Plantation
http://www.plimoth.org/

Redwood National and State Parks
http://www.nps.gov/redw

Rocky Mountain National Park
http://www.nps.gov/romo

Saint Louis Art Museum
http://www.slam.org/

San Diego Zoo
http://www.sandiegozoo.com/

San Francisco Museum of Modern Art
http://www.sfmoma.org/

Shedd Aquarium
http://www.sheddaquarium.org/

Smithsonian Education
http://www.smithsonianeducation.org/

Smithsonian: Science and Technology
http://www.si.edu/Encyclopedia_SI/science_and_technology/

Space Center Houston
http://www.spacecenter.org/

Tennessee Aquarium
http://www.tennis.org/

United States Holocaust Memorial Museum
http://www.ushmm.org/

University of California Museum of Paleontology
http://www.ucmp.berkeley.edu/

The White House Historical Association
http://www.whitehousehistory.org/

Yellowstone National Park
http://www.nps.gov/yell

Yosemite National Park
http://www.nps.gov/yose

Zion National Park
http://www.nps.gov/zion

High-Frequency Words

High-Frequency Words	UNIT/WEEK
I	Start Smart Week 1
can	Start Smart Week 2
we	Unit 1 Week 1
the	Unit 1 Week 2
like	Unit 2 Week 1
a	Unit 2 Week 2
see	Unit 3 Week 1
go	Unit 3 Week 2
to	Unit 4 Week 1
have	Unit 4 Week 2
is	Unit 5 Week 1
play	Unit 5 Week 2
are	Unit 6 Week 1
for	Unit 6 Week 2
you	Unit 6 Week 2
this	Unit 7 Week 1
do	Unit 7 Week 1
and	Unit 7 Week 2
what	Unit 7 Week 2
little	Unit 8 Week 1
said	Unit 8 Week 1
here	Unit 8 Week 2
was	Unit 8 Week 2
she	Unit 9 Week 1
he	Unit 9 Week 1
has	Unit 9 Week 2
look	Unit 9 Week 2
with	Unit 10 Week 1
my	Unit 10 Week 1
me	Unit 10 Week 2
where	Unit 10 Week 2

Oral Vocabulary

Week		Theme Words	Oral Vocabulary Card Words	
1	The Bus For Us	vehicle transportation	glide continue rapidly	transportation vehicle
2	On the Go	travel journey	prepare relax familiar	travel journey
3	Duck on a Bike	wheel adventure	haul attach massive	wheel adventure

Language Transfers:

The Interaction Between English and Students' Primary Languages

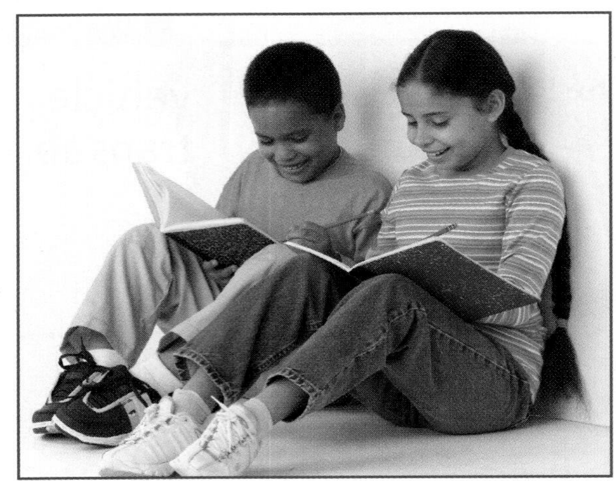

Dr. Jana Echevarria
California State University, Long Beach

Dr. Donald Bear
University of Nevada, Reno

It is important for teachers to understand why English Language Learners (ELLs) use alternative pronunciations for some English words. Many English sounds do not exist or transfer to other languages, so English Language Learners may lack the auditory acuity to "hear" these English sounds and have difficulty pronouncing them. These students are not accustomed to positioning their mouth in a way the sound requires. The charts that appear on the following pages show that there is variation among languages, with some languages having more sounds in common and thus greater transfer to English than others.

For example, an English speaker may be able to pronounce the /r/ in the Spanish word *pero* ("but"), but not the /rr/ trill in *perro* ("dog"). The English speaker may also lack the auditory acuity to detect and the ability to replicate the tonal sounds of some Chinese words. Similarly, a Vietnamese speaker may have difficulty pronouncing /th/ in words such as *thin* or *thanks*.

Further, English Language Learners make grammatical errors due to interference from their native languages. In Spanish, the adjective follows the noun, so often English Language Learners say "the girl pretty" instead of "the pretty girl." While English changes the verb form with a change of subject (*I walk. She walks.*), some Asian languages keep the verb form constant across subjects. Adding /s/ to the third person may be difficult for some English Language Learners. Students may know the grammatical rule, but applying it consistently may be difficult, especially in spoken English.

When working with English Language Learners, you should also be aware of sociocultural factors that affect pronunciation. Students may retain an accent because it marks their social identity. Speakers of other languages may feel at a social distance from members of the dominant English-speaking culture.

English Language Learners improve their pronunciation in a nonthreatening atmosphere in which participation is encouraged. Opportunities to interact with native English speakers provide easy access to language models and give English Language Learners practice using English. However, students should not be forced to participate. Pressure to perform—or to perform in a certain way—can inhibit participation. In any classroom, teacher sensitivity to pronunciation differences contributes to a more productive learning environment.

Phonics, word recognition, and spelling are influenced by what students know about the sounds, word structure, and spelling in their primary languages. For example, beginning readers who speak Spanish and are familiar with its spelling will often spell short *o* with an *a*, a letter that in Spanish makes the short *o* sound. Similarly, English Language Learners who are unaccustomed to English consonant digraphs and blends (e.g., /ch/ and *s*-blends) spell /ch/ as *sh* because /sh/ is the sound they know that is closest to /ch/. Students learn about the way pronunciation influences their reading and spelling, beginning with large contrasts among sounds, then they study the finer discriminations. As vocabulary advances, the meaning of words leads students to the sound contrasts. For example, *shoe* and *chew* may sound alike initially, but meaning indicates otherwise. Students' reading and discussions of what they read advances their word knowledge as well as their knowledge in all language and literacy systems, including phonics, pronunciation, grammar, and vocabulary.

Phonics Transfers

Phonics Transfers:

Sound Transfers

This chart indicates areas where a positive transfer of sounds and symbols occurs for English Language Learners from their native languages into English. This symbol (✔) identifies a positive transfer. "Approximate" indicates that the sound is similar.

Sound Transfers	Spanish	Cantonese	Vietnamese	Hmong	Korean	Khmer
Consonants						
/b/ as in bat	✔	approximate	approximate	approximate	approximate	✔
/k/ as in cake, kitten, peck	✔	✔	✔	✔	✔	✔
/d/ as in dog	✔	approximate	approximate	✔	approximate	✔
/f/ as in farm	✔	✔	✔	✔		
/g/ as in girl	✔	approximate	✔	approximate	approximate	
/h/ as in ham	✔	✔	✔	✔	✔	approximate
/j/ as in jet, page, ledge		approximate	approximate		approximate	
/l/ as in lion	✔	✔	✔	✔	✔	
/m/ as in mat	✔	✔	✔	✔	✔	✔
/n/ as in night	✔	✔	✔	✔	✔	✔
/p/ as in pen	✔	✔	✔	approximate	✔	✔
/kw/ as in queen	✔	approximate	✔		✔	✔
/r/ as in rope	approximate					✔
/s/ as in sink, city	✔	✔	✔	✔	✔	approximate
/t/ as in ton	✔	✔	approximate	approximate	✔	✔
/v/ as in vine	✔		✔	✔		
/w/ as in wind	✔	✔			✔	✔
/ks/ as in six	✔				✔	✔
/y/ as in yak	✔	✔		✔	✔	✔
/z/ as in zebra			✔			
Digraphs						
/ch/ as in cheek, patch	✔	approximate		✔	✔	✔
/sh/ as in shadow			✔	✔	✔	
/hw/ as in whistle					✔	✔
/th/ as in path	approximate		approximate			
/TH/ as in that	approximate					
/ng/ as in sting	✔	✔	✔	✔	✔	approximate

Sound Transfers	Spanish	Cantonese	Vietnamese	Hmong	Korean	Khmer
Short Vowels						
/a/ as in cat	approximate		approximate	✔	✔	
/e/ as in net	✔	approximate	approximate		✔	
/i/ as in kid	approximate	approximate			✔	
/o/ as in spot	approximate	approximate	approximate	approximate	approximate	✔
/u/ as in cup	approximate	approximate	✔		✔	✔
Long Vowels						
/ā/ as in lake, nail, bay	✔	approximate	approximate	approximate	✔	✔
/ē/ as in bee, meat, cranky	✔	approximate	✔	✔	✔	✔
/ī/ as in kite, tie, light, dry	✔	approximate	✔	✔	✔	✔
/ō/ as in home, road, row	✔	approximate	approximate		✔	
/ū/ as in dune, fruit, blue	✔	approximate	✔	✔	✔	✔
/yü/ as in mule, cue	✔	approximate			✔	
***r*-Controlled Vowels**						
/är/ as in far	approximate	approximate				
/ôr/ as in corn	approximate	approximate				
/ûr/ as in stern, bird, suburb	approximate	approximate				
/âr/ as in air, bear						
/îr/ as in deer, ear						
Variant Vowels						
/oi/ as in boil, toy	✔	approximate	approximate		✔	✔
/ou/ as in loud, down	✔	approximate	✔	approximate	✔	✔
/ô/ as in law	approximate	✔	✔	approximate	approximate	✔
/ô/ as in laundry	approximate	approximate	✔	approximate	approximate	✔
/ôl/ as in salt, call	approximate	approximate			approximate	✔
/ü/ as in moon, drew	✔	approximate	approximate	✔	✔	✔
/ů/ as in look		approximate	approximate		approximate	✔
/ə/ as in askew			approximate		✔	

Phonics Transfers:
Sound-Symbol Match

Sound-Symbol Match	Spanish	Cantonese	Vietnamese	Hmong	Korean	Khmer
Consonants						
/b/ as in bat	✔		✔			
/k/ as in cake	✔		✔			
/k/ as in kitten	✔		✔	✔		
/k/ as in peck						
/d/ as in dog	✔		✔	✔		
/f/ as in farm	✔			✔		
/g/ as in girl	✔		✔			
/h/ as in ham			✔	✔		
/j/ as in jet, page, ledge						
/l/ as in lion	✔		✔	✔		
/m/ as in mat	✔		✔	✔		
/n/ as in night	✔		✔	✔		
/p/ as in pen	✔		✔	✔		
/kw/ as in queen			✔			
/r/ as in rope	approximate					
/s/ as in sink, city	✔		✔			
/t/ as in ton	✔		✔	✔		
/v/ as in vine	✔		✔	✔		
/w/ as in wind	✔					
/ks/ as in six	✔					
/y/ as in yak	✔			✔		
/z/ as in zebra						
Digraphs						
/ch/ as in cheek, patch	✔					
/sh/ as in shadow						
/hw/ as in whistle						
/th/ as in path			✔			
/TH/ as in that						
/ng/ as in sting	✔		✔			
Short Vowels						
/a/ as in cat			✔	✔		
/e/ as in net	✔		✔			
/i/ as in kid						
/o/ as in spot			✔	✔		
/u/ as in cup						

Sound-Symbol Match	Spanish	Cantonese	Vietnamese	Hmong	Korean	Khmer
Long Vowels						
/ā/ as in lake						
/ā/ as in nail						
/ā/ as in bay						
/ē/ as in bee						
/ē/ as in meat						
/ē/ as in cranky						
/ī/ as in kite, tie, light, dry						
/ō/ as in home, road, row						
/ū/ as in dune			✔	✔		
/ū/ as in fruit, blue						
/yü/ as in mule, cue						
***r*-Controlled Vowels**						
/är/ as in far	✔					
/ôr/ as in corn	✔					
/ûr/ as in stern	✔					
/ûr/ as in bird, suburb						
/âr/ as in air, bear						
/îr/ as in deer, ear						
Variant Vowels						
/oi/ as in boil	✔		✔			
/oi/ as in toy	✔					
/ou/ as in loud						
/ou/ as in down						
/ô/ as in law						
/ô/ as in laundry						
/ôl/ as in salt	✔					
/ôl/ as in call						
/ü/ as in moon, drew						
/ů/ as in look						
/ə/ as in askew						

How to Use the Phonics Transfer Charts

To read and speak fluently in English, English Language Learners need to master a wide range of phonemic awareness, phonics, and word study skills. The Phonics Transfer Charts are designed to help you anticipate and understand possible student errors in pronouncing or perceiving English sounds.

1. **Highlight Transferrable Skills** If the phonics skill transfers from the student's primary language to English, state that during the lesson. In most lessons an English Language Learner feature will indicate which sounds do and do not transfer in specific languages.

2. **Preteach Non-Transferrable Skills** Prior to teaching a phonics lesson, check the chart to determine if the sound and/or spelling transfers from the student's primary language into English. If it does not, preteach the sound and spelling during Small Group time. Focus on articulation, using the backs of the small **Sound-Spelling Cards**, and the minimal contrast activities provided.

3. **Provide Additional Practice and Time** If the skill does NOT transfer from the student's primary language into English, the student will require more time and practice mastering the sound and spellings. Continue to review the phonics skill during Small Group time in upcoming weeks until the student has mastered it. Use the additional resources, such as the extra decodable stories in the **Teacher's Resource Book**, to provide oral and silent reading practice.

Teaching Supports for Students Transitioning from Spanish to English

The **Sound-Spelling Cards** have been created to assist you in working with English Language Learners. For example:

1. The dotted border on many of the cards indicates that the sound transfers from Spanish to English. On these cards, the same image is used in both English and Spanish (e.g., *camel/camello*). Therefore, students learning the sound in Spanish can easily transfer that knowledge to English.

2. Students whose primary language is not English will need additional articulation support to pronounce and perceive non-transferrable English sounds. Use the articulation photos on the backs of the Sound-Spelling Cards and the student-friendly descriptions of how to form these sounds during phonics lessons.

Sound-Spelling Cards

Transfer Skill Support

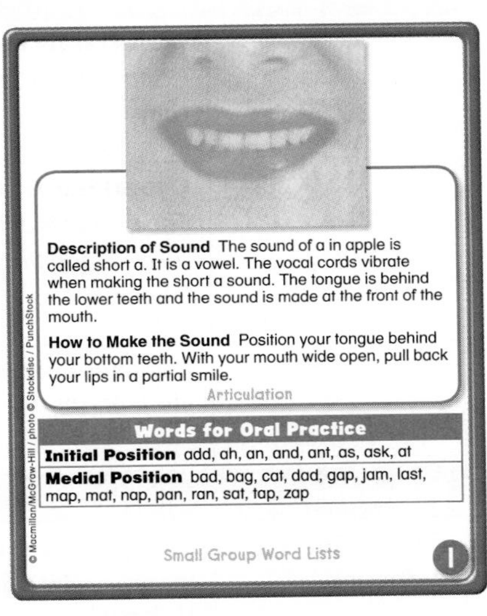

Description of Sound The sound of a in apple is called short a. It is a vowel. The vocal cords vibrate when making the short a sound. The tongue is behind the lower teeth and the sound is made at the front of the mouth.
How to Make the Sound Position your tongue behind your bottom teeth. With your mouth wide open, pull back your lips in a partial smile.
Articulation
Words for Oral Practice
Initial Position add, ah, an, and, ant, as, ask, at
Medial Position bad, bag, cat, dad, gap, jam, last, map, mat, nap, pan, ran, sat, tap, zap
Small Group Word Lists

Articulation Support

Grammar Transfers

Grammar Transfers:

Grammatical Form

This chart can be used to address common mistakes that some English Language Learners make when they transfer grammatical forms from their native languages into English.

Grammatical Form	Transfer Mistakes in English	Native Language	Cause of Difficulty
Nouns			
Plural Marker -*s*	**Forgets plural marker -*s*** *I have 3 sister.*	Cantonese, Haitian Creole, Hmong, Korean, Vietnamese, Khmer	Native language does not use a plural marker.
Countable and Uncountable Nouns	**Confuses countable and uncountable nouns** *the homeworks* or *the informations*	Haitian Creole, Spanish	Countable and uncountable nouns are different in English and native language.
Possessives	**Uses prepositions to describe possessives** *the book of my brother* as opposed to *my brother's book*	Haitian Creole, Hmong, Spanish, Vietnamese	Possession is often described using a prepositional phrase.
	Avoids using *'s* *dog my father* as opposed to *my father's dog*	Haitian Creole, Vietnamese, Khmer	A noun follows the object in the native language.
Articles			
	Consistently omits articles *He has book. They want dog not cat.*	Cantonese, Haitian Creole, Hmong, Korean, Vietnamese, Khmer	There is no article in the native language or no difference between *the* and *a*.
	Overuses articles *The English is difficult. The soccer is popular in the Europe.*	Haitian Creole, Hmong, Spanish	Some languages use articles that are omitted in English.
a/an	**Mistakes *one* for *a/an*** *She is one nurse.*	Haitian Creole, Hmong, Vietnamese	The native language either does not use articles or uses articles differently.
Pronouns			
Gender-Specific Pronouns	**Uses pronouns with the inappropriate gender** *He is my sister.*	Cantonese, Haitian Creole, Hmong, Korean, Spanish, Khmer	The third person pronoun in the native language is gender free, or the personal pronoun is omitted.
	Uses inappropriate gender, particularly with neutral nouns *The day is sunny. She is beautiful.*	Spanish	Nouns have feminine or masculine gender in the native language, and the gender may be carried over into English.

Grammatical Form	Transfer Mistakes in English	Native Language	Cause of Difficulty
Pronouns			
Object Pronouns	**Confuses subject and object pronouns** *Her talks to me.*	Cantonese, Hmong, Khmer	The same pronoun form is used for subject and object in the native language.
	Omits object pronouns *That girl is very rude, so nobody likes.*	Korean, Vietnamese	The native language does not use direct objects.
Pronoun and Number Agreement	**Uses the wrong number for pronouns** *I saw many red birds. It was pretty.*	Cantonese, Korean	The native language does not require number agreement.
Subject Pronouns	**Omits subject pronouns** *Mom isn't home. Is at work.*	Korean, Spanish	Subject pronouns may be dropped because in the native language the verb ending gives information about the number and/or gender.
Pronouns in Clauses	**Omits pronouns in clauses** *If don't do homework, they will not learn.*	Cantonese, Vietnamese	The native language does not need a subject in the subordinate clause.
Pronouns and Nouns	**Overuses pronouns with nouns** *This school, it very good.*	Hmong, Vietnamese	This is popular in speech in some languages. The speaker mentions a topic, then makes a comment about it.
	Avoids pronouns and repeats nouns *Carla visits her sister every Sunday, and Carla makes a meal.*	Korean, Vietnamese	In the native language, the speaker repeats nouns and does not use pronouns.
Pronoun *one*	**Omits the pronoun *one*** *I saw two dogs, and I like the small.*	Spanish	Adjectives can stand alone in the native language, but English requires a noun or *one.*
Possessive Forms	**Confuses possessive forms** *The book is my.*	Cantonese, Hmong, Vietnamese	Cantonese and Hmong speakers tend to omit the final *n* sound, which may create confusion between *my* and *mine.*

Grammar Transfers:
Grammatical Form

Grammatical Form	Transfer Mistakes in English	Native Language	Cause of Difficulty
Verbs			
Present Tense	**Omits -*s* in present tense, third person agreement** *He like pizza.*	Cantonese, Haitian Creole, Hmong, Korean, Vietnamese, Khmer	Subject-verb agreement is not used in the native language.
Irregular Verbs	**Has problems with irregular subject-verb agreement** *Tom and Sue has a new car.*	Cantonese, Hmong, Korean, Khmer	Verbs' forms do not change to show the number of the subject in the native language.
Inflectional Endings	**Omits tense markers** *I study English yesterday.*	Cantonese, Haitian Creole, Hmong, Korean, Vietnamese, Khmer	The native language does not use inflectional endings to change verb tense.
Present and Future Tenses	**Incorrectly uses the present tense for the future tense** *I go next week.*	Cantonese, Korean	The native language may use the present tense to imply the future tense.
Negative Statements	**Omits helping verbs in negative statements** *Sue no coming to school.*	Cantonese, Korean, Spanish	The native language does not use helping verbs in negative statements.
Present-Perfect Tense	**Avoids the present-perfect tense** *Marcos live here for three months.*	Haitian Creole, Vietnamese	The native language does not use the present-perfect verb form.
Past-Continuous Tense	**Uses the past-continuous tense for recurring action in the past** *When I was young, I was talking a lot.*	Korean, Spanish	In the native language, the past-continuous tense is used but in English the expression *used to* or the simple past tense is used.
Main Verb	**Omits the main verb** *Talk in class not good.*	Cantonese	Cantonese does not require an infinitive marker when using a verb as a noun. Speakers may confuse the infinitive for the main verb.
Main Verbs in Clauses	**Uses two or more main verbs in one clause without any connectors** *I took a book went studied at the library.*	Hmong	In Hmong, verbs can be used consecutively without conjunctions or punctuation.
Linking Verbs	**Omits the linking verb** *He hungry.*	Cantonese, Haitian Creole, Hmong, Vietnamese, Khmer	In some languages, *be* is implied in the adjective form. In other languages, the concept is expressed with a verb.
Helping Verb in Passive Voice	**Omits the helping verb in the passive voice** *The homework done.*	Cantonese, Vietnamese	In Cantonese and Vietnamese, the passive voice does not require a helping verb.

Grammatical Form	Transfer Mistakes in English	Native Language	Cause of Difficulty
Verbs			
Passive Voice	**Avoids the passive voice** *They speak English here.* *One speaks English here.* *English is spoken here.*	Haitian Creole	The passive voice does not exist in the native language.
Transitive Verbs	**Confuses transitive and intransitive verbs** *The child broke.* *The child broke the plate.*	Cantonese, Korean, Spanish	Verbs that require a direct object differ between English and the native language.
Phrasal Verbs	**Confuses related phrasal verbs** *I ate at the apple.* *I ate up the apple.*	Korean, Spanish	Phrasal verbs are not used in the native language, and there is often confusion over their meaning.
Have* and *be	**Uses *have* instead of *be*** *I have thirst.* *He has right.*	Spanish	Spanish and English have different uses for *have* and *be.*
Adjectives			
Word Order	**Places adjectives after nouns** *I saw a car red.*	Haitian Creole, Hmong, Spanish, Vietnamese, Khmer	Nouns often precede adjectives in the native language.
	Consistently places adjectives after nouns *This is a lesson new.*	Cantonese, Korean	Adjectives always follow nouns in the native language.
***-er* and *-est* Endings**	**Avoids *-er* and *-est* endings** *I am more old than you.*	Hmong, Korean, Spanish, Khmer	The native language shows comparative and superlative forms with separate words.
***-ing* and *-ed* Endings**	**Confuses *-ing* and *-ed* forms** *Math is bored.*	Cantonese, Korean, Spanish, Khmer	Adjectives in the native language do not have active and passive meanings.
Adverbs			
Adjectives and Adverbs	**Uses an adjective where an adverb is needed** *Talk quiet.*	Haitian Creole, Hmong, Khmer	Adjectives and adverb forms are interchangeable in the native language.
Word Order	**Places adverbs before verbs** *He quickly ran.* *He ran quickly.*	Cantonese, Korean	Adverbs usually come before verbs in the native language, and this tendency is carried over into English.
Prepositions			
	Omits prepositions *I like come school.*	Cantonese	Cantonese does not use prepositions the way that English does.

How to Use the Grammar Transfer Charts

The grammar of many languages differs widely from English. For example, a student's primary language may use a different word order than English, may not use parts of speech in the same way, or may use different verb tenses. The Grammar Transfer Charts are designed to help you anticipate and understand possible student errors in speaking and writing standard English. With all grammar exercises, the emphasis is on oral communication, both as a speaker and listener.

1. **Highlight Transferrable Skills** If the grammar skill transfers from the student's primary language to English, state that during the lesson. In many lessons an English Language Learner feature will indicate which skills do and do not transfer.

2. **Preteach Non-Transferrable Skills** Prior to teaching a grammar lesson, check the chart to determine if the skill transfers from the student's primary language into English. If it does not, preteach the skill during Small Group time. Provide sentence frames and ample structured opportunities to use the skill in spoken English. Students need to talk, talk, and talk some more to master these skills.

3. **Provide Additional Practice and Time** If the skill does NOT transfer from the student's primary language into English, the student will require more time and practice mastering it. Continue to review the skill during Small Group time. Use the additional resources, such as the grammar lessons in the **Intervention Kit** (K–3) or review lessons, in upcoming weeks.

4. **Use Contrastive Analysis** Tell students when a skill does not transfer and include contrastive analysis work to make the student aware of how to correct their speaking and writing for standard English. For example, when a student uses an incorrect grammatical form, write the student sentence on a **WorkBoard**. Then write the correct English form underneath. Explain the difference between the student's primary language and English. Have the student correct several other sentences using this skill, such as sentences in their Writer's Notebooks.

5. **Increase Writing and Speaking Opportunities** Increase the amount of structured writing and speaking opportunities for students needing work on specific grammatical forms. Sentence starters and paragraph frames, such as those found in the lessons, are ideal for both written and oral exercises.

6. **Focus on Meaning** Always focus on the meanings of sentences in all exercises. As they improve and fine-tune their English speaking and writing skills, work with students on basic comprehension of spoken and written English.

To help students move to the next level of language acquisition and master English grammatical forms, recast their responses during classroom discussions or provide additional language for them to use as they respond further. Provide leveled-language sentence frames orally or in writing for students to use as they respond to questions and prompts. Below are samples.

English Language Learner Response Chart

Beginning (will respond by pointing or saying one word answers)	**Sample Frames** (simple, short sentences) *I see a* ______. *This is a* ______. *I like the* ______.
Early Intermediate (will respond with phrases or simple sentences)	**Sample Frames** (simple sentences with adjectives and adverbs added, and compound subjects or predicates) *I see a* ______ ______. *The* ______ *animal is* ______. *There are* ______ *and* ______.
Intermediate (will respond with simple sentences and limited academic language)	**Sample Frames** (harder sentences with simple phrases in consistent patterns; some academic language included) *The animal's prey is* ______ *because* ______. *The main idea is* ______ *because* ______. *He roamed the park so that* ______.
Early Advanced (will begin to use more sophisticated sentences and some academic language)	**Sample Frames** (complex sentences with increased academic language, beginning phrases and clauses, and multiple-meaning words) *When the violent storm hit,* ______. *As a result of the revolution, the army* ______. *Since most endangered animals are* ______, *they* ______.
Advanced (will have mastered some more complex sentence structures and is increasing the amount of academic language used)	Use the questions and prompts provided in the lessons for the whole group. Provide additional support learning and using academic language. These words are boldfaced throughout the lessons and sentence starters are often provided.

Cognates

Cognates are words in two languages that look alike and have the same or similar meaning (e.g., *school/escuela, telephone/teléfono*) and can be helpful resources for English Language Learners. This list identifies some Spanish cognates for the academic language used during the lessons.

Students must also be aware of false cognates—words that look similar in two languages, but have different meanings, such as *soap* in English and *sopa* (meaning *soup*) in Spanish.

accent	*acento*	**context**	*contexto*
action	*acción*	**contrast**	*contrastar*
action verb	*verbo de acción*	**definition**	*definición*
adjective	*adjetivo*	**demonstrative**	*demostrativo*
adverb	*adverbio*	**denotation**	*denotación*
alphabetical order	*orden alfabético*	**description**	*descripción*
analogy	*analogía*	**dialogue**	*diálogo*
analyze	*analizar*	**dictionary**	*diccionario*
antecedent	*antecedente*	**direct**	*directo*
antonym	*antónimo*	**effect**	*efecto*
apostrophe	*apóstrofe*	**evaluate**	*evaluar*
article	*artículo*	**event**	*evento*
author	*autor*	**example**	*ejemplo*
cause	*causa*	**exclamation**	*exclamación*
classify	*clasificar*	**family**	*familia*
combine	*combinar*	**fantasy**	*fantasía*
compare	*comparar*	**figurative**	*figurativo*
complex	*complejo*	**fragment**	*fragmento*
comprehension	*comprensión*	**future**	*futuro*
conclusion	*conclusión*	**generalization**	*generalización*
confirm	*confirmar*	**generalize**	*generalizar*
conjunction	*conjunción*	**glossary**	*glosario*
connotation	*connotación*	**Greek**	*Griego*
consonant	*consonante*	**homophone**	*homófono*

idea	*idea*	**prefix**	*prefijo*
identify	*identificar*	**preposition**	*preposición*
illustration	*ilustración*	**prepositional**	*preposicional*
indirect	*indirecto*	**present**	*presente*
introduction	*introducción*	**problem**	*problema*
irregular	*irregular*	**pronunciation**	*pronunciación*
language	*lenguaje*	**punctuation**	*puntuación*
Latin	*Latín*	**reality**	*realidad*
myth	*mito*	**relationship**	*relación*
negative	*negativo*	**sequence**	*secuencia*
object	*objeto*	**singular**	*singular*
opinion	*opinión*	**solution**	*solución*
order	*orden*	**structure**	*estructura*
origin	*orígen*	**subject**	*sujeto*
paragraph	*párrafo*	**suffix**	*sufijo*
part	*parte*	**syllable**	*sílaba*
perspective	*perspectiva*	**synonym**	*sinónimo*
persuasion	*persuación*	**technique**	*técnica*
phrase	*frase*	**text**	*texto*
plural	*plural*	**theme**	*tema*
possessive adjective	*adjetivo posesivo*	**verb**	*verbo*
predicate	*predicado*	**visualize**	*visualizar*
prediction	*predicción*	**vowel**	*vocal*

ELL ENGLISH LANGUAGE LEARNERS

The **English Language Learners** in your classroom have a variety of backgrounds. An increasing proportion of English Language Learners are born in the United States. Some of these students are just starting school in the primary grades; others are long-term English Language Learners, with underdeveloped academic skills. Some students come from their native countries with a strong educational foundation. The academic skills of these newly arrived students are well developed and parallel the skills of their native English-speaking peers. Other English Learners immigrate to the United States with little academic experience.

These English Learners are not "blank slates." Their oral language proficiency and literacy in their first languages can be used to facilitate literacy development in English. Systematic, explicit, and appropriately scaffolded instruction and sufficient time help English Learners attain English proficiency and meet high standards in core academic subjects.

Beginning

This level of language proficiency is often referred to as the "silent" stage, in which students' receptive skills are engaged. It is important that teachers and peers respect a language learner's initial silence or allow the student to respond in his or her native language. It is often difficult for teachers to identify the level of cognitive development at this stage, due to the limited proficiency in the second language. It is important to realize that these beginning students have a wide range of abilities in their first language. They are able to transfer knowledge and skills from their first language as they develop English and learn grade-level content. Beginning students include those with limited formal schooling: young students just starting school, as well as older students. Other beginning students have had schooling in their native language and are academically parallel to nativeEnglish-speaking peers.

The Beginning Student...

- recognizes English phonemes that correspond to phonemes produced in primary language;
- is able to apply transferable grammar concepts and skills from the primary language;
- initially demonstrates more receptive than productive English skills;
- produces English vocabulary to communicate basic needs in social and academic settings;
- responds by pointing to, nodding, gesturing, acting out, and manipulating objects/pictures;
- speaks in one-or two-word responses as language develops;
- draws pictures and writes letters and sounds being learned.

Early Intermediate

At this level, students are considered more advanced beginning English Learners. They are developing early production skills, but their receptive skills are much more advanced than their speaking ability. At this stage it is critical that the students continue to listen to model speakers.

The Early Intermediate Student...

- recognizes English phonemes that correspond to phonemes produced in primary language;
- is able to apply transferable grammar concepts and skills from the primary language;
- understands more spoken English than the beginning student;
- speaks in one- or two-word utterances;
- may respond with phrases or sentences;
- produces English vocabulary words and phrases to communicate basic needs in social and academic settings;
- begins to ask questions, role-play, and retell;
- begins to use routine expressions;
- demonstrates an internalization of English grammar and usage by recognizing and correcting some errors when speaking and reading aloud;
- increases correct usage of written and oral language conventions.

Intermediate

Students at this level begin to tailor their English language skills to meet communication and learning demands with increasing accuracy. They possess vocabulary and knowledge of grammatical structures that allow them to more fully participate in classroom activities and discussions. They are generally more comfortable producing both spoken and written language.

The Intermediate Student...

- pronounces most English phonemes correctly while reading aloud;
- can identify more details of information that has been presented orally or in writing;
- uses more complex vocabulary and sentences to communicate needs and express ideas;
- uses specific vocabulary learned, including academic language;
- participates more fully in discussions with peers and adults;
- reads and comprehends a wider range of reading materials;
- writes brief narratives and expository texts;
- demonstrates an internalization of English grammar and usage by recognizing and correcting errors when speaking and reading aloud.

Early Advanced

Students at this language proficiency level possess vocabulary and grammar structures that approach those of an English-proficient speaker. These students demonstrate consistent general comprehension of grade-level content that is presented.

The Early Advanced Student...

- applies knowledge of common English morphemes in oral and silent reading;
- understands increasingly more nonliteral social and academic language;
- responds using extensive vocabulary;
- participates in and initiates more extended social conversations with peers and adults;
- communicates orally and in writing with fewer grammatical errors;
- reads with good comprehension a wide range of narrative and expository texts;
- writes using more standard forms of English on various content-area topics;
- becomes more creative and analytical when writing.

Advanced

The student at this language proficiency level communicates effectively with peers and adults in both social and academic situations. Students can understand grade-level text but still need some English language development support, such as preteaching concepts and skills. While the English language proficiency of these students is advanced, some linguistic support for accessing content is still necessary.

The Advanced Student...

- understands increasingly more nonliteral social and academic language;
- responds using extensive vocabulary;
- communicates orally and in writing with infrequent errors;
- creates more complex narratives and expository writing in all content areas.

English Language Learner Profiles
Facilitating Language Growth

Beginning

Student's Behaviors	Teacher's Behaviors	Questioning Techniques
▪ Points to or provides other nonverbal responses ▪ Actively listens ▪ Responds to commands ▪ Understands more than he or she can produce	▪ Gestures ▪ Focuses on conveying meanings and vocabulary development ▪ Does not force students to speak ▪ Shows visuals and real objects ▪ Writes words for students to see ▪ Pairs students with more proficient learners ▪ Provides speaking and writing frames and models	▪ Point to the _______. ▪ Find the _______. ▪ Put the _______ next to the _______. ▪ Do you have the _______? ▪ Is this the _______? ▪ Who wants the _______?

Early Intermediate

Student's Behaviors	Teacher's Behaviors	Questioning Techniques
▪ Speaks in one- or two-word utterances ▪ Uses short phrases and simple sentences ▪ Listens with greater understanding	▪ Asks questions that can be answered by yes/no ▪ Asks either/or questions ▪ Asks higher-order questions with one-word answers ▪ Models correct responses ▪ Ensures supportive, low-anxiety environment ▪ Does not overtly call attention to grammar errors ▪ Asks short "wh" questions	▪ Yes/no (Did you like the story?) ▪ Either/or (Is this a pencil or a crayon?) ▪ One-word responses (Why did the dog hide?) ▪ General questions that encourage lists of words (What did you see in the book bag?) ▪ Two-word responses (Where did I put the pen?)

Intermediate

Student's Behaviors	Teacher's Behaviors	Questioning Techniques
▪ Demonstrates comprehension in a variety of ways ▪ Speaks in short phrases or sentences ▪ Begins to use language more freely	▪ Provides frequent comprehension checks ▪ Asks open-ended questions that stimulate language production	▪ Why? ▪ How? ▪ How is this like that? ▪ Tell me about _______. ▪ Talk about _______. ▪ Describe _______. ▪ What is in your book bag?

Early Advanced

Student's Behaviors	Teacher's Behaviors	Questioning Techniques
▪ Participates in reading and writing activities to acquire information ▪ Demonstrates increased levels of accuracy and correctness and is able to express thoughts and feelings ▪ Produces language with varied grammatical structures and academic language ▪ May experience difficulties in abstract, cognitively demanding subjects	▪ Fosters conceptual development and expanded literacy through content ▪ Continues to make lessons comprehensible and interactive ▪ Teaches thinking and study skills ▪ Continues to be alert to individual differences in language and culture	▪ What would you recommend/why? ▪ How do you think this story will end? ▪ What is this story about? ▪ What is your favorite part of the story? ▪ Describe/compare _______. How are these similar/different? ▪ What would happen if _______? ▪ Why do you think that? Yes, tell me more about _______.

Fostering Classroom Discussions

Strategies for English Language Learners

One of the most effective ways in which to increase the oral language proficiency of your English Language Learners is to give students many opportunities to do a lot of talking in the classroom. Providing the opportunities and welcoming all levels of participation will motivate students to take part in the class discussions. You can employ a few basic teaching strategies that will encourage the participation of all language proficiency levels of English Language Learners in whole class and small group discussions.

☑ WAIT/DIFFERENT RESPONSES

- Be sure to give students enough time to answer the question.
- Let students know that they can respond in different ways depending on their levels of proficiency. Students can
  - answer in their native language;
  - ask a more proficient ELL speaker to repeat the answer in English;
  - answer with nonverbal cues (pointing to related objects, drawing, or acting out).

Teacher: Where is Charlotte?

ELL Response: (Student points to the web in the corner of the barn.)

Teacher: Yes. Charlotte is sitting in her web. Let's all point to Charlotte.

☑ REPEAT

- Give positive confirmation to the answers that each English Language Learner offers. If the response is correct, repeat what the student has said in a clear, loud voice and at a slower pace. This validation will motivate other ELLs to participate.

Teacher: How would you describe the faces of the bobcats?

ELL Response: They look scared.

Teacher: That's right, Silvia. They are scared. Everyone show me your scared face.

☑ REVISE FOR FORM

- Repeating an answer allows you to model the proper form for a response. You can model how to answer in full sentences and use academic language.
- When you repeat the answer, correct any grammar or pronunciation errors.

Teacher: Who are the main characters in the story *Zathura*?

ELL Response: Danny and Walter is.

Teacher: Yes. Danny and Walter <u>are</u> the main characters. Remember to use the verb <u>are</u> when you are telling about more than one person. Let's repeat the sentence.

All: Danny and Walter <u>are</u> the main characters.

REVISE FOR MEANING

- Repeating an answer offers an opportunity to clarify the meaning of a response.

Teacher: Where did the golden feather come from?

ELL Response: The bird.

Teacher: That's right. The golden feather came from the Firebird.

ELABORATE

- If students give a one-word answer or a nonverbal cue, elaborate on the answer to model fluent speaking and grammatical patterns.
- Provide more examples or repeat the answer using proper academic language.

Teacher: Why is the girls' mother standing with her hands on her hips?

ELL Response: She is mad.

Teacher: Can you tell me more? Why is she mad?

ELL Response: Because the girls are late.

Teacher: Ok. What do you think the girls will do?

ELL Response: They will promise not to be late again.

Teacher: Anyone else have an idea?

ELICIT

- Prompt students to give a more comprehensive response by asking additional questions or guiding them to get to an answer.

Teacher: Listen as I read the caption under the photograph. What information does the caption tell us?

ELL Response: It tells about the butterfly.

Teacher: What did you find out about the butterfly?

ELL Response: It drinks nectar.

Teacher: Yes. The butterfly drinks nectar from the flower.

Making the Most of Classroom Conversations

Use all the speaking and listening opportunities in your classroom to observe students' oral language proficiency.

- Response to oral presentations
- Responding to text aloud
- Following directions
- Group projects
- Small Group work
- Informal, social peer discussions
- One-on-one conferences

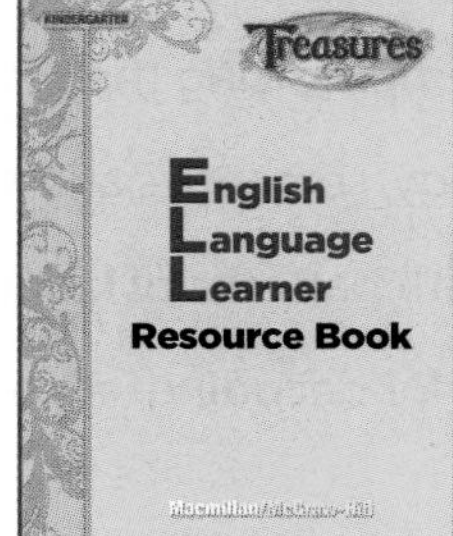

The **English Language Learner Resource Book** provides Speaking and Listening Checklists to help you monitor students' oral language proficiency growth.

Support for Students with Dyslexia

Characteristics of Dyslexia

A student with dyslexia is a student who continually struggles with reading and spelling but displays an ability to learn when there are no print materials involved. Even though the student receives the same classroom instruction as most other students, he continues to have difficulties with reading and spelling.

Students identified with dyslexia often have difficulties in the following areas

- reading words in isolation
- decoding nonsense words accurately
- oral reading (slow and inaccurate)
- learning to spell

The difficulties in these areas are usually the result of student's struggles with:

- phonological awareness: segmenting, blending, and manipulating words
- naming letters and pronouncing their sounds.
- phonological memory
- rapid naming of the letters of the alphabet or familiar objects

Effective Instruction

To address the needs of a student with dyslexia, instruction should be delivered in small groups. The instruction should be explicit, intensive, employ multisensory methods, as needed, and be individualized. It should include instruction on:

- phonemic awareness that has students detect, segment, blend and manipulate sounds
- phonics, emphasizing the sound/symbol relationships for decoding and encoding words
- morphology, semantics and syntax
- fluency with patterns of language
- strategies for decoding, encoding, word recognition, fluency and comprehension

Resources:
The International Dyslexia Association Website: www.interdys.org
The Dyslexia Handbook: Procedures Concerning Dyslexia and Related Disorders (Revised 2007) Texas Education Agency, Austin, TX, Publication Number: GE8721001

Treasures Reading and Language Arts Program

Treasures is a scientifically-based core program that offers sequential, explicit, and effective instruction in phonological awareness, phonics, morphology, fluency, vocabulary, and reading comprehension. Students are given many opportunities to practice and review these skills to help prevent reading difficulties before they begin.

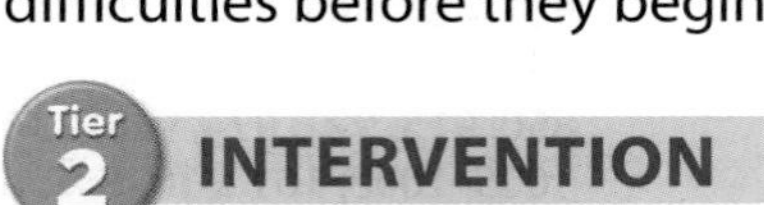

Tier 2 INTERVENTION

Weekly Small Group Lessons Intervention Teacher's Editions

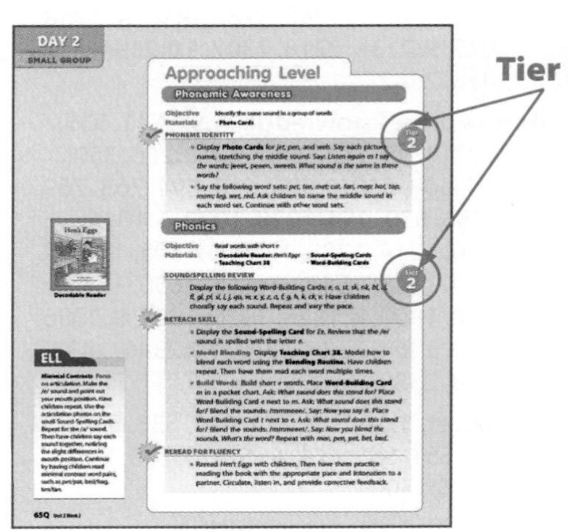

Tier 2 Instruction is provided in weekly small group lessons in the ***Treasures* Teacher's Editions**. These lessons provide targeted instruction in priority skills taught in the week. ***Tier 2 Intervention* Teacher's Editions** provide additional instruction for struggling students in the areas of phonemic awareness, phonics, vocabulary, fluency, and comprehension, grammar and writing.

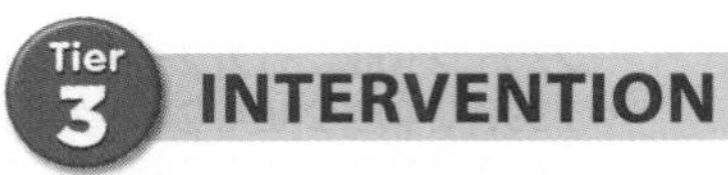

Tier 3 INTERVENTION

Reading Triumphs Intervention Program

Reading Triumphs provides intensive instruction. Explicit, sequential lessons delivered through clear instructional routines for all the key components of reading are embedded in the program. The "no assumption instruction" allows for both teacher and student success.

A

Key 1 = Unit 1

B

Index

C

Key 1 = Unit 1

D

E

Key 1 = Unit 1

F

Key 1 = Unit 1

I

Key 1 = Unit 1

L

Index

M

N

O

P

Key 1 = Unit 1

Index

Key 1 = Unit 1

Index

Index

R

S

Key 1 = Unit 1

T

U

V

Index

Index

W

Key 1 = Unit 1

"Duck on a Bike" by David Shannon. Copyright © 2002 by David Shannon. Published by arrangement with The Blue Sky Press, an imprint of Scholastic, Inc.

"Let's Ride" from CIRCLE TIME ACITIVITES FOR YOUNG CHILDREN by Deya Brashears & Sharron Werlin Krull. Copyright © 1981 by Deya Brashears & Sharron Werlin Krull. Reprinted by permission of Circle Time Publishing. (Original Title: Let's Play Automobile).

"My Bike" from SING A SONG OF POETRY. Copyright © 2004 by Gay Su Pinnell and Irene C. Fountas. Reprinted by permission of Heineman, a division of Reed Elsevier Inc.

"On the Go" by Ann Morris, photographs by Ken Heyman. Text copyright © 1990 by Ann Morris. Photographs copyright © 1990 by Key Heyman. Published by arrangement with William Morrow & Company, an imprint of HarperCollins Publishers.

"Take a Trip" adaptation by Wendy Flemming Raby from RESOURCES FOR CREATIVE TEACHING IN EARLY CHILDHOOD EDUCTION by Darlene Softley Hamilton and Bonnie Mack Flemming. Copyright © 1990 by Harcourt Brace Jovanovich. Used by permission.

"The Bus for Us" by Suzanne Bloom. Text and illustrations copyright © 2001 by Suzanne Bloom. Published by Caroline House, published by arrangement with Boyds Mills Press, Inc.

"The Little Red Caboose" by Bernice Johnson Reagon. Copyright ©1989 Songtalk Publishing Company (BMI). Used by permission.

"Transportation is the Way!" from MCGRAW-HILL SING–ALONG CHART. Lyrics by Becky Manfredini and Jenny Della Penna. Copyright © 2003. Reprinted by permission of The McGraw-Hill Companies, Inc.

Book Covers

A LONG WAY. Reprinted by permission of Candlewick Press.

ALPHABEEP: A ZIPPING, ZOOMING ABC. Reprinted by permission of Holiday House.

BEAR ON A BIKE. Reprinted by permission of Barefoot Books.

CITY SIGNS. Reprinted by permission of Kids Can Press.

CLICKETY CLACK. Reprinted by permission of Penguin Putnam Books for Young Readers.

I LOVE BOATS. Reprinted by permission of Candlewick Press.

SCHOOL BUS. Reprinted by permission of Greenwillow Books, a division of HarperCollins Publishers.

TWO LITTLE TRAINS. Reprinted by permission of HarperCollins Publishers.

WHEELS ON THE BUS. Reprinted by permission of Random House, Inc.

Photography Credits

All Photographs are by Ken Cavanagh or Ken Karp for Macmillan/McGraw-Hill (MMH) except as noted below:

xiii: Veer. 521: Brad Perks Lightscapes/Alamy. 528: Blue Trimarchi. 612: Blue Trimarchi. 696: Blue Trimarchi. 773: Pixtal/PunchStock.

Teacher Notes

Use this page to record lessons that work well or need to be adapted for future reference.

Lessons that work well.

Lessons that need adjustments.

Use this page to record lessons that work well or need to be adapted for future reference.

Lessons that work well.

Lessons that need adjustments.

Teacher Notes

Use this page to record lessons that work well or need to be adapted for future reference.

Lessons that work well.

Lessons that need adjustments.